THE ANTHROPOLOGY OF DONALD TRUMP

The Anthropology of Donald Trump is an edited volume of original anthropological essays, composed by some of the leading figures in the discipline. It applies their concepts, perspectives, and methods to a sustained and diverse understanding of Trump's supporters, policies, and performance in office. The volume includes ethnographic case studies of "Trump country," examines Trump's actions in office, and moves beyond Trump as an individual political figure to consider larger structural and institutional issues.

Providing a unique and valuable perspective on the Trump phenomenon, it will be of interest to anthropologists and other social scientists concerned with contemporary American society and politics as well as suitable reading for courses on political anthropology and US culture.

Jack David Eller is Head of Global Anthropology of Religion at the Global Center for Religious Research. His research interests include anthropology of religion, psychological anthropology, violence and culture, and Australian Aboriginal cultures. His most recent book is *Trump and Political Theology: Unmaking Truth and Democracy*.

The Anthropology of Now
Series Editor: Jack David Eller

The Anthropology of Donald Trump
Culture and the Exceptional Moment
Edited by Jack David Eller

https://www.routledge.com/Anthropology-of-Now/book-series/ANTHNOW

THE ANTHROPOLOGY OF DONALD TRUMP

Culture and the Exceptional Moment

Edited by Jack David Eller

LONDON AND NEW YORK

Cover image: © Gage Skidmore (CC BY-SA 2.0)

First published 2022
by Routledge
2 Park Square, Milton Park, Abingdon, Oxon OX14 4RN

and by Routledge
605 Third Avenue, New York, NY 10158

Routledge is an imprint of the Taylor & Francis Group, an informa business

© 2022 selection and editorial matter, Jack David Eller; individual chapters, the contributors

The right of Jack David Eller to be identified as the author of the editorial material, and of the authors for their individual chapters, has been asserted in accordance with sections 77 and 78 of the Copyright, Designs and Patents Act 1988.

All rights reserved. No part of this book may be reprinted or reproduced or utilised in any form or by any electronic, mechanical, or other means, now known or hereafter invented, including photocopying and recording, or in any information storage or retrieval system, without permission in writing from the publishers.

Trademark notice: Product or corporate names may be trademarks or registered trademarks, and are used only for identification and explanation without intent to infringe.

British Library Cataloguing-in-Publication Data
A catalogue record for this book is available from the British Library

Library of Congress Cataloging-in-Publication Data
A catalog record has been requested for this book

ISBN: 978-0-367-71591-5 (hbk)
ISBN: 978-0-367-71592-2 (pbk)
ISBN: 978-1-003-15274-3 (ebk)

DOI: 10.4324/9781003152743

Typeset in Bembo
by SPi Technologies India Pvt Ltd (Straive)

CONTENTS

List of Figures   vii
Notes on the Contributors   viii
Acknowledgements   xi

1   Introduction: on anthropology of the contemporary generally and of Trump specifically   1
Jack David Eller

PART I
Ethnographies of Trump country   19

2   Stigmatized identity motivating right-wing populism: how the tea party learned to love Donald Trump   21
William H. Westermeyer

3   The reddest of states: fieldnotes from Trumplandia   40
Michael E. Harkin

4   Making the Cuban American dream great again: race and immigrant citizenship in Miami   59
Ariana Hernandez-Reguant

5   "We're on the same team, right?": political polarization and social connections in "Trump country"   75
Claudine M. Pied

PART II
Performing and representing Donald Trump   93

6   Indexing ambivalence: laterality and negation
    in Donald Trump's co-speech gestures   95
    Daniel Lefkowitz

7   Trump the Caudillo: tapping into already-existing
    populist unrest   115
    Micah J. Fleck

8   Lying as a cultural system   125
    Jack David Eller

9   Orange candles and shriveled Cheetos: symbolic representations
    of Trump in the anti-Trump witchcraft movement 141
    Julia Coombs Fine

PART III
Donald Trump versus social institutions   159

10 "I don't think the science knows, actually": the biocultural
    impacts of Trump's anti-science and misinformation rhetoric,
    the mishandling of the COVID-19 pandemic, and
    institutionalized racism   161
    Benjamin J. Schaefer

11 Trumping the past, Trumping the future: how political
    messianism and violent conspiracy cultism come front and
    center in American politics   182
    Bruce Knauft

12 Hindutva and Donald Trump: an unholy relation   203
    Raj Kumar Singh

13 The events at the capitol and the Trump mediation: America's
    uncivil war and new authoritarian totalitarian possibilities 219
    Bruce Kapferer and Roland Kapferer

Afterword: authoritarianism after Trump   233
Jeff Maskovsky

Index   239

FIGURES

6.1	The two most common variants of former President Barack Obama's precision grip gesture. (Source: PBS coverage of Barack Obama's State of the Union speech, 26 January 2001: https://www.youtube.com/watch?v=-RSjbtJHi_Q&t=1047s, 0:11:00 & 0:11:12, respectively.)	99
6.2	Example of Biden's Lateral Gestures	103
6.3	Typical sequence of Lateral Gestures in Trump's debate speech. (0:29:05–0:29:32)	109
9.1	Orange candle stub and unflattering photograph. Image credit: Kaleigh Donnelly @901Tarot	147
9.2	Tarot cards. Image credit: Amber Love, @amberunmasked; Cards copyright MJ Cullinane (@crowtarotmjcullinane)	147
9.3	Baby carrot. Image credit: @boredofwords	148
9.4	"#yourefired." Image credit: @cameragirlsf	153
9.5	"#CheetoInChief." Image credit: @SeebeeNarra	154
11.1	Life-sized gilded statue of Donald Trump holding the US Constitution and a star scepter, at the Conservative Political Action Conference (CPAC), Orlando, FL, February 26, 2021	182

NOTES ON THE CONTRIBUTORS

Jack David Eller is Head of Global Anthropology of Religion at the Global Center for Religious Research. His research interests include anthropology of religion, psychological anthropology, violence and culture, and Australian Aboriginal cultures. His most recent book is *Trump and Political Theology: Unmaking Truth and Democracy*.

Julia Coombs Fine is a sociocultural linguist working on language, power, and social justice. Her research focuses on discourses of climate justice, political resistance, and Indigenous language revitalization. She is currently a postdoctoral fellow in Environmental Studies at the College of St. Benedict and St. John's University.

Micah J. Fleck is an anthropologist and neuro researcher who has written on topics such as education, the arts, populist movements, and group selection theory as they pertain to sociopolitical systems and human motivation. He holds degrees from Columbia University and Harvard University and is also the author of *Anthropology for Beginners* and *Privileged Populists: Populism in the Conservative and Libertarian Working Class*.

Michael E. Harkin is professor of anthropology at the University of Wyoming. He has conducted fieldwork in British Columbia, Wyoming, France, Romania, and Greece and has held fellowships at Karl Franzen University in Graz, Austria; the University of Otago in Dunedin, New Zealand; and Babes-Bolyai University in Cluj-Napoca, Romania. He was a visiting professor at Shanghai University. He has received three awards from NEH and two Fulbright awards. He is past president of the American Society for Ethnohistory and editor-in-chief of *Reviews in Anthropology*.

Notes on the Contributors **ix**

Ariana Hernandez-Reguant is a visiting research assistant professor of Latin American Studies at Tulane University. She has published widely on ideology and the media in contemporary Cuba, as well as about civic participation and political ideologies in Cuban Miami.

Bruce Kapferer is Emeritus Professor in Social Anthropology at the University of Bergen. He is also Professorial Fellow, Anthropology, University College London; Professorial Fellow, Cairns Institute; Director ERC Advanced Project Egalitarianism. Currently, he is a roving anthropologist and ethnographer with field experience in Africa, South Asia and Australia.

Roland Kapferer is Lecturer, Anthropology, Deakin University. Additionally, he is a musician, filmmaker, and social philosopher focusing on the anthropology of new technologies.

Bruce Knauft is Samuel C. Dobbs Professor of Anthropology at Emory University. Author of ten books and edited collections and thirty journal articles, Dr. Knauft has special interest in issues of inequality in relation to subjectivity and political economy and in larger considerations of social and cultural theory. Originally trained as an ethnographer of rainforest New Guinea—an interest he actively maintains—Dr. Knauft has also conducted research and engaged anthropology project work in East and West Africa, the Himalayas, Inner Asia, and Southeast Asia. His application of critical theory perspectives to the US is reflected in work concerning American neo-imperialism during the period of the Iraq War and, in recent years, publications and blog-posts concerning the dynamics of Trump and Trumpism.

Daniel Lefkowitz is Associate Professor of Linguistic Anthropology and Middle East Studies at the University of Virginia. He is the author of *Words and Stones: The Politics of Language and Identity in Israel* (2004). His current work focuses on the language of the media, primarily television and Hollywood cinema. He is at work on a book that looks at the history of changing representations of dialect in the character dialogue of American movies.

Jeff Maskovsky is Professor and Executive Officer (Chair) of the PhD Program in Anthropology at the Graduate Center, and Professor of Urban Studies at Queens College, at the City University of New York. His research and writing focus on poverty, welfare, health, security and governance in the urban United States. His latest book is the anthology, *Beyond Populism: Angry Politics and the Twilight of Neoliberalism*, co-edited with Sophie Bjork-James (2020).

Claudine M. Pied is Associate Professor of Sociology and Anthropology at the University of Wisconsin-Platteville. Her research has focused on intersections of politics, economics, and identity in rural communities in the United States. She is currently working on two projects related to changing land ownership and access:

one on the politics of forestland access in the northeast and the other on the effects of agricultural land consolidation in Wisconsin.

Benjamin J. Schaefer is a Queer, Non-Binary, Millennial doctoral candidate in Biological Anthropology at the University of Illinois at Chicago and The Field Museum of Natural History. Additionally, he holds an affiliation with the Latin American and Latino Studies program at UIC. He has collaborated on numerous bioarchaeological and forensic field projects, lab work, and publications. His other research interests include global health, the social embodiment of disease, archaeological biogeochemistry and paleogenomics, paleoepidemiology, ritual violence and warfare, and mummy studies, all through the intersections of Black, Indigenous, Queer, Crip, and Feminist theory.

Raj Kumar Singh is a PhD Scholar in the Department of Anthropology, University of Delhi. His research interests include the anthropology of religion with specialization in anthropology of Buddhism and economy, economic anthropology, and political anthropology. He is currently pursuing his PhD research on the topic of the relationship between refugee Tibetan Buddhism and the economy in Dharamshala, Himachal Pradesh, India.

William H. Westermeyer is Assistant Professor of Anthropology at the University of South Carolina, Aiken. He is author of *Back to America: Identity, Political Culture, and the Tea Party Movement*.

ACKNOWLEDGEMENTS

A volume like this is the accomplishment of many people, both visible in the book and not. My first thanks go to Alexandra McGregor and Katherine Ong at Routledge for believing in the project, initially when it was just an idea, then a list of contributors, and eventually a fully-realized manuscript. Also thanks to the anonymous reviewers, who provided important guidance on shaping the project. I am also appreciative of all of the anthropologists, including those not featured in the collection (many of whom are discussed in the introduction), who have made the anthropology of Donald Trump a viable enterprise and who inspired the volume. I am grateful to all of the contributors who dedicated their time and expertise to the collection, but especially to the authors who joined the project late but submitted quality work under great time constraints. Finally, I owe special gratitude to Jeff Maskovsky for his helpful and insightful commentary on the manuscript; he made the project better, but any remaining flaws are my own.

1
INTRODUCTION

On anthropology of the contemporary generally and of Trump specifically

Jack David Eller

In late 2020 and early 2021, the most common word in American discourse was "unprecedented." Trump's refusal to concede defeat (which he has still never done and never will); his baseless claims of election fraud and insistence that he won; his myriad frivolous and rejected lawsuits; his recorded request of Georgia election officials to "find" enough votes to hand him the state; the open suggestion by former and current staffers to deploy the military to invalidate the election and hold another; his demand that Vice President Pence overrule the Congressional count of electoral votes, leading to an insurrection to prevent certification of Joe Biden's victory; and his boycott of Biden's inauguration—all of these were "unprecedented." Even before these stunning (in both senses of the term) events, scholars from various disciplines were analyzing and critiquing Trump's presidency and re-election campaign, including of course political scientists but also sociologists (e.g. the characteristics of Trump voters), historians (e.g. the exceptionalism of his administration relative to American presidential history), psychologists (e.g. the pathologies behind his bizarre speech and behavior), and theologians (e.g. the curious relationship between evangelicals and Trump or the Republican party overall). As usual, anthropologists were relatively absent from the public conversation. Some might argue that anthropology, the quintessential science of "tradition"—that is, behavior that follows precedent—is not designed for exceptional moments and actors. This raises the question of whether an anthropology of Trump is possible. And given that the reign of Trump has ended, a second question is whether an anthropology of Trump is still relevant.

To the first question we can offer a resounding yes. There is, of course, no reason why any "anthropology of X" should be impossible. Anthropology is a perspective, a method, and a disciplinary tradition that can be applied to any topic. More, by 2016 and 2017 there were several initiatives already underway, including *American Ethnologist*'s "Anthropology of Trump," *Cultural Anthropology*'s "Cultural

DOI: 10.4324/9781003152743-1

Anthropology Responds to Trump," *Anthropology Now*'s "Trump Watch," Zero Anthropology's "Trump and Anthropology," Anthro Everywhere's "Anthropology of Trump," and Open Anthropology Cooperative's "Invitation to a Discussion: Anthropologists on the Trump Election." Additionally, numerous anthropologists had written articles or essays with titles like "Anthropology of Trump" (Pickles 2017; Stoller 2017), "Trump Studies" (Taussig 2017), and "Anthropology of Trumplandia" (Huhn 2018).

In other words, an anthropology of Trump is not only conceivable but already in existence. Much of this work, however, has been consigned to academic journals or blogs where it received too little attention from pundits and the public. Second, much of it is relatively short-form, consisting of brief analyses, commentaries, and opinion pieces. The thoughts conveyed therein are important and original, often missed by other disciplines, but they are not developed into journal article or book chapter length. The present volume aims to correct this omission, by inviting anthropologists—many of whom are the authors of these earlier pioneering publications—to expound in greater detail on their data and analyses and to update their findings in light of the four years of Trump's administration and his ultimate rebuke by the electorate in 2020.

This leaves us with the second question: now that Trump is out of office, does an anthropology of Trump remain relevant? *Prima facie* the question is almost trivial: more than a century after their appearance, do Malinowski's *Argonauts of the Western Pacific* or Spencer and Gillen's *The Native Tribes of Central Australia* still matter? Certainly they do. In fact, much of social science (and all of history) is retrospective. Further, it could be argued that a volume like this one could only be assembled after the Trump phenomenon, as the necessary primary literature first had to emerge and then the authors solicited and gathered to contribute their new and fully-realized writings. And the fact that the Trump regime is over—and that it did not die gracefully—affords a perspective that was not available during his term.

If this volume were merely an anthropological postmortem on the Trump presidency, a snapshot of a cultural moment, that would be enough to justify it. Beyond this, though, Trump is not gone, any more than the Trobriand Islanders or the Australian Aboriginals are gone, even—or maybe especially—if they are not who they were a hundred years ago, and Trumpism most surely endures. Trump remains a force, commanding loyalty among voters and Republican Party officials (so much so that they displayed a golden idol of him at the February 2021 Conservative Political Action Conference [CPAC]), threatening to campaign against "weak" Republicans who did not support him during his second impeachment, and holding out the prospect of a presidential bid in 2024. But more to the point, despite its title, this volume is not particularly or even primarily about Trump the man; it is not psychology or biography. It is about Trump as a cultural system, to paraphrase Geertz. The Trump movement and presidency did not suddenly emerge out of nowhere, nor did it vanish in January 2021. Trump was a product of deep beliefs and values that helped form him and deliver him into power—precisely the sort of thing that anthropology was invented to investigate.

Likewise, the effects of Trump will be felt in the United States long after his departure from the political scene (whenever that is). He instilled his doubts, suspicions, and conspiracies into a society that was well primed for them, that already accepted them or it would not have accepted them from him. And he demonstrated, without possessing any theoretical understanding of the matter, the fragility and contingency, the instability and vulnerability, of the sorts of cultural topics that have preoccupied anthropologists, such as traditions, laws, and institutions. He was a walking exercise in the construction of society and the (anti)social construction of reality.

The Trump phenomenon, as many have recognized, says at least as much about American society and culture as it does about Trump the person. Indeed, to study Trump anthropologically is to engage in an anthropology of American culture, as we will elucidate below. Nor was Trump an isolated American cultural and political effect; to study Trump anthropologically is to engage in an anthropology of the current global moment, in which right-wing, authoritarian, and populist parties and leaders preside in many countries, most surprisingly in countries where democracy was considered strong or where authoritarian (usually socialist/communist) regimes were only recently deposed. An anthropology of Trump as a global process speaks to the contradictions, limitations, and failures of other concepts long dear to anthropology and other social sciences—globalization, neoliberalism, liberalism, and democracy itself. In a word, an anthropology of Trump throws notions and predictions of the present and the future in the air, wondering where and if they will land.

The anthropology of the contemporary

The reputation of anthropology, deserved or not, has emphasized a single-minded focus on the "traditional," the remote, if not the "primitive." No less a figure than A. R. Radcliffe-Brown, one of our field's founders, defined anthropology in 1965 as "the study of what are called primitive or backward peoples" (1965: 2), and the equally venerable E. E. Evans-Pritchard asserted three years prior that anthropology was the branch of social science "which chiefly devotes itself to primitive societies" (1962: 11), adding belatedly that the discipline "embraces all human cultures and societies, including our own" (4).

Although anthropology has allowed itself to be assigned to the "savage slot" (Trouillot 1991) of the small, remote, traditional or indigenous society, it has never allowed itself to be trapped or restricted there, and fortunately even at the moment when Radcliffe-Brown and Evans-Pritchard opined on the nature of anthropology they were wrong and had been for decades. No later than 1931 W. Lloyd Warner, after doing conventional fieldwork in Aboriginal Australia, turned his sights to the Western Electric Company, studying how the workplace environment affected labor productivity; in 1946 he joined other experts in founding Social Research Incorporated, an anthropological consulting firm with such clients as Sears, Roebuck and Company. Shortly thereafter, Hortense Powdermaker (1950) shined the anthropological light on the American spectacle known as Hollywood and the movie industry, after conducting research in mid-twentieth-century Mississippi in her 1939 *After Freedom: A Cultural Study in the Deep South*.

Insofar as anthropology remained the science of "natives" in the middle of the last century, Malinowski appreciated that it was and must be the science of "the changing Native," because "what exists nowadays [and he was writing in 1945] is not a primitive culture in isolation but one in contact and process of change" (1961: 6). In the same year, as the title of his edited volume asserted, Ralph Linton (1945) reframed anthropology as "the science of man in the world crisis," leading Stanley Diamond, in another volume designed to reinvent anthropology, to rethink the definition of the discipline as "the study of man in crisis by man in crisis" (1972: 401). To be sure, humanity was in crisis by the 1900s and continues in crisis today.

Another misconception about anthropology, fostered by Geertz himself but definitively disproven by all of the examples above, is that anthropologists "study in villages" (1973: 22). To the extent that this was true, it was an artifact of the kinds of societies that anthropologists studied most often. But of course humans do not live in village settings exclusively, and anthropology follows them where it finds them. No later than the 1960s an urban anthropology was forming, although Ulf Hannerz (1980) reckoned that the first book with the title *Urban Anthropology* only appeared in 1968; by 1972 there was a journal of the same name. However, before that time anthropologists were discovering and describing society and culture in cities, for instance in the well-known "Copperbelt" of Africa, where "tribal" affiliations and identities were often recast if not cast off.

Anthropologists were further driven out of the village precisely because locals were driven out of it or chose to leave it. George Marcus exploded the "intensively-focused-upon single site" methodology of sitting in one village in favor of "multi-sited ethnography" (1995: 96). People do not stand still, nor do ideas, objects, and practices; rather, they are all implicated in "chains, paths, threads, conjunctions, or juxtapositions" (105) that send anthropologists on translocal, sometimes global, expeditions. At the extreme, anthropologists have acquired the facility, because they must, to examine culture and social interaction when there is no "site" whatsoever, as with "virtual communities" such as Facebook or online gaming platforms like Second Life (Boellstorff 2008) or World of Warcraft (Nardi 2010). Inspired by Bruno Latour's (e.g. Latour 2005) "actor network theory," anthropologists actually accept that social interaction is not restricted to humans but instead that our tools and instruments participate in society such that "objects too have agency."

We are far from Radcliffe-Brown's and Evans-Pritchard's science of the primitive but not yet far enough. Anthropology's commitment to "culture" has tended to make it seem backward-looking, past-oriented, and tradition-obsessed. Joel Robbins (2007), probably in a salutary way, accused anthropology of "continuity thinking," that is, of emphasizing the continuity between the past and present and therefore overlooking or underestimating the discontinuities in the modern world (he particularly argued that continuity thinking made it difficult for anthropology do deal with Christianity, which often advocates if not accomplishes a radical break with the past). But like many criticisms, this one is probably somewhat overstated.

Anthropologists increasingly grasp that culture is not only about the past or even the present but also or primarily the future. Hence the anthropological literature increasingly contains studies of planning, design, decision-making, invention, imagination, aspiration, uncertainty, emergence, risk, hope (and too often hopelessness), nostalgia, waiting, boredom, and so forth (see e.g. Eller 2020a). The insight is that culture does not pre-exist and independently exist but is emergent, often quite differently than the past and "tradition" (see e.g. Fischer 2003, 2009). One of the clearest places to witness this is in the growing field of "design anthropology." Humans inhabit a designed world; virtually everything we own, use, or interact with—from clothing and food to cars and computers—has been designed by someone, ever more often with the input of anthropologists, who find that design is a quite intentional and systematic aspect of contemporary life. From innovation labs and think tanks to consumer-behavior and "user experience" studies, professionals ask, "How can things be different?" and set about to make it so (Mazé 2016: 50). In formal design settings, or merely in situations like that reported by Jan Patrick Heiss (2018) in which a Hausa man had to decide whether to migrate with his family and thus leave his father and his land behind, culture does not and cannot make decisions for us or compel any specific decision; instead, culture is a resource in planning and design, *and sometimes culture is an obstacle*.

Finally, as anthropological participation in design work and other planning projects illustrates, anthropologists are no longer entirely passive observers. As skilled scholars, and as full citizens, anthropologists often join in the processes of change, of the construction of future culture. This raises the issue of another subdiscipline or impulse within the discipline, so-called "engaged anthropology." Almost a century ago Malinowski (1929) urged anthropologists to be "practical" as well as academic (especially in the practice of colonial management), and a year earlier Franz Boas in *Anthropology and Modern Life* (1928) expressed deep concern with practical social issues like racism, nationalism, eugenics, criminology, and education.

Some like David Maybury-Lewis, the founder of Cultural Survival, get involved in indigenous issues, a natural extension and complement of anthropology's basic orientation. Others lend their energies to "action anthropology" such as Brian McKenna's (2013) work on/against the influence of Dow Chemicals on higher education in Michigan. One of the most high-profile engaged or activist anthropologists is Nancy Scheper-Hughes, who turned her interest in health issues into Organs Watch, an organization to document and combat illegal organ trafficking. Many others belong to the Society for Applied Anthropology which, according to its website (appliedanthro.org), explicitly promotes "the application of [anthropological] principles to contemporary issues and problems." Meanwhile, a good proportion of anthropologists work outside of the academy altogether, using their methods and skills to serve industry, government, medicine, community development, or other causes. More than a few anthropologists have eschewed if not openly opposed such activity, often on the premise that it violates anthropology's prime directive of objectivity and relativism. However, as members of our societies and not only scholars, we have every right to enter the social fray, and besides, objectivity does not mean neutrality: objectivity entails how one arrives at a position, not the position that one arrives at, much less not arriving at a position at all.

Toward an anthropology of Trump

Anthropology has more than confirmed its capability to handle the contemporary world and its relevance to comprehending and constructing modern life. But what of our second question and challenge, of the relevance of an anthropology of Trump, particularly in the aftermath of his administration? We have already addressed the complaint of timing, insisting that such a volume was hardly possible until now and that Trump will remain a viable subject of analysis and criticism for the foreseeable future. But to fully confront and evaluate the importance of an anthropology of Trump, it is essential to contemplate what such a research project would be. What exactly are the foci of an anthropology of Trump, and how does this volume begin to approach them? There are a number of clear areas of investigation, all of which anthropologists are already exploring.

The identity of Trump supporters

Probably the most obvious, and to outsiders the most puzzling, question is who Trump's "base" was and what attracted them to him. Here anthropology's signature method, participant observation, is invaluable. Most of the studies and commentaries of Trump voters took one of two forms. In one form, they generalized and homogenized Trump's support, often echoing Hillary Clinton's "basket of deplorables" assessment and stigmatizing them as racists, xenophobes, Islamophobes, homophobes, and irrationalists who live in a sequestered world of white privilege, right-wing-media-induced unreality, or both. In the second form, they employed "big data" to paint statistical pictures of this constituency, discovering correlations between approval of Trump and education and income (both low) as well as race (white), religion (evangelical Christianity), and various personality traits, for instance "authoritarian aggressiveness" or hatred of certain groups and "support for leaders who target those same groups" (Smith and Hanley 2018: 197).

For instance, it is true that Trump commanded an impressive percentage (81 percent) of the evangelical vote in 2016, but this was not inconsistent with Republican success in recent elections (Mormon Mitt Romney and born-again George W. Bush carried 79 percent in 2012 and 2004, respectively, and the more secular John McCain won 73 percent in 2008). But a closer look uncovers confounding facts: there was an odd inverse relation between church attendance and Trump support, such that non-born-again Christians who attend church regularly *disapproved* of Trump by a margin of 49 versus 46 percent (Gorski 2018). We find similar anomalies or overgeneralizations in other allegedly central variables, like race and income: while Trump appealed to white voters, a majority (60 percent) of Clinton's voters were also white, and Trump's constituents actually had higher average incomes than Clinton's, only 35 percent of Trump fans earning less than $50,000.

Anthropological fieldwork among Trump's supporters revealed a much more complex, interesting, and potentially troubling landscape. Playing on Susan Harding's (1991) memorable essay about Christian fundamentalists as the "repugnant other," Myles Lennon adds significant nuance to the portrait of Trump voters, learning firstly that Trump voters are not necessarily Trump supporters. He introduces three unlikely characters who voted for Trump—a woman whose political inclinations are more liberal than conservative, a white military veteran who previously avoided politics on principle, and, most strangely, a male gay porn actor. Each for his/her own reason voted for Trump although they disagreed with him or, in the case of the porn star, considered his views "reprehensible" (Lennon 2018: 445). The military retiree got behind Trump as a reaction to supposed anti-white, anti-male mobilization among blacks; the liberal woman wanted to "push back" against "liberal smugness"; and, most incongruously, the gay actor made some kind of self-defeating point about "the chasm between his political ideals and the country's political reality, as he perceives it" (445). The lesson that Lennon takes from this experience—and a profound lesson it is—is that voters are "by no means ideologically coherent, and contradictions, illegibility, and inconsistences" often characterize their political opinions and actions (442).

While anthropological work in "Trump country" complicates any simple depiction of his people, it also suggests some concrete conclusions. Morgan Ramsey-Elliot's research on truck-owning families in Texas and Colorado put him inadvertently in the middle of Trump country, where a notable set of "small-town American community values" led them to endorse Trump. Although there is nothing small-town or rural about the wealthy New Yorker, they recognized and liked "his persona— straight-shooting, unpretentious, seemingly benevolent and both individual and familiar in his celebritydom" (Ramsey-Elliot 2017: 25). More than anything, they approved of his expression of loyalty and commitment to the "team" (even if the team was disgruntled white people). Christine Walley pinpoints a similar cultural divide, one that transcends race and class and relates more to region (rural versus urban or "heartland" versus "coastal elite"), although it comes in two local flavors. In Louisiana, working-class whites displayed "resentment about the perceived disdain of coastal liberals" and, for historical reasons, identified "up" to wealthy white which "strengthened support for 'pro-business' (if anti-Wall Street) Tea Partiers and for Donald Trump" (Walley 2017: 233). The dynamics in the Eastern and Midwestern Rust Belt were different, with the same result: while less inclined to identify with local rich whites, working-class whites helped flip several normally Democratic states to the Trump camp, indicating "the centrality of economic concerns for many white voters, the 'white privilege' of those who could register economic grievances by voting for Trump without having to fear the bigotry his campaign was unleashing, and the channeling of economic resentments against Others [due, for instance, to competition with African Americans and new immigrants for scarce factory jobs]" (234).

Unsurprisingly, several chapters of the present volume offer ethnographic glimpses into specific Trump constituencies. In fact, the entire first part, or roughly one-third of the volume, consists of such studies. To open the ethnographies, William Westermeyer takes aim at the Tea Party in North Carolina and the shift in outlook sparked by Trump. Michael Harkin moves us to Wyoming, a solid Trump state, to meet working-class white males. Hispanics in Florida would perhaps seem an unlikely Trump demographic at first, but Ariana Hernandez-Reguant explains the appeal of Trump to first-generation Latinx inhabitants of Miami. Claudine Pied offers a lesson in possible coexistence of Americans with different political ideologies in rural New England, where she finds a model of solidarity despite disagreement.

Trump as performance and representation

Much attention and anxiety have been directed toward Trump's presentational style, particularly his speech patterns and manual gestures. In both regards he was an unusual, even abnormal president, gleefully refusing to respect norms of the office or to "act presidential." Like many others, Paul Stoller (2017) judges the Trump performance as "the embodiment of celebrity culture—a world filled with glitz, fantasy and illusion":

> It is culture in which shallow perception is more valuable than deep insight. If you watch Donald Trump perform his shtick, you hear pretty much the same thing. Mr. Trump comes on stage, recites his poll numbers, insults his opponents, invites famous supporters to the stage to sing his praises, and then talks, without giving concrete factual examples, about how bad things are and how he's the man to make things better.
>
> Each event is a tightly controlled theatrical production that is designed to reinforce the myth of Mr. Trump's fearless strength, his invincibility and his inevitability—a real strong man.

This was an act perfected over a lifetime of real estate deals and years of television hosting, and it apparently played well to a large segment of the audience/citizenry (prompting us to ask whether the citizenry has become or been replaced by the audience).

Whether orally or in writing—that is, in his torrential tweets—Trump's communication style was uncompromisingly grandiose, insulting, and "popular," if not vulgar. Although an Ivy-League-educated East Coast billionaire, Trump talked like one of the masses, down to his locker room banter about grabbing women's genitals. This self-representation was prophesied by scholars of authoritarianism in the 1950s, when the experience was fresh and novel. In their unfortunately neglected study of the "American agitator," Leo Lowenthal and Norbert Guterman described how the political agitator seldom behaves seriously, preferring to tread the twilight zone "between the respectable and the forbidden,… to use any device, from jokes to doubletalk to wild extravagances" to whip his listeners into a frenzy (1949: 5). Often bringing to the role the reputation as "the indefatigable businessman" but always "a suffering martyr" who sacrifices much—his wealth, his empire—purportedly to serve the people, he is a salesman (if not a huckster) who "does not hesitate to advertise himself," since he is his own main product (118). Whether he plays the part of the "great little man" or "bullet-proof martyr"—or alternates between them—his posture is "an exceptionally gifted man who knows and even admires his own talent," a "tough guy… physically powerful and something of a terrorist to boot," who "has access to secret and highly important information, the source of which he is careful not to disclose. He quotes mysterious 'sources' (sometimes just what 'many people' say) and cryptically refers to information he will reveal in some unspecified future" (132). When it comes to his opponents and enemies, he is quick to pelt them with labels like "hoax, corrupt, insincere, duped, manipulate" (13). One almost wonders if Trump modeled himself after Lowenthal and Guterman's agitator or if he is merely a predictable political type.

As for Trump's Twitter tirades, they were just print versions of his in-person style. Adam Hodges (2017) rates them "formulaic" and summarizes the formula: (1) selecting from a short list of condescending nouns such as "clown, disaster, dummy, joke, liar," and, as we know too well, "hoax"; (2) adding on disparaging adjectives like "biased, boring, corrupt, crazy, crooked, disgraceful, disgusting, dumb, failed… and, of course, sad, stupid, terrible, weak"; (3) dosing the language with "intensifiers—semantically vacuous adverbs," including "very, totally, so, really" and "100%," often in all caps; and then (4) repeating ad infinitum. Facetiously, Hodges anticipates Trump's response tweet to his analysis: "Biased and 100% irrelevant. Has zero credibility. Written by a failing dopey writer. Knows NOTHING! What a clown. Don't read #TrumpedUpWords."

Along with his words, anthropologists and other scholars have pondered his gestures and associated physical antics. In an influential article on "the hands of Donald Trump," Kira Hall, Donna Goldstein, and Matthew Ingram attribute much of Trump's political success to the "comedic entertainment" of his physical performances, "particularly his use of gesture to critique the political system and caricature his opponents" (2016: 71), even if those caricatures, like his mocking of a disabled journalist, are crude and mean-spirited. His "impersonations of political opponents at campaign rallies" (73) were of a piece with his name-calling, including "Lying Ted [Cruz]," "Crooked Hillary [Clinton]," and "Sleepy Joe [Biden]." "To watch a Trump speech," they reckon, "is to experience something like standup comedy. His words, gestures, repetitions, and interactive style tag his routines as comedic, if also crude and bawdy. Indeed, prominent comedians such as Samantha Bee, Trevor Noah, and John Oliver have themselves noted that Trump's routines mirror a comedic format" (77). His condescending parodies of rivals and critics, from the "wrist-flailing reporter" to the "food-shoveling governor" and "border-crossing Mexican," violated our expectations of a sober politician, but that was precisely the point: "Trump uses gestural excess to convey the impression he is a new kind of politician, unconstrained by petty rules and competent at accomplishing daunting tasks" (84)—and unafraid to be un-PC. Ultimately,

> Trump's gestures are part of a complicated mediation of Trump's celebrity image as it relates to his overall brand. Trump is known as a famous figure with a long career of entertaining the mass US audience through performative humor. His humor works because it incorporates that central Bakhtinian trope called vulgarity. In Trump we find a Rabelaisian character that deploys bawdy humor to entertain his audience. He provides carnivalesque moments as he pokes fun at other candidates, at their bodies, at their fluids, at their stiffness. Like Rabelais, Trump understands that crude humor has the power to bring down the princely classes—aka, the political establishment—as well as anyone who opposes him.
>
> (82)

The four chapters in the second part of the present volume scrutinize performance and representation in the Trump phenomenon. Building on the work of Hall, Goldstein, and Ingram, together with the linguistic analysis of Jennifer Sclafani (2018) in *Talking Donald Trump*, Daniel Lefkowitz concludes that the contrast of verbal and gestural meanings gives Trump's interaction style its uniquely complex and contradictory resonances for different elements of its American audience. Micah J. Fleck likens Trump to a Latin American caudillo or political/military strongman (Trump has even praised himself as "the baddest hombre") exploiting pre-existing race- and class-based grievances, a profile that fits better than the standard fascist or populist label. Jack David Eller tackles one of Trump's most characteristic verbal tropes—his extraordinary dishonesty—arguing that, rather than (or at least in addition to) condemning it as a personality disorder, anthropologists should think seriously about lying as social interaction, as a mark of authenticity and a display of power, and as a challenge to institutions and a social construction (or destruction) of reality. Finally, coming from a very different angle, Julia Fine discusses how the witchcraft movement resists and inverts Trump's performance, choosing symbols and nicknames to critique and "bind" Trump's perceived materialism, artificiality, and misogyny.

Executive versus institution

In his epochal reformulation of political theology, Carl Schmitt declared, "Sovereign is he who decides the exception" (2005: 5). Schmitt meant that laws and institutions are never self-guaranteeing nor ever rest fully on norms and constitutions but always depend upon and arise from *a decision*. A decision, and therefore a willful decider, bring laws and constitutions into being, and a willful decider can ignore them, annul them, or re-write them.

One of the more prominent, and alarming, features of the Trump presidency was his willingness to disregard limitations of or legal/constitutional checks on the office. He literally believed, or behaved like he believed, that he was a Schmittian sovereign: "Let me tell you, the one that matters is me. I'm the only one that matters, because when it comes to it, that's what the policy is going to be," he boasted, much more the decider than George W. Bush ever claimed to be (CNN 2017). For such an egotistical executive, laws, traditions, institutions, conventions—all the stuff that is so central to anthropology and social science in general—were a distraction if not a barrier.

In this, he betrayed his populist inclinations. Populism has been on the anthropological radar since 1969 if not earlier, when Ernest Gellner co-edited a volume titled *Populism: Its Meaning and National Characteristics* (Ionescu and Gellner 1969). Since then, populism has been the subject of much scholarly reflection. One of the best definitions comes from political scientists Cas Mudde and Cristóbal Kaltwasser, who call it

> a thin-centred ideology that considers society to be ultimately separated into two homogeneous and antagonistic groups, "the pure people" and "the corrupt elite," and which argues that politics should be an expression of the *volonté générale* (general will) of the people… This means that populism is in essence a form of moral politics, as the distinction between "the elite" and "the people" is first and foremost moral (i.e. pure vs. corrupt), not situational (e.g. position of power), socio-cultural (e.g. ethnicity, religion), or socio-economic (e.g. class). Moreover, both categories are to a certain extent "empty signifiers"…, as it is the populists who construct the exact meanings of "the elite" and "the people."
>
> (2012: 8–9)

By "thin-centred" they stress that it is an ideology that can be readily attached to many other and contradictory ideologies and identities, both right-wing and left-wing, including nation, class, race, ethnicity, religion, or some combination of these factors.

At the heart of populism, in its diverse guises, is a triad of "the people," those who are not "the people" or are the veritable enemies of "the people," and the leader. Of course, in all democracies and indeed some autocracies and monarchies, the leader alleges to represent the people and to govern in their name (if not always their interest). However, most analysts of modern populism stress the *lack of mediation* between leader and people, what William Mazzarella calls "a direct and immediate presencing of the substance of the people and, as such a reassertion, a mattering-forth of the collective flesh" in the person of the leader (2019: 49). This "politics of immediation" goes a long way to accounting for three traits of Trump. The first was his "popular" style of communication, as discussed above; by his common, comedic, and iconoclastic manner (or lack of manners), he conveyed that he was "one of the people," no matter how rich and distant he may be. The second was his Twitter governance and overall neglect and denunciation (as "fake news") of the mainstream media, which, as the name suggests, mediated between him and the people; he explicitly recognized that Twitter allowed him to speak directly to America without any mediation or filter. The third, of course, was his wanton contempt for laws, traditions, and institutions, which restrain the will of the people (which, ideally, was embodied in his will) and which was interpreted, not just by him but by all populists, as part of the "establishment" or "elite" plot against the people.

The irony of populism, as political theorist and philosopher Ernest Laclau points out, is that "the people" does not really exist, certainly not as a concrete entity prior to the populist movement. "The people," like any collectivity such as the nation or the ethnic group, is a product of what Laclau terms "a practice of naming" (2005: 113), that is, is interpellated by the populist leader and movement, is an imagined community in the same sense, and by many of the same processes, as Benedict Anderson construes the modern nation. To be sure, there are more and less likely ways to frame "the people," but, as Jeff Maskovsky and Sophie Bjork-James warn in their recent volume on "angry politics," the people "is almost always constituted as a raced, classed, and gendered political subject" (2020: 7)—to which we might add ethnicized, regioned/geographized (see the rural/urban division above), and culturized or civilizationized (e.g. Western/Christian civilization against Eastern/Muslim, etc. civilization… or no civilization at all). In other words, "the people" and therefore populism are inevitably *exclusionary* concepts, naming who the movement, the government, and the law itself are for and who they are against. Almost always, certain classes (the upper classes, the elite, the nobility), races (non-whites), ethnicities (immigrants from non-European countries and language groups), and religions (especially Jews and Muslims) are excluded or vilified and demonized. Meanwhile, internal differences within "the people" are erased, creating an ideal or myth of homogeneity and harmony of "the people" and their manifest will, the leader.

In the present volume, Bruce Knauft examines how candidate and president Trump extended and undermined the Republican Party and American party politics by encouraging extremism and conspiratorial thinking (and violence) against liberal governance; he foresees a dangerous trajectory of alt-right threats to democracy. Inspired and outraged by the assault on the Capitol in January 2021, Bruce Kapferer and Roland Kapferer perceive Trump or what they call "events Trump" as mediating a fundamental creative/destructive dynamic related to global capitalism and fascism/authoritarianism, resonating with somber fictional futures envisioned by Orwell and Huxley. Physical anthropologist Benjamin Schaefer seizes the COVID-19 pandemic to scrutinize Trump's corrosive impact on science and what Schaefer rightly calls the oldest and most endemic American disease of all—racism. Raj Singh ranges beyond America's border to compare Trump to India's own right-wing populist leader, Narendra Modi, arguing not only that there are similarities but that the Trump effect diffused to India, feeding Hindu-nationalist sentiments on the other side of the planet.

Trump as a lens on American and global politics and culture

There are many other broad issues that an anthropology of Trump could and should study and, in most cases, has already begun to study. Two related topics of international import are the turn against neoliberalism and globalization and the worldwide rise of right-wing populist parties and leaders, as mentioned previously. Trump marked a break with decades of Republican endorsement of neoliberalism and globalization, first championed by conservatives like Ronald Reagan and Margaret Thatcher, not to mention conservative economists like Milton Friedman and his "Chicago boys" who inflicted it on countries such as Chile in the 1970s and 1980s, with devastating consequences. Interestingly, Trump's condemnation of internationalism left Democrats, long critics of neoliberal policies, somehow holding the bag for it. Trump in many ways resembled the typical nationalist populist countercurrent to neoliberalism and globalization (including international institutions like the World Health Organization), denouncing them as threats to American culture and sovereignty and to the future of American "winning."

Anthropologists have long been analysts and critics of neoliberalism and globalization (perhaps because of the impact on the indigenous peoples with whom we are so closely associated), although our critiques diverge from Trump's and there is no evidence that he is aware of anthropology's pronouncements. David Harvey's (2005) classic *A Brief History of Neoliberalism* characterized it as a political-economic theory and practice that puts markets and private property and interests at the center of society and diminishes the role of the state. In the years immediately before and after, many anthropologists commented on contemporary governmentality, James Ferguson and Akhil Gupta (2002), Kregg Hetherington (2011), Tanya Li (2007), and Aihwa Ong (2006)—the last with the wonderfully Schmittian title *Neoliberalism as Exception*—to name but a few. Among the many angles that plumb the heart of the relationship between Trump and the revolt against neoliberalism is Gregory Morton's proposal that Trump's victory signaled not a nostalgia for the 1950s manufacturing economy but an adjustment to the new era of corporate domination, precarity, and the gig economy:

> Neoliberalism is dead… The market is in retreat… People are now learning to mediate social relations through the bureaucracy of corporate structure, and corporations are serving as the intermediaries between workers and markets… And Donald Trump is the voice, the sign, of the new corporate world—our new big boss.
>
> (2018: 209)

Trump, Morton concludes, "speaks like a boss"—which he was in fact accustomed to being—and under CEO Trump the United States was "the biggest business of them all" (216). He reasons that Trump's presidency embedded "the rhetoric of power and powerlessness, domination and submission, and humiliation and restoration that Donald Trump *borrows from his global conservative peers*" (212, emphasis added). Here he invokes our second point, that Trump was one drop, and a late drop, in a wave—what Morton calls "the 'white tide,' cresting early in Hungary, Poland, and Britain"—of elected executives who are "anti-neoliberal conservatives" (214). Among the current generation of right-wing populists in power are India's Modi, Jair Bolsonaro (Brazil), Viktor Orbán (Hungary), Recep Tayyip Erdoğan (Turkey), Rodrigo Duterte (Philippines), and of course Vladimir Putin (Russia), while Marine

Le Pen and Geert Wilders plan their path to power in France and the Netherlands, respectively. All of these figures speak the same language as Trump, the language of nationalist, racist, civilizational populism or of what Orbán, the most theoretically articulate of the class, has proudly dubbed *illiberal democracy* in which, once again, the interests of "the people" (raced, classed, and gendered) supersede everything—not just the rights of minorities and immigrants but also the norms of democratic elections and institutions.

As noted, two of the present chapters (Fleck and Singh) deal with comparisons between Trump and other current or recent strongmen, and Michael Fischer (2017) puts the "populist backlash" on the to-do list for anthropologists, who "have longitudinal and multilevel expertise in monitoring the ebb and flow of such movements" and should therefore join others "who have long warned that democracy is no longer a sufficient slogan, that voting without institutional checks and balances is a recipe for disaster." An exclusionary, wall-building, and at its worst hate-mongering politics, such populist disengagement from the world of cultural diversity constitutes a dis-integrative revolution, an undoing of the integrative revolution that many anthropologists like Geertz perceived and celebrated. And it is (mis)informed by the cardinal anthropological sin, ethnocentrism, which Theodor Adorno et al. (1950) put at the crux of the authoritarian personality.

In the best anthropological tradition of holism, one insight leads to another. Anthropologists of democracy (e.g. Appadurai 2002; Cole 2007; Graeber 2013; Paley 2008) can and must unite with ethnographers of political parties (e.g. Faucher 2020; Klein and Stern 2004; Shafer 1986) to diagnose the long-term trajectory of the Republican Party, the state of America's unusual two-party system, and the fragility of the concept of democracy, fully grasping that democracy is not the inevitable destination of history and only survives, like every facet of culture, so long as it is valued and practiced; see again Knauft in this volume. The anthropological gaze must reach to emerging right-wing institutions like the Proud Boys, the Oath Keepers, and the far-right alternative to Twitter called Parler.

Perhaps most crucially at this moment in American society, anthropologists of Trump must accentuate the question of race, a cultural construct that anthropologists have critiqued since the days of Boas, Melville Herskovits, and Ashley Montagu, the latter of whom (Montagu 1945) called it humanity's most dangerous myth (although humanity has produced many dangerous myths). Race—a topic raised prominently in this volume by Harkin, Hernandez-Reguant, and Schaefer and mentioned by others—is a conspicuous dividing line in American politics, Trump carrying only *8 percent* of the African-American vote in 2016 and 28 percent of the Hispanic vote while *winning a majority (58 percent) of white votes*. Within the solid evangelical block we see the same split: *white evangelicals* supported Trump almost unanimously, but in 2019 just 29 percent of nonwhite evangelicals approved of him and a mere 7 percent of black evangelicals (Enten 2020). Race relations have not been worse, and hate crimes higher, in recent memory than during the Trump years, with high-profile accusations of police brutality, street protests, and "hashtag activism" in the form of #HandsUp, #JusticeforMichaelBrown, and, most importantly,

#BlackLivesMatter, inspiring "hashtag ethnography" among anthropologists in response (Bonilla and Rosa 2015). Meanwhile, Trump's worrying popularity among white nationalists renders urgent our ethnographic understanding of these individuals and organizations, begun, for instance, by Sophie Statzel's (2006) work on the white nationalist online group Stormfront, Nancy Scheper-Hughes' (2017) reflections on racial hatred, Claudine Pied's (2018) analysis of the white working class, and Jeff Maskovsky's (2017) thoughts regarding "white nationalist postracialism." A kindred scholar from just outside anthropology and from outside the US, S. Romi Mukherjee (2018), concludes that Trump's signature slogan "Make America Great Again" amounted to a "white political theology" (see also Eller 2020b on Trump and political theology).

These citations as well as others not included here, and the chapters in the present volume, demonstrate that the anthropology of Trump is not only possible but is alive and thriving and that it is not only relevant but essential for understanding this moment in American and global history and culture. In the end, whatever one thinks of Trump, it is clear that anthropology must and can think of him and that he is, to borrow from Lévi-Strauss, good to think. And as whenever anthropology has blazed trails into new territory, that territory becomes more legible to us, as anthropology itself grows in robustness and value.

References

Adorno, Theodor W., Else Frenkel-Brunswick, Daniel J. Levinson, and R. Nevitt Sanford. 1950. *The Authoritarian Personality*. New York: Harper & Row.

Appadurai, Arjun. 2002. "Deep Democracy: Urban Governmentality and the Horizon of Politics." *Environment & Urbanization* 13 (2): 23–43.

Boas, Franz. 1928. *Anthropology and Modern Life*. New York: W. W. Norton & Company, Inc.

Boellstorff, Tom. 2008. *Coming of Age in Second Life: An Anthropologist Explores the Virtually Human*. Princeton, NJ: Princeton University Press.

Bonilla, Yarimar and Jonathan Rosa. 2015. "#Ferguson: Digital Protest, Hashtag Ethnography, and the Racial Politics of Social Media in the Unites States." *American Ethnologist* 42 (1): 4–17.

CNN. 2017. "Trump: I'm the Only One That Matters." https://www.cnn.com/videos/politics/2017/11/03/trump-im-only-one-that-matters-fox-sot.cnn, accessed May 24, 2020.

Cole, Kimberly. 2007. *Democratic Designs: International Intervention and Electoral Practices in Postwar Bosnia-Herzegovina*. Ann Arbor: University of Michigan Press.

Diamond, Stanley. 1972 [1969]. "Anthropology in Question." In Dell Hymes, ed. *Reinventing Anthropology*. New York: Random House, Inc., 401–29.

Eller, Jack David. 2020a. *Cultural Anthropology: Global Forces, Local Lives*, 4th ed. London and New York: Routledge.

———. 2020b. *Trump and Political Theology: Unmaking Truth and Democracy*. Denver, CO: Global Center for Religion Research Press.

Enten, Harry. 2020. "White Evangelicals Love Trump. Religious Voters? Not so Much." https://www.cnn.com/2020/01/01/politics/evangelical-support-trump/index.html, accessed April 25, 2020.

Evans-Pritchard, E. E. 1962. *Social Anthropology and Other Essays*. New York: The Free Press.

Faucher, Florence. 2020. "An Anthropology of Contemporary Political Parties: Reflexions on Methods and Theory." *Ephemera: Theory & Politics in Organization*. http://www.ephemerajournal.org/contribution/anthropology-contemporary-political-parties-reflexions-methods-and-theory, accessed November 19, 2020.

Ferguson, James, and Akhil Gupta. 2002. Spatializing states: Toward an Ethnography of Neoliberal Governmentality. *American Ethnologist* 29 (4): 981–1002.

Fischer, Michael M. J. 2003. *Emergent Forms of Life and the Anthropological Voice*. Durham, NC and London: Duke University Press.

——— 2009. *Anthropological Futures*. Durham, NC and London: Duke University Press.

——— 2017. "First Responses: A To-Do List." https://culanth.org/fieldsights/first-responses-a-to-do-list, accessed April 4, 2020.

Geertz, Clifford. 1973. *The Interpretation of Cultures*. New York: Basic Books.

Gorski, Philip S. 2018. "Christianity and Democracy after Trump." *Political Theology* 19 (5): 361–2.

Graeber, David. 2013. *The Democracy Project: A History, a Crisis, a Movement*. New York: Spiegel & Grau.

Hall, Kira, Donna M. Goldstein, and Matthew Bruce Ingram. 2016. "The Hands of Donald Trump: Entertainment, Gesture, Spectacle." *HAU: Journal of Ethnographic Theory* 6 (2): 71–100.

Hannerz, Ulf. 1980. *Exploring the City: Inquiries Toward an Urban Anthropology*. New York: Columbia University Press.

Harding, Susan. 1991. "Representing fundamentalism: The Problem of the Repugnant Cultural Other." *Social Research* 58 (2): 373–93.

Harvey, David. 2005. *A Brief History of Neoliberalism*. Oxford and New York: Oxford University Press.

Heiss, Jan Patrick. 2018. "A Hausa Man Makes a Decision: A Contribution to the Anthropological Perspective on Decision-Making." *Anthropological Forum* 28 (3): 236–54.

Hetherington, Kregg. 2011. *Guerilla Auditors: The politics of Transparency in Neoliberal Paraguay*. Durham, NC: Duke University Press.

Hodges, Adam. 2017. "Trump's Formulaic Twitter Insults." *Anthropology News* 58 (1).

Huhn, Arianna. 2018. "Anthropology of Trumplandia." https://storify.com/AriannaHuhn/anthropologyoftrumplandia, accessed May 5, 2020.

Ionescu, Ghita and Ernest Gellner. 1969. *Populism: Its Meaning and National Characteristics*. London: Weidenfeld & Nicolson.

Klein, Daniel B. and Charlotta Stern. 2004. "Democrats and Republicans in Anthropology and Sociology: How Do They Differ on Public Policy Issues?" *The American Sociologist* 35 (4): 79–86.

Laclau, Ernesto. 2005. *On Populist Reason*. New York: Verso.

Latour, Bruno. 2005. *Reassembling the Social: An Introduction to Actor-Network-Theory*. Oxford and New York: Oxford University Press.

Lennon, Myles. 2018. "Revisiting 'The Repugnant Other' in the Era of Trump." *HAU: Journal of Ethnographic Theory* 8 (3): 439–54.

Li, Tanya. 2007. *The Will to Improve: Governmentality, Development, and the Practice of Politics*. Durham, NC: Duke University Press.

Linton, Ralph, ed. 1945. *The Science of Man in the World Crisis*. New York: Columbia University Press,

Lowenthal, Leo and Norbert Guterman. 1949. *Prophets of Deceit: A Study of the Techniques of the American Agitator*. New York: Harper & Brothers.

Malinowski, Bronislaw. 1929. "Practical Anthropology." *Africa: Journal of the International African Institute* 2 (1): 22–38.
———. 1961 [1945]. *The Dynamics of Culture Change: An Inquiry into Race Relations in Africa.* New Haven, CT and London: Yale University Press.
Marcus, George. 1995. "Ethnography In/Of the World: The Emergence of Multi-Sited Ethnography." *Annual Review of Anthropology* 24: 95–117.
Maskovsky, Jeff. 2017. "Toward the Anthropology of White Nationalist Postracialism: Comments Inspired by Hall, Goldstein, and Ingram's 'The Hands of Donald Trump.'" *HAU: Journal of Ethnographic Theory* 7 (1): 433–40.
Maskovsky, Jeff and Sophie Bjork-James. 2020. "Introduction." In Jeff Maskovsky and Sophie Bjork-James, eds. *Beyond Populism: Angry Politics and the Twilight of Neoliberalism.* Morgantown: West Virginia University Press, 1–19.
Mazé, Ramia. 2016. "Design and the Future: Temporal Politics of 'Making a Difference.'" In Rachel Charlotte Smith, Kasper Tang Vangkilde, Mette Gislev Kjaersgaard, Ton Otto, Joachim Halse, and Thomas Binder, eds. *Design Anthropological Futures.* London and New York: Bloomsbury, 37–54.
Mazzarella, William. 2019. "The Anthropology of Populism: Beyond the Liberal Settlement." *Annual Review of Anthropology* 48: 45–60.
McKenna, Brian. 2013. "Dow Chemical's Knowledge Factories: Action Anthropology against Michigan's Company Town Culture." In Sam Beck and Carl A. Maida, eds. *Toward Engaged Anthropology.* New York and Oxford: Berghahn Books, 55–74.
Montagu, M. F. Ashley. 1945. *Man's Most Dangerous Myth: The Fallacy of Race*, 2nd ed. New York: Columbia University Press.
Morton, Gregory Duff. 2018. "Neoliberal Eclipse: Donald Trump, Corporate Monopolism, and the Changing Face of Work." *Dialectical Anthropology* 42 (1): 207–25.
Mukherjee, S. Romi. 2018. "Make America Great Again as White Political Theology." *Revue LISA/LISA E-Journal.* https://journals.openedition.org/lisa/9887, accessed November 21, 2020.
Nardi, Bonnie. 2010. *My Life as a Night Elf Priest: An Anthropological Account of World of Warcraft.* Ann Arbor: University of Michigan Press.
Ong, Aihwa. 2006. *Neoliberalism as Exception: Mutations in Citizenship.* Durham, NC: Duke University Press.
Paley, Julia, ed. 2008. *Democracy: Anthropological Perspectives.* Santa Fe, NM: SAR Press.
Pickles, Anthony J. 2017. "The Anthropology of Trump: What to Do When the Court Jester Takes Charge." http://theconversation.com/the-anthropology-of-trump-what-to-do-when-the-court-jester-takes-charge-80925, accessed April 4, 2020.
Pied, Claudine. 2018, "Conservative Populist Politics and the Remaking of the 'White Working Class' in the USA." *Dialectical Anthropology* 42 (2): 193–206.
Powdermaker, Hortense. 1939. *After Freedom: A Cultural Study in the Deep South.* New York: Viking.
———. 1950. *Hollywood, The Dream Factory—An Anthropologist Looks at the Movie-Makers.* Boston, MA: Little, Brown.
Radcliffe-Brown, A. R. 1965 [1952]. *Structure and Function in Primitive Society.* New York: The Free Press.
Ramsey-Elliot, Morgan. 2017. "From Trucks to Trump: The Role of Small-Town Values in Driving Votes." *Anthropology Now* 9 (1): 53–7.
Robbins, Joel. 2007. "Continuity Thinking and the Problem of Christian Culture: Belief, Time, and the Anthropology of Christianity." *Current Anthropology* 48 (1): 5–38.
Scheper-Hughes, Nancy. 2017. "Another Country? Racial Hatred in the Time of Trump: A Time for Historical Reckoning." *HAU: Journal of Ethnographic Theory* 7 (1): 449–60.

Schmitt, Carl. 2005 [1985/1934]). *Political Theology: Four Chapters on the Concept of Sovereignty*. George Schwab, trans. Chicago, IL: The University of Chicago Press.

Sclafani, Jennifer. 2018. *Talking Donald Trump: A Sociolinguistic Study of Style, Metadiscourse, and Political Identity*. London and New York: Routledge.

Shafer, Byron E. 1986. "Republicans and Democrats as Social Types: Or, Notes toward an Ethnography of the Political Parties." *Journal of American Studies* 20 (3): 341–54.

Smith, David Norman and Eric Hanley. 2018. "The Anger Games: Who Voted for Trump in the 2016 Election, and Why?" *Critical Sociology* 44 (2): 195–212.

Statzel, R. Sophie. 2006. "The Apartheid Conscience: Gender, Race, and Re-imagining the White Nation in Cyberspace." *Ethnic Studies Review* 29 (2): 20–45.

Stoller, Paul. 2017. "The Anthropology of Trump: Myth, Illusion and Celebrity Culture." https://www.huffpost.com/entry/the-anthropology-of-trump_b_9366242, accessed April 4, 2020.

Taussig, Michael. 2017. "Trump Studies." https://culanth.org/fieldsights/trump-studies, accessed April 4, 2020.

Trouillot, Michel-Rolph. 1991. "Anthropology and the Savage Slot: The Poetics and Politics of Otherness." In R. Fox, ed. *Recapturing Anthropology: Working in the Present*. Santa Fe, NM: School of American Research Press, 18–44.

Walley, Christine J. 2017. "Trump's Election and the 'White Working Class': What We Missed." *American Ethnologist* 44 (2): 231–36.

PART I
Ethnographies of Trump country

2
STIGMATIZED IDENTITY MOTIVATING RIGHT-WING POPULISM

How the tea party learned to love Donald Trump

William H. Westermeyer

Introduction

In the summer of 2016, I was reinterviewing some of the Tea Party members with whom I had been researching since 2010. The Tea Party Movement (TPM) had been in decline since its peak in 2011, and most of the groups I had participated with no longer met. Many participants had simply moved on to other activities while some had become more active in local and state politics. Sandra was one of the primary organizers of one of these defunct county-level groups. A fifty-year-old office worker, Sandra still embraced her Tea Party identity. She spoke about issues in the context of the Constitution. She saw America in decline because of the rejection of "founding principles" espoused by revolutionary-era American leaders, and she was mistrustful of politicians—both Republican and Democrat—who had betrayed those principles. At her vacation cabin at a lakeside community, she even had her own golf cart made to look like a Gadsden flag, the bright yellow ensign with coiled rattlesnake and the words DON'T TREAD ON ME that had been a symbol of the movement.

Our interview that summer was overshadowed by a new political phenomenon—the rise of Donald Trump as a viable presidential candidate. Sandra was not impressed to say the least.

> What he says is so empty. When he talks about policy. You really think you can go down there and build a wall? Is that gonna happen? No. He hasn't really spoken about the issues… about how Americans can come back together and get companies to stay here. And how we can build things up. He just flies off these little things that are empty. He doesn't really say anything. To me he talks like a kindergartener. I know middle school kids who have better ideas [and] who know what's going on better than he does. Doesn't make sense….

DOI: 10.4324/9781003152743-3

> And I do believe he is a divider not because he says racial things. Ronald Reagan. He built people up; He made people proud to be an American. He made people feel good about where we live. About prosperity. We are great people. I think Obama has brought us down. He just rips us. America's terrible. I think Trump will do the same thing.

In that conversation she also stated that she didn't feel that Trump knew or even read the Constitution or that he was truly a self-made billionaire like he claimed. Yet when I spoke with Sandra again in 2020 her attitude had changed dramatically.

> Based on all the information that has come out and a lot of the digging that I've done, Trump could not do anything [to lose my support] because I do not believe that Trump is pulling the wool over America's eyes. Trump is trying to wake people up… America is sitting up on a pedestal because we're a Republic [and] because of our Constitution. Because of our capitalism. Our country has been blessed very well. But the greed and destruction of family and good moral values is tearing our country down.

This quote illustrates a dramatically different conclusion than four years earlier yet is explicable by how it frames her support in the context of her Tea Party involvement. She articulates the sense of culture loss that was common with my Tea Party informants as well as the importance of the Constitution and the free market. And although it's only implied in this quote, her and others' later utterances will show how "wake people up" points to an acceptance of Trump's transgressive style and how he represents and expresses a transcendent truth.

Looking back, support for Donald Trump seems a logical continuation of Tea Party activism as the movement declined in significance. Of course, both movements are contemporary examples of right-wing populism, a political formation that one could trace back to the "know-nothings" of the mid-19th century (Berlet and Lyons 2000). However, in early 2016 this articulation was far from certain. Then, many of my informants were either ambivalent or openly hostile toward Trump, and, more broadly, there didn't appear to be a "Trumpist" collective identity to affiliate with. There are distinct qualities of the Tea Party cultural world that complicate an easy transition from Tea Party to Trump. Yet reflecting what Michael Kazin (2016) terms "old whine in new bottles" at the same time there are definite themes of contemporary right-wing populism shared by both the Tea Party and Trumpism.

In this chapter I will show that Trump offered a more forceful political *style* that allowed Tea Party supporters to address grievances and failures left unresolved by their earlier movement. To understand the shift in outlooks by my Tea Party supporters I will merge the terms *grievance* and *style*. Grievances are the problems that collective actors seek to change. Grievances may be specific, such as higher taxes or low wages, or more general, such as revitalization movements and religious fundamentalism.

I use the term style as a combination of both tactics and aesthetics. Tactics begin with the assumption that mobilization of social movements is based on underlying characteristics of the culture. Sidney Tarrow (1994) writes that social movements draw upon aspects of culture and history. Leaders of movements will collect cultural resources and adapt them to their circumstances to overcome constraints to mobilization. These tactics reflect factors discussed in classic social movement theory, such as resource mobilization or political opportunity.

But social movements are more than just repositories of cultural information. Social movements also draw upon, construct, and shape meaning both within the movement and in the wider society (Johnston and Klandermans 1995; Swidler 1986). Some theorists have drawn upon Stuart Hall (1982), describing social movements as agents of "signifying practice." One such practice is framing, the process of matching grievances and actions to the established meanings in the wider culture. According to Snow et al., framing enables individuals "to locate, perceive, identify and label occurrences within their life space and the world at large" (1986: 464). Populism is especially effective in ordering and figuring experiences and action among individuals and groups (Bonikowski 2017; Laclau 2005). However, beyond merely framing experience, social movements also construct or form the basis of powerful collective identities in which meanings and repertoires of action are embodied within political actors (Escobar 2008; Holland et al. 2008; Strauss and Friedman 2018).

Movements also structure emotions, creating "affective solidarity" (Yang 2000) between movement participants. Anthropologists studying the mass protests of the alter-globalization movement identified different affinity groups or blocs—black blocs, pink blocs, clowns, white overalls (Juris 2008; Graeber 2009). The blocs drawing upon different frames and cultural resources allowed participants to associate with groups that aggregated people from different political identities and expressing different emotions (rage, play, satire, etc.). Buddhist monk protests in Myanmar and Trump rallies frame conflicts and actions, draw upon cultural resources and identities, and are characterized by different emotional registers.

The different affinity groups of the alter globalization movement also point to the second aspect of style, aesthetics. Crispin Sartwell (2010) writes that understanding and judging political formations is more than simply understanding ideology and texts. Politics is also "multi-sensory aesthetic surround and context." The most vibrant example he uses is the films of Leni Riefenstahl depicting the Third Reich. One could also point to the songs derived from the African-American spiritual that characterized the civil rights movement that T. V. Reed terms "the halfway house of commitment" (2005: 28).

Essentially, while grievances are central to social movement mobilization, movements are also dynamic cultural formations which signify and assign meaning to people and events, are characterized by different emotional registers, and are actively constructed and interpreted through multiple senses. The grievances of the Tea Party—culture loss, political dispossession, and stigma—aligned well with the grievances articulated by Donald Trump. The style—history and patriotism, political and cultural fundamentalism, and emotional measures of indignation—largely did not. All populism to some degree "disrupts the normal dinner table, much to the discomfort, even alarm, of the usual patrons" (Oliver and Rahn 2016), yet Trump's style went beyond those of most of the Tea Partyists I knew. Some aspects of the style dropped off while others were strengthened and made more belligerent by Trump. And though many of my Tea Party consultants sometimes resisted the belligerent style, the loyalty they expressed toward Trump became unshakable and, in some cases, made them more extremist.

I offer two related explanations for the shift in support by my Tea Party supporters that became apparent when considered in the context of the long-term engagement I had with Tea Party activists. First, Trump offered a political style that counteracted the sense of defeat Tea Partyists felt regarding their movement. Second, Trump broke the sense of stigma Tea Partyists felt about their style and how they were viewed by wider American society. Trumpism provides a new language and demeanor to express, perform, and address their grievances. I will close with ideas of what this transformation and the expressions of my Tea Party informants teach us about the current state of American political culture.

Tea party style/grievance

I will first explain more fully the cultural world of my Tea Party consultants to show both how support for Trump is a natural extension of their political outlook and how it isn't. The Tea Party cultural world consists of three primary grievance/style themes: history and patriotism; cultural and political fundamentalism; and structured emotional registers (Westermeyer 2016, 2019).

The Tea Party Movement (TPM) emerged at a distinct historical conjuncture of social forces and discourses in early 2009. Populist movements, including the TPM, often emerge from a combination of economic, demographic, and cultural dislocation (Bonikowski 2017). Conservative Americans were experiencing an ongoing sense of political and cultural dislocation that began in the George W. Bush administration and supplemented by demographic and ethnic changes occurring in the United States. By early 2009, there was a severe economic recession and a new, biracial United States president who had been thoroughly vilified through conservative media and who was instituting what seemed the largest intervention of government into the economy in their lifetimes.

Media such as Fox News and talk radio, corporate-backed large conservative advocacy groups such as the Koch network, and everyday conservative individuals began organizing in a loose network of protests which formulated a meaning system combining grievances and a unique style to express those grievances. The dislocation and fear were identified with the declining value of what they saw as an idealized American cultural identity. This identity was characterized as independent, driven by individual success and the distinct combination of individualism and fundamentalism that characterizes American patriotism (Westermeyer 2016, 2019). The identity was also implicitly (and sometimes explicitly) white and Christian. While the initiation of the TPM is conjunctural, the style was arguably put in motion by CNBC reporter Rick Santelli's "rant" in January of 2009. Santelli effectively framed the grievances in the context of the founding fathers and what was seen as their "founding principles" of individualism and personal responsibility that they enshrined in the United States Constitution.

Style and grievance merged. The root of American decline is the rejection of the values that made America not only unique but the greatest nation and to many, a nation with a divine mission defined by God. A return to greatness requires a firm adherence to the Constitution which is seen as the near-sacred document containing the genetic code of American exceptionalism. This package of frames, symbols, and discourses was conveyed in an emotional register of indignation, mistrust of politicians and vigilance toward further erosion of liberty. Paul, one of my Tea Party consultants from Western North Carolina, put it well.

> But the ideas that we're standing for are not stupid ideas. It's what built this country. It's what built the greatest country. I know this is hard for a lot of certain progressives in power—is [that] our nation is set apart in its achievement if nothing else. We believe it is set apart in its destiny. In its achievement. Nobody's done what America has done around the world. That's because of freedom and innovation.

Much of the blame lies with individual Americans, yet the source lies in political leadership, what Oliver and Rahn (2016) term a "representation gap" or Lipset (1959) terms "crisis of legitimacy"—Democrats and RINOs (Republicans in Name Only) who fail to follow "founding principles," who have weakly yielded their liberty to the "nanny state," embraced dependency, and been silenced by political correctness.

The TPM is an example of a twenty-first-century right-wing populist movement which could be defined as a political formation that identifies a "people" as opposed to an "other." This other could be refugees and immigrants admitted to European countries and the politicians that welcome them, or, in the case of the Tea Party, undocumented immigrants, RINOs and progressives.[1]

The second point regarding right-wing populism is its relationship to fundamentalism (Herriot 2020; Westermeyer 2021). Both fundamentalism and populism identify an other and a people. Yet, to fundamentalists, the other is not only outside the group and value system but an enemy who is actively seeking to destroy it (Nagata 2001). Often right-wing populism is portrayed as associated with ethnonationalism, a bounded and ascribed cultural identity (Bonikowski 2017). While accurate, Mudde (2007) seeks a more "holistic" definition of nationalism as both ethnic and civic. In returning to my conversation with Paul, this Tea Party civic nationalism is based in values.[2]

> I hate to say this to a progressive, I'm not quite sure you would say you're progressive, but I like you, Bill. I think you're a good person, but the belief

systems of the progressives are evil. I don't think they're just bad—bad plans… [Because of them] we are rejecting truth and we are actually turning truth into the enemy.

The words "evil" and "truth" were used by several informants to analyze their opponents. Speaking with Linda who sees the enemy as progressive and elitist, she said, "The people didn't understand where it was coming from. It's not about Trump or Obama. I think the biggest problem is that so many people are so freaking dumbed down, they're not even paying attention. It's good versus evil." I ask her to explain evil because it is a term I didn't understand. She replies, "That's what's wrong with the left (referring to me). There is no right or wrong. They don't believe some things are evil."

For the Tea Party, this fundamentalism is also political. By political I mean the Tea Party is characterized by an unwillingness to compromise what they see as founding principles (as demonstrated by the taxing and spending stalemates which led to the debt ceiling crisis of 2011 and the government shutdown in 2013) and the elevation of the US Constitution to that of a sacred document that must be interpreted in its original and literal context.

Based upon this style, I was initially puzzled by my Tea Party consultants' support because I saw Trump supporters and Tea Party supporters as two discrete groups within the socio-political right. Most Tea Partyists were aligned with candidates who had cultivated Tea Party support from early in the movement's emergence, primarily Senator Ted Cruz and Dr. Ben Carson. In November of 2015 I attended an Iowa-style caucus amongst Tea Party supporters in the western Piedmont of North Carolina, and Ted Cruz and Ben Carson split nearly the entirety of the 200 votes evenly with only one supporter for Trump. However, less than a year later many of my supporters had come around to being strong supporters of Trump.

Granted, much of this may be attributed to the decline of the TPM after 2012, which left many newly activated conservatives without a strong vibrant growing movement. Moreover, Trump's opponent, Hillary Rodham Clinton, had been made a villain through twenty-five years of right-wing talk radio. Tea Partyists could easily support Trump given there was no real alternative. Nonetheless, the shift I saw requires a stronger explanation than just lack of choices.

Conflicts of style and matching grievances

Although initially Trump seemed to be addressing some of the same grievances as my Tea Party informants, there were distinct warning signs presented by Trump. Tea Party grievances which I describe as fundamentalist are based in values and uncompromising firmness. Trump possessed no ideological consistency according to my Tea Party consultants in 2016. Furthermore, his conservative bona fides were equally questionable. His multiple marriages, his long-term financial support of Democratic candidates (including Hillary Rodham Clinton), and his past support for abortion rights (Schwarz 2015) all raised red flags among conservatives in general. Trump also did not adhere to other basic tenets of Tea Party fundamentalism, such as the strict adherence to the Constitution and the framing of grievances in the context of the founding fathers and their enduring principles. At the same time Trump's uncompromising stance toward undocumented immigration was popular among Tea Partyists. We see this ambivalence when I asked Paul his stance on Trump.

> By and large. I think there are things that are better about Trump than Hillary [Clinton]. I think you have a wolf in wolf's clothing which is Hillary and a wolf in sheep's clothing which is Trump. I think there's certain things I can agree with Trump on. But I don't think he has a moral compass. He's not pegged to anything. Except maybe Trump. Maybe he's pegged to himself.

He continues,

> Trump is concerning to me because I don't know what his values are. I think that Trump potentially could turn into [a person I could support]. Every nation needs borders. We seem to be the only country where we're supposed to ignore ours… If Trump goes in there if he does those things, those things will have some benefit. But ultimately Trump is on many issues progressive. I could give you examples of him giving to liberals and stuff.

To a large degree Paul is concerned about grievance mentioning borders and values. Tea Partyists also had, and continue to have, a problem with his style. Issues were usually framed in the context of the Constitution, the founders etc. As Sandra said later in our 2016 conversation,

> Do I think he is a constitutional conservative? No. I don't think he even knows the Constitution. I really don't. The reason why he's doing so well is that people are fed up. They're just fed up. We want somebody to say what they think.

Evoking that people are fed up and want someone to say what they think shows the grievance/style of the Tea Party. Desiring the quality of saying what one thinks implies there are people who don't *and* can't say what they think. Throughout my research with Tea Partyists there was a persistent sense of stigma. They felt that displays of their vision of idealized America had no place in a multicultural and "woke" home. The free expression of patriotism was one indication of a return to the idealized American culture. Roberta lamented, "But when I grew up, we put your hand over your heart for the Pledge of Allegiance. We sang 'God Bless America,' and we sang religious songs. I learned all the armed services songs. Today it is considered poor taste. Are you going to step on somebody's toes?" It was more than just patriotism; it was also cultural values, according to Paul.

> You watch MSNBC or read some of the newspapers on the left… we're just buffoons, we're morons, we're idiots. We're deniers, whatever. We are intellectually racist. Whatever. And it's just not true. We may disagree on some things but were not stupid people. There are intelligent people on both sides.

This was echoed by Glenn, a sixty-year-old salesman:

> I mean we're just tired of being beat down and a lot of these problems that society faces… our side gets a lot of grief. We're called homophobic and we're called bigoted. We don't care if somebody's gay or not—well, some people do—but we just don't want it in our face. Go do what you wanna do but we shouldn't have to be forced to bless you and what you're doing.

There was a definite racial resentment to some as well. To a large degree, the Tea Party identity was an example of whiteness, a social identity of privilege which is unmarked (Hartigan, Jr. 1997; Westermeyer 2018). With the election of Donald Trump and the rise of the Black Lives Matter Movement many Americans were being forced to confront their own whiteness. The silencing imposed by political correctness was also seen as discrimination against whites. As one consultant related to me, "Though conservatives may be more tough love, the point is that there is a better life out there. But if I talk about people taking care of themselves, I am termed a racist." Race is an underlying theme for Sandra, and on this occasion in 2016 she expressed a pointed racial resentment.

> But now as a white person I'm walking on pins and needles. If I say something that's wrong and to look at them wrong. It's just unreal… we've got this issue that has risen up now saying that we're (whites) being discriminated against more. And it's really creating a divide. I'm to a point now where I try to avoid being around groups of black people because this can turn into an issue. You could say something wrong or do something. [There is an] entitlement thing going on too. If something's not going someone's way, what's the first thing they're going to say? You are racist.

These Tea Partyists were all expressing grievances that were not simply about changing culture but also about being silenced or what Pierre Bourdieu (Bourdieu and Thompson 1991) would term "symbolic violence" in their resistance to it. During the years of my research, due to symbolic violence, Tea Partyists expressed these values in specific contexts, most often in what Melucci (1989) would term "submerged spaces," small local regularly-held meetings of Tea Party groups. Here, meetings always began with the Pledge of Allegiance and the Christian prayer. They were separate, and to a degree pre-figurative, spaces where people freely discussed the Constitution and American history and performed patriotism and conservative social values.

My Tea Party informants conceptualize a wider conflict between good and evil and that evil is winning the culture war because it is silencing them. For Linda, it was a sociopolitical and cultural elite. For Paul, it was more generally progressives. Sandra and Glenn were more focused upon identity politics. All felt that they were being made to feel as "strangers in their own land" (Hochschild 2016).

A final factor still prominent to my Tea Party informants is the negative sense of their movement's success. I and others have argued that the Tea Party was a successful social movement by moving the national Republican Party more to the right (Skocpol and Williamson 2011), building long-term political skills among neophyte activists (Westermeyer 2019), creating new spaces for women in politics (Burke 2016), and having dramatic effects on local political controversies (Trapenberg Frick 2013). Moreover, several of my Tea Party informants with no prior political experience prior to 2009 have run for elected office, and a few have even won. However, many of my consultants did not see the movement as successful. The representation gap remained. Some said that they now realized that their efforts had been futile all along, while others believed that the Tea Party was not aggressive enough. In other words, the grievances were still worthwhile, but the style had been woefully lacking.

From patriot to deplorable

From my experiences at Trump rallies and through social media and scholarly writing, I interpreted a different political style characteristic of Trump and his supporters. Instead of emulating the Constitution and history in a distinct style of nationalism and patriotism, Trump supporters expressed a more explicit nationalism emphasizing nativism and xenophobia (Oliver and Rahn 2016). Though they embrace a similar mistrust of political elites and fear of multiculturalism, there is no grounding in foundational principles of cultural citizenship tracing a legacy to the Constitution and founding fathers. Trump supporters, as opposed to Tea Partyists, didn't seem to care how Ben Franklin would have felt about the Affordable [health] Care Act or undocumented immigrants. Moreover, while I was accustomed to the relatively measured and consistent emotions of indignation, patriotism, and self-righteousness by the Tea Party, the Trump rallies were more unruly and restive, with a suppressed and unpredictable rage which could easily (and did sometimes) turn to violence. Finally, there was a different demographic at the Trump rallies. Whereas Tea Partyists were typically older, upper-middle-class and white, the Trump crowds that I witnessed, while still primarily white, contained a much larger group of working-class and 18-to-35-year-old males.

Donald Trump seemed anathema to many of the aspects of the Tea Party cultural world that I had been studying and writing about. However, as I continued speaking to some of my consultants, I began to understand the shift in outlook. And in fact, when looking at the broad outlines of the Tea Party's cultural world and the symbolic and discursive components of Tea Partyists' movement identities, there is a distinct connection between Tea Party activists and Donald Trump supporters. The point I will make in this section is that while the grievances of the Tea Party are reflected in the actions of Donald Trump, it was the acceptance of the shift in style that brought my Tea Party supporters so strongly to him.

Between mid-2015 and the spring of 2017, most of my consultants' outlooks on Trump had shifted from indifference or opposition to strong support. With the election won, my Tea Party consultants were firmly in the Trump camp. Among my informants the shift in support can be attributed to two primary factors. First and most simply, Trump provides hope to those who believed that the Tea Party movement was not a success. As Diane said to me in mid-2020,

> I think that's part of [Trump's] appeal. He doesn't answer to anybody. Romney has turned out to be such a… I'd like to get a hold of him. They all turned out to be turncoats. We worked so hard for McCain and Romney I was heartbroken when they didn't win. And then they turned out being so bad. I understand McCain's hatred of Trump. Things that were said and all. It's a shame that neither of them could see the big picture.

But more importantly it is the shift in style. Trump's belligerence and pugilism is necessary to defeat the powerful, entrenched hegemony of evil left-wing ideas such as socialism, cultural relativism, and the dominance of elites.

The simplest path to explain the support of Donald Trump by Tea Partyists is through the response to their sense that the Tea Party wasn't successful. Trump offered a style that they saw as effective due to its disruptive quality. Paul connects the idea of losing and being burned out with the hope he feels with the rise of Donald Trump. He also provides a clue to something deeper motivating my former Tea Partyists.

> I think a large portion of folks are at that point in the fight. Everybody in this fight gets to this point. We're against the Goliath… Will we win? We will win in the end because we know how the Bible ends. Will we win that fight politically? If I had to guess right now, I would say that we are so outgunned and so outnumbered. They have the marketing appeals and everything… I think a lot of people in the Tea Party look at Trump. They see he's bad. They see him as not part of the system that's in place. The people who are driving the agenda of the left. They go, "I'm not big enough I don't have a big enough voice. But that big man there is the biggest man on the block and he's spoiling for a fight always. He's a bully and we need a bully."

As noted, Sandra's attitude toward Trump changed dramatically between 2016 and when I interviewed her again in 2020. I asked her if she thought that Trump's political style made people more aggressive in their politics.

> You're right, here's the thing. Being nice is over. We tried to be nice. We tried to lead on the middle ground. We tried to come to the table. The Democrats they just keep beating us down and beating us down and beating us down. There's no being nice anymore. Stick to the Constitution. And this immoral… And don't do these backroom deals. This is just over. That is what people like

about Trump. Trump is trying to fight back. You have the spineless Republicans that are doing nothing… When Bill Clinton was president, he had Newt Gingrich as speaker. Newt Gingrich was hard-core, and he made a mockery of him and stuff got done. That's not the case anymore. When you get these anti-American, America-hating people in there—the American people are awake.

Sandra's quote is telling when compared to her first quote in the opening vignette. Whereas Sandra favored the unity of Ronald Reagan in 2016, in 2020 she valued the combat of Newt Gingrich. And another interviewee, Linda, also stresses combat.

Right now, I think he's brilliant with what he's doing the tweets and all. He knows exactly what he's doing. He's not accidentally [letting his true feelings show]. He is getting them all worked up. And then they concentrate on that stupid tweet. Then he changes things over here and over there. He's distracting them in their attacking him and that's what they're taught to do. That's what the left does attack attack attack attack and take the bait.

Tea Partyists were welcoming toward a fighter and rule breaker, yet we get a sense again of fundamentalism that is a significant factor in my Tea Partyists' political outlook. The specific word "truth" or its implicit meaning appears throughout my interviews. This focus upon truth shows that there are truths and lies with a strict moral boundary between them that cleaves American society, and that is the root of American decline. Trump exposes the lie, fulfilling a prophetic function (Melucci 1989). Truth, such as the Tea Party grievances mentioned in the prior section, had been hidden away by a rapidly changing America and the political and cultural elites enabling those changes.

I think regular people wanted to see some action not a bunch of crap. People ready to hear the truth. I don't care what you say he comes across as the truth. In their regular lives he resonated with what he was talking about. So, whether you like him or not he was brutally honest.

Essentially Linda is saying that Trump makes the left elites react and be defensive in contrast to being on the offensive. However, in Paul's quote above he mentions a crucial aspect of how many Trump supporters see their place in American society: "He's not part of the system." In the context of that quote, he is referring to mainstream American political culture and the hegemony of (evil) left-wing ideas. However, more generally he is referring to a different class of people who control what is said and done in America. While speaking with Linda, I was struck by one thing that she said to me. Referring to why she supported Trump she said, "He's never been at the table with those powerful people." The sentence puzzled me because we were discussing a billionaire who operated within circles of many other billionaires, who could buy anything he desired and had given a fortune to Democrat and Republican candidates alike. However, on further reflection it began to make sense in the context of the grievance/style of the Tea Party and offered a clue as to how some Tea Party supporters eventually became diehard Trump supporters.

Essentially, instead of powerful people characterized solely by material wealth, Linda was referring to a cultural and political elite, a class of Americans apart from them who, as Paul had said, set the political and cultural agenda for the nation.

> He's not one of them. For whatever reason. Probably because he asked questions, he's not always fallen in line. And these elites. These families of some of these people, they nurture their own. This is the monarchy. Their kids get into the best schools. You think these kids get into the schools whether they're smarter not? They end up in the Harvard's for whatever. They are all part of a destined. Who knows? Maybe Trump's bloodline wasn't right. Maybe he wasn't cooperative. So, I don't think he ever had a seat at the table. I think he puts ketchup on his steak and does weird things. Like when you hear somebody like [former senator from Massachusetts and Secretary of State John] Kerry and how he talks. That kind of elitism. It's cultural; you're born right; you're in the right bloodline.

The power of this class is recognized as setting the standards of political correctness, gender roles, multiculturalism, and, more generally, a hegemonic liberal conception of American cultural identity. Moreover, while setting this agenda, they are all the while looking down their noses at patriotic, conservative, typically non-urban and Christian, Americans, the unrefined and traditionalists. Linda continues,

> It's one thing to have money. But it's different for you to feel you're smarter and know best. And there is an elite element in our world. People that know best and they run everything. They're the public masters. Certain people think they know best. You have them in all different parts of life.

The "ruling class" had been a recurring theme in my research. For many, Tea Party activism was triggered by a crisis of representation. Could a conception of class based upon culture provide an explanation for Tea Party activists' shift in outlook and the broader attraction of Trump to many Americans? Simply, Linda was referring to a definition of power not connected with wealth and more firmly Weberian, grounded in ideas of status, prestige, and belonging. I have written previously of how the Tea Party had used different categories of class than the typical Marxian perspective of control of the means of production. Sociologist Stanley Aronowitz (2003) writes that classes have historicity; they are unique formations based on the structural conditions of time and place. To understand class in contemporary society, one needed to consider class as the control of both material and *immaterial* production. In the case of my Tea Party consultants, the immaterial production was culture and politics—policies, agendas, and trends. To Tea Partyists, it is produced by a political and cultural elite with their own set of faulty values. Bourdieu wrote of how human cultures construct structures and categories that legitimize and naturalize unequal relations of power. These power relations are negotiated and constructed in fields where different forms of capital are accumulated and valued. He broadly referred to these forms of power as cultural capital. The immaterial production is the structure that assigns value to cultural capital. The perceived lack of symbolic capital leads to stigma and a resentment toward those who seemingly possessed it. Trump, on the other hand, shatters the sense of stigma felt by Tea Partyists who feel they lack the cultural capital that has value in current American society.

While Donald Trump may operate effortlessly in the cultural field of billionaire real estate developers, he lacks and embellishes his lack of cultural capital recognized in the cultural-political field. He is seen by his supporters favorably by being outside the circles of those possessing high levels of cultural capital, what some would call the "cultural elite." Trump lacks measured language, has never been a benefactor of the arts, is proud of his lack of political correctness, and makes no apologies for his aversion to healthy eating habits. He is the bourgeois, anti-cultural elite, and his utterances and gestures signal this to his supporters (Hall et al. 2016).

Trump supporters demonstrate a different response to a lack of cultural capital than the sense of symbolic violence felt by my Tea Party consultants. Many Trump supporters are not self-censored but rather embrace their lack of cultural capital. The best example is the 2016 speech by Hillary Rodham Clinton in which she declared that half of Trump supporters are in a "basket of deplorables." Her label did not reinforce symbolic violence but just the opposite. The label was embraced and provided a cultural resource used in the forging of a Trumpist collective identity. Soon there were T-shirts proclaiming one to be a "PROUD MEMBER OF THE BASKET OF DEPLORABLES" or Facebook group titled UNITED DEPLORABLE'S FOR TRUMP with over a quarter of a million likes. In other words, it is the style of how one responds and acts within the habitus of American culture. Trump doesn't accommodate it. He directly confronts it. He doesn't speak truth to power; Trump "speaks truth about power" (Hahl et al. 2018). Diane, who runs a small business with her husband, expressed the stigma and the desire to break it.

> I wish I could be more that way. Even now I put a Trump sticker on my car. I have to go to Raleigh tomorrow I wonder if I should take it off. Because I really am afraid that I might get attacked or something. But there's another part of me that wants to be in your face. I am a Trump supporter; deal with it.

Glenn, like Linda describing Trump's Twitter habits, sees Trump as a reaction to the left.

> We have our set ideals, and the left has their set ideals. We need someone to fight for our ideals like Donald Trump does. The left doesn't give up—single payer healthcare; The left stands up for what they believe in. We should be just as proud in the way we defeat it and go back to a market-based solutions for healthcare problems and we don't need to be shrinking away from that. And

> I think Trump realizes that you know he has never been one to shrink away from a fight and get a slap upside the head. But he is more resolved to pass things.

And, finally, Sandra who again frames her resentment in slightly racialized terms.

> A lot of them say that they're glad that Trump is exposing a lot of this that's going on. As the Tea Party tried to get a lot of this exposed but Trump has brought it out in front of everybody and we see the evil trying to fight back against him. People are scared. People are scared to say or do anything because if you're conservative and a Trump support you get attacked. You're automatically called a racist. The people are living in fear now because they're scared they're going to be called a racist. I say so what! People can call you names. Whatever. We have to get back to the fundamentals of things.

In the context of style, it is apparent that there was a desire by Tea Partyists to be more extreme in their pursuit of ends. As noted in the first vignette of this chapter, Sandra said that nothing Trump could do would cause her to not support him. Diane made a similar statement:

> I loved what he said and now I'm behind him 100% and I still am. Just like other people I cringe sometimes and really wish they would take his Twitter account away for a while. There's nothing a man can do to lose me. There's really nothing I can imagine him doing that would change my mind.

While one could doubt this statement in the literal sense, it nonetheless shows that unlike other political figures who have invariably let these Tea Partyists down, Trump can't. The point, though, is that Trump isn't a politician in the sense that he is a leader who compromises and is beholden to "evil" interests.

A second point is the idea of norm breaking. The American political culture has undergone stress and change during the four years of the Trump presidency. Granted, norms, customs, and unwritten rules of governance have been severely eroded before Trump by the Republican leadership during the Obama administration. But Trump has made social discourses that were once unsayable and undoable before sayable and doable now (Hahl et al. 2018; Hall et al. 2016) and earned the undying loyalty of his supporters.

Conclusion

In April of 2020 I attended a protest in front of the South Carolina statehouse called "Operation Gridlock." South Carolina and much of the rest of the world were in the midst of the first of several surges in the COVID-19 pandemic which would eventually sicken or kill tens of millions of people including killing over 600,000 Americans. Operation Gridlock was one of the many protests by what I term "reopen activists" (Westermeyer 2021) staged across the nation opposing government restrictions meant to stem the spread of the virus. At the time, states across the country were closing all but essential businesses and, depending upon the jurisdiction, asking or ordering people to shelter at home and to don face coverings.[3] I wanted to see for myself these new conservative activists that had arisen with the rise of Donald Trump and solidified with the COVID-19 pandemic.

As I faced the state capitol building and its wide, open plaza, I experienced something familiar. On the five wide steps between the floor of the plaza and the capitol entrance flew a bright yellow Gadsden flag with its coiled rattlesnake and words "DON'T TREAD ON ME." Here, it hung on a short pole beside a microphone stand framed on the opposite side by an American flag. In front of the microphone and down the steps two people stood with a long blue banner with white letters that read:

> TRUMP-PENCE 2020
> MAKE AMERICA GREAT AGAIN

Without the Trump banner, the scene and symbolism were strikingly similar to the Tea Party rallies I had attended a decade before. As I listened to the succession of short speeches, I heard familiar themes of liberty, market fundamentalism, Judeo-Christian values, conspiracy narratives, and mistrust toward institutions, government, and expertise that characterized the TPM. And though there were no three-corner hats and revolutionary-era garb, there was the occasional protest sign with a quote from a founding father.

I began to write this paper in late 2019 to trace the transition of Tea Partyists to Trumpists. As described here in April, it seemed that the Tea Party style had come full circle though in different form. Tea Party themes and symbols appeared to be useful in framing people's resistance to government-imposed restrictions and regulations to prevent the spread of a pandemic. This years-long process shows how grievances and styles employed by social movements inform each other, shift, and re-form under different historical circumstances.

But something more profound and grave was becoming apparent. As I spoke to some of these activists and former Tea Partyists who largely shared the views of reopen activists, the style I have discussed had become even more extreme. Observing right-wing populism surrounding the COVID-19 pandemic has uncovered more elaborate and numerous conspiracy theories and higher degrees of suspicion and mistrust toward leaders and expertise. When I studied the Tea Party a decade ago, I was intrigued by deciphering their logic. But today, finding a logic among Trump supporters, whether former Tea Partyists or the newer reopen activists, is much more difficult. A large part of this is due to the insular world of Trump supporters in which the exegesis of their experience and existence is so completely opposite of my mine. And while diving into difference is, of course, what we do as anthropologists, I found it troubling that these opposed realities with little common ground were widening between people sharing a history, national identity, and most importantly, the same polity.

Many explanations have emerged (and will emerge) on this political phenomenon, but I want to focus back on my use of the concept of fundamentalism. Our political culture currently is rife with conflict—some of the greatest conflict since the 1960s. But this conflict is not simply driven by populism. It is not just a "people" versus an "other." It is the very nature of how that other is conceived. Contemporary right-wing populism typically frames the other in ethnic and racial terms, typically groups of marked individuals who do not belong. And while this is definitely a mark of cultural fundamentalism, in our current situation, the Muslim and the undocumented immigrant are secondary. The primary other is Americans, people of color *and* white, on the opposite side of the political spectrum. As mentioned, my informants often evoked the sense of truth and how their struggle was to uncover truth. But the opposite of truth to many of them is not falsehood; it is evil, iniquity and malignancy. We have seen hints of this from political science with observations that have been variously labelled as "negative partisanship" (Abramowitz and Webster 2018), affective partisanship (Iyengar and Krupenkin 2018), and "political sectarianism" (Finkel et al. 2020) in which political positionality today is more often based in the people one is opposed to rather than the issues one favors.

The larger question, though, is what are the sources of these dramatic and disturbing changes in the political culture? Much has been written on the media influence on right-wing politics and the creation of media bubbles. Yet media consumption also establishes and maintains not only the content but *the space* of political and cultural fundamentalism. Richard Antoun (2001) writes that one aspect of fundamentalism's "quest for purity" is separation. Separation could be considered in the literal sense, such as a separate, insular religious community, or more metaphorically, such as the wearing of a particular style of dress. But media have become a form of separation. As Paul said early in the chapter, "Truth has become the enemy." Many Trump supporters and former Tea Partyists have found a place where truth isn't the enemy or rather a place with different truths that are more conducive to their grievances and style. Fox News and talk radio have been those separate spaces for years. However, in late 2020 the media universe became even more insular. Primarily since the 2020 election handed Trump electoral defeat, truth for Trump supporters has become the enemy, even in parts of their own media universe such as Fox News, which, in their eyes, perpetuated a lie by declaring Trump's electoral defeat soon after the election. Many Trump supporters have moved from Fox News to One America News Network and Newsmax TV—news sources unbound by journalistic standards and functioning more as social movement organizations in the wider right-wing social movement (Grynbaum and Koblin 2020; Isaac and Browning 2020).[4] A similar exodus has occurred from Facebook and Twitter, which have now banned Trump altogether, to Parler. In short, the epistemic closure of the right-wing media universe creates separation, not simply separate information systems but prefigurative spaces where the world they envision is modeled. Moreover, it is possible that this separation has become wider in 2020 and 2021 due to the COVID-19 pandemic's isolation and social distancing. Everyday conversations at the grocery store or at workplaces have been severely curtailed. These discourses between citizens are crucial aspects for a functioning pluralistic and democratic society.

Yet, regardless of the sources, America has been led by a charismatic leader with authoritarian tendencies loved by many for not being grounded to political or even democratic norms. However, due to the changes in the political culture, Americans to a large degree no longer agree what those norms are. Insular spaces with different truths, coupled with the demonization of loyal opposition, impede reaching mutual understandings and increase the fragility and contingency of a nation, even one as supposedly stable as the United States.

Notes

1. The term "progressive" is understood by people on the left as those espousing the most dramatic and deep changes to increase social and economic democracy. To those on the right, progressive is used much as the term liberal was in the 1980s—as a pejorative term to label anyone who is not conservative as an extremist.
2. This is not meant to imply that the Tea Party did not have ethno-nationalist tendencies and beliefs. I will discuss race further below yet the more explicit example of ethno-nationalism within the Tea Party was toward Latino immigrants, specifically undocumented ones. But this outlook is more complex than simple xenophobia. Tea Party racism and ethnic prejudice is a complex phenomenon (Westermeyer 2016, 2019).
3. The term reopen activist fails to adequately capture the breadth of this protest movement. Beyond simply demanding that government no longer force businesses to close due to the pandemic, we're strongly opposed to wearing masks and circulated doubt regarding the source and severity of COVID-19.
4. Rebekah Mercer, a member of a billionaire family of GOP donors, is a primary funder of the Parler social network (Hagey 2020).

References

Abramowitz, Alan I., and Steven W. Webster. 2018. "Negative Partisanship: Why Americans Dislike Parties but Behave Like Rabid Partisans." *Political Psychology* 39 (S1): 119–35. doi: 10.1111/pops.12479.

Antoun, Richard T. 2001. *Understanding Fundamentalism: Christian, Islamic, and Jewish Movements*. Walnut Creek, CA: AltaMira Press.

Aronowitz, Stanley. 2003. *How Class Works: Power and Social Movement*. New Haven, CT: Yale University Press.

Berlet, Chip, and Matthew Nemiroff Lyons. 2000. *Right-Wing Populism in America: Too Close for Comfort*. New York: Guilford Press.

Bonikowski, Bart. 2017. "Ethno-Nationalist Populism and the Mobilization of Collective Resentment." *The British Journal of Sociology* 68 (S1): S181–213.

Bourdieu, Pierre, and John B. Thompson. 1991. *Language and Symbolic Power*. Cambridge, MA: Harvard University Press.

Burke, Meghan A. 2016. *Race, Gender, and Class in the Tea Party: What the Movement Reflects about Mainstream Ideologies*. Lanham, MD: Rowman & Littlefield.

Escobar, Arturo. 2008. *Territories of Difference: Place, Movements, Life, Redes*. Durham, NC: Duke University Press.

Finkel, Eli J., Christopher A. Bail, Mina Cikara, Peter H. Ditto, Shanto Iyengar, Samara Klar, Lilliana Mason, et al. 2020. "Political Sectarianism in America." *Science* 370 (6516): 533–36. doi: 10.1126/science.abe1715.

Graeber, David. 2009. *Direct Action: An Ethnography*. Edinburgh and Oakland, CA: AK Press.

Grynbaum, Michael M., and John Koblin. 2020. "Newsmax, Once a Right-Wing Also-Ran, Is Rising, and Trump Approves." *The New York Times*, November 22, 2020, sec. Business. https://www.nytimes.com/2020/11/22/business/media/newsmax-trump-fox-news.html.

Hahl, Oliver, Minjae Kim, and Ezra W. Zuckerman Sivan. 2018. "The Authentic Appeal of the Lying Demagogue: Proclaiming the Deeper Truth about Political Illegitimacy." *American Sociological Review* 83 (1): 1–33. doi: 10.1177/0003122417749632.

Hall, Kira, Donna M. Goldstein, and Matthew Bruce Ingram. 2016. "The Hands of Donald Trump: Entertainment, Gesture, Spectacle." *HAU: Journal of Ethnographic Theory* 6 (2): 71–100.

Hall, Stuart. 1982. "The Rediscovery of Ideology: Return of the Repressed in Media Studies." In *Culture, Society and the Media*. Michael Gurevitch, Tony Bennett, James Curran, and Janet Woollacott (eds). London: Methuen & Co. http://www.davidryfe.com/here/wp-content/uploads/2013/01/hallch03culture.pdf.

Hartigan Jr., John. 1997. "Establishing the Fact of Whiteness." *American Anthropologist* 99 (3): 495–505.

Herriot, Peter. 2020. *Populism, Fundamentalism, and Identity: Fighting Talk*. Cham, Switzerland: Palgrave Macmillan. doi: 10.1007/978-3-030-42509-8.

Hochschild, Arlie Russell. 2016. *Strangers in Their Own Land: Anger and Mourning on the American Right*. New York: The New Press. http://worldcat.org/oclc/953867247.

Holland, Dorothy, Gretchen Fox, and Vinci Daro. 2008. "Social Movements and Collective Identity: A Decentered, Dialogic View." *Anthropological Quarterly* 81 (1): 95–126.

Horwitz, Jeff, and Hagey. 2020. "Parler Makes Play for Conservatives Mad at Facebook, Twitter." *Wall Street Journal*, November 15, 2020, sec. Tech. https://www.wsj.com/articles/parler-backed-by-mercer-family-makes-play-for-conservatives-mad-at-facebook-twitter-11605382430.

Isaac, Mike, and Kellen Browning. 2020. "Fact-Checked on Facebook and Twitter, Conservatives Switch Their Apps." *The New York Times*, November 11, 2020, sec. Technology. https://www.nytimes.com/2020/11/11/technology/parler-rumble-newsmax.html.

Iyengar, Shanto, and Masha Krupenkin. 2018. "The Strengthening of Partisan Affect." *Political Psychology* 39 (S1): 201–18. doi: 10.1111/pops.12487.

Johnston, Hank, and Bert Klandermans. 1995. *Social Movements and Culture*. Minneapolis: University of Minnesota Press.

Juris, Jeffrey. 2008. *Networking Futures: The Movements against Corporate Globalization*. Durham, NC: Duke University Press.

Kazin, Michael. 2016. "Trump and American Populism: Old Whine, New Bottles." *Foreign Affairs* 95: 17.

Laclau, Ernesto. 2005. *On Populist Reason*. London and New York: Verso.

Lipset, Seymour Martin. 1959. "Some Social Requisites of Democracy: Economic Development and Political Legitimacy." *The American Political Science Review* 53 (1): 69–105.

Melucci, Alberto. 1989. *Nomads of the Present: Social Movements and Individual Needs in Contemporary Society*. Philadelphia, PA: Temple University Press.

Mudde, Cas. 2007. *Populist Radical Right Parties in Europe*. Cambridge: Cambridge University Press. doi: 10.1017/CBO9780511492037.

Nagata, Judith. 2001. "Beyond Theology: Toward an Anthropology of 'Fundamentalism'." *American Anthropologist* 103 (2): 481–98.

Oliver, J. Eric, and Wendy M. Rahn. 2016. "Rise of the Trumpenvolk: Populism in the 2016 Election." *The ANNALS of the American Academy of Political and Social Science* 667 (1): 189–206. doi: 10.1177/0002716216662639.

Sartwell, Crispin. 2010. *Political Aesthetics*. Ithaca, NY: Cornell University Press.

Schwarz, Hunter. 2015. "The Many Ways in Which Donald Trump Was Once a Liberal's Liberal." *Washington Post*, July 9, 2015. https://www.washingtonpost.com/news/the-fix/wp/2015/07/09/ths-many-ways-in-which-donald-trump-was-once-a-liberals-liberal/.

Skocpol, Theda, and Vanessa Williamson. 2011. *The Tea Party and the Remaking of Republican Conservatism*. Oxford and New York: Oxford University Press.

Snow, David A., E. Burke Rochford Jr., Steven K. Worden, and Robert D. Benford. 1986. "Frame Alignment Processes, Micromobilization, and Movement Participation." *American Sociological Review* 51 (4): 464–81.

Strauss, Claudia, and Jack R. Friedman, eds. 2018. *Political Sentiments and Social Movements: The Person in Politics and Culture*. New York: Palgrave Macmillan.

Swidler, Ann. 1986. "Culture in Action: Symbols and Strategies." *American Sociological Review* 51 (2): 273–86. doi: 10.2307/2095521.

Tarrow, Sidney. 1994. *Power in Movement: Social Movements, Collective Action and Politics*. New York: Cambridge University Press.

Trapenberg Frick, Karen. 2013. "The Actions of Discontent: Tea Party and Property Rights Activists Pushing Back Against Regional Planning." *Journal of the American Planning Association* 79 (3): 190–200. doi: 10.1080/01944363.2013.885312.

Westermeyer, William H. 2016. "Local Tea Party Groups and the Vibrancy of the Movement." *PoLAR: Political and Legal Anthropology Review* 39 (S1): 121–38.

———. 2018. "Progressives' Plantation: The Tea Party's Complex Relationship with Race." In Claudia Strauss and Jack R. Friedman, eds. *Political Sentiments and Social Movements: The Person in Politics and Culture*. Cham: Springer International Publishing. doi: 10.1007/978-3-319-72341-9_3.

———. 2019. *Back to America: Identity, Political Culture, and the Tea Party Movement*. Anthropology of Contemporary North America. Lincoln: University of Nebraska Press.

———. 2021. "Freedom over Fear: Fundamentalist Populism and the Challenge of COVID-19." *Open Anthropological Research*. 1 (1): 116–28. doi: 10.1515/opan-2020-0106.

Yang, Guobin. 2000. "Achieving Emotions in Collective Action: Emotional Processes and Movement Mobilization in the 1989 Chinese Student Movement." *The Sociological Quarterly* 41 (4): 593–614. doi: 10.1111/j.1533-8525.2000.tb00075.x.

3
THE REDDEST OF STATES
Fieldnotes from Trumplandia

Michael E. Harkin

This chapter will explore the crisis of liberal democracy from two perspectives: a theoretical consideration of the current crisis of liberalism from the point of view of anthropology and philosophy, and an ethnographic description of "Trumplandia," based on my fieldwork in Wyoming among white male Trump supporters. Here the global and local truly intersect. The collapse of the neoliberal order, occurring in places as diverse as Hungary, the United Kingdom, the United States, and Italy, is founded on unrest and dissatisfaction among working-class people, primarily men, who make up the rank and file of the *gilets jaunes* and Trump supporters. Living in Wyoming, I have had considerable contact with the latter; so much so that I predicted a Trump victory in July 2016 in a lecture given in New Zealand (Harkin 2016).

Anthropology, philosophy, and the crisis of democracy

Anthropology and philosophy are intertwined over the centuries like two strands of DNA. Although anthropology's disciplinary history is truncated in comparison to that of philosophy, many common themes are broached. At the very beginning of what would become the Western philosophical tradition, Socrates considered the question of variation across political formations. As Plato writes in Book VIII of the *Republic*, we can see a succession of political forms following on the collapse of Aristocracy. Timocracy constitutes rule by warriors and military leaders, which further devolves into Oligarchy, rule by those who accumulate wealth. This, in turn, produces among the younger generation of oligarchs the desire to enjoy wealth without constraint, which is the impetus for Democracy, characterized above all by the liberalization of social norms. Thus, Democracy, rather than being the apotheosis of a process of political and cultural evolution, is instead the penultimate stage in a devolution of political formations. Only Tyranny, the inevitable successor

DOI: 10.4324/9781003152743-4

of Democracy, in which the tyrant increasingly pushes out the elements who still value traditional virtues, remains, although Kakistocracy, government by the worst, a term enjoying much currency today but not found in the *Republic*, could be said to be the nadir of this devolution.

This is remarkably relevant to our situation today, when in many democratic societies we see a movement toward Tyranny and Kakistocracy. The frequent resignations of White House officials possessing substantial experience in government or related fields, and said to be the "adults in the room," and their replacement by sycophants with only a background in media, is clearly a mechanism for achieving this undesirable end point. I will come back to this question later, but my real interest here is in demonstrating the utility of anthropology as a lens through which to view these events.

It is interesting that Socrates/Plato chose not only to address the variation in political and cultural formations, which anthropologists today also do, but to do so in the classic anthropological mode of change through time. On the surface, the devolutionary model of the *Republic* would seem to be opposite that of the nineteenth-century evolutionists. For them, we are told, the story was a happy one, technically a comedy, an aria sung in a major key, culminating in patriarchal, Christian, bourgeois society. However, this is to ignore important strains of anthropological evolutionary thought. Lewis Henry Morgan, for instance, concludes *Ancient Society*, a treatise on political evolution seen through the lens of property and inheritance—a theme emphasized as well in the *Republic*—with a rumination on the unfettered rise of private property, as a spectral figure threatening to swallow humanity itself (Morgan 1877). This strain was, of course, picked up by Marx and Engels, and played a considerable role in their model of the development of capitalism. Others who used a version of evolutionism, notably Durkheim and Freud, similarly saw at the very least a downside—increasing *anomie* and alienation—in the modern condition.

This all makes sense to us at the end of the "long twentieth century," when the political and cultural assumptions, inherited from the Enlightenment and refined by the Victorians, are no longer current. The depredations of Trump et al. threaten the oldest modern democracies and very much resemble the decline envisioned in the *Republic*. For a variety of reasons, which I will explore below, the people in these societies are alienated not only from the means of economic production but also from the means of political production and social reproduction. The willingness of common people in the US and the UK, and elsewhere, to vote against their own self-interest in order to produce a rift in the social and political order is extraordinary if not, as Plato tells us, unprecedented. (Or as Trump would have it "unpresidented"!)

In their recent bestselling book, *How Democracies Die*, political scientists Steven Levitsky and Daniel Ziblatt examine a range of cases in which democratic regimes have been threatened, on some occasions surviving the threats, others not (Levitsky and Ziblatt 2018). They note that there are two main modes by which democracies die: suddenly and dramatically, such as with the military attack on the regime of Juan Peron in Argentina, or gradually. The former cases are rare; it is the latter that are more common and insidious. The rise of Hitler and Mussolini is shown to be a gradual affair. Crucially, in both cases, the ascendance of a populist outsider, whose charisma gave them a substantial political base but far from an electoral majority, was facilitated by the assistance of insiders, those who represented the very systems that would be placed under threat and eventually destroyed by these outsiders. King Victor Emmanuel III, beset by leftist protests, felt it was in his own interest to welcome the charismatic outsider Mussolini into the inner sanctum of state power. So do "gatekeepers" often open up a little to dangerous forces that will ultimately enslave or destroy them (Levitsky and Ziblatt 2018: 12–13).

Structure of the conjuncture

The great American anthropologist Marshall Sahlins developed a theoretical model for understanding the way in which cultural structures—imagined, to one degree or another, as permanent features of a particular cultural order—and the event interact (Sahlins 1981). Events may be pure contingency such as a weather disaster or may be directed by an agent of some sort. In both cases, as Sahlins says, history is not determined by culture, but it is shaped by it. Thus, for instance, a devastating earthquake may be viewed very differently within a Buddhist context than a Christian one. For the former it may be taken as affirmation of the nature of earthly existence as suffering; for the latter, of God's wrath over imagined sin.[1]

And yet these very attempts to rein in a random event within the cultural structure leave that structure open to change and even destruction from within. Such events are familiar to anthropologists and historians: When the French navigator La Pérouse appeared off the coast of British Columbia in 1786 in a ship perceived as a giant bird by the natives on the shore; when Hernan Cortés arrived, amidst prophecy and rumor, in Mexico City in November 1519; when Captain Cook made a right-hand circuit around the island of Hawai'i in 1779. Such structures of the conjuncture are simultaneously continuous and discontinuous with the pre-existing structure. Indeed, the extraordinary nature of these exogenous events often leads to at least a temporary doubling-down on structure; while Hawai'ian priests had been content to slay the agricultural god Lono symbolically in every previous iteration, when Cook, perceived as the literal embodiment of Lono, arrives, it becomes necessary to carry out the sacrifice in literal fashion.

Plus la même chose, plus ça change, as Sahlins says. In such situations, we have a case where, given the threat to the cultural order, those in positions of authority feel the need to play their assigned roles correctly and convincingly. Even so, such crises create openings for forces opposed to the existing cultural order, often in the form of human agents. The self-interested player, the holy fool, the stranger king: all have the capacity to alter the very structure in which they are participating. Julius Caesar used the rules of republican politics to fashion an imperial political formation, which would easily survive his own assassination.

Here we must return briefly to our present circumstance of the Trump administration and the changes wrought to the American democratic formation. Trump arrived as an outsider, who made no bones about operating according to narrow self-interest, very much at odds with the values of American democracy, where leaders have always at least paid lip service to the idea of public service. In many other ways—temperament, experience, education, intellectual ability—Trump proved the inversion of a traditional political leader. (To be sure, a certain amount of deviation from the ideal was acceptable, if one brought great strengths in other areas; think of Winston Churchill, John F. Kennedy, and Bill Clinton). At the same time, the formal rules were followed: Trump won enough Republican primaries to legitimately assume the nomination, the Electoral College followed its constitutional mandate (although some argued that it had a duty to provide a check on an unsuitable candidate); the gatekeepers, doing their job, allowed someone whose character proved a threat to those very institutions whose normal functioning allowed for Trump's accession to power.

In *How Democracies Die*, Levitsky and Ziblatt present a table of "four key indicators of authoritarian behavior." These include: 1. Rejection of (or weak commitment to) democratic rules of the game, 2. Denial of the legitimacy of political opponents, 3. Toleration or encouragement of violence, 4. Readiness to curtail civil liberties of opponents, including media (Levitsky and Ziblatt 2018: 23–4). Obviously Trump meets all these criteria, some to a degree not seen even in other contemporary post-liberal societies. Trump's support, for instance, for neo-Nazi violence in Charlottesville, Virginia, is alone a threat to American democracy unprecedented in my lifetime.

Democracy and liberalism

A second term that we hear much about in the current climate is "liberalism" and the threats it faces, possibly even greater than those of democracy itself. It is worth pausing for a moment to consider the meaning of this term and to then return to the question of democracy itself. Liberalism has typically been considered to be inseparable from democracy, as the two co-evolved from Enlightenment roots. John Stuart Mill, Jeremy Bentham, and generations of subsequent philosophers and politicians sought to extend both the franchise and the benefits of modern society itself to increasingly large groups: non-landowners, non-whites, women, children, ethnic and religious minorities, etc. In an important sense, this is the genealogy of our present political formation. Liberals, until they were warned off this term by voices both from the left and right, embraced this steady extension of the politics of inclusion and cosmopolitanism, to the end point of what Richard Rorty calls, somewhat tongue in cheek, "postmodern bourgeois liberalism," a promised land of multicultural tolerance, relative prosperity, and the guarantee of stable democratic institutions (Rorty 1983). At this point we could ask ourselves what went wrong with this vision (Islamist terrorism, increasingly dysfunctional partisan politics in the major democracies, the apotheosis of social media, for a start), but instead, I think it is more useful here to look at contradictions inherent to liberalism itself.

Why are relatively few people, at least in the English-speaking world, who share my general position and worldview willing to call themselves "liberals"? A small part of it is the campaign by right-wingers since the days of Reagan and Thatcher to stigmatize the word, making it more difficult to adopt than a term such as "progressive." More significant, though, is the changing semantic environment, in which "liberal" increasingly became equated with what we now call "neoliberal," a political economic philosophy based on at once the easing of regulations regarding capital, and hence elites, while tightening controls—through surveillance, auditing, discipline, and punishment—on those below. It produces what Wacquant (2012) calls a "Centaur state," in which the formation of the top segment is very different from the bottom. Now certainly this represents a particular stage in a structure of the *longue durée*, in which increasing liberalization of corporations and global trade, for instance, becomes directly opposed to the equally liberal project of extending the benefits of an open society to all its citizens, but it also reflects a fundamental problem of semantic definition. Liberal is always a relative concept; it always pertains to the situation in which one finds oneself at a particular place and time. Thus, the racially "liberal" politicians of the American South during the 1960s and 1970s would seem much less so today, perhaps even to the point of not being considered liberal at all. "Liberal" would seem to be the very best example to offer for Jacques Derrida's concept of *différance*, in which meaning is produced through structural opposition, as in Saussure's model of semiotics, but is also always endlessly deferred, as any meaning arrived at will always be provisional, and subject to further reassessments down the line (Derrida 1982).

I would argue that this is why it is easy for conservatives to make fun of liberals, as they have no fixed political positions but rather engage in whatever the issue *du jour* is (marriage equality, trans rights, etc.) on the side of the angels, while conservatives have maintained a fairly fixed agenda of opposition to such things. Of course, conservatism is itself relative, which we see quite clearly in the case of the religious right in the United States supporting Trump despite accusations of infidelity and sexual abuse. However, the authoritarian nature of conservatism allows for the illusion of continuity to take precedence over the reality of change. As Lévi-Strauss (1966) said of "cold societies," it is not that they do not change but rather that they like to think that they do not.

"Liberal" is thus a concept requiring considerable mental agility and a relativistic perspective—neither of which is in great abundance in the era of Trump and Brexit. The inevitable decline of liberalism has a knock-on effect on the various institutions considered as its manifestations and defenders: a free media, the rule of law equally applied to all, insurance against the corruption of democracy by those wishing to restrict the franchise and tilt electoral results (as, again, we viewed in high definition in 2016). In certain circles it is supposed that it is possible to maintain "illiberal democracies," as in Poland, Turkey, and Viktor Orbán's Hungary. These societies may have abandoned the liberal project, it is thought, but remain democracies, which may one day choose to pursue a different path. However, as the eminent political scientist Jan-Werner Mueller has argued, this formulation is not realistic, as the hard institutional mechanisms of democracy require the soft mechanisms of convention, tradition, and culture (Mueller 2018). Even better, from my perspective, are the two terms introduced by Levitsky and Ziblatt, "mutual toleration" and "forbearance," that is, the ability to accept one's rival (in their understanding, partisan opponent, but easily extendable to various social others), and unwillingness to use any means necessary to crush them (2018: 101–17). Without an ethos of liberalism, the institutional structure of democracy rots from the inside. This would seem to be a good description of where we are likely headed today.

Fieldnotes from Trumplandia

Loïc Wacquant begins his piece on "actually existing neoliberalism" with discussion of an ethnographic context: an African-American boxing club on the South Side of Chicago, presumably adjacent to Hyde Park and the University of Chicago. To say this article is light on ethnography would be an understatement, much to my disappointment. Nevertheless, his theorizing and conclusions do ring true to me, as one who lived in that neighborhood and participated in similar activities. Here I will, space permitting, present my own ethnographic sketch of a group of white males in Wyoming who lean heavily toward Trump. A note about the term "Trumplandia": this is derived from the popular American television program *Portlandia*, a comedy of manners examining the thoroughly "liberal" ethos of Portland, Oregon, a place in which feminism, lesbianism, political radicalism, and New Age spirituality act as Bourdieuian markers of distinction within a bourgeois-bohemian context. It is significant to this case because, although opposite values appear in Trumplandia, the mechanisms by which they are both conserved and extended—not just Bourdieuian distinction, but Batesonian schismogenesis—are quite similar. The hyperlocalization of political cultures seems more characteristic of the American West than of other regions, but this is a topic for another day.

My findings are congruent with other recent work on "deplorables," white working-class Trump devotees (Hochschild 2016). However, my state of Wyoming is unusual in many regards, far too many to list here. But it is the most rural state in the "lower forty-eight," among the whitest, and the one that voted for Trump by the largest margin in 2016, so these three factors alone make it an important case for our consideration. In addition, a significant portion of its workforce is involved in energy and mineral extraction, one of Trump's main talking points. Thus the ideal for most men (such work is heavily gendered) is to obtain a well-paid job working in a coal mine or gas field. The mineral and energy industry both pays high wages and contributes vast amounts to the state budgets, to the degree that Wyoming lacks a state income tax and has low levels of other taxes, while maintaining one of the best public education systems in the country. The contradiction between these two facts and their attendant cultural mythology—that of the lone frontiersman and the "socialism" of a low-tax, high-benefits state—is one of the driving forces of the state's self-identity. Another factor comes into play here: given the high-quality K-12 education offered, and the extremely low tuition charged by the state's university and colleges, many first-generation students graduate from university. Ironically, the conditions that made this possible have also resulted in a lack of employment opportunities for those with university degrees, meaning that Wyoming tends to export university graduates while it imports blue-collar workers. This determines that the ethos of the state is defined by masculine blue-collar work, viewed as extracting value from nature. The most popular sport is none of the major international or American ones but rather rodeo, which symbolizes humanity's struggle against a resistant nature.

The micro-context in which I have conducted fieldwork over the past four years is a series of settings in Laramie, the home of the University of Wyoming. As with Wacquant's field site, I have chosen places on the margins of the university, which attract people unaffiliated with it, as well as a mix of students and university employees. This project began by looking at the culture of craft beer, which is one national trend in which Wyoming participates enthusiastically (Harkin 2017b). Even in that study, I ran into issues of Bourdieuian distinction as it related to social class and political perspective (Bourdieu 1984). In particular, I found a link between rejection of elite definitions of taste (even if proposed by merely a local brewer or connoisseur) in beer as well as in political opinion. These people were, by the time of the general election, almost uniformly pro-Trump, although a surprising number of them had supported Bernie Sanders during the Democratic nomination campaign. I am by no means certain that these people actually voted for Trump; indeed, several of the men have had their voting rights terminated due to criminal convictions, and they are on the whole disinclined to vote and view politics with great cynicism. If they did vote, their motivation was intense dislike for Hillary Clinton, who represents for them a nightmarish version of liberalism: cultural liberalism (coded as "political correctness" by these men) combined with globalist neoliberalism. On the other end of the spectrum, those who were willing to open themselves up to the novel gustatory experiences they would find in craft beer—and which was not always positive—were more willing to assume a "liberal" position in other aspects of their lives. The arguments for drinking mass-produced beer and voting for Trump were quite similar; no one said that either was inherently superior to its opposite, rather that they were more comfortable sticking with what was familiar and reassuring.

The general group of people with whom I have worked over the past four years is diverse—surprisingly so for a state as homogenous as Wyoming. Women, LGBT persons, people of color, etc., have constituted a portion of my sample approaching 50 percent, and considerable variation in age, religious affiliation, educational attainment, etc. can be seen. However, the subset of Trump supporters is much more homogenous: uniformly male, white, middle-aged (ranging from mid-30s to 70s), and with a blue-collar occupation or background. A number of other factors unite them, but one does above all: gun ownership.

These men are at different points in their lives and vastly different educational levels. Although most lack a university degree, several are working toward one. Although all have held blue-collar jobs such as truck driving, others have at times worked in areas such as tech and marketing. Several of the men were raised in affluent circumstances; however, their relationships with parents are often strained. One factor is common: almost all have experienced failed marriages and relationships, and all who have children are estranged from them, often by court order. That is, they feel a strong sense of both being victims of forces beyond their control (notably lawyers and the courts), as well as being unable to fulfill the paternal responsibilities that they believe to be a central part of masculine identity. There exists a wound at the center of their being, which they attempt to compensate for in various ways, in particular through the possession of guns and other markers of a blue-collar masculine ideal, such as large pickup trucks.

Many of these men are on Social Security disability, which for many of them provides the funds that allow them to attend university. Several have had life-threatening injuries related to work. As many other writers have noted, this is a prime example of voting against one's material self-interest, as Republicans regularly attempt to defund Social Security and other safety net programs. Many of these disabilities are physical, although certainly psychological factors such as addiction and depression factor into it. One informant, whom I will call Bill, a man in his mid-30s, once had a job that he loved: he was a "smoke jumper" (firefighter) for the US Forest Service. Although he was not proud of working for the federal government, a body viewed with suspicion by most Wyomingites, he enjoyed working outside in a heroic, highly masculine role. It was dangerous, though, and he was seriously injured in a plane crash, forcing him to spend years in rehabilitation. He will never hold another job requiring intense manual labor; hence his decision to return to university, despite the inevitable dissonance of this experience.

Bill is, among a group of avid hunters and fishers, probably the most avid. He holds long conversations with his mates about hunting and fishing experiences, punctuated with cell phone videos he has taken or has downloaded from social media. And, inevitably, the discussion turns to guns, both those used for hunting and those used for massacres. I have asked him why he wants to own the latter—and I have no doubt that he would never use any of his guns on another person—and the response is a shrug, rather than an argument. I have heard him, and others, say that they do not want to live in California (where Bill had lived during his Forest Service years) because they would "take away" his guns. I can only think that guns are seen, within the experience of this group, as an affirmation of personal autonomy, despite the reality of their own life experience. For it is not only in the matter of child support payments and restraining orders that these men have experienced state power. Other encounters with the criminal justice system, most commonly drunk driving and other alcohol-related offenses, have sent several of these men to state prison. (If Bill has done, he has not volunteered this information.) They, like Wacquant's informants, are on the wrong side of the Centaur state.

One of the endearing sides of Bill is his custom of food-sharing. He always gets at least one elk in the fall and is constantly obtaining smaller game and fish, including the gourmet delight of walleye. He will routinely bring in steaks, fish filets, ground meat, and jerky, and distribute them to people at the bar that he frequents.[2]

(I am occasionally included but usually awarded only jerky.) In particular, there is an older retired man whom everyone especially likes, who is likely to receive elk filet mignon and other prestigious food. In this way, Bill is a provider, an alpha male who is recognized within his group and beyond it as someone who is highly capable as well as generous, who understands his responsibility to the less able (despite him being legally disabled himself), and who participates in a just society, which is made so by an individual's moral choices. Guns are not problematic for Bill and his ilk, because these men—white, Christian, living according to a rural, working-class ethos—believe that they will never abuse their responsibilities. This is reminiscent of the "poetics of manhood" in Cretan society, so richly described by Michael Herzfeld (1985).

In my conversations with Bill and other gun owners, including some who express liberal political positions, guns are seen as a fact of life, indeed a necessity, for a variety of purposes. The idea of nature as inherently threatening is a large part of this formulation. Indeed, since the first writing, Bill suffered a serious injury while hiking in the mountains. Bears, lions, and other predators threaten humans; to go to such places without a gun is considered foolhardy. For those men with a background in ranching, guns are indispensable for protecting their herd from predators. Guns also underwrite a sort of social contract. There exists an internet meme, "Welcome to Wyoming: Assume Everyone is Armed," which neatly expresses this. It is an idealized view of the autonomous, armed man or woman (although male is clearly the unmarked category), whose ability to protect themselves is assumed. A further claim is made: those "good guys with guns" are the guarantors of security and indeed of the social order itself. They point to the fact that no mass shooting has ever occurred in Wyoming. Bill, in particular, is fond of posting to Facebook examples where an armed wrongdoer was killed or disarmed by a "good guy with a gun." Recently (August 2019) a local incident reinforced this belief among many people. A man angrily left a bar and vowed to return and "shoot the place up." Although he was met upon return by the police, many people averred that he would have been gunned down by one of the armed patrons or employees had the police not been present.

The political implications of this self-image and worldview are clear. The linguist George Lakoff has identified separate liberal and conservative social-political models, both based on the nuclear family. For liberals, it is the model of the egalitarian, nurturing family that prevails: from each according to their ability, to each according to their need. For conservatives, it is the model of the stern authoritarian family, in which the patriarch sets rules and standards for behavior (Lakoff 2016). It is clear that men like Bill and his mates both long for and, in their own way, attempt to model the latter. Voting for Trump was thus not a rational choice but an expression of identity.[3]

Race

Early on in my work with my white, working-class Wyoming men, I was told an anecdote that encapsulates a certain version of Wyoming attitudes toward race. It took place at a roadhouse bar between Cheyenne and Laramie. A Black man entered and ordered a beer and then proceeded to take out his phone. The bartender told him, "You'll have to stand over there," pointing to a location away from the other customers. The man looked confused and then angry. Then the bartender said, "Yeah, our cell service sucks out here—that's the only place you can use your phone." The point of the story is obvious. The Black man, maybe from nearby F.E. Warren Air Force Base, but certainly not from Wyoming, was expecting racist treatment from the local rednecks but was instead treated to Wyoming's famous hospitality. This is of a piece with stories about strangers being rescued from the side of the road in a snowstorm, out-of-state hunters getting lost in the deep wilderness, and the like. It is an important part of the self-image of the state and, given the reality of living in a deeply rural and unforgiving environment, based on reality. It also of course provides a ready-made "alibi," in Barthes's sense: a mythos that covers up underlying conflict.

This mythos draws on a second element as well: the individualism of the frontier. Although cowboys were low-paid corporate employees, and most settlements in Wyoming were organized around a single company (the railroad, mining interests) or religion (Mormonism), the myth of the individual is paramount. One aspect of this belief is the idea that all people should be treated and judged as individuals rather than as representatives of a group. Again, there is some truth to this: the venue where I usually met these men attracted a diverse crowd, including a fairly high percentage of racial and ethnic minorities for Wyoming. I never observed any overt racist behavior toward these people individually. Indeed, I know several Black men who came to Wyoming originally for college from big cities such as Chicago and Detroit and who remained in large part because of the relative lack of overt racism in Laramie. However, in telling stories of their experiences in places such as Denver, where minority populations were large enough to make them feel uncomfortable, they resorted to typically racist tropes. One man spoke of his encounter with a "nigger cop," an image that condensed irrational fear of other races with the rational fear of unrestrained state power.

However, even in Wyoming such open displays of racism are not uncommon. A friend of mine, a Black woman who grew up in Laramie before moving to northern Colorado, was attacked in Laramie with a knife by a group of Whites shouting racial epithets. Although the ringleader was charged with assault and a hate crime, she was acquitted. Another friend of mine, a large Indigenous man, was repeatedly arrested for public intoxication, despite the fact that White students in the same situation rarely were. Famously, in a case that happened in 2018, a White sheriff's deputy chased down and shot and killed a local Hispanic man who was unarmed and trying to flee to his house.

It is probably fair to say that race is an issue that is not foregrounded in Wyoming as it is in most other places in the US. However, the armature of racist ideology exists here as well. It is mostly latent but can be activated under the right circumstances. During the summer of 2020 Laramie experienced marches in support of Black Lives Matter. These marches attracted counter-protestors carrying automatic weapons. On a few occasions these weapons were pointed at marchers. Many of the armed men were of course wearing MAGA gear and displaying Trump and Gadsden flags from their pickup trucks. Indeed, in the Trump era racist and homophobic attacks have increased across Wyoming, as they have elsewhere in the US. Trump has been the catalyst for this in several ways. Since his descent down the golden escalator he has racialized White people's fears and frustrations, rooted in economic and social decline. He has instilled a sense of victimhood in Whites who culturally identify with a rural, Christian identity. His rallies provided a cathartic expression of this White identity in a way that had not been socially acceptable before. The trope of "political correctness" partially displaces the racial animus underlying Trumpism onto the White "liberals" who, in various institutional settings, impose and enforce regimes of "diversity" in the workplace, which Trumpists correctly associate with other mechanisms of the neoliberal order, such as drug testing and excessive policing.

Anthropology as a technology of liberalism

Social science famously began as a tool of the state. Economics, statistics, and sociology were all created with the idea of giving governments the means to achieve a more perfect society. Saint-Simon and Comte, in particular, saw the challenge as one of harnessing the new industrial technology and the findings of science to create a society that would be more just, wealthier, and founded on secular, not religious, principles. (Much of this is highly reminiscent of the discussions we are having now about information technology and its implication for work, happiness, and the nature of society.) One of the most famous and important of these social science interventions was Émile Durkheim's *Suicide*, which looked at the problem in the context of urbanization, declaring that the increase in suicide rates were the result of increasing feelings of *anomie* among city-dwellers (Durkheim 1897). Durkheim proposed a modern society based upon secular principles, and the "organic" division of labor among different classes and occupations (Durkheim 1893).

At about the same time that Durkheim was proposing a secular, socialist state that would supersede the entrenched prejudices of the past, Franz Boas, the great German-American anthropologist, was using anthropological methods to describe the changing American society that he saw in New York. In particular, the issue at hand was immigration, which had been a prominent phenomenon in American society from the beginning. However, as the sources of immigration shifted from the British Isles and northwestern Europe, to southern and eastern Europe, leading conservative voices objected, as they feared weakening the gene pool of American society. At the same time, the Jim Crow era in the American South produced the Great Migration northward so that cities such as New York appeared remarkably more diverse than they had a generation before. Boas employed his findings in physical anthropology to demonstrate that physical type was much more fluid than had been assumed, and much more subject to environment. Race thus becomes a scientifically questionable concept.

Even more important from Boas's perspective was what we would now call the relativism of culture: the idea that cultures have different norms and values but that no one culture may be considered inherently superior. These ideas were developed, at least in part, with Boas's colleague at Columbia, the great pragmatic philosopher John Dewey (Harkin 2017a). Together they taught a course on "comparative ethics," looking at a range of cultures culled from the ethnographic record. Despite coming from rather different intellectual traditions—Boas was influenced by German Romanticism and the work of Johann Gottfried Herder, among others, while Dewey was more in the mainstream of Anglo-Saxon thought—they developed a modus operandi. Anthropological students of that seminar came to identify themselves as "Deweyans" as well as "Boasians."

While very little remains from that seminar, we can surmise some of the main themes from Boas's correspondence with Dewey and, especially, his contemporary tome *The Mind of Primitive Man* (Boas 1911). It was, first and foremost, a skeptical critique of both evolutionism and scientific racism, as personified by Francis Galton. In both instances Boas injects elements of doubt, questioning unspoken assumptions. This technique of "negative capability" allows him to reject these positions in favor of what we can properly call a liberal sensibility. This form of liberalism embraces cultural difference by seeking to understand it from an anthropological perspective. He envisions not only differences between societies—as Kant did in an earlier iteration of anthropology—but differences within societies, as the reality of an immigrant population such as that of New York City in the early twentieth century pressed upon him.

An important distinction can be made here between the methods of sociology and the other social sciences, and those of anthropology, as regards the question of the liberal society. For the former, the task was to gather data on social problems and suggest policies that would ameliorate them. For anthropology, the task was more exploratory—more ethnographic—to inform not so much public policy (although Boas would make recommendations regarding immigration and other policies) but rather to communicate to the citizens themselves, directly, through means such as writing (Boas was a frequent author of letters to the editor of major newspapers) and museum display. At the American Museum of Natural History, Boas attempted to represent the diversity of both American and global populations which were, in New York, becoming increasingly merged. Anthropology was thus a social science situated firmly within society itself, speaking of and to that society: immanent, in other words.

Thus, for Boas, as for Kant before him, anthropology was a means to achieving a democratic ideal: for Kant, this involved relations among nations, for Boas, the creation of something entirely new, Rorty's "postmodern bourgeois liberalism." In this social formation, cultural difference was not stigmatized but seen as a positive benefit. Different cultures could interact within an overarching liberal, multicultural context, which became in effect the guarantor of democracy itself. The logic is a progressive one: various groups that had been shut out on ethnic, racial, religious, and, later, gender and sexual criteria, were to be included in that happy society.

Democracy, rather than the penultimate stage of decline, was a natural and permanent state that more faithfully represented the actual state of affairs than any other possible form.

A half-century later, in Greece, a similar attempt was made to introduce anthropology into a society undergoing rapid change. Prince Peter's small tome *The Science of Anthropology* introduced an Anglo-Saxon version of anthropology to a wide Greek audience (Papamichaeil Harkin 2019). The book echoes in many ways Boas's *The Mind of Primitive Man*, to a similar purpose: to inform a broad public of existing cultural and biological diversity within society, and anthropological (rather than racialist or xenophobic) means of understanding it. A half-century further along many societies of the West, who have come to valorize rather than condemn democracy, our patrimony from the ancient Greeks, wonder whether it can be preserved, and with it the idea of a liberal pluralistic society comfortable with itself. If such an accomplishment is possible, it will require an anthropological intervention, a re-inscribing, as Rorty calls it, of society along realistic, which is to say scientific, lines.

From Centaur to Minotaur?

The Centaur state provides the conditions of possibility of Trumpism and related phenomena of reactionary populism. But, as we have seen with Trump, the Centaur state has only grown greater with the ascendency of such leaders. The two major actions Trump has taken merely reinforce the existing structure: tax cuts for the very rich make their condition even more enviable, while the security apparatus has become more robust, especially as applied to immigrants and people of color. This has the perverse effect of heightening the original conditions that led to the election of Trump in the first place. While most liberals assume that Trump's failure to ease the conditions that caused white working-class people to vote for him will cost him their votes, this is by no means certain. Indeed, among Wyoming Trump voters there seems to be a doubling-down on Trump, especially as elite opinion is increasingly scathing of him. It is possible that Trumpism will outlive Trump, with another avatar of right-wing populism running for president in 2024.

What this will entail is unknowable. It depends to a large degree on the ability of institutions outside government, in particular the press and higher education, to maintain autonomy and continue to exercise their legitimate functions. However, one way to think about this future is the rise of a Minotaur state, in which the functions of government are increasingly deployed for destructive purposes. That is, destruction is not a mere side effect of the security state but its actual purpose. We see hints of this already in the situation at the southern border, where it is clear that the mistreatment of migrant families is a feature, not a bug, of the system. As the Minotaur devoured Athenian youth—considered by many scholars to be a reference to the tributary status Athens held in relation to the Minoan polity—so the sacrifice of young people at the border is valued for its demonstration effects. As was the case with the shooter in El Paso, it is clear that such effects reach far beyond government, although they originate with it.

The Minotaur state represents the penultimate stage on the way toward totalitarian fascism, with full-on genocide, terror, and the ultimate destruction of the social order. At this stage no one, not even those who were protected from the security apparatus of the Centaur state, will be immune from its destruction. Indeed, at the risk of overburdening the metaphor, the Minotaur state, like its namesake, is becoming preternaturally sensitive to those within its labyrinth. Facial recognition, digital tracking, and similar technologies make it increasingly difficult, if not impossible, to avoid surveillance by the state and by private organizations. It is fitting that we have arrived at a situation best described by a classical monster. Episodes of monstrosity have abounded in the age of Trump, beginning with the man himself, who presents an uncanny simulacrum of a human being.

The monstrousness of Trump

He emerged as if from the national id, a grotesque and loathsome creature. In a theatrical reversal of this trope, he actually descended on a golden elevator, optically signaling that for the next five years, up would be down, black white. Freud introduced the concept of the uncanny a century ago, as a way of explaining the quality associated with objects of fear. They are recognizable, familiar even, but in some subtle ways are just different enough from the norm as to cause unease and anxiety. Thus, the popular culture figure of Slenderman is human in basic form but with unusually long, attenuated limbs that one does not notice until close, that is, until it is too late. Trump presents a human form as well, although with his small hands, large belly, absurd hair, orange skin, and excessively long tie, he is a grotesque figure. At the first presidential debate of 2016, he played this role to his benefit. By looming and lurching behind Hillary as she was speaking, he looked menacing and evil. This was, unfortunately for the nation, what many people wanted to see. The monster threatened only those who deserved it and, after all, the monster was strong, a national golem. With Chekhovian certainty, we knew that this particular weapon would not remain unused, but would be aimed at the body politic in direct assault.

Monsters operate in culture as a sort of anthropology in reverse. While they may be physically similar to humans (or not), they represent a moral inversion of what it means to be a human being living in society. Thus in *Beowulf*, Grendel is a humanoid figure, although unnaturally strong, but is the inversion of all of the values of Danish society, epitomized by the king, Theoden, and the hero, Beowulf. Rather than share meat freely, as Theoden does at the mead hall, Grendel takes these men as meat. Rather than openly and bravely engage in fair combat, like Beowulf, Grendel attacks in the dead of night while the Danes sleep. So too with Trump, we see an inversion of the formal and informal norms of presidential behavior, indeed, norms that would be expected at any level of government or business. We do not expect, to say the least, our leaders to be accused of rape, to use the office for corrupt personal benefit, to lie openly and repeatedly, to attempt to corrupt and subvert the mechanisms of government itself, most notably the system of criminal justice, to have a completely intemperate character; all of these qualities were on display before he was elected. As many commentators noted, it was unbelievable that the release of the video in which Trump was heard boasting about assaulting women right before the election did not end it all there.

Monsters such as Grendel have didactic value. These stories are associated with childhood because they provide models of what not to be as a responsible adult. The Greeks associated childhood with idiocy (in the sense of idiosyncratic) and adulthood with puberty (in the sense of being capable of acting in public). The monster plays on the paradox of being physically an adult, but lacking the moral and emotional qualities that allow one to act in an ethical and responsible way. Trump's cruelty has been oft noted. It is part of a personality complex described well by his niece Mary Trump, a clinical psychologist, as a narcissistic disorder. He can be brazenly cruel because he literally has no sense of empathy. He could willfully expose thousands of his supporters and staff to a deadly disease because they only existed for the benefit of Trump. If they got sick and died, it was because they, unlike Trump, were "weak."

If the figure of Trump exists as a structural inversion of the norm, in which we view the president as a sort of national father figure (although liberals and conservatives have very different notions of what that means, as Lakoff has noted), what can this possibly mean? Do many of us believe that the nation is irredeemably decadent and we need to be punished by a Krampus-like figure? This is, indeed, a common theme in oral literature; in Northwest Coast mythology an ogress, Dzonokwa, would take naughty children and place them in her backpack, never to be seen again. Or, is it not the nation as a whole but those who aren't "real Americans," the educated, urban, nonwhite, not heterosexual, etc. who need to be punished? In fact, I believe that both factor in; Trump appeals equally to both masochistic and sadistic ideations.

Concluding thoughts

As of this writing, it is impossible to know what the ultimate outcome of the Trump phenomenon will be. We still have an unstable maniac with eight days remaining of his term and the ability to start war, assassinate enemies, to wreck American democracy. That said, it looks as though the challenge to the democratic system has, for now, been met, although undoubtedly some reforms in the system, particularly in terms of congressional oversight of the executive branch, are inevitable. Another point, made by many but particularly well by Heather Cox Richardson on her daily blog, *Letters from an American*, is that none of this is new; echoes of 1877 and 1898, the end of Reconstruction and the coup against the government of Wilmington, North Carolina, respectively, were there on January 6. The tale of progress and increasing inclusiveness of American society is only partly true.

As anthropologists we are interested less in the mechanics of political systems—although we have necessarily had to consider them in recent years—than in structures of the *longue durée*, in underlying social forces, in hidden causes and correlations. One theory of social unrest that has gained currency recently, with prominent articles in *The Atlantic* and *The Economist*, comes from the research of the mathematical ecologist turned macrohistorian, Peter Turchin. Turchin argues, from an analysis of what he claims is ten thousand years of historical and archaeological records, that the controlling variable in societal collapse is the overproduction of elites. This has a certain commonsense appeal to it. We do know, for example, that the collapse of classic Mayan civilization took the specific form of a rebellion against the elites, who make up a disproportionate number of the victims analyzed by bioarchaeologists. For the modern day, Turchin argues that this overproduction of elites is the result of an excess of credentials and institutions that grant them, primarily prestigious universities. Already this has a whiff of what he is purportedly attempting to explain—anti-intellectual right-wing populism—about it. But he makes a case that is superficially plausible. Too many people get too many advanced degrees from elite universities, but there are not enough positions at white-shoe law firms, Ivy League universities, hedge funds, tech start-ups, and higher echelons of government for this credentialed multitude to find satisfying employment. Again, this seems about right. As one who went through such an elite education but finds himself teaching at a middling university, this is a commonplace of academics of my generation and younger. I know many people with similar backgrounds who are underemployed or unemployed. The taxi driver I met in Las Vegas who had a graduate degree from the University of Chicago and a huge chip on his shoulder comes to mind.

Turchin argues that such people form the core of what he calls the "anti-elite," a wannabe elite that will seize any opportunity to join the actual elite. They do this by uniting with the proletariat, who similarly are experiencing the reality of diminished opportunity (although in their case it is material and not merely status anxiety). He gives as an example Steve Bannon, a Harvard graduate of working-class background who made his fortune in investing but remained an outsider to the Groton–Yale nexus. He was Trump's most important early advisor, who pushed him into the sphere of "fuck-the-system" neofascism. Similarly, many other Trump advisors and aides hail from such backgrounds and welcomed the opportunity to gain employment with the Trump administration that would have been impossible with anyone else, because Trump himself was not connected to the establishment networks from which someone like Biden can draw his appointees. Again, much of this is demonstrable. In addition to Bannon we could mention Michael Savage, the right-wing radio personality. Savage, born Michael Alan Weiner, befriended such countercultural figures as Timothy Leary and Alan Ginsburg. He received degrees in both anthropology and botany, completing a PhD in ethnobotany at Berkeley in 1978. He was unable to find academic employment but went on to become an immensely popular far-right radio personality and podcaster. One could extrapolate out to thousands of Savages—all of those hopeful members of the boomer and subsequent generations, often liberal and antinomian in their youth, whose ambitions were quashed by their lack of social, as opposed to academic, qualifications. Certainly some of them would gravitate toward populist positions, either of the left or the right.

The problem with this argument is that not enough of these people exist to explain anything. For one so grounded in the mathematical principles governing human history, Turchin seems uncurious about the frequency with which such people are created. For every one Michael Savage there are literally scores of Rush Limbaughs—ignorant, uneducated, mentally unstable, superstitious people who never had any chance at being part of the establishment. In my fairly wide network of professional friends and associates I can think of only one who went this route. The others facing unemployment or employment outside the academy have channeled their energies into more conventional and predictable activities, such as community service, politics, and creative activities. Beyond my limited world, there are few direct data on this question, but we could look to political polls as something of a proxy for the "anti-elite" hypothesis. In 2018 and 2020 polls showed that higher education increasingly correlated with support for the Democratic Party. Although the 2020 polls were contradicted by the performance of down-ticket candidates, they largely held with regard to the top of the ticket. These data are not granular enough to be able to tell who received what degree from what university, and how this might constitute an elite credentialing, but in general it would seem unlikely that there are a significant number of these "anti-elites" living among us and supporting fascists.

What seems a more reasonable hypothesis to me also involves the increasing production of people with elite credentials. It rests not in the attitudes of disappointed would-be elites themselves but in their impact on their families and communities. People with advanced degrees and/or degrees from elite institutions necessarily absorb the culture of those institutions. This culture—the "liberal" side of neoliberalism—is at odds with the traditional culture of rural White America. This divide is clear in a place such as Laramie, where the younger and more educated share a common perspective in which equality among gender, race, sexual orientation, and so forth is a given. To the older, less educated, such ideas are anathema. And it is not only college towns where these liberals are to be found. Increasingly, small towns throughout the rural West have colonies of them, often because of access to public lands or burgeoning artistic communities. Small towns in Wyoming such as Lander and Ten Sleep have such communities. They function as a social irritant in these places. Repeated thousands of times in places in the South and West such as Marfa, Texas or Hillsborough, North Carolina, we can imagine the degree to which conservative communities have felt threatened and felt the need to respond.

Another line of thought, which is supported richly by my own research, is the lack of social capital possessed by many of the Trump supporters. Conservative pollster Daniel Cox (2020) found low levels of social trust and high levels of alienation among Trump supporters. Many of them are close followers of QAnon and other conspiracies because it gives them a sense of community lacking in their non-virtual lives. One of the most fraught issues of the moment for conservatives has had to do with social media. In addition to Trump, many of his supporters have been "de-platformed." The Facebook alternative Parler has just gone dark, perhaps permanently. A small incident on my own Facebook page, in which a Trumpist commenter drew heavy criticism from my other "friends," causing him to delete his account, was typical. Wyoming as a state has one of the highest suicide rates in the country. The level of *anomie* outside a few select places, such as Laramie and Jackson Hole, is high. Certainly, among the men I have talked to over the past five or six years, this was a prime cause for feelings of oppression and low self-worth.

That Trump—a figure as lacking in empathy as any in history—would provide comfort for such people is at first surprising but can be understood as a means of lashing out against those who have much higher degrees of social capital, i.e., the elites, however one defines them. The professors in Laramie or the billionaires in Jackson Hole: both possess a higher degree of social capital, to go along with higher levels of cultural and economic capital. The acquired taste, the ability to exercise *distinction*, separates these elites from the masses, a group that under the regime of neoliberalism, in the age of COVID-19, feels itself losing ground in both symbolic and material ways. To quote Hannah Arendt, whose insights into fascism are remarkably relevant:

> The truth is that the masses grew out of the fragments of a highly atomized society whose competitive structure and concomitant loneliness of the individual had been held in check only through membership in a class. *The chief characteristic of the mass man is not brutality and backwardness, but his isolation and lack of normal social relationships.* Coming from the class-ridden society of the nation-state, whose cracks had been cemented with nationalistic sentiment, it is only natural that these masses, in the first helplessness of their new experience, have tended toward an especially violent nationalism, to which mass leaders have yielded against their own instincts and purposes for purely demagogic reasons.
>
> (Arendt 1973: 317, emphasis added)

An atomized society—one characterized by *anomie* and its attendant ills, notably suicide and domestic violence, both prevalent in Trumplandia—is a precondition for the rise of fascism, as fascism seeks to rectify this isolation through the promise of race- and religion-based forms of identity and solidarity. The virulent reaction against mask-wearing can be understood as a rejection not just of elites but of the forced anonymity many have endured since the breakdown of the modern-era social contract.

Notes

1 This latter example was chosen intentionally, as many American evangelical Protestants who support Trump hold such views.
2 I have raised the issue of Chronic Wasting Disease (CWD), a prion disease of the brain that can be transmitted through eating game. Bill and others view this as an example of "fake news," which Bill also applies to reporting on mass shootings.
3 Bill's openness to voting for Bernie Sanders and his friendship with me, also a social democrat, indicate that the left–right axis is essentially irrelevant to understanding the Trump phenomenon.

References

Arendt, Hannah. 1973 [1951]. *The Origins of Totalitarianism*. San Diego, CA: Harvest Books.

Bourdieu, Pierre. 1984. *Distinction: A Social Critique of the Judgement of Taste*. Richard Nice, trans. Cambridge, MA: Harvard University Press.

Cox, Daniel. 2020. "Could Social Alienation among Some Trump Supporters Help Explain Why Polls Underestimated Trump Again? FiveThirtyEight." https://fivethirtyeight.com/features/could-social-alienation-among-some-trump-supporters-help-explain-why-polls-underestimated-trump-again, accessed January 11, 2021.

Derrida, Jacques. 1982. *Margins of Philosophy*. Alan Bass, trans. Chicago: The University of Chicago Press.

Durkheim, Émile. 1893. *De la Division du Travail Social*. Paris: Presses Universitaires de France.

———. 1897. *Le Suicide*. Paris: Ancienne Libraire Germer Baillière.

Harkin, Michael E. 2016. "The Trump at the End of the World: Monsters and Marvels in Our Parlous Age." William Evans Lecture, University of Otago. Dunedin, New Zealand, July 2016.

——— 2017a. "I Believe We Are Also One in Our Concept of Freedom: The Dewey-Boas Correspondence and the Invention of Postmodern Bourgeois Liberalism." In Regna Darnell and Frederic Gleach, eds. *Historizing Theories, Identities, and Nations*. Lincoln: University of Nebraska Press, 41–60.

———. 2017b. "The Strange Life and Presumed Death of *Homo Economicus*." In Sarmistha Sarma, ed. *Global Observations of the Influence of Culture on Consumer Buying Behavior*. Hershey, PA: IGI International, 136–45.

Herzfeld, Michael. 1985. *The Poetics of Manhood: Contest and Identity in a Cretan Mountain Village*. Princeton, NJ: Princeton University Press.

Hochschild, Arlie Russell. 2016. *Strangers in their Own Land: Anger and Mourning on the American Right*. New York: The New Press.

Lakoff, George. 2016. *Moral Politics: How Liberals and Conservatives Think*. Chicago: University of Chicago Press.

Lévi-Strauss, Claude. 1966. *The Savage Mind*. Chicago: The University of Chicago Press.

Levitsky, Steven and Daniel Ziblatt. 2018. *How Democracies Die*. New York: Crown.

Morgan, Lewis Henry. 1877. *Ancient Society*. Chicago: Charles H. Carr.

Mueller, Jan-Wenner. 2018. "Democracy Still Matters." *The New York Times*, March 5, 2018.

Papamichaeil, Elly Maria and Michael Harkin. 2019. "I Enigmatiki Morfi tou Pringipa Petrou." *Istoria Eikonografimeni*, July 2019.

Rorty, Richard. 1983. "Postmodern Bourgeois Liberalism." *Journal of Philosophy* 80 (10): 583–9.

Sahlins, Marshall. 1981. *Historical Metaphors and Mythical Realities: Structure in the Early History of the Sandwich Islands Kingdom*. Ann Arbor: University of Michigan Press.

Wacquant, Loïc. 2012. "Three Steps to a Historical Anthropology of Actually Existing Neoliberalism." *Social Anthropology* 20 (1): 66–79.

4
MAKING THE CUBAN AMERICAN DREAM GREAT AGAIN

Race and immigrant citizenship in Miami

Ariana Hernandez-Reguant

A few days before the November 2020 presidential election, Carlos Otero, a popular Miami television host, announced live on his evening show on América TeVé that he had voted. As he proudly waved his "I voted" sticker on camera, his co-host, comedian Boncó Quiñongo, hummed the viral salsa hit, turned official Trump campaign song, "I am going to vote for Donald Trump." Being both Cuban, speaking to their own cohort of post-Soviet immigrants, in a local Spanish-language station aimed at Cubans, the statement was safe to make. The audience was solidly Red, and the predicted bluing of the South Florida Cuban electorate was not going to happen after all, despite trends pointing in that direction for years.

A just-released poll from Florida International University (Grenier and Lai 2020) showed that it was no longer the old exiles of the 1960s, reliable Republican voters at least since Reagan, who were responsible for the community's electoral choices. South Florida is home to about a million people who self-identify as Cuban, approximately two-thirds of whom were born in Cuba. Over half of those have arrived since 1990, that is, after the fall of the Soviet Union, having grown up, if adults, under state socialism. To everyone's surprise, it was these recent immigrants, who by the turn of the millennium surpassed them in numbers, who went all in for Trump. These new citizens were not aggrieved blue-collar workers whose fortunes had turned south. They were ambitious people who grew up in Cuba and who, in many cases, risked their lives to reach the "land of the free." Having lived under socialism a good chunk of their lives, they were presumed to be socially liberal. Confronted with their Trumpian endorsement, one could venture that it was their diasporic post-socialist subjectivity and not a neoliberal citizenship that paved the way for their embrace of alt-right populism. And indeed, there was that, but it was secondary. In this article, I focus on something more obvious, and it is that for immigrants, Trumpism signified the activation of an American Dream long dormant.

DOI: 10.4324/9781003152743-5

Carlos Otero himself was an immigrant who, despite having been a TV star in his native Cuba, never had a breakthrough in Miami beyond the ethnic enclave. He and Quiñongo, for years the only Black face on local Spanish-language television, went back a long way as veterans of the megapopular variety show *Sabadazo* on Cuban television. Both in South Florida since the late 2000s, they replicated the familiar formula of live music guests, celebrity news, and comedy skits typical of Latin American television, honoring América TeVé's nickname as "Cubavisión in exile." Thanks to them, the station built a loyal audience that had been underserved—recent Cuban immigrants who longed for the stars and fads they left behind. América TeVé also became a reliable source of employment for expatriate professionals. With a mixed programming of news magazines and entertainment programs, it operated as a school of citizenship, introducing immigrants to the habitus of US capitalism.

Looking straight at the camera, Otero continued, "I voted for Cuba." "A vote for Cuba," he said, "is a vote for Donald Trump." Then, addressing viewers in Cuba, where copies of the show circulated digitally, he explained himself. "Remember: during Obama, all eight years, you underwent a lot of hardship. More than today. And today you are also in need, and we are in pain to see our kinfolk in Cuba suffer. This is why I voted for Donald Trump. Because it is a vote for Cuba." Why a vote for Trump, who just prohibited direct remittance transfers that sustained families, would be a vote for Cuba was not self-evident. Quiñongo explained that those remittances "only benefit the government," presumably because of taxes and fees thereby collected, and urged people to get creative and send money in other ways.

This position was a curious ideological shift for professionals who made a career in Miami thanks to increased transits to and from the island. Merely five years earlier, in 2015, Otero had sent an open letter to Obama, asking him to ease immigration hurdles for Cubans. And later he sent another to the new president Trump to request a reinstatement of the "Wet Foot, Dry Foot" policy that automatically paroled Cubans into the country as refugees from Communism and that his predecessor eliminated. Their very television station, América TeVé, built its audience and business thanks, precisely, to the relaxation of travel and cultural exchanges that ensured an influx of new on-air talent for the shows, and therefore ratings and advertising.

Yet by 2020, the community was galvanized in vociferous support for President Trump Fidel Castro finally dead but the Cuban regime going strong after Obama's rapprochement policies, it was perhaps time to move on and actively join an American polity that offered promise instead of defeat. A growing number of Spanish-language, mostly Cuban, webzines, social media pages and YouTube influencers—some, like Ota Ola, garnering hundreds of thousands of viewers—created an echo chamber for Trumpism in South Florida, as it never existed before, catering to the young. And so Trump the South Florida Cuban vote handsomely—Hialeah by about 75 percent of the vote, sometimes surpassing, in the same precincts, Clinton's vote four years prior by over twenty points. This time, Cuban Americans in South Florida went out to vote en masse, and they did so for Donald Trump.

Why did Cubans, and particularly those most accented—the immigrants that Trump seemed to loathe—go all in for him? What was the allure of Trumpism for new citizens who had for years been civically disengaged and voted without fanfare or not at all?

After a decade of ethnographic fieldwork among Cubans in Hialeah, dozens of formal interviews, and about two months of daily canvassing for the local Democratic Party prior to the 2020 election, knocking on thousands of doors and talking to hundreds of residents, I came to the conclusion that no one single issue either sealed or broke the deal. Neither the economy, nor the Second Amendment, immigration, jobs, law and order, the coronavirus, or US Cuban policy were definitive. Trumpism was not a policy calculation. It was not the result of resentment either, as scholars have argued in relation to other groups, like Rust Belt workers or rural dwellers (Cramer 2016; Hochschild 2016).

Rather, it was a structure of feeling that cut across sociological categories, an emergent political subjectivity that transcended party and redefined nation not as a pre-existing condition but as a project defined by the individual. Its development may be understood within a double axis. One corresponds to immigrant aspirations for upward mobility that rejects ideals of equality in favor of hierarchy. The other one responds to a very different tendency that may be described as "anti-politics" and that emerges as a reaction to the Communist experience, espousing ideals of individual liberty in rejection of a system of majority rule. It is the first that is the focus of this chapter.

Walking the Hialeah dream

In late 2020, Hialeah was ebullient with Trump flags and banners. As soon as its central library opened for early voting, residents, overwhelmingly Cuban and white, and outfitted with MAGA hats and t-shirts, lined up outside at all hours of the day. Its parking lot, usually vacant, was a jungle of US flags and Trump banners. Los 3 de La Habana's viral hit, "*Yo voy a Votar por Donald Trump*" (I am going to vote for Donald Trump) blasted without pause. The Hialeah Republican Club, founded two years earlier by a former Hialeah mayor to boost Trump's candidacy, occupied the back area with its pickup trucks and a life-sized cardboard cutout of Donald Trump. Its raucous members, all Cuban and Spanish-speaking, shouted slogans through their megaphones, passed around literature to passers-by, and improvised dance circles. A little girl was standing around with a full-head rubber Trump mask. A teenager was zooming by in his skateboard carrying a triple flag that included Trump's as well as a marijuana one.

An older Black man in blue gym wear with the word "Cuba" embroidered in red attracted the attention of onlookers with his spectacular rumba moves. I inquired about his unusual outfit: "I brought it with me from Cuba," he explained, adding that he used to be an elite weightlifter. "They don't make anything this good here," he rejoiced. A white man in his fifties, sitting close by at a folding chair, laughed at the incongruence, mumbling that nothing was good under socialism. He, by contrast, had arrived in the US empty-handed. "When I arrived from Cuba in 2000, I was practically homeless. But I worked hard and now I own a $400,000 house." To underscore his point, another man, also a recent emigré, handed me a magazine entitled "The One Percent." "Those are the millionaires!" I joked. "Like us, one day," he replied.

This scene was unusually lively and eventually attracted the national press. Hialeah's central library was the epicenter of Cuban Florida, and the enthusiasm was on Trump's side. Up until then, Hialeah, located in northwest Miami-Dade County, population 230,000—96 percent white Hispanic, two-thirds Cuban, and, more than that, foreign-born—was far from a haven for political activism. A whites-only area since its incorporation in the 1920s, Cubans began to settle there in significant numbers in the 1970s to be close to the many small textile and other manufacturing plants that provided employment. As non-Hispanics fled to the suburbs, the city eventually displaced Little Havana as the Cuban "ethnic enclave," in terms of both demographic concentration and economic activity, all the while maintaining the geographical lines of racial segregation intact. In 2017, the city acquired the dubious honor of being the fourth-least diverse city in America (Hussain 2017). In 2019, according to the mini-census, 93 percent of the households spoke Spanish at home, and the city remained firmly white, with over 95 percent of residents reporting as such (Census Reporter 2019c). Black Cubans traditionally skirted Miami for other regions of the country, or, alternatively, settled in Miami's African American and other diverse neighborhoods.

In addition to class and race lines of segmentation in the Cuban community, there was one less obvious to outsiders, and that was cohort. The exiles who arrived in the region early on after the 1959 revolution were initially slow to take on US citizenship, since they hoped to return. They prided themselves on being a model minority, were recipients of numerous aid programs, and never thought of themselves as anything other than racially white. The 1980 Mariel boatlift began to threaten that self-image. Differently from their predecessors, the *Marielitos* were viewed as hardened brown men as reflected in the Scarface. Antonio López (2012) has beautifully explained that the Hollywood rendition of a Cuban American drug lord as an Italian American (Al Pacino) donning brownface signaled the prospect of a generalized "darkening" that would translate in social descent for the entire Cuban American community. The 1994 Balsero crisis and the mass migration ensuing Cuba's loss of Soviet support that decade were the nail in the coffin, in terms of reshaping the national community away from the island, in line with other working-class Latin American and Caribbean immigrant groups.

After Mariel, the upwardly mobile exiles organized politically to counteract a social backlash that lumped them in the same group as their alien countrymen. By then well-established and economically stable, they helped drive the area toward the Republican Party. "Being a Republican," said to me a Miami-born Cuban, "was part of the culture." "Because I am Cuban" became the most frequent explanation for a Republican vote. Indeed, from the early 1980s onward, Hialeah's mayor and council members, as well as those of the city of Miami, as well as county, state, and federal representatives have all been Cuban, mostly Republican, and mostly male. Into the 2020s, they still were, but what was less obvious was that they also continued to belong to the cohorts of exile or their American-born offspring.

By then, most residents, however, had reached US shores in the 1990s or later, escaping the economic disarray after the fall of the Soviet Union. Raised under revolutionary socialism, their language and speech, upbringing and life experiences, class and popular culture set them apart from their exiled forebears. Among these recent immigrant cohorts, views of the political process ranged from indifferent to skeptical to contemptuous. Voter turnout was typically very low: in the 2014 mid-terms, for instance, participation in central Hialeah precincts was in the single digits. Presidential elections always saw a spike, but 2016 had been subdued, perhaps because none of the Cubans, Cruz and Rubio, or Florida's own Jeb Bush made the presidential nomination. Then, few houses featured electoral signs, and the Trump campaign office on 49th Street was easy to miss, with only a small window poster and a tiny staff of elderly English-speaking out-of-towners. Occasional "Cubans4Trump" flash mobs would take place at well-to-do suburbs but were mostly attended by US-born and/or -raised families (Hernandez-Reguant 2016). In 2020, by contrast, the euphoria was shared by all, established exiled families and recently-arrived immigrants, whites and Blacks, young and old. Trump united a community otherwise divided by class and culture in a common project that, for the first time, was not the Cuban nation.

Precisely to get beyond the statistics, as well as phone surveys with predetermined questions, while also being ethnographically constrained by a raging pandemic, I decided to make mine a method from political activism: canvassing. In the early fall 2020, I volunteered to canvass the city of Hialeah on behalf of a candidate for county mayor, a Democrat in a non-partisan race. That allowed me easy access to voting data, as well as the legitimacy to knock on thousands of doors and engage people of various political leanings—although targets were mostly Democrats and Independents—in conversation about their voting preferences. I walked hundreds of city blocks, usually from mid-day to the early evening, every day of the week, and talked to thousands of people, almost all Cuban.

Hardly anyone was out during the day, when the sun blasted the treeless sidewalks. Only the corner malls that dotted the most suburban areas of single-family homes had traffic in and out of big-box chain and discount stores. In the residential streets, front and back yards were often paved or had fake grass, more friendly to barbequing than the native South Florida brush. Only the sound of air conditioners betrayed human habitation in the middle of the day. Children and youths were often home now, attending school online because of the pandemic, but it was the elderly who usually opened the door: some were visiting from Cuba to take care of babies and toddlers. Fast-tracked for residency thanks to the Cuban Adjustment Act, they would stay in Miami only to get their residency papers and then return, initiating an annual back and forth. "Do you know when I will get my social security card? asked one who was apparently on the last flight to Miami before the pandemic shut down air travel. "I can't wait to go back," he told me. He was from a rural area and felt both bored and constrained in the concrete desert, spending his days repairing an out-of-order van he bought for cheap and missing his friends and extended family.

The next person on my canvassing list that day was also an elderly one, but she was not home. According to my data, the demographic segments under twenty-five and over seventy were more likely to be Democrat, but in multi-generational households, it was common to find both different migratory cohorts and party affiliations. "That's my grandmother, she's in Cuba," said the youth who opened: "She will not be back in time to vote because of the pandemic." For these and most other households in the area, the connection with Cuba was very much alive. Through the Obama years, many traveled to and from the island regularly as well as sending a good chunk of their earnings as remittances—in the order of between $4 billion and $8 billion annually, mostly originating in Florida (US Cuba Trade and Economic Council 2020). In November 2020, the Trump administration forced Western Union to eliminate the service, effectively banning direct transfers in a move that was billed as a punishment for the Cuban government rather than for recipient families. A few doors over, the man I asked about, also a retiree, was also in Cuba but not just visiting. He had moved back with a new wife for good, only to return every so often to cash his Social Security checks, but the pandemic confinement was keeping him overseas for now. "And my mother and I are voting for Trump," grumbled his ex-wife. When the person who came to the door was not who I was looking for, we engaged in conversation just the same.

In the late afternoon, driveways began to fill up, and neighbors came out. They washed their cars, swept their front steps, emptied out their mailbox, or set up a camping table from which to sell homemade croquetas and jams. "Things are tough right now," said one in Spanish, which is the sole language spoken in 96 percent of Hialeah homes. As I walked by, one called me to ask if I understood English, then handed me a handwritten letter she just received for me to translate: it was signed by a Republican Party volunteer from Minnesota urging her to vote. Across the street, a grandfather sitting at a beach chair guarded a pickup truck loaded with watermelons and papayas outside his son's reggaeton-blasting house. Area residents appreciated the convenience after a long day's work.

Trump houses were easy to spot. Picket fences and dog warnings often demarcated property lines, and their Trump banners, and Blue Lives Matter, QAnon and plain US flags competed for space with traditional altars dedicated to San Lázaro or la Virgen de la Caridad, and with over the top Halloween decorations. At times, boats parked on the yards dwarfed the houses themselves. A man with a Goya Foods polo shirt got off his Maserati as I reached his doorway. Conspicuous displays of luxury purchases boasted a propertied citizenship that went hand in hand with the political subjectivity of Trumpism. As Alain Badiou remarked in a 2017 essay on Trumpism, private property was the structuring principle for an ambitioned society where equality took a back seat. To be a member of the polity entailed owning property, or at least being a conspicuous consumer. Also recall "The One

Percent" mentioned at the beginning of this section. "One day we too may be rich," asserted the member of the Hialeah Republican Club who was handing it out at the Hialeah central library. Meanwhile, Los 3 de La Habana sang lines like "How sharp is Melania, with her bag and her dress from Louis Vuitton," while their accompanying video showed images of sharply dressed white people tossing dollar bills around and partying on a yacht.

Democratic homes seemed to be more subdued. Often, these voters did not actually live in the house but rented carriage-type studios or "efficiencies" around the sides or the back, that were typical in the area, built to generate extra income from renting to new immigrants of modest means and often lacking in creditworthiness. Walking the streets without venturing into the properties, these small quarters were easy to miss, and a stratification that was not just of income but of migratory cohort remained hidden. I had to duck under a huge Trump banner to reach one: "Shhhh, I don't want them to know that I am for Biden," a middle-aged lady said, popping her head out to make sure nobody heard me. She and her elderly mother were inside, away from the bright sun, watching an enormous wall-mounted TV. They were new citizens and had never voted before. She held up the mail-in ballots as proof. "We don't know how to fill them out," she sighed, looking at them as if they were written in alien script. "We were not planning on voting." I offered to give them an impromptu class, and she immediately turned off the TV and sat me in their best La-Z-boy. They took profuse notes ("so that we have the instructions for next time"), and finally tongue-sealed the envelopes. They were all smiles as they waved me goodbye.

I found more new citizens in the old, dilapidated apartment complexes of West Hialeah, where Trump signs were few. More people were home, some out of work. Already before the pandemic, 21.3 percent of residents lived below the poverty line, and 40 percent of the households received food stamps (Census Reporter 2019b). The city's labor force was evenly divided among manufacturing and transportation, construction, sales, services, and small businesses, most of which were heavily hit by the pandemic slump (Census Reporter 2019a). Now, tired-looking couples sat on their balconies all day long, smoking cigarettes or just glancing in the distance. In these places, everybody knew each other and were quick to direct me to the right door, only for another neighbor to pop out and tell me all about the one who was not home. Oftentimes, distant voices encouraged me to push the door, "Come in, don't be shy, do you want a coffee?" I hesitated but I often obliged. It was the scarce Black families who often ushered me in; the mother or the grandmother would be lying on the couch, too tired from work to get up. They seemed as likely as whites to vote for either party. "We don't vote Black. We vote Cuban," said one.

A great deal of people who affirmed they would vote for Trump did not know what party they were registered with ("it must have been when I became a citizen, that they put that down") or which one was Trump's. "Are you with Trump?" they inquired. "With the Democrats," I responded. "Is that Trump's party?" "No, it is the other one." "Oh, we are not interested." They did not vote in primaries or belong to party clubs. Others acknowledged to have voted Democrat in the past, both for Hillary Clinton in 2016 and for Obama in 2012, but this time they were changing course.

When pressed, people would explain that they supported Trump because their 401k was doing better under his government or because Hialeah should become great again, like it was before the factories left for China and "you could get a job just like that," according to a woman who had three jobs to make ends meet. Or because they approved of restricting immigration, just because "*no hay cama pa' tanta gente*" ("there's no room for so many people"), as some folksily put it. Or because they did not agree with paying taxes to cover other people's welfare, education, health and housing. "My children are not disabled, why should I pay for my neighbor's disabled kid?," argued one. A retired forklift operator ranted against the politics of identity that other minorities allegedly used to seek favors and get ahead.

Voting for Trump was seldom a vote for Cuba. In this election, policy seemed an afterthought. Trumpism was at the time an empty vessel, a framework for policy rather than policy itself. This is why the young man who spent his days skateboarding around the Hialeah central library with the double Marijuana/Trump flag could shrug off the apparent contradiction. His view was that the Republican Party might oppose legalization, but Trump could get behind it if that's what people wanted. Trump offered an open space where policy was transactional and contingent, as the extension of a free market of favors. In other words, Trump signified total capitalism. And that was the America post-socialism immigrants desired. Trumpism thus connected with a structure of feeling that, to simplify Raymond Williams' (1980) original theorization, both emerged from and gave sense to their immigrant experience and that was culturally articulated on the basis of their socialist and post-socialist mental mappings.

The populist ingredient was, of course, also there. The socialism Cubans fled was an authoritarian one, personified in one leader who demanded undying loyalty. That was a familiar framework. President Trump both demanded and elicited a fierce loyalty, and there is no doubt that his constant media presence leading up to the election, as well as his vulnerabilities and flaws, earned people's sympathies. "He does not need to knock on doors to remind anyone to go to vote," an older woman said with scorn. In true populist fashion, people often referred to him without naming him: Trump was just "he" or "him." "He will fix things," "I am voting for 'him.'" "For him, who?" "Well, for Trump." I had a déjà vu that became uncanny when a man referred to him as "*el caballo*" (the horse, which is the number one in the Cuban numerical charade and used to refer to Fidel Castro, also often alluded to in Cuba as, simply, "He"). For various informants, He was handsome, He cared about the poor, He was being mistreated, He was not a politician, He was the everyday man with the same flaws as the average person. In sum, He was a Big Man in the anthropological sense, a "prince among men" (Sahlins 1963). His commanding power was personal before it could become political. This is why He, Trump, supplanted He, Fidel; an affective substitution visually materialized at a Little Havana's bloc party to celebrate Castro's passing. It was late November 2016, and the popular funeral party was coronated by huge luminous signs spelling TRUMP. Four years later, the previously ubiquitous Cuban flag had all but disappeared from Hialeah, replaced, for the first time, by the US flag.

In this worldview, elections were not about the minutiae of policy but about competing visions of self and the future. The roadmap that Trump offered was uncharted, but one thing was certain: it took Cubans in the United States farther away from the Cuba they left behind. They were new Americans insofar as they were also Cubans anew, breaking free from the old country. "Raise your hands if you are both Cuban and American," sang Los 3 de La Habana. They did not call on their audience as every Cuban dance band used to do, by shouting names of Cuban towns and Havana's neighborhoods. Instead, they called on those who were US citizens. "If you are proud of being both Cuban and American, raise your hands," the lyrics went on. Their official video, which was contracted by Latinos for Trump after their impromptu chorus, "I am going to vote for Donald Trump" went viral, featured US, Thin Blue Line, and Trump flags, but not a Cuban one. Voting for Trump was a not a vote for Cuba. It was a vote for America.

But voting for America required some adjustments, not necessarily on the envisioned America but on the portrayal of self. The model minority image that early Cuban exiles had crafted broke into pieces with the 1980 Mariel boatlift and again with the next mass influx in the 1990s and beyond. While the Mariel group, with lower levels of education and racially diverse, fueled a widespread social panic in South Florida, the constant trickling of new transplants, raised under socialism, throughout the 1990s and the twenty-first century, further fragmented the Cuban community. Upbringing, ethos, accent, education, class, networks of power, and views of self and others sometimes seemed, all together, like an insurmountable cultural divide—with the added complication of the group made up of exiles' US-born and -educated, English-speaking offspring, who, no longer lived in the ethnic enclave. As recent immigrants became the most numerous segment, Hialeah became the butt of all jokes for its quirky visual and personal aesthetics and forms of speech (Hernandez-Reguant 2020). The only literary title that bore its name was "How to Leave Hialeah" (Capó 2009). There was no pride in being from there, and Hialeah was consistently ranked at the bottom of the country in terms of liveable places (Lipcomb 2019). It was not the embrace of a generic Latinidad that would save these new Americans from social descent, but rather, the embrace of Cuban exile values, including whiteness.

A bifurcated citizenship

When former Miami-Dade County mayor and freshman US Representative Carlos Giménez proclaimed on Fox News that undocumented immigrants seeking citizenship "oughta really go back to their country of origin and get in line," the irony was not lost on the local press (Cardona 2021). Born in Cuba, Giménez himself had been a direct beneficiary of generous immigration policies. More to the point, the metaphor he used, "to get in line," aligned him immediately with a very specific ideology that, according to Hochschild's (2016) and Cramer's (2016) respective studies of rural voters, was intrinsic to Tea Party supporters' mental mappings. The Libertarian worldview resolved the tension between democracy and liberalism—between the call for equality and the privileging of a possessive individualism linked to free market—in favor of the latter. That is, it naturalized social stratification as determined not by structures of inequality but by their negation, placing all agency on the individual. Even though these voters blamed the government for selectively enabling privilege on the basis of identity politics, they directed their resentment toward those social groups that allegedly "cut the line" by relying on public programs, namely immigrants and African Americans. Accordingly, they faulted the poor for their own predicament, attributing an alleged lack of individual entrepreneurship to a culture that was in their view interchangeable with race.

In his book on the American alt-right, Neiwert (2017) referred to this narrative as "producerism": the idea that hard working "producers" are "beset by a two-headed enemy: a nefarious elite suppressing them from above, and a parasitic underclass of 'others,' reliant on welfare and government benefits… sucking them from below." This view, which leads to racist and anti-immigrant conclusions, is at the base of a right-wing populism that has become a global phenomenon. In Israel, for instance, the Mizrahi Jews, who are mostly working class, support right-wing parties, while resenting the Ashkenazi middle as well as upper classes who represent the ideal of a liberal nation (Mautner 2016). Despite their own disenfranchisement, the Mizrahin reject a social equality that would demand solidarity with a Palestinian underclass, undermining their claim to ethnic and religious privilege. Similarly, in Western Europe, native whites resent their wealthy cosmopolitan elites, all the while denying rights to racialized immigrants and former colonial subjects (Brown 2018). In all instances, essentializing stratification was necessary to prevent further social descent, as well as the ascent of others at the margins. This is also an American story. Irish immigrants in nineteenth-century Philadelphia, not considered white at the time, donned blackface to harass African Americans so as to distance themselves from the one impediment to upward mobility—Blackness (Roediger 1999). At the turn of the twenty-first century, history repeated itself in Miami, and not as a farce.

This link between citizenship and racialization could not be more evident in some of the comedic skits that for years were bread and butter of local Spanish-language immigrant television in Miami. Seven years before Carlos Otero trumpeted his Trump vote on live television, he had made a related announcement, also from his show on América TeVé. It was Independence Day 2013, or rather the day before, when it was taped. I was in attendance, as part of my ethnographic fieldwork at the time. Otero informed the audience that he had just been honored with US citizenship, only five years after being paroled into the country. To celebrate, he was wearing an Uncle Sam hat and was all smiles when the studio audience clapped and the house band played celebratory chords. "How many stars are there in the flag?," his co-host playfully asked, imitating the citizenship examiner. Otero faltered. "Fifty-two," he said. The producer gasped, but the schedule was tight and there was no time to re-tape. Quickly, all on-air talent present—hosts, dancers, actors, musical guests—were summoned to the set for the opening and closing segments. Standing next to each other, they swayed their hips to the beat, clapped, and waved to the panning cameras. There were only two black faces among the twenty or so people—a visiting actress from Cuba and Juancito, a small actor introduced as the only "true Yuma" (slang for true American) in the house. Born in Key West to Cuban exile parents and perfectly bilingual, he was donning blackface.

The next segment was a comedy skit, also to be included in the following day's broadcast of TN3. Entitled *"Los Asaltantes"* (The Assailants), it was the story of a down-and-out white Cuban couple with two Black kids, one played by the aforementioned Juancito. This July Fourth episode took place at a state unemployment office, but others did at various sites of immigrant life, like welfare and medical offices, public transportation, a funeral home, a botanica, a cell phone store or a Disneyworld box office. There, always humiliated with charges that they could not afford—whether $100 for sleeping pills, $800 for a Santeria consultation, $120 for the welfare application, $500 for a cell phone, $900 for a medical procedure, or $400 for a Disney ticket—the husband, Manolo, dressed in black tights and turtle neck, and wearing a black bonnet like a cartoon thief, pulled out a gun and attempted a stick-up. Victims would plead with him, arguing that "we are penniless," or "there is no money here, only food stamps," or "I only make minimum wage," or "when have you seen that people with money will take the bus," or would explain that they were retired or jobless, or sick or old, to no avail. At that point, Juancito typically entered the scene.

"Daddy, daddy!," he would cry, walking toward Manolo. He was never welcome. Manolo would push him away, loudly denying any acquaintance, at times forced to explain that the "black thing" was not his son but his sister's "who was raped by a Black man." Then he would tell Juancito that he was not his father but "merely adopted him from an African tribe." His wife, albeit admitting to her sexual attraction toward Black men, would, however, dismiss his paternity doubts: "Don't you see that he has your same face, same smile, same charisma?" "We don't have the same skin color, *coño*!," he would grumble, "he could not be any darker…," and then splash whipped cream or talcum powder on Juancito so as to whiten him. In the US, differently from Cuba, the one-drop rule flipped white into Black in one step and there was no way back. Manolo's fear was not so much of a degraded manhood, as of a degraded whiteness.

A degraded whiteness, in essence, amounts to a degraded citizenship. Scarface's browning of the new Cuban Americans was becoming a prophecy come true. Hence Manolo's quixotic battle against this dramatic social precipice was waged not in the bedroom but in the spaces of dependent citizenship that had become arenas of competition between Cubans and African Americans. "The Assailants" was a perfect example of class fear, played as a fear of Blackness. As Hochschild (2016) perceptively noted, while for the Left, the theater of conflict is Wall Street, or, I would add, a Black neighborhood where a Wall Streeter gets lost—as in Tom Wolfe's

The Bonfire of the Vanities—for the Right it is the welfare office, the space where the white working poor come together with a racialized underclass.

In one episode at the Department of Children and Families, Manolo impatiently cut the line in front of a tired-looking Black mother (a white actress donning brownface) only to be scolded by his wife: "Don't you see that she has a Black child, just like us?" Manolo snapped: "This is the United States. There is no racism here and I do not care if he's white, Chinese or Black." A moment later, Manolo asked the lady, already clutching two babies, to hold his for a moment, only to then walk away with one of hers. "Excuse me, sorry," he said handing her the baby, "I took the wrong negro, I mean… *niño*." His early statement that the US was a color-blind society was obviously facetious, for color is all there is, erasing any hope for individuality and therefore of agency. Juancito and his baby brother's Blackness constituted a defacement, in turn characteristic of an inexorable social descent.

"The Assailants" was one of many skits on TN3 and other local Spanish-language television shows that used blackface during the 2000s, when several local stations catered to the recently-arrived Cuban audience. In most cases, this performative device was intended to transport viewers to a colonial era of supposed racial harmony, and thus convey a nostalgia for a lost nation (Hernandez-Reguant 2017). But in the 2010s, a new modality sought to emasculate not the "embraceable" (to borrow from Helan Page, 1997) Afro-Cuban but the unruly African American, whose fate increasingly became the yardstick against which to measure immigrant success. For instance, in another episode, Manolo is outrun by a knife-wielding African American youth (another blackface actor) more skilled than he is with the weapons that are their means of production. Whether as a father or as a provider, Manolo is always beaten at his game by a black man. Without Cuban exceptionalism, there is only an immigrant that has to get in the back of the line.

The series, written by two white Cuban comedians, brutally pushed against the rag-to-riches exile narrative of upward mobility that for decades sustained the myth of the Cuban American Dream. As immigrants, the newcomers measured their social accomplishments and economic mobility by the standards of those who climbed up the ladder before them. But by the 2010s, almost a quarter of all Hialeah households lived below the poverty level, quickly catching up to the 32 percent of all Black households in the county that did too (Census Reporter 2019c). As the decade came to a close, the gap between the working class and the, disenfranchised masses was closing. The images of African American protests that captured front pages and television screens through 2020 heightened immigrants' fear of belonging to a failed polity. It became clear that there were two divergent paths to US citizenship. One, linked to enterprise and possessive individualism, was white. Another, linked to state dependency and petty criminality, was Black. A claim to whiteness—to the old Cuban, Hispanic, European whiteness—and its associated respectability became common sense. This is also why the 95.5 percent of residents of Hialeah would claim to be Hispanic and white, turning the one-drop rule on its head.

At the same time, the Blackness being delegitimized in public discourse, including parody, was that of the unruly African American. América TeVé, along with most local Spanish-language media aimed at Cubans (exile talk radio, newspapers, webzines, and YouTube influencers), constantly stressed the connection between African American Blackness and criminality. By contrast, Black Cubans were kindly portrayed as Cuban first and Black second or not at all. This is why an alt-right white supremacy group like the Proud Boys could have a Black Cuban as president. His famous arrest was, precisely, for desecrating African American Blackness—for vandalizing a historically Black church and burning its Black Lives Matter banner. In this worldview, whiteness stood not only for skin color but for personal visual and aural aesthetics, as well as, in a circular logic, for the rejection of a very specific kind of blackness that was viewed as threatening to white, including white Hispanic, hegemony.

Against this scenario, Trump offered a hope that Obama, viewed as president of the line-cutters, did not deliver. Obama's elimination of the "Dry Foot, Wet Foot" policy that sustained Cuban exceptionalism and the fiction of exile was his ultimate betrayal because he forced Cubans, precisely, to get in line. Trump did not reverse the policy, but he did offer something better. Rather than strengthening a transnational Cuban community, he allowed Cubans to partake, as individuals, of that which they wanted to become and join in a national project, not as Cubans but as Americans.

Trumpism lives

At the closing of this writing, Jacques Rancière (2021) published a short article entitled "The Fools and the Wise," seeking to explain, in retrospect and after the Capitol riots, the allure of Trumpism. There, he made two key points. The first was that sociological explanations have fallen short. That is, no demographic characteristics, identity markers, or socioeconomic indicators are predictors of an embrace of the populist alt-right. And that is because, in his view, Trumpism is not the expression of a pre-existing community. Rather, it is people-making. It creates a community that looks not at the past but at the future. The second, related point that Rancière makes is that these voters are not aggrieved, as is often stated, nor do they resort to a politics of resentment, as Cramer (2016), among others, have argued of Tea Party followers. Instead, many Trump supporters are fighting to maintain a privilege that is perceived to be in jeopardy, and they do so vis-à-vis other groups they deem as less deserving.

Both arguments are validated by this ethnography of Cuban immigrants in South Florida, particularly in the enclave of Hialeah. This article makes, in addition, a third argument, and that is that in the United States, the claim to privilege is made on the basis of rights, and it entails the racialization of others. That is, on the one hand, the narrative of entitlement requires a dreamworld of progress that gives purpose to the migrant passage and that entails a centering of individual rights—namely possessive individualism—as the structuring principle for political subjectivity. On the other hand, a claim to self-righteousness entails the denial of others', and that takes place through their racialization.

Cubans in the United States are far from a homogeneous community. One of their deepest cleavages concerns migratory cohort. There are significant ideological, class, and cultural differences among exiles, from those who mostly arrived in the 1960s fleeing Communism, to their US-born English-speaking offspring, to post-1980 immigrants who grew up under socialism and were acculturated into it. This latter group now populates the ethnic enclave. While exiles possessed political, financial, and social capital in the region, recent immigrants have stronger and more active ties with the island and are more bound by family and work obligations than by civic duties.

For all of them, property is key to political subjectivity. As Badiou (2019) described, in the Libertarian worldview, one who is neither a proprietor nor a consumer is a non-entity—what I would describe as a "bare" citizen. For Cuban immigrants in South Florida, the American Dream means the realization of material advancement on the basis of individual enterprise. It means, therefore, an identification with those propertied ones accepted into white society and the rejection of the dispossessed, typically racialized as African Americans and Latinos. The precarious balance between democracy and liberalism, between equality and individualism, is definitely resolved toward the latter.

Los 3 de La Habana, a popular band back in Havana, and, for that reason, well known to the immigrant cohorts of the new millennium, brought home the rags-to-riches myth that had seemed increasingly unattainable. As they recounted in a television interview with Carlucho, a popular comedian from their same generation and migration cohort, the pandemic had shuttered their livelihood, giving them no choice other than to apply for unemployment. Then an acquaintance hired them to play at a private party but warned them that the neighbor, a Democrat, might call the police on the crowd. In response, they playfully improvised a chorus, specially to defy the neighbor: "I am going to vote for Donald Trump." Before they knew it, the live feed had gone viral. Even President Trump himself retweeted it, and his campaign eventually hired them to play at rallies while also using their song in campaign ads. The naturalized music trio, in the United States since 2007, came to embody the powerful vision of the self-made immigrant realized, merely by embracing that ideal. Their full membership in the nation only occurred when Trump, president of their adopted country, rewarded their innate talent with work, money, and fame. The marriage of political populism and celebrity status was, precisely, the emblem of the new anti-politics.

Trump won Florida and the Cuban vote but lost the election, leaving, however, the legacy of three loyalists, all Cuban, to represent Miami-Dade county in Congress, including a well-known television anchor who unseated Democrat Donna Shalala. Their votes against certifying the presidential election and against the Equality Act, as well as their extremely conservative positions, most Cubans in South Florida will never know. Trumpism was not about the minutiae of policy or the administration of government. It offered a grand narrative from which to make sense of the world, of self and others. It was a structure of feeling whose participants were not subjects but free individuals webbed together by nothing more than contingent, contractual agreements.

Finally, Trumpism offered a foreign-born community the opportunity to reconstruct a collective mental mapping founded no longer on exile loss but on immigrant gain. For the first time, revolution-raised Cuban expatriates could join in a community of purpose that did not look toward Cuba but toward the United States, joining in the project with innumerable other individuals from all walks of life. Trump allowed for a guilt-free severance of the homeland's umbilical cord. If you were a Cuban immigrant, being American under Trump was about making a leap forward into a new dreamworld of progress. One expat spelled it out, "We are here to make America great. This is why we came." It was also about having the opportunity to jump up into wealth and fame, with the luck of a lottery winner. No president, much less a presidential candidate including Trump himself four years prior, had offered such a palatable vision. And all without leaving Hialeah, the most Cuban place outside of Cuba.

References

Badiou, Alain. 2019. *Trump*. Cambridge, UK and Medford, MA: Polity Press.

Brown, Wendy. 2018. "Neoliberalism's Frankenstein: Authoritarian Freedom in Twenty-First Century 'Democracies'." In Brown, W., Gordon, P.E., and Pensky, M. *Authoritarianism. Three Inquiries in Critical Theory*. London: Verso, 7–43.

Capó, Jenine. 2009. *How to Leave Hialeah*. Iowa City: University of Iowa Press.

Cardona, Alexi. 2021. "Cuban Immigrant Carlos Giménez to Undocumented U.S. Citizenship Seekers: 'Get in Line'" *Miami New Times*. https://www.miaminewtimes.com/news/us-rep-carlos-gimenez-opposes-biden-immigration-plan-11824020, accessed 27 January 2021.

Census Reporter. 2019a. "Hialeah, FL. Industry by Occupation." https://censusreporter.org/data/table/?table=B24050&geo_ids=16000US1230000&primary_geo_id=16000US1230000, accessed 12 December 2020.

———. 2019b. "Hialeah, FL. Public Assistance Income or Food Stamps in the Past 12 Months for Households (in 2020)." *Table B19058* https://censusreporter.org/data/table/?table=B19058&geo_ids=16000US1230000&primary_geo_id=16000US1230000, accessed 12 December 2020.

——— 2019c. "Hialeah, FL. Poverty line." https://censusreporter.org/profiles/16000US1230000-hialeah-fl, accessed 12 December 2020.

Cramer, Katherine J. 2016. *The Politics of Resentment. Rural Consciousness in Wisconsin and the Rise of Scott Walker*. Chicago: The University of Chicago Press.

Grenier, Guillermo J. and Qing Lai. 2020. *2020 FIU Cuba Poll: How Cuban Americans in Miami view U.S. policies toward Cuba*. Miami: Florida International University. https://cri.fiu.edu/research/cuba-poll/2020-fiu-cuba-poll.pdf, accessed 1 November 2020.

Hernandez-Reguant, Ariana. 2016. "Cubans 4 Trump and the Battle for the Nation." *Cuba Counterpoints*. https://cubacounterpoints.com/archives/4399.html, accessed 20 February 2021.

———. 2017. "Miami Minstrels: A Farewell to the Cuban Nation." In Pierre Sean Brotherton, ed. *Cuba as Dreamworld or Catastrophe*. Cultural Anthropology, Hot Spots Series. https://culanth.org/fieldsights/miami-minstrels-a-farewell-to-the-cuban-nation, accessed 26 February 2021.

———. 2020. "Meeting Cubans 4 Trump." https://nacla.org/news/2020/10/31/cubans-4-trump, accessed 30 October 2020.

Hochschild, Arlie. 2016. *Strangers on their Own Land. Anger and Mourning in the American Right.* New York: The New Press.

Hussain, Selima. 2017. "Hialeah One of Nation's Least Diverse Cities, Study Says." *Sun Sentinel.* https://www.sun-sentinel.com/features/fl-reg-hialeah-least-cultural-diverse-america-20170222-story.html, accessed 24 February 2021.

Lipcomb, Jessica. 2019. "Why Is Hialeah Always Ranked the Worst City for Everything?" *Miami New Times,* Jan 16, 2019. Https://www.miaminewtimes.com/news/why-is-hialeah-always-ranked-the-worst-city-for-everything-11047893, accessed September 3, 2021.

López, Antonio. 2012. *Unbecoming Blackness.* New York: NYU Press.

Mautner, Menachem. 2016, "Liberalism in Israel. Between the 'Good Person' and the 'Bad Citizen'." *Israel Studies Review* 31 (1): 6–35.

Neiwert, David. 2017. *Alt-America: The Rise of the Radical Right in the Age of Trump.* London: Verso.

Page, Hélan. 1997. ""Black Male" Imagery and Media Containment of African American Men." *American Anthropologist* 99 (1): 99–111.

Rancière, Jacques. 2021. "The Fools and the Wise." https://www.versobooks.com/blogs/4980-the-fools-and-the-wise, accessed 23 January 2021.

Roediger, David R. 1999. *The Wages of Whiteness: Race and the Making of the American Working Class.* London: Verso.

Sahlins, Marshall. 1963. "Poor Man, Rich Man, Big-Man, Chief: Political Types in Melanesia and Polynesia." *Comparative Studies in Society and History* 5 (3): 285–303.

U.S. Cuba Trade and Economic Council. 2020. "Western Union Data for Transfers to Cuba". *Economic Eye on Cuba.* https://www.cubatrade.org/blog/2020/11/17/kpjlhqqsng-ty2v8u4nwc41u2d6a1q6, accessed 19 November 2020.

5

"WE'RE ON THE SAME TEAM, RIGHT?"

Political polarization and social connections in "Trump country"

Claudine M. Pied

I have known Scott for more than ten years. We are both from the same rural region of Maine, and we met there when I was doing research on political responses to changes in the economy. For most of the time I have known him, he has had a tenuous relationship with his brother. They connect with each other through a mutual interest in fishing. They go on trips, share stories of backwoods streams, and buy each other lures for Christmas. In fact, they have talked almost exclusively about hunting and fishing for the last several decades. When a conversation veers toward anything that may be perceived as political, they both try to make a quick statement and then move on, but the Trump years have been hard.

I was writing this chapter on January 6, 2021, when Trump supporters, white supremacists, and conspiracy theorists, motivated by Trump's claim that a rigged election robbed him of a second term, took over the US Capitol building. Like many Americans, I read my Facebook feed while watching live reporting of the event. A Marine-veteran friend in Maryland referred to the riots as a "disgrace to our nation" and asked where the police were who had pelted her with rubber bullets when she was at a Black Lives Matter protest. A New York City friend posted a picture of a man with a "Camp Auschwitz" shirt and referred to rioters as "Deliverance deplorables." My friends from home battled with their neighbors, co-workers, and high school classmates in the comments: "sedition is a serious felony"; "we have the right to overthrow the government"; "Trump is responsible for all of this"; "the whole government is corrupt and we just sit back and take it and pay them more as our friends and neighbors can't eat"; "Antifa and BLM [were there] by the busloads wearing MAGA hats." Scott's brother, like many Trump supporters, criticized those who were concerned about the events in Washington but were not concerned when "BLM, Antifa and the Defund the Police movement were burning and looting our cities." His post was followed by dozens of supportive comments from friends, including high school teachers, small business owners, and a sheriff.

DOI: 10.4324/9781003152743-6

When I called Scott and shared the post, he fluctuated between rage and tears, saying, "I don't know how much longer I can keep doing this."

In the decades since the contested 2000 presidential election, elections coverage has presented color-coded geographic political divisions—the blue coasts and cities versus the red heartland and countryside—and popular books have lamented over culture wars and political polarization (Hunter 1992; Klein 2020). Voters in rural regions and suburbs of small cities supported Donald Trump (and other Republicans) at higher rates than urban areas (Scala and Johnson 2017), but color-block maps and media depiction of "Trump Country" ignore political diversity within these regions and relationships that cross political lines. This chapter explores these connections and divisions by drawing from ethnographic fieldwork in the rural counties of inland Maine. National stereotypes and cultural tropes about liberals and conservatives indeed exacerbated political divisions there, culminating in talk of civil war in the summer of 2020. But friends and neighbors with divergent political beliefs also continued to connect with each other, whether by openly "talking politics," avoiding politics, or forming new political solidarities.

The end of the Trump era has led to calls to minimize polarization by uniting under nationalist banners or pushing politics aside. In this context, this article draws attention to the existing social connections without naming the connections themselves as the solution. As Scott's case suggests, personal and political conflicts can linger below the surface of these social connections. Seeking consensus or cohesion without asking which class, race, or religious interests the consensus serves could contribute to further polarization by ignoring the social forces and institutions that underlie these divisions.

The politics of political polarization

Political scientists have long debated the degree of political polarization in the United States. Some argue that polarization is a myth, that most Americans have moderate views about issues like abortion and gay rights (Fiorina, Abrams, and Pope 2004), while others document that political parties and elites have become more clearly sorted along ideological lines (Baldassarri and Gelman 2008). There is overwhelming evidence, though, that Americans increasingly feel animosity and distrust toward people who belong to the opposing party (Iyengar et al. 2019). Labels like "liberal" or "conservative" become identities that people organize around or against (Mason 2018). This affective polarization both contributes to and is exacerbated by sorting into social groups on the basis of social factors like religion, class, race, or age. Consequently, since the mid-twentieth century, survey respondents have increasingly reported that they would be unhappy if their child married someone of the opposing political party (Iyengar, Sood, and Lelkes 2012).

Though people tend to follow the political ideas of those who are similar to them (DellaPosta, Shi, and Macy 2015), cultural differences are also manipulated and exaggerated by industry and political leaders. This occurs when leaders promote an issue by linking it to identity and describing opponents as a threat to this identity. Anti-abortion activists, for example, have described abortion and pro-choice politics not only as an attack on religious identity but also as a threat to the traditional family, patriotism, and gun rights (Franklin and Ginsburg 2019). Extractive industries similarly connect coal to a nostalgic era of strong manufacturing, masculinity, and nationalism and describe environmentalists as opposed to this culture (Kojola 2019). Increasingly politically divisive media (Grossmann and Hopkins 2018) attract viewers by reinforcing inaccurate images of wealthy urban liberals and working-class rural conservatives (Gelman et al. 2007), leading to common misunderstandings of political parties and the people who support them (Ahler and Sood 2018).

Conservative populist politics and facile depictions of "white working-class" Trump supporters have contributed to polarization by reinforcing racialized cultural caricatures (Pied 2018). In the years following Trump's election, media, pundits, and scholars almost exclusively depicted Trump voters as bitter rural "white working-class" voters. According to post-election surveys, about 60 percent of "white working-class" voters supported Trump in 2016, but only 31 percent of Trump voters were white people without college degrees earning below-median incomes (Carnes and Lupu 2020). Also, rural and urban places are more overlapping and interconnected than popular portrayals of "Trump country" imply (Blanchette and Laflamme 2019). Writing in the wake of the 2016 election, anthropologist Jessica Smith described media representation of Trump supporters as a spectacle "that entertained liberals by constructing an impossibly idiotic, illiberal rural electorate" (Smith 2017). This helps to explain why Trump voters described feeling controlled, belittled, or patronized by liberal politicians and their liberal neighbors (Lennon 2018).

The electability of a right-wing populist is, in part, a symptom of political polarization in the years leading up to 2016 (Campbell 2018). The Tea Party movement, for example, developed a coalition of support for many of the ideas that Trump capitalized on, including a return to the fictive American glory days (Westermeyer 2019). But Trump exacerbated polarization by using lies and rumors to create a spectacle that forged and solidified political communities (McGranahan 2017). Linguist Normal Mendoza-Denton explains how Trump's tweets and speeches contributed to polarization "[b]y verbally nudging his supporters in the direction of pre-established discursive divisions in society, and by creating new patterns through which the groups can attack each other" (Mendoza-Denton 2020: 50).

Evidence of political polarization may seem to contradict previous characterizations of a "post-political" neoliberal era, in which conflict is removed from the public sphere as decisions are made by technocrats deemed to have the expertise to solve problems (Swyngedouw 2010). So too does the surge of white nationalism seem to contradict theory about a post-Civil Rights-era racism that is covert and "color blind" (Bonilla-Silva 2003). But both of these theories demonstrate how governance that minimizes conflict without addressing inequalities can exacerbate these inequalities. Chantal Mouffe's response to post-political theory explains how this happens. Optimistic scholars looked to a post-political era as a new modernity that will move beyond left/right political antagonisms and social divisions as part of a global proliferation of democracy. Mouffe, though, identified a coalescing of political parties in Europe around a neoliberal political center and explained that it was leading to "antagonisms which put into question the very parameters of the existing order" (2005: 6). The "consensus in the center," according to Mouffe, created a bloc of political elite that controlled the government, leaving room for populist extremists to provide an alternative anti-establishment vision and a much-needed outlet for collective identity. Though Mouffe was analyzing global trends rather than social interactions, if consensus indeed contributes to the rise of extremist politics on the national stage, simply "getting along" may not be the solution to political polarization.

Methodological note

My analysis of political connections and divisions draws from several years of research in the small towns and rural areas of northwestern Maine. In 2006, 2007, and 2014, my research focused on community response to economic change and in 2019 and 2020, I studied forestland ownership and access in a broader region of northwestern Maine and northern New Hampshire. I interviewed more than one hundred people for these projects, almost always including questions about political ideology and social divisions. For this chapter, I analyzed the coded fieldnotes and transcripts from this previous research.

Maine is politically divided between the liberal-leaning southern counties and the more conservative northern counties, where this research was conducted. The state has a history of supporting independent and centrist politicians for national positions. Approximately 52 percent of the people in the region voted for Obama in 2012 and the same percentage voted for Trump in 2016. This region is approximately 98 percent white and has one of the oldest populations in the country. Following the rise of the Tea Party, in 2010, the state elected a populist governor, Republican Paul LePage, who described himself as "Donald Trump before Donald Trump became popular" (Seelye 2018). Despite the history of independent politics, the region was dominated by Trump signs leading up to the 2020 election and indeed supported Trump by nearly 60 percent.

Political polarization in rural Maine

National stereotypes of urban elite liberals versus conservative rural white workers influence sociopolitical divisions in Maine. When I was studying how class and politics affected community development plans in 2007 and 2014, for example, a division developed between a group perceived as liberal young outsiders wanting to promote tourism, farming, and the arts and longtime residents wanting to preserve the town and protect its finances. Though the political ideology was often discussed with coded language, a teacher who volunteered on development committees addressed it directly:

I think there is sort of liberal people doing things and conservative people wanting to make sure the town isn't going to have to pay for it [laughter]. I mean that's my opinion. Maybe you can phrase that a different way so that it doesn't sound bad.

In a different part of the state with a strong recreational tourism economy, a community leader described the divisions as "the skier crowd versus the skidder crowd," adding "you don't say it too loudly in a public room." When I asked interviewees to describe community divisions, I often heard about the "haves" and the "have nots," the social cliques that had been around since high school, or some version of "everybody knows each other," but only the teacher quoted above explicitly brought up political divisions. Though politics were imbricated in class and status-based divisions, by 2019 political tensions were at the forefront of people's concerns. Interviewees often identified extremism, divisions, or partisan politicians as "the biggest problem facing our country." When I was taking a hunter's safety course, the Korean War veteran instructor managed to work into his lecture that he had built a cannon in 2016 so that he would be prepared if Hillary Clinton had won the presidency. I was not sure if he was joking, but he unveiled the two-foot-high wooden weapon in the kitchen as we were serving ourselves plates of cold cuts and cheese.

Affective polarization and ideas about Republicans and Democrats influence relationships with neighbors and acquaintances, even when they have similar cultures or identities. In the summer of 2020, I was at an outdoor gathering with a small group of people who were largely opposed to Trump but who had many connections with friends, family, and coworkers who were Trump supporters. We had not been talking about politics when I complained that my neighbor had been target practicing for hours on end. Jason, a middle-aged Mainer who owned a construction business, said that his neighbor down the road, the one with the Trump sign, had a massive gun collection and also shoots incessantly. "You want people to target practice," I said, "so they can be good hunters." "Oh yeah. I'm a hunter." Jason responded, "I don't have any problem with guns. But it's something about the combination of the constant target-shooting and the Trump sign. If it comes to a civil war," he joked, "he'd be the first person I'm taking out. He'll think I'm going over to borrow a cup and sugar and 'bam!'" Everyone laughed. "And then you would have all his guns," someone else added. To be clear, Jason was not saying this in anger, and he mocked the idea of a civil war. Still, this interaction demonstrates how the neighbor's support for Trump, when combined with his penchant for target practicing, implied, for Jason, that he was a certain type of person. They were both white gun owners from the same part of Maine, but they would not be on the same side of a civil war.

Early summer of 2020 was a particularly divisive time, yet political divisions were still interwoven with social connections. The response to the coronavirus was becoming increasingly politicized, such that following mask and social distancing guidelines symbolized Democratic Party affiliation (Clinton et al. 2020). In the wake of the murder of George Floyd, Black Lives Matter (BLM) protests had been growing around the country, and several violent clashes linked to anti-fascist movements (antifa) garnered media attention. In an address from the White House, Trump described an "overrun" police precinct, vandalized national memorials, an historic church "set ablaze," and people "afraid to leave their homes." He promised to commit resources toward "ending the riots and lawlessness that has spread throughout our country" and to "protect the rights of law-abiding Americans, including your Second Amendment rights" (Trump 2020). With the help of social media, then, Trump amplified fears that racialized urban violence and white liberal protesters were threatening the safety of American suburbs and small towns across the country.

All of this was happening when I talked to Mike as part of my research on changes in forestland ownership and access. Several people had recommended I talk to him because he worked in the woods and also liked to hunt and fish. He was originally from Massachusetts but had been coming up to Maine to go hiking and hunting since he was a kid and had been living in this small town of less than a thousand people for decades. He owned a successful business that built roads for forestry companies. Mike and I had been at a couple different meetings together, but we really met for the first time during the interview. He had looked me up, he said, so he was a bit skeptical and wanted to make sure I did not have a predetermined agenda with my research. I quote at length from this interview because several interactions with community members illustrate how, even in the midst of describing political polarization, he is interacting with and maintaining connections with people known to have different political ideologies. In addition, the lengthy excerpt helps to more clearly explain Mike's politics in his own terms. We sat outside in front of a restaurant and talked over coffee. He said politics was "driving huge wedges" between people, and that some people would no longer talk to him because of his beliefs. He blamed media misrepresentation of Donald Trump and the divisiveness of social media and then began talking about how these politics were affecting the community:

MIKE: There was a, [pause] there was a Black Lives Matter protest in town and there was probably a hundred people there. And I said, "Good for them. Good. Our town has spoken up." And most people were pretty respectful of it. Now were a couple of idiots riding around with Confederate flags in the back of the truck. Yes. But is that the exception? Yes. Most people were like thumbs up. Good for you. Your right to free speech and protest. It was fine. There was no violence. They had a couple of cops here because they heard it was going to be a protest. So they had one on this end of town, the other end of town. It was fine. It was fine. [A young man with scraggly hair who I had seen walking around downtown since the protest walks by with a sign that said something about ending the police state.] It was well done. And just like they protested, somebody else should be able to protest on the other end of town. You know, we need to be respectful. [A well-known participant of the BLM protest walks by] Hey, Sandy. How are you? [Turning back to me.] I think our right to free speech is under attack. If ten people are standing here and I oppose what they're talking about, you know, I'm vilified. I see a divide in our country. I don't like it at all.

CLAUDINE: Can you think of anything that should be done differently?

MIKE: Responsible. Be responsible. If you've got an agenda—it's those things right there [points to his cell phone] and everybody's on those… You know, try to be positive. Positive things, as opposed to everybody attacking everybody else. It's kind of a sad time right now. It really is. And I'm an upbeat person, but—I have another hat I wear. It's a black and white flag with one red stripe and it's to support firefighters. And, where the hell was I? Walmart or something. This guy comes up to me and says, [with angry tone] "what does that mean?" I says, "what?" He says "Your hat." He says, "I don't like it." I said, "I support firefighters." He says, "Well, I don't think that's what it means. I think you're a pro-Trumper." What are you talking about? You know? I was just like, "argh" [sounding exasperated] "get out of my way." So with police, they have the same flag with a blue stripe, "support your local police." My wife bought it for me. And I like it. It's a great hat. But I have to be careful where I wear it… But you know something, my dad was a World War II Veteran, you know? Prisoner of war shot down in his last mission. Fought hard. When I see someone taking a [US] flag—I was driving through town one day and I missed it by about two minutes. They were burning the flag. I won't put up with it for a second. I mean, my dad fought, gave his life, you know, and that flag means a lot to us. It flies in my house all the time. And so, when people disrespect the flag, start to take down our patriotism, that's where my horns come out. That's where I draw the line… I can't, that, that just means so much. [his voice gets a little shaky] People have died for that flag, you know? [A pickup truck pulls up. It is a young woman who owns a store in town that specializes in organic produce. She is wearing a hat with the old Maine flag.] Nice hat.

STORE OWNER: I hope the mask thing didn't make you not come in the other day.

MIKE: I just didn't have one.

STORE OWNER: I was like, "oh, I'll bring stuff out to you."

MIKE: No, no. That's all right. I'll come back.

STORE OWNER: Well, my dad has diabetes, so I have to be super careful.

MIKE: Gotcha. [He waves and she drives off. He turns to me again.] Yeah, but politically, I just think, I think we're in a bad place. I think people are trying to tear things down. You know, are we headed to a civil war? Boy. I'd like to think not, but people say it more and more. And the people in, where was it? Coeur d'Alene, Idaho. Antifa was like, "We're coming to Coeur d'Alene. We're coming and we're gonna protest and we're going to show you what it's all about." And Coeur d'Alene, Idaho is just a cowboy town. And all the business owners and anybody that was local, on Friday night, was out there, armed to the hilt. They were all wearing their guns. Not doing anything bad, not threatening anybody, but saying, "we're here to protect that property. This is our property." They [antifa] showed up and just kept right on going.[1] You know, now is that a good thing? No, but I think people are being pushed to the brink. If someone's going to come here and they're going to protest? This is my business. And they're going to burn my building and take the windows out? I'm gonna defend my property. And that's what I'm seeing more and more is people are right to here [gesturing to the top of his head]. It's happening in the cities but when you start to get out away from there? Naw, people aren't going to put up with it. I mean, you've got people talk here locally there that are like, "What are we going to do if this happens in our town?" I don't wanna say forming a militia but talking in that direction. And it's not about doing bad, it's about, let's protect our old people, let's protect the people, let's protect our community. And you know, I can't say that I support it, but I can't say I'm against it either.

Within these few minutes of conversation, Mike is identifying political conflict in his community, connecting with people with opposing political ideas, and contemplating preparing for a civil war with leftist radicals. The tensions surrounding COVID, racism and policing, and protests created an environment in which strangers in Wal-Mart or a corner store aggressively reacted to symbols of political ideology, whether a "thin red line" hat, with Mike's example, or a COVID mask. In another case, for example, a young woman said she was called a "liberal bitch" for wearing a mask in a gas station. These types of interactions with neighbors and strangers contributed to a palpable political polarization and hostility. In addition, Trump's White House speech informed Mike and his friends' interpretation of protest violence as a potential threat to small towns.

Nevertheless, even while talking about his conservative friends preparing for a civil war and taking up arms, Mike's interactions with Sandy, the Black Lives Matter protester, and the store owner demonstrate the connections that he maintains despite known political differences. Though Mike may have been frustrated about the need for a mask in the store, for example, the store owner reaches out to him to assure he will come back to the store. As I describe below, these types of interactions in which community members connect with each other without explicitly addressing politics, are an important point of connection in an era of increased polarization.

Talking politics

Though friendships and social connections tend to form among people with similar political ideologies, when longtime friends, co-workers, or social media contacts develop or recognize their differing political beliefs, they negotiate these differences by avoiding them or finding respectful ways to talk about them. Anthropologists have studied how social connections and experiences create political solidarities. Danny Kaplan, for example, explored the role of friendships and social networks in creating political solidarities or transitioning from personal connections to "collective intimacy" (2014). Others have shown how historical events re-align relationships to remake friends and neighbors into enemies (Holtzman 2017). Between these extremes are social connections that continually cross political differences without creating new political subjectivities.

As communications scholar Stephen Coleman describes in post-Brexit Britain, "talking politics" with friends, family, and acquaintances is a process that often requires fragile negotiations around cultural norms (2020). In this case, I am describing "the political" as an ethnographic category (Candea 2011), referring to the emic sense of politics as political parties, leaders, or policy issues known to create conflict. Sarah, an administrative assistant, was someone who liked talking politics with her friends, at least when we first talked in 2013. At that time, she had a weekly dinner with a group of women. They were all single, and several of them were "real junkies when it comes to political stuff." Someone would often find an article online, print it out and share it with the group. They had been talking a lot about the Tea Party and the role of government. Sarah was a registered Republican who found herself drifting to the left as she got older, but her friends were both more conservative and more liberal than she was. If Sarah disagreed with one of her friends, she would explain her point of view, unless the debate was particularly heated. If people were no longer listening to each other, she said, "then there's no point in trying to converse." The debates were worth it, according to Sarah, because "at least you can understand why they feel that way and maybe understand the world better." People continued to "talk politics" during the Trump years but were more likely to do so with people who had similar political beliefs (Butters and Hare 2017).

Social media has largely contributed to polarization by reflecting information that confirms people's existing beliefs and connecting people to those with similar ideas (Bakshy, Messing, and Adamic 2015). Still, several people I talked to reported having enjoyable or constructive debates online with former classmates or other political adversaries. A nurse in her fifties who is committed to preventing the development of wind towers, for example, would often get into heated debates in Facebook comments. When we talked about it during an interview, she smiled and said, "I have fun with it" and described a couple of people she enjoys engaging with, adding that "eventually we agree to disagree." A retail worker in her forties frequently tried to correct misinformation on Facebook about COVID-19, resulting in debates with friends and strangers. She said that she had lost some connections due to political debates but did not consider it a loss if she had been respectful and forthright in stating her opinions. She also described making new connections, even with people she disagreed with, after having "honest, sincere, and direct" conversations.

Direct acknowledgement and engagement with political differences also occurs among longtime friends with opposing political beliefs through joking and competitive banter. Linguist Deborah Cameron demonstrates how Trump's crude masculine banter helped him to connect with supporters as a "man of the people," bridging the class differences between him and his supporters (2020). Political banter, such as taunting a friend after their candidate lost an election, also provides a way to "talk politics" and connect with political adversaries. For example, I overheard a Trump supporter threatening to wear a MAGA hat to an event he was going to with a Trump opponent and longtime friend. The Trump opponent responded by laughingly saying, "Fuck you!" Though this is not a policy debate, it acknowledges differences while maintaining connections. Banter is aggressive, as participants challenge each other about differences or perceived weaknesses, but it is also affectionate in that it requires a level of trust and connection (Easthope 1990). Mike, who was quoted at length above, described growing political divisions nationally and locally, but when I asked if he had any friendships that he maintained despite political differences, he said, "absolutely" and described this sort of political banter:

> My best friend. Yeah. My best friend. We've been opposed politically forever, and we'll sit in the boat fishing and we'll have this heated discussion back and forth. And my son goes, he goes, "If I didn't know any better, I'd think you guys were going to kill each other." [Mike chuckles] And I said, part of it's an act. And we play this bantering thing, but I respect his beliefs and he respects mine, you know? And every once in a while, he'll say, "okay, I get it. I get it."

In this example of Mike's relationship with his best friend, bantering drifts into political debate. When there is mutual respect in the relationship, banter provides a means to "talk politics" or acknowledge political differences without conceding or threatening the relationship.

Avoiding politics

In addition to political banter and debate, residents of rural Maine maintained relationships across political divisions by avoiding political talk. These types of connections include the relationship between Scott and his brother, from the beginning of the chapter, and more informal interactions, as with Mike and the store owner in the excerpt above. In fact, avoidance is how most people say they approach relationships with friends and family with opposing political beliefs. Jen, a high school teacher who listens to NPR and votes overwhelmingly Democratic, maintains most of her friendships by avoiding talking about politics. She and her husband share many political beliefs, but their friends are mostly conservative Trump supporters. They grew up with many of their friends. They help each other out on house projects and rally support for each other in times of tragedy, and now their kids are growing up together. And, Jen explained, their conservative friends are fun. Still, when Trump was elected, she and her husband fantasized about moving to a different country. Jen was not interested in getting into debates about Trump or his politics, but every so often a comment or conversation would remind her of her friends' beliefs. In the summer of 2020, I asked what it was like to be spending time with people with such different political beliefs at this particularly divisive time. "I think most people have a sense of our politics," she said, "so they know not to bring it up." Instead, they talked about their children, sports, or anything else they had in common.

Well before the Trump presidency, small business owners, whether restaurant owners or mechanics, made efforts to develop apolitical connections with their customers and town leaders, knowing that in a town with a limited customer base, ostracizing any particular group could be detrimental to the business. In his analysis of lineage meetings in Sierra Leone, anthropologist William Murphy described leaders gaining support by creating an appearance of consensus among some groups, while talking about different factors or disagreement in other contexts (Murphy 1990). Focusing on similar interests or political values that people share in common is also a strategy used by local politicians, business leaders, and friends in order to maintain their connections.

But, again, the Trump years have been hard. I brought up questions about politics in almost all of my interviews, beginning in 2006, whether asking about national problems or local policies. In 2019 and 2020, though, these questions were increasingly tense, especially before an interviewee assessed whether it was safe to reveal their opinion of Donald Trump. And as Mike indicated above, some people described losing friends or increasingly avoiding politics to maintain connections. I followed up with Sarah, the woman who had weekly dinners with friends in 2013, to ask if they still got together to talk politics. COVID had changed things, of course, but these open debates had become less common. She still had a few friends with opposing politics who were willing to engage, but she found it more difficult to talk politics because people were moving to the "edges of liberal and conservative views." For these friends, she avoids bringing up particular topics. Avoidance of "political talk" is both an indication of political polarization and tension, and a technique used to maintain relationships with political adversaries.

Creating new solidarities

The type of social connections discussed so far cross political subjectivities without forming a collective intimacy that leads to new solidarities. Though social and environmental problems are often politicized, rural residents sometimes come together to address shared concerns (Ashwood 2020), forming networks that cross political divisions and creating new shared experiences and social bonds (Holston 2019). When researching forestland access and ownership, for example, I came across several politically diverse groups of people who shared a connection to and interest in the Maine woods, whether in conservation, preserving access, or preventing a particular type of development. Several research participants spoke specifically of the tension of political polarization and an interest in finding common ground with people who have differing politics. This was true of an environmentalist working to preserve access to Maine's forestland in ecologically important regions. In the following excerpt he shows his excitement about forming alliances with otherwise political adversaries, emphasizing the importance of compromise.

> Rich who, you know, is a proud LePage guy, proud Trump guy—maybe not as proud, but anyway. I've always thought of myself, I'm more middle of the road: I'm not knee-jerk, flaming liberal and I'm not ultra conservative, but

I guess if I tilted one way, you'd start checking off my value sets and be like, "oh, you sound a little left, but not extreme." But I think it's great that I can work with Rich and hear him say something like, "I'd rather have fifty percent access to my favorite forest and hunting grounds, and have it owned by a federal entity, than have it have zero access because some a-hole from Massachusetts or New York bought it and closed it off." I was like, "yeah, that's what I think!" That is so important to all these discussions, getting out of your corner of ideals and principles that you'll die for dramatically and saying, "okay, we can fight about this forever and accomplish nothing. Or we can say, let's keep [this parcel] open for harvesting, let's keep it open for all those extractive values, but let's also acknowledge that sometimes we're going to need federal dollars to do that."

In addition to consensus and compromise, bipartisan political solidarities were motivated by a shared connection to place and a common frustration with the technocratic power of state/corporate/NGO alliances (Pied 2021). In response to a Massachusetts request for renewable energy sources, Central Maine Power (CMP) proposed a 150-foot-wide electrical transmission line, fifty-three miles of which would cut through Maine's northern forest. The CMP Corridor, as opponents called it, would transmit power from massive hydroelectric dams in Quebec, through Maine, to Massachusetts. Opposition to the corridor brought together a diverse set of constituencies, including environmental organizations, the biomass industry, and people who fish, camp, snowmobile, and whitewater raft in the northern forest. Trump supporters and Trump opponents worked alongside each other, motivated by a shared interest in protecting this region, distrust of CMP and its Spain-based parent company, and, often, a shared belief in the corruption of the corporate and government agencies in charge of the project.

At a public event organized to recruit opponents to the corridor, a large man with a beard approached me and asked if I was "against this thing." My response must have been convoluted because he asked for clarification, "So, we're on the same team, right?" "Yes," I said. His body relaxed and he took a step forward, ready for a conversation. The corridor debates created new "teams" that reshuffled familiar right/left conflicts. Those opposing the corridor often spoke with pride about the nonpartisan solidarity of the movement. They collected petitions together, met for coffee or beer, planned volunteer parties, and travelled around the state trying to prevent the project. A middle-aged woman who opposed the project because of its negative effect on the forests and mountains described working with people while speaking against the project at public hearings and then looking at their Facebook page and realizing, "I would never connect with this person if it wasn't for the corridor." When a debate breaks out on the Facebook page—as it often did when someone posted something about corridor proponent Governor Mills—administrators remind participants that "this is not a Republican or Democrat issue." In the words of a woman who I met an organizing event, "It's really refreshing, it's people all over the political spectrum that are against this."

But formations of political solidarities involve internal conflicts as well as processes of exclusion and dispossession (Postero and Elinoff 2019). One corridor opponent described the protection of "my land" (in this case, the Northwoods of Maine) as something that unites left- and right-wing activists, though he distanced himself from right-wing opponents by describing himself as peaceful and those on the right as angry defenders of their property. Though some corridor opponents worked with Indigenous peoples in Maine and Quebec in opposition to the project, there was little critical assessment of the sense of ownership of the Northwoods. Some corridor opponents brought an even more restrictive (racist and anti-immigrant) meaning of "our" in "our land." At a town meeting a man stood up and argued that the CMP corridor is a national security issue because it is going to create a "yellow-brick road" for immigrants coming over the Canadian border. He explained that Muslims and Mexicans were now trying to get to the United States through Canada. A number of residents rolled their eyes or laughed uncomfortably, but his point was not refuted. Similarly, when collecting signatures for a referendum, activists patiently listened to a diatribe from a man who claimed that the corridor was a national security threat because Maine power would depend on Canada. He talked with the volunteers for more than an hour, explaining that the Canadian prime minister was Muslim and instituting sharia law. After he left, they labeled him a conspiracy theorist, but again we did little to challenge his assertions and instead focused on his opposition to the corridor. Confronting activists that used nationalist or xenophobic arguments, formal collaborations with Indigenous groups, and "talking politics" were all discouraged due to their potential threat to the solidarity of the movement.

Conclusion

In the summer of 2020, in the midst of the politicization of the COVID-19 pandemic, a Minneapolis police officer killed George Floyd, and people around the country protested against racism in policing. Some residents of a Maine small town responded by organizing their own Black Lives Matter protest, while others talked about organizing a militia to protect their community from radical leftists. But the woman who helped to organize the protest and the man who talked about taking up arms still worked together in community development meetings and checked in with each other at the grocery store. And Scott still goes fishing with his brother. Previous research on Trump voters and journalistic dives into "Trump Country" tend to reinforce the dichotomous representation of urban/liberal and rural/conservative cultures. Social and political divisions occur both between and within rural and urban areas and occur differently in different regions (Koch et al. 2021). Yet polarization is often studied through national surveys, with less attention to social connections and divisions of liberal and conservative people in the rural United States. In the wake of the Trump presidency, as politicians and pundits call for national unity, it is important to recognize that in towns and neighborhoods around the country people already work, socialize, and debate with people who have differing political ideologies.

Bipartisan social connections, though, should not be understood as, in themselves, a solution to political polarization. Despite social interactions across party lines, Mainers reported feeling increasingly disconnected from each other. The type of social connection described above as "talking politics" was becoming less common. Sarah, for example, who would get together with her friends to talk politics in 2013, by 2020 had learned to avoid certain topics as many of her friends had increasingly extreme political beliefs. Old friends, co-workers, and neighbors with differing political ideologies might share day care duties, plow each other's driveways, or go on hikes with each other but avoid talking politics while they do so. Groups that created a consensus that crossed left/right political divisions or that developed new political solidarities based on shared connection to place, as with the CMP corridor opponents' connection to the Northwoods, also avoided conflict that could threaten this solidarity.

Previous analyses of the problems of "post-political" politics and "color-blind" discourse serve as warnings to avoid addressing polarization by promoting an elite consensus or talk of multiculturalism rather than racism. Covert racisms "facilitate the denial of racism and conceal the inner workings of the social system," such that racial inequalities are seen as individual or cultural failures (Mullings 2005: 679). Racism is not housed in the bodies of Trump voters and will not recede when white supremacists are no longer in the news. Rather, it is reproduced through systemic racism, good intentions, and "seemingly non-racial policies" (Bonilla-Silva 2019: 24). Chantal Mouffe argued that the left/right political consensus under neoliberalism in fact contributed to the rise of extremism, explaining that "when the channels are not available through which conflicts could take an 'agonistic' form, those conflicts tend to emerge on the antagonistic mode" (Mouffe 2005: 5). In this context, according to Mouffe, political adversaries can become moral enemies. Encouraging social connections that cross political divisions, then, or uniting under a shared national identity, will not prevent political polarization without addressing the racism, economic precarity, and power inequalities that underlie these divisions.

Note

1 The impromptu militia formed in Coeur d'Alene to protect the city from antifa was based on a specific online rumor (Stanley-Becker and Romm 2020).

References

Ahler, Douglas J., and Gaurav Sood. 2018. "The Parties in Our Heads: Misperceptions about Party Composition and Their Consequences." *Journal of Politics* 80 (3): 964–81. https://doi.org/10.1086/697253.

Ashwood, Loka. 2020. "'No Matter If You're a Democrat or a Republican or Neither': Pragmatic Politics in Opposition to Industrial Animal Production." *Journal of Rural Studies* https://doi.org/10.1016/j.jrurstud.2020.05.011.

Bakshy, Eytan, Solomon Messing, and Lada A. Adamic. 2015. "Exposure to Ideologically Diverse News and Opinion on Facebook." *Science* 348 (6239): 1130–32. https://doi.org/10.1126/science.aaa1160.

Baldassarri, Delia, and Andrew Gelman. 2008. "Partisans without Constraint: Political Polarization and Trends in American Public Opinion." *American Journal of Sociology* 114 (2): 408–46. https://doi.org/10.1086/590649.

Blanchette, By Alex, and Marcel Laflamme. 2019. "Introduction: An Anthropological Almanac of Rural Americas." *Jounral for the Anthropology of North America* 22 (2): 52–62. https://doi.org/10.1017/S0021853718000804.

Bonilla-Silva, Eduardo. 2003. *Racism Without Racists: Color-Blind Racism and the Persistence of Racial Inequality in the United States*. Lanham, MD: Rowman & Littlefield.

———. 2019. "'Racists,' 'Class Anxieties,' Hegemonic Racism, and Democracy in Trump's America." *Social Currents* 6 (1): 14–31. https://doi.org/10.1177/2329496518804558.

Butters, Ross, and Christopher Hare. 2017. "Three-Fourths of Americans Regularly Talk Politics Only with Members of Their Own Political Tribe." *Washington Post*, May 1, 2017.

Cameron, Deborah. 2020. "Banter, Male Bonding, and the Language of Donald Trump." In Janet McIntosh and Norma Mendoza-Denton, eds. *Language in the Trump Era: Scandals and Emergencies*. Cambridge: Cambridge University Press, 158–67.

Campbell, John L. 2018. *American Discontent: The Rise of Donald Trump and the Decline of the Golden Age*. Oxford: Oxford University Press.

Candea, Matei. 2011. "'Our Division of the Universe': Making a Space for the Non-Political in the Anthropology of Politics." *Current Anthropology* 52 (3): 309–34. https://doi.org/10.1086/659748.

Carnes, Nicholas, and Noam Lupu. 2020. "The White Working Class and the 2016 Election." *Perspectives on Politics*, 1–18. https://doi.org/10.1017/S1537592720001267.

Clinton, J., J. Cohen, J. Lapinski, and M. Trussler. 2020. "Partisan Pandemic: How Partisanship and Public Health Concerns Affect Individuals' Social Mobility during COVID-19." *Science Advances* 7 (2): 1–7. https://doi.org/10.1126/sciadv.abd7204.

Coleman, Stephen. 2020. *How People Talk About Politics: Brexit and Beyond*. London: Bloomsbury Publishing.

DellaPosta, Daniel, Yongren Shi, and Michael Macy. 2015. "Why Do Liberals Drink Lattes?" *American Journal of Sociology* 120 (5): 1473–1511. https://doi.org/10.1086/681254.

Easthope, Antony. 1990. *What a Man's Gotta Do: The Masculine Myth in Popular Culture*. Boston, MA: Unwin Hyman.

Fiorina, Morris, Samuel Abrams, and Jeremy Pope. 2004. *Culture War? Culture War? The Myth of a Polarized America*. New York: Pearson.

Franklin, Sarah, and Faye Ginsburg. 2019. "Reproductive Politics in the Age of Trump and Brexit." *Cultural Anthropology* 34 (1): 3–9. https://doi.org/10.14506/ca34.1.02.

Gelman, Andrew, Boris Shor, Joseph Bafumi, and David Park. 2007. "Rich State, Poor State, Red State, Blue State: What's the Matter with Connecticut?" *Quarterly Journal of Political Science* 2 (4): 345–67.

Grossmann, Matt, and David A. Hopkins. 2018. "From Fox News to Viral Views: The Influence of Ideological Media in the 2018 Elections." *Forum* 16 (4): 551–71. https://doi.org/10.1515/for-2018-0037.

Holston, James. 2019. "Metropolitan Rebellions and the Politics of Commoning the City." *Anthropological Theory* 19 (1): 120–42. https://doi.org/10.1177/1463499618812324.

Holtzman, Jon. 2017. *Killing Your Neighbors : Friendship and Violence in Northern Kenya and Beyond*. Oakland, CA: University of California Press.

Hunter, James Davison. 1992. *Culture Wars: The Struggle To Control The Family, Art, Education, Law, and Politics In America*. New York: Basic Books.

Iyengar, Shanto, Yphtach Lelkes, Matthew Levendusky, Neil Malhotra, and Sean J. Westwood. 2019. "The Origins and Consequences of Affective Polarization in the United States." *Annual Review of Political Science* 22: 129–46. https://doi.org/10.1146/annurev-polisci-051117-073034.

Iyengar, Shanto, Gaurav Sood, and Yphtach. Lelkes. 2012. "Affect, Not Ideology: A Social Identity Perspective on Polarization." *Public Opinion Quarterly* 76 (3): 405–31. https://doi.org/10.1093/poq/nfs038.

Kaplan, Danny. 2014. "The Architecture of Collective Intimacy: Masonic Friendships as a Model for Collective Attachments." *American Anthropologist* 116 (1): 81–93. https://doi.org/10.1111/aman.12070.

Klein, Ezra. 2020. *Why We're Polarized*. London: Avid Reader Press/Simon & Schuster.

Koch, Insa, Mark Fransham, Sarah Cant, Jill Ebrey, Luna Glucksberg, and Mike Savage. 2021. "Social Polarisation at the Local Level: A Four-Town Comparative Study on the Challenges of Politicising Inequality in Britain." *Sociology*. 55 (1): 3–29. https://doi.org/10.1177/0038038520975593.

Kojola, Erik. 2019. "Bringing Back the Mines and a Way of Life: Populism and the Politics of Extraction." *Annals of the American Association of Geographers* 109 (2): 371–81. https://doi.org/10.1080/24694452.2018.1506695.

Lennon, Myles. 2018. "Revisiting 'the Repugnant Other' in the Era of Trump." *HAU: Journal of Ethnographic Theory* 8 (3): 439–54. https://doi.org/10.1086/700979.

Mason, Lilliana. 2018. "Ideologues without Issues: The Polarizing Consequences of Ideological Identities." *Public Opinion Quarterly* 82 (S1): 280–301. https://doi.org/10.1093/poq/nfy005.

McGranahan, Carole. 2017. "An Anthropology of Lying: Trump and the Political Sociality of Moral Outrage." *American Ethnologist* 44 (2): 243–48. https://doi.org/10.1111/amet.12475.

Mendoza-Denton, Norma. 2020. "'Ask the Gays': How to Use Language to Fragment and Redefine the Public Sphere." In Janet McIntosh and Norma Mendoza-Denton, eds. *Language in the Trump Era*. Cambridge: Cambridge University Press, 47–51.

Mouffe, Chantal. 2005. *On the Political (Thinking in Action)*. London: Routledge.

Mullings, Leith. 2005. "Interrogating Racism: Toward an Antiracist Anthropology." *Annual Review of Anthropology* 34: 667–93. https://doi.org/10.1146/annurev.anthro.32.061002.093435.

Murphy, William P. 1990. "Creating the Appearance of Consensus in Mende Political Discourse." *American Anthropologist* 92 (1): 24–41. https://doi.org/10.1525/aa.1990.92.1.02a00020.

Pied, Claudine M. 2018. "Conservative Populist Politics and the Remaking of the 'White Working Class' in the USA." *Dialectical Anthropology*. 42 (2): 193–206. https://doi.org/10.1007/s10624-018-9501-1.

——— 2021. "Negotiating the Northwoods: Anti-Establishment Rural Politics in the Northeastern United States." *Journal of Rural Studies* 82: 294–302. https://doi.org/10.1016/j.jrurstud.2021.01.020.

Postero, Nancy, and Eli Elinoff. 2019. "Introduction: A Return to Politics." *Anthropological Theory* 19 (1): 3–28. https://doi.org/10.1177/1463499618814933.

Scala, Dante J., and Kenneth M. Johnson. 2017. "Political Polarization along the Rural-Urban Continuum? The Geography of the Presidential Vote, 2000–2016." *Annals of the American Academy of Political and Social Science* 672 (1): 162–84. https://doi.org/10.1177/0002716217712696.

Seelye, Katharine Q. 2018. "Paul LePage Was Saying Whatever He Wanted Before That Was a Thing." *New York Times*, August 13, 2018.

Smith, Jessica. 2017. "Blind Spots of Liberal Righteousness." *Fieldsights*. https://culanth.org/fieldsights/1044-blind-spots-of-liberal-righteousness, accessed June 12, 2018.

Stanley-Becker, Isaac, and Tony Romm. 2020. "Armed White Residents Lined Idaho Streets amid 'antifa' Protest Fears. The Leftist Incursion Was an Online Myth." *Washington Post*, June 4, 2020. https://www.washingtonpost.com/national/protests-armed-white-vigilantes/2020/06/04/09e17610-a5bb-11ea-b619-3f9133bbb482_story.html, accessed December 9, 2020.

Swyngedouw, Erik. 2010. "Apocalypse Forever? Post-Political Populism and the Spectre of Climate Change." *Theory, Culture & Society* 27 (2–3).

Trump, Donald. 2020. "Statement by the President." June 1, 2020 Rose Garden Statement. 2020. https://www.whitehouse.gov/briefings-statements/statement-by-the-president-39, accessed January 3, 2021.

Westermeyer, William H. 2019. *Back to America: Identity, Political Culture, and the Tea Party Movement*. Lincoln: University of Nebraska Press.

PART II
Performing and representing Donald Trump

6
INDEXING AMBIVALENCE
Laterality and negation in Donald Trump's co-speech gestures

Daniel Lefkowitz

Introduction

As I compose this essay, in the wake of an insurrectional mob's attack on and brief occupation of the US Capitol on January 6, 2021, a cable television news story features speculation about whether Donald J. Trump's hand gestures carry coded signals to his extremist—and at that point frenzied—followers. In a brief segment aired January 14, 2021, CNN anchor Alisyn Camerota interviews Arieh Kovler, identified as a political consultant with expertise on social-media-based political extremism. Camerota elicits from Kovler his claim that Trump's supporters "parse his words to within like a syllable, I mean as though he's some oracle, and they listen for exactly what he says and what he doesn't say," and Kovler elaborates:

> Inside these pro-Trump forums, there's a lot of confusion right now. They really thought Donald Trump was going to win. Until really a few days ago, they haven't had months to process the election results and they don't understand what's supposed to happen next. They saw this video from the President last night, and they—they're not sure. They think maybe he's warning them to stay in their homes because the military is going to conduct a coup for him. There are some people who were even going as far as to parse his hand movements. And he did this hand signal a couple of times. And some of them think that's Morse Code… [T]he people involved in the QAnon movement thought that he was signaling something related to that. Maybe the letter "q," maybe some other letter. I mean you can't be doing Morse Code with your hands, so I don't really understand the theory.
>
> (CNN 2021)

DOI: 10.4324/9781003152743-8

Trump supporters may or may not be discerning support for QAnon in his hand gestures, but this essay will argue that his idiosyncratic style of co-speech gesturing does signal significant things about his political identity. Unpacking the contribution gesture makes to Trump's overall communicative style will, I claim, help explain something that scholars and commentators have struggled to explain the past several years: what it is that makes Trump's way of speaking so peculiar and yet so effective. As Hall, Goldstein, and Ingram put it:

> Donald Trump Jr.'s description of his father as a "blue-collar billionaire" during the 2016 Republican primary season highlighted a contradiction that has puzzled commentators on both sides of the political spectrum since the beginning of Trump's rise in the election polls: How does a businessman situated in the uppermost tier of American wealth capture the allegiance of the working classes?
>
> (Hall et al. 2016: 71)

Hall, Goldstein, and Ingram answer the question they pose for themselves by pointing to the entertainment value in Trump's peculiar speaking style and, in particular, his unorthodox reliance on iconic gestures. In this chapter, I would like to broaden this insightful analysis to incorporate some of linguist Jennifer Sclafani's observations about Trump's non-iconic (or pragmatic) gesturing, namely his preference for symmetrical, open-handed gestures that move laterally toward the sides of his body. In doing so I will focus on the lateral movement common to so many of Trump's hand motions during public speaking, like his debate performances with Joe Biden, linking this observation with Adam Kendon's interpretation of such lateral, horizontal motion as evoking negation, withdrawal, denial, or negative assessment (Kendon 2004). Though my analysis remains preliminary, I would like to argue that the pattern of lateral movements, indexically associated with forms of negation, works to doubly voice his utterances (in the sense of Bakhtin 1981), suggesting both what is explicitly said and its opposite, introducing both plausible deniability (see Hodges 2020) and a playful artistry that helps establish the entertainment key identified by Hall and her colleagues (Hall et al. 2016).

The argument proceeds along the following path: A close transcription of his co-speech gestures during the second presidential debate with Joe Biden during the 2020 presidential campaign shows a preponderance of gestures involving lateral movement (in dramatic contrast to the co-speech gestures of Biden, who shows the much more common pattern of outward and downward movement for a forcefully speaking figure of authority and power). Work on the structure and function of co-speech gesture strongly associates lateral motion with negation, an association that will be demonstrated with reference to examples taken from the second Trump–Biden debate. Trump's generalization of this specific function to become an aspect of gestures widely divorced from any specific negation entextualizes

(Briggs and Bauman 1992) a style that indexes negation, and frequent use of this style contributes to Trump's branding of himself as playful and oppositional (see Lempert 2011). Finally, I will draw on the theoretical work of linguist Anthony Woodbury on rhetorical structure (Woodbury 1985; Woodbury 1987) to suggest a way of thinking about the relations between vocal speech, bodily gesture, and performances of identity in the public sphere, and the stimulating work of literary critic Stephen Booth on the role of "nonsense" in poetically structured discourse to explain the connection between a paradoxically double-voiced communicative style and the paradox of Trump's rhetorical power.

Gesture in political oratory

Let me begin with a description of the phenomenon I am interested in. Politicians, like other Americans, use their hands, faces, and bodies in many ways while they are engaged in talk. We tend to think of such gestures as we think of "body language" more generally, as para-linguistic, tangential to the serious business of communicating (especially on such serious matters as politics). In recent decades, however, a number of scholars have focused attention on the embodiment of language in general and specifically on the systematic ways in which gesture, or "visible bodily activity" in Kendon's phrasing (2004: 110), is integrated with the words and sounds that we most commonly identify as human language (see, e.g. Kendon 2004; McNeill 2016; Streeck et al. 2011). Kendon identifies the combination of gesture and speech as an "ensemble," insisting that what we call an "utterance" encompasses both the vocal and gestural components, which together convey meaning in communication. As Kendon notes, "This is not to say that speech and gesture express the same meanings. They are often different. Nevertheless, the meanings expressed by these two components *interact*…" (Kendon 2004: 108).

Visible bodily activity encompasses a great deal more than manual gestures, of course, including facial expression, body posture and proxemics, among other phenomena, but, in this essay, I will focus on the manual gestures, of which there are several kinds. Much has been made—in the popular press and consultant literature, as well as in scholarly linguistic anthropology literature—of mimetic gestures, the way that Trump uses dramatic hand and arm depictions in his public speech, often thereby commenting derisively on conjured foes. Kira Hall and her colleagues, for example, describe Trump's mimetic depiction during a 2016 campaign rally in Myrtle Beach, South Carolina, of *Washington Post* reporter Serge Kovaleski, who is "afflicted by a muscular condition that involves contracture of the body muscles and joints." Trump depicted Kovaleski, while commenting on him, as a sequence of flailing hands and wrists, conjuring up stereotypical images of disability (Hall et al. 2016: 86). Their important point was that Trump's mimetic gesturing helped construct his speaking events as theatrical, spectacular, and entertaining, which, in turn, produced a wide intertextual gap (Briggs and Bauman 1992) with the general norms for such events as serious political discussion.

As scholars of gesture have shown, however, manual gestures have many other important functions in talk interactions. Kendon distinguishes between *referential gestures*, such as the mimetic gestures described above, which contribute to the meaning of utterances, and *pragmatic gestures*, which "contribute to or constitute the acts or moves accomplished by utterances" (Kendon 2004: 225). He identifies three kinds of pragmatic gesture, differentiated by how they function in utterances (158–9). Gestures can function *performatively*, as when a speaker makes their locution into an offer by extending the hands, palm up, out toward the interlocutor. Gestures have a *parsing* function—as is extremely common in political rhetoric—when speakers jab a podium or point an index figure coincident with stressed constituents of the vocal locution, punctuating discourse to demarcate information structure. And a gesture is functioning *modally* when it "alters in some way the frame in terms of which what is being said in the utterance is to be interpreted" (159). In what follows I will be especially interested in the modal function, especially inasmuch as Trump's gestures operate on the vocal locution so as to suggest that it be interpreted negatively.

Central to the systematic investigation of gesture systems has been the descriptive technology pioneered by Adam Kendon for gesture morphology, which I will describe here briefly. Individual gestures are classified in terms of handshape, orientation, and movement. Noting that speakers' hands tend to remain in some neutral "home position" (2004: 111)—whether down at their sides during casual conversation, or resting on a podium during formal lectures or debate—Kendon defined a *gesture unit* as the motion excursions the hands undergo between such moments of being "at rest." A gesture unit, in turn, comprises one or more *gesture phrases*, which include initial motions that bring the hands into position for the gesture (the *preparation*), and the final motions that return the hands to the home position (the *recovery*), together bracketing the *stroke*, which is what we intuitively recognize as the gesture itself. The gesture stroke is the usually quick, distinct motion toward a point of maximal excursion (displacement from the home position), where the handshape takes its most distinctive form, and where the temporal alignment with vocal speech is often most clearly defined. Speakers often maintain the hands in the shape and position of the stroke for some time, a phenomenon Kendon labelled the *post-stroke hold*. While some actual gestures show this morphology clearly, variation is as central to the gesture system as it is to phonological or prosodic systems of speech.

Central to Kendon's work on gesture is the notion of a *gesture family*, which he defines as "a group of gestures that have in common certain kinesic features [of]… hand shape and hand orientation" (2004: 281) and which share a "semantic theme," or contribution to the meaning of an utterance. One such family is what Kendon called the "precision grip" gestures, in which a speaker brings thumb into contact with the tip of the index finger. Speakers often, and especially in formal discourse, use the precision grip for a parsing function, moving the hand downward, or outward (toward a real or conjured interlocutor), coincident with points of focus in the information and phonetic structure of the spoken utterance. As Michael Lempert

FIGURE 6.1 The two most common variants of former President Barack Obama's precision grip gesture: thumb tip contacting tip of index finger on the left and thumb tip contacting first joint of index finger on the right. (Source: PBS coverage of Barack Obama's State of the Union speech, January 26, 2001: https://www.youtube.com/watch?v=-RSjbtJHi_Q&t=1047s)

(2011) notes, this particular handshape contributes the meaning of conciseness and precision to the parsing function (which can be performed with many different handshapes). In his brilliant analysis of former President Barack Obama's use of this gesture, Lempert notes that Obama used (at least) four variants of the gesture, two of which are pictured as Figure 6.1.

Lempert shows that Obama's use of the precision grip gesture in the 2008 presidential debates involves at least three levels of indexicality. A first-order indexicality emerges from the frequent co-occurrence in Obama's debate speech of the precision-grip gesture with vocal words that explicitly express precision, specificity, or exactness. Lempert's first example (249), reproduced here, is illustrative:

```
that's why I have s- uh proposed
[specific tax relief now immediately]
P        p    p     P    P
```

In this example, the square brackets delimit a gesture unit, and each "P" identifies an instance of a gesture phrase in which Obama moves his precision-grip shaped hand downward and outward in synchrony with the vocal pitch-accents aligned with the stressed syllable of each of the spoken words, "specific," "tax," "relief," "now," and "immediately." As Lempert explains, the first-order indexicality evident in the association of the precision grip gesture with the (focused) words "specific," "now," and "immediately," becomes second-order indexicality when the gesture co-occurs with "tax" and "relief," which are not semantically specified for precision. Here the phrase as a whole is interpreted as a speech act of precision, generating the interpretations 'specific-tax' and 'precise-relief'. Lempert argues that Obama's frequent use of this gesture (in its various forms and contexts) throughout the debate generates a third-order indexicality of himself as a precise and specific person, and a fourth-order indexicality of a candidate branded in terms of dedication to precision and specificity (258).

Gestures in the Trump–Biden presidential debates of 2020

Lempert's analysis of the branding of Obama through patterns of co-speech gesture use raises the intriguing question as to what an equally distinctive but very different pattern of co-speech gestures—those of Donald Trump in his debates with Joe Biden during the 2020 presidential campaign—comes to mean. Jennifer Sclafani, author of *Talking Donald Trump*, devotes a section to "his idiosyncratic use of gesture and facial expressions in public speaking events" (2018: 58), specifically contrasting Trump's gesture style to that of Obama. Whereas Lempert held up the precision grip gestures as diagnostic of Obama's gestural code, Sclafani points to a family of Trump gestures that she identifies as "large, two-handed, and open-handed" (61), which she argues contribute messages of vagueness and imprecision diametrically opposed to the precision and sharpness Obama communicates with his precision-grip gestures (62).

In order to investigate Trump's manual gestures in greater detail, a recording of the second presidential debate was analyzed in terms of the gesture units and component gesture phrases (in relation to spoken locutions) produced by the two candidates.[1] The debate was held at Belmont University in Nashville, Tennessee, on October 22, 2020, and lasted about 90 minutes. Each gesture phrase produced by the candidates was identified and coded for handshape, handedness (right hand, left hand, or two-handed), and hand motion, and these data were entered into a searchable database. A total of 2,122 gesture phrases were identified, of which roughly two-thirds (1,366) were produced by Trump and one-third (756) by Biden.

The dramatic difference between Trump's use of gesture and Biden's in this debate is immediately apparent. As the summary statistics indicate, Trump gestured a great deal more than did Biden. Indeed, Donald Trump gestured with his hands almost constantly during his turns at talk, while Biden used hand gestures to punctuate his speech periodically. Consistent with Sclafani's observations, Trump also dominated visual space with his gestures much more than did Biden, and these were, in turn, dominated by a family of gestures that loosely fit her description, many of them being two-handed, open-handed, and large in terms of the sweep of motion and the space they occupied (Sclafani 2018: 58).

A closer look at the data from the corpus of Trump and Biden gestures gives further insight into the dramatic difference between the two candidates' gesture codes. Table 6.1 tabulates information on the hand motion for each of the coded gesture phrases (lumping together gestures that involve different handshapes and handedness). Table 6.1 includes only the four most common hand motions: downward motion, as when a speaker moves their hand vertically downward, as if to pound on a table with emphasis; outward motion, as when a speaker projects their hand out in front of their body, toward an interlocutor; pointing motion, where the speaker moves their hand in the direction of, while referring to an interlocutor or an object present in the physical space of the debate; and lateral motion, in which the speaker moves their hand or hands horizontally sideways out toward the side of the body. Together these four categories account for 81 percent of Trump's gestures and 80

TABLE 6.1 Statistics on Motion of Gestures by Trump/Biden

Gesture Phrase Motion (% of Total Phrases)		
Hand Motion	Donald Trump	Joe Biden
Downward	14	40
Outward	4	18
Pointing	10	15
Lateral	53	7

percent of Biden's. The data in Table 6.1 show that over half (53 percent) of all of Trump's gestures involved lateral movement, compared to only 7 percent of Biden's. In contrast, 68 percent of Biden's gestures involved either downward or outward motion, compared to the 18 percent of Trump's gestures that involved these two otherwise common hand motions.

The repertoire of gestures Joe Biden deployed during his debate with Donald Trump is recognizable as what Hall et al. called "the gestural prescriptivism that has dominated the American political arena" (Hall et al. 2016: 74). Drawing on Juergen Streeck's (2008) analysis of the co-speech gestures of candidates participating in a debate during the 2004 Democratic primary race, Hall and colleagues characterize this genre as avoiding depictive gestures while preferring pragmatic gestures that "accentuate or illustrate the rhetorical structure of speech" (74). Streeck emphasizes the generic similarity of candidates' gestural repertoires, what he calls "a shared gesture code" (Streeck 2008: 156). The debate he analyzed involved several Democratic candidates for president, including Dick Gephart, Joe Lieberman, Carole Mosely Braun, John Edwards, John Kerry, Al Sharpton, and Howard Dean. Dean presents a very interesting exception, which I'll discuss below. For all other candidates, though, the repertoire of gestures was almost entirely limited to the four handshapes that Streeck labels "slice," "pointing," "precision grip/ring," and "power grip."[2] These different handshapes were deployed primarily in a rhythmic downward (or forward) movement and timed to coincide with words so as to delineate and demarcate information and discourse structure (Streeck 2008).

The striking outlier is Howard Dean, who gestured a lot but who used only a single handshape, an index finger extended vertically, which Streeck labels descriptively as a "finger wag" (179). Moreover, Streeck argues for considering Dean's use of his hands more a "posture" than a gesture because Dean does not move the hand and does not alter the gesture. This handshape, when embedded in a motion that together would constitute a co-speech gesture, often has pedagogical function, conveying something like "what I am saying is important; it is something that I know and you should heed." As Streeck observes, however, when used, as Dean does in this debate, "over and over and over again," the pattern comes to embody a claim on the part of candidate Dean that "everything he had to say was of special importance and in need of heightened audience attention" (179). Streeck provocatively suggests that Dean's self-representation with gestural claims to superiority and a haughty, scolding demeanor may have cost him his frontrunner status in the early polling—a sudden and catastrophic fall in popularity that has generally been blamed on Dean's odd and slightly hysterical "whoop" during a jubilant primary victory speech.

Trump, like Howard Dean before him, stands out among presidential candidates (and most politicians) for deploying a very different regime of co-speech gesturing. Remarkable (and, I argue, salient) about Trump's gesturing is the pervasive use of lateral motion, in sharp contrast to the predominantly downward (or slightly outward) beats of Biden's gestures. This essay speculates on the meaning indexed by this idiosyncratic pattern.

I begin my discussion of Trump's gestures in his debate with Joe Biden by looking closely at an example of Biden's gesturing. Figure 6.2 transcribes a representative segment of Joe Biden's debate speech, in which he deploys the kind of lateral gesture that is relatively uncommon in Biden's discourse but that predominates in Trump's utterances. The topic of conversation has been healthcare, and Biden has been given a short amount of time to respond to comments Trump made on the issue. Biden utters the four-phrase rejoinder transcribed below that is heard to be rather emphatic (**boldface and underlined** type indicates syllables bearing pitch-accents):

> There's **no** way he [referring to Trump] could protect pre-existing con**di**tions
> **None**
> **Zero**
> You can't do it in the **e**ther.
>
> (0:46:46–0:46:52)

Figure 6.2 illustrates the sequence of gestures, their morphology and alignment with the spoken locution for this set of utterances. In this and other gesture illustrations in this essay, gesture phrases are numbered sequentially within each example (G1, G2, etc.). The initial (left-most) images show the preparatory phase of the gestures, while the final (right-most) images show the end point of the stroke phase for each gesture phrase.[3] I include the initial images in order to give an impression of the (lateral) motion involved in the gestures.

With reference to Figure 6.2, notice that Biden begins with his hands more or less at home position on the podium (image G1a). As he begins speaking, Biden also begins to raise his right arm slowly up and out to his right (image G1b) in preparation for his upcoming gesture. Simultaneous with vocalizing the word "conditions," Biden straightens the fingers of his right hand and extends his elbow slightly so that his now open hand moves laterally outwards, further to his right side (image G1c), effecting a pointing motion because it is in the general direction of his interlocutor, Trump, the referent of "he." This is the gesture's stroke, which is then held through the end of the word "conditions."

The utterance transcriptions below the images adapt Kendon's (2004) system for representing the structure and alignment of locution (aural) and gesture (visual).

Indexing ambivalence **103**

The pipe symbol ("|") demarcates the boundaries of gesture phrases. Tildes ("~") indicate when the speaker is moving his hands in preparation for a gesture, and underscores ("_") indicate when this preparatory motion is held prior to the beginning of the gesture proper. The gesture identifier (here "G1") marks the stroke phase and is aligned with the transcription of the words, indicating when in the segmental sequence of the utterance the main action of the gesture occurred. Asterisks ("★") indicate a "post-stroke hold," where a speaker maintains the handshape and position for some time after completing the gesture stroke.[4]

Returning to the utterances represented in Figure 6.2, note that Biden repeats this lateral pointing gesture two more times (G2 and G3), coincident with the words "none" and "zero," though these latter gesture phrases are less pronounced. He then changes the handshape of his right hand, bunching the fingers into a fist, and draws his hand inward toward his shoulder (image G4a) in preparation for the stroke of the G4 gesture, a lateral motion out towards his right side that coincides with the stressed syllable on the word "ether" (image G4b).

FIGURE 6.2 Example of Biden's Lateral Gestures.

```
There's no way he could protect pre-existing conditions.
|~~~~~~~~~~~~~~~~~~~~~~~~~~~~~~~~~~~~~~~~~~ G1 *** |
None.
|~ G2 |
Zero.
|~ G3 |
```

```
You can't do it in the ether.|~~~~~~~~~~~~~~~ G4 *** |
```

Biden's co-speech gesture sequence works in at least two ways. He is in part pointing to Trump, reinforcing the pronominal reference ("he") to his interlocutor, but the sideways gesture, repeated four times, also coincides with four semantic negatives: "no way," "none," "zero," and "can't." This association of the lateral gestures with negative particles, statements, or ideas is typical for speakers of American English (and many other languages as well). As Kendon notes, there is a common family of gestures, which he labels Open Hand Prone gestures, that "function in ways similar to negative particles" (2004: 281). Kendon elaborates:

> The hand is moved in a rapid horizontal lateral movement, away from the midline of the speaker's body. These gestures may be performed with one hand or with two. The contexts in which these gestures are used can all be interpreted as involving a reference to some line of action that is being suspended, interrupted, or cut off.
>
> (255)

Bressem and Müller (2014) build on Kendon's initial observations in discussing a broader category of gestures that they call "away gestures." Diverging from Kendon's focus on gesture families determined in large part by similarity of handshape, Bressem and Müeller point to the significant parallels among gestures belonging to various gesture families that are linked by commonality in motion. In particular, they note that all gestures, regardless of handshape or orientation, that involve hand motion away from the speaker's body also seem to share a semantics of rejection, refusal, negative assessment, or negation (2014: 1596)—a common meaning component of *away gestures* that stems from an underlying semantics of sweeping or clearing objects from the body space, or blocking the approach of objects from the body space (1600).

The statistical preponderance in Trump's utterances of a gesture component that involves lateral hand motion (see Table 6.1) thus presents an intriguing interpretive question: What does it mean for a public speaker to be inflecting more than half of his locutions with a co-incident gesture whose general meaning is negation? Figure 6.3 (provided as an Appendix because of its length) takes a closer look at the pattern of locution and gesture in a typical sequence of Trump's debate utterances. The broader context for this excerpt is Trump's extended reaction to questions posed by the debate moderator about his taxes. Trump has been contesting the claim that he does not pay enough in tax, and he pivots to suggest financial malfeasance on the part of Biden. The locutions of the debate excerpt are re-presented here for convenience (with the lines numbered to correspond to the numbering of the gesture phrases in Figure 6.3).[5]

1. **I** don't make money from **Chi**na?
2. **You** do
3. **I** don't make money from U**krain**e?
4. **You** do
5. **I** don't make money from **Russia**
6. **You** made **three** and a half million **dollars, Joe**?
7. And your **son gave** you—
8. They **e**ven have a **state**ment

Indexing ambivalence   **105**

9. That ... we have to give **10** per**cent**
10. To the **big** man
11–12. **You're** the **big** man, I **think**
13. **I** don't **know, may** be you're **not**
14–15. But **you're** the **big** man, I **think**
16. Your **son** said we have to give **10** per**cent** to the **big** man
17. **Joe**, what's that all a**bout**, it's **ter**rible

In Figure 6.3 each line corresponds to a single prosodic phrase of the spoken locution. Most of Trump's prosodic phrases correspond to single gesture phrases, with the exception of gestures G11 and G12, which occur within the same prosodic phrase, as do gestures G14 and G15. As with the example of Biden's gesturing discussed above, the images in Figure 6.3 are intended to highlight the lateral motion, illustrating, in most cases, the preparation phase and stroke phase of each gesture phrase. Since many (though not all) gesture phrases within a gesture unit begin with the hands held in the position where the previous phrase ended (the post-stroke hold), the final (right-most) image in one row will often be identical to the initial (left-most) image in the succeeding row (as is true, for example, for gestures G1 and G2).

In the first four lines of this fragment, Trump poetically alternates negations about self ("I don't...") with emphatic assertions about Biden ("You do"). As we might expect from the previous discussion, the explicit negatives coincide with lateral gestures synchronized with the stressed syllables of focused words. Gesture G1, for example, is a prototypical example of the kind of "away gesture" Kendon classified as the Open Hand Prone Palm Horizontal (or ZP). Trump's hands are in the open-hand shape, and his forearms are oriented so that the palms would be prone (palms facing down) were his wrists not torqued, positioning the palms in an oblique angle pointing partially outward (toward an interlocutor) and partially facing each other (image G1a). Trump then moves his hands symmetrically laterally outward (image G1b) in alignment with the stressed word "**I**", recovers (image G1c), and moves them laterally again in alignment with the stressed syllable of "**Chi**na" (image G1d). This emphatic negation at the level of locution is reinforced by the gesture associated with negation.

Trump's second utterance, however, also deploys lateral movement (images G2a and G2b) despite coinciding with a positive assertion in the locution. In this case the lateral motion coincides with a pointing function, since Trump is pointing in the direction of Biden's podium (note Trump's head and eyes pointing in Biden's direction as well), but nearly all gestures in this sixteen-utterance fragment of discourse involve lateral movement, while only two others (G5 and G13) co-occur with explicitly negative locutions. In the remainder of this turn-at-talk, Trump constructs the following four grammatically positive assertions about Joe Biden (some of which are fragmented and/or repeated):

- You made three and a half million dollars
- Your son said we have to give 10 percent to the big man

- You're the big man
- It's terrible.

Each of these assertions is accompanied by horizontal lateral hand movements that index negation. In each case the explicit statements suggest an ironic reading, such that what is conveyed is more or less the opposite of what is said. For example, the explicit claim that Biden made $3.5 million (G6) is stated neutrally but intended derisively, essentially "You should not have earned this money." Similarly, Trump's locution "You're the big man" (note the focal stress on "big") suggests its opposite, namely that Biden is an odd fit as a mob boss. And the line "…we have to give 10 percent to the big man" drips with disdain for the implication of actions attributed to Biden that a politician should not do. In each case the ironically-interpreted assertions receive an inflection of negation from the co-occurring gesture indexically linked to negation.

Kendon's discussion of lateral movement gestures and negation provides an explanation for the above association, when he points out that the motivation underlying the gestures' meaning, namely the action of sweeping physical objects away from the speaker's body space, is often applied metaphorically to what is implied or presupposed by the locution (2004: 255). His example comes from a recorded conversation in which a woman selling cheeses tells her customer that she has only a limited supply of the brie he wants to buy, saying, in part "and then it's the finish of that particular brie," and deploying the two-handed lateral gesture on her word "finish." Kendon notes that the gesture corresponds to an implied negation, "there will be no more of that brie" (257).

Discussion

While many particular instances of lateral away gestures in Trump's discourse carry either direct, first-order indexicality (co-occurring with explicit negation) or indirect, second-order indexicality (inflecting positive assertions with negative subtexts), what I find most important is the broader pattern of Trump's co-speech gestures in public speaking contexts, namely the overwhelming preponderance of lateral gestures in his gestural repertoire. I would like to interpret these facts through the lens of two theoretical constructs from neighboring disciplines: the linguist Anthony Woodbury's notion of rhetorical structure and the literary critic Stephen Booth's notion of nonsensical coherence in texts.

Set out initially in 1985 and 1987 papers, Woodbury embedded his close analysis of Central Alaskan Yupik (CAY) intonational phrasing in a broad descriptive framework that viewed prosody, phonology, syntax, and other dimensions of talk as independent-but-interacting levels of (socio)linguistic structure:

> I take a rhetorical structure *component* to be any well-defined recurrent, hierarchic organization that is present in a stretch of discourse and distinct from

other such organizations… the notion also predicts… that rhetorical structure components in texts… will somehow *interact*.

(1987: 178–9)

A text's rhetoric, then, often involved mutual reinforcements of meaning from the various levels, as when phrasing constituency coincides with syntactic constituency. Woodbury, however, was equally interested in what he called enjambments (following Jakobson 1960), where levels conflicted with each other. Woodbury himself did not discuss gesture, but it certainly lends itself to his framework. Much of the literature on co-speech gesture has focused on the relations of reinforcement between speech and gesture, as when rhythmic gestural "beats" reflect the prosodic or information structure of speech. Less attention has been paid to the creative and playful possibilities of clash between gesture and speech and the rich communicative possibilities contained therein.

Literary critic Stephen Booth's analysis of "nonsense," articulated especially elegantly in the introductory essay to his 1998 book *Precious Nonsense*, can be seen to apply Woodbury's framework to the interpretation of texts of all kinds. Booth provocatively suggests that what makes "great literature" (such as Lincoln's Gettysburg Address) great is not the ideational (sense) structure of the text but, rather, its points of cohesion that do not rely on sense-relations—and often actually create logical conflicts or conundrums. His elegant argument that Lincoln's great speech appears nonsensical upon close textual analysis complements his shocking comparison to less "great" (but deeply known) texts, like "Little Boy Blue" (Booth 1998: 4), in drawing our attention to the way that texts that entertain, give pleasure, remain meaningful in peoples' lives, tend to be those that establish a paradox, a riddle, a puzzle needing to be solved. The unforgettable nursery rhyme suggests, for example, connecting the "blue" in the boy's name to the "blow" on the horn, to the "blew" that comes to mind when thinking of blow, etc. These formal connections generate pleasure, in part through the puzzles they construct. In Booth's words:

> What does the human mind ordinarily want most? It wants to understand what it does not understand. And what does the human mind customarily do to achieve that goal? It works away—sometimes for only a second or two, sometimes for years—until it understands. What does the mind have then? What it wanted? No. What it has is understanding of something it now understands. What it wanted was to understand what it did not understand. I suggest that, by giving us the capacity casually, effortlessly to accept "The sheep's in the meadow" as self-evidently distressing news, "Little Boy Blue" does something comparable to the impossible: it gives us understanding of something that remains something we do not understand.
>
> (5–6)

Taken together these two strands of thought go a long way toward explaining the paradoxical power-cum-incoherence of Trump's rhetoric. Many scholars have wrestled with paradox in Trump's discourse, including Robin Lakoff, who begins her 2017 essay "Hollow Man" citing the journalist Salena Zito's famous line, "The press takes Trump literally but not seriously. Trump's supporters take him seriously but not literally" (Zito 2016, cited in Lakoff 2017: 595). For Lakoff hollowness comes from irreconcilable paradox, as, for example, in her interesting observations about Trump and masculinity. Lakoff notes that much of what Trump says constructs a hyper-masculine self, while the way that he says it (using effeminate gestures, superlatives, comparatives like "so" and "such," etc.) constructs an effeminate self (2017: 598).[6]

Similarly, Adam Hodges (2020) has pointed to Trump's penchant for creating "plausible deniability" in his speech. Similarly paradoxical, Trump's proclamations are often both bombastically assertive and thoroughly vague. Often caught saying things that draw extensive criticism, for example, like his pressure on former FBI director James Comey to abandon the FBI investigation of Michael Flynn, or his equivocation on the violence that erupted in Charlottesville in August of 2017, Trump then succeeds at denying that his statement(s) meant what they were universally interpreted to mean.

The broad pattern of gestural negation overlaid on statements that are sometimes actual negation but often are not creates precisely the kind of plausible deniability Hodge describes. Trump effectively conveys to listeners a message the valence of which is simultaneously interactively clear and plausibly deniable. The pattern can also explain the insights of Hall et al. (2016) that began this essay: statements that are simultaneously asserted and negated are classic forms of entertainment, carnivalizing discourse, in the sense of Bakhtin (1981), as they bring pleasurable contemplation of an ever-multiplying set of puzzles, in the sense of Booth (1998), to the reception of his texts. This, it seems to me, is at the heart of Trump's distinctive communicative style, the peculiar (and perplexing) power of his words.

Transcription conventions

Gestures are transcribed using a modification of Kendon's system (Kendon 2004: 363), in which:

| | represents the boundary of a gestural phrase
~~~ represent preparatory hand motion in advance of the gestural stroke
___ represents holds within the preparatory phase
G# boldface numbered gestures stand for the gesture stroke and are positioned to indicate temporal alignment with the syllable on which they begin
(G#) parenthesized numbered gestures indicate the rough starting point for the gestural motion. These images are provided mainly to highlight the motion involved in the gesture stroke phases. They are positioned to indicate temporal alignment with spoken syllables
★★★ represents post-stroke hold
ether Bold/Underlined segments represent syllables receiving a pitch-accent.

Indexing ambivalence **109**

Appendix

FIGURE 6.3 Typical sequence of Lateral Gestures in Trump's debate speech.

```
. . . . . . . . . . .  I don't make money from China?
|~~(G1a)_____(G1b)_____(G1c)_____G1d***|
```

```
You do
|G2b**|
```

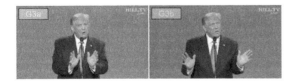

```
I don't make money from Ukraine?
|~~~(G3a)~~~~G3b****************|
```

```
You do
|G4b**|
```

```
I don't make money from . Russia
|~~(G5a)_____G5b***|
```

```
You made three and a half million dollars Joe?
|(G6a)___G6b*********************************|
```

```
And your son gave you—
|~(G7a)___G7b**********|
```

```
They even have a statement
|~~~_____G8b******|
```

```
That . we have to give 10 percent
|~~(G9a)_____G9b********|
```

Indexing ambivalence **111**

```
To the big man
|(G10a)G10b***|
```

```
You're the big man I think
|G11******|G12************|
```

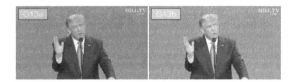

```
I don't know maybe you're not
|(G13a)_G13b*****************|
```

```
But you're the big man I think
|~~(G14a)_____G14b|_____G15**|
```

```
Your son said we have to give ten percent to the big man
|(G16a)~~(G16b)_____G16c*********************|
```

```
Joe what's that all about it's terrible
|(G17a )__G17b *****************************************|
```

Acknowledgement

I would like to acknowledge the contributions made to this project by students in my Speech Play and Verbal Art seminar, with special thanks to Will Norton and Margaret Oldham.

Notes

1 The Hill.TV digital recording of the full (90-minute) debate was accessed from YouTube.com (https://www.youtube.com/watch?v=EQMpwLZFyEM&t=1917s) on October 30, 2020. Compared to the recordings available on youtube.com from better-known networks, such as cnn.com or pbs.com, Hill.TV added much less visual material, like titles, scrawls, or other special effects that tended to obscure candidates' hand motions. The YouTube video was converted to mp4 format and saved to my computer using the website www.clipconverter.cc. ELAN software was used to transcribe the words and gestures.
2 The slice gesture involves an open hand held out in front of the body with thumb pointing upward that is moved downward, as if slicing a loaf of bread. It is often produced two-handed. Pointing gestures involve extending the index finger. The ring gesture is a variation of the precision grip, in which the non-index fingers are extended so that thumb and index form a circle. Power grip involves the hand made into a fist, with the thumb on top.
3 Note that Kendon (2004) introduces an unfortunate point of confusion into his terminology by using the very similar terms "phase" and "phrase" for somewhat different ideas. Phase refers to the structural components (preparation phase, stroke phase) of the gesture phrase.
4 A more detailed description of these transcription conventions is provided as an Appendix to this chapter.

5 I've included images from each of the lines in the example stretch of Trump's speech for the sake of completeness. Due to the change in camera angle during the phrases coinciding with Gestures #5, 6, and 7, it is difficult to see the lateral motion from the sequence of still images. The actual video does indicate clear lateral movement of Trump's hands in each of those gesture phrases.
6 Another rhetorical structure component, prosody, seems to work in just this way. Trump's utterances are often bombastic at the level of words, yet performed in a strikingly unemphatic prosody. His declarative, assertive phrases often end in phrase-final rises that are associated with uncertainty, desire for acknowledgement, and subordination, and his phrase-final falls often fail to reach the lower end of his pitch range (which would lead to an interpretation of decisiveness). And his voice quality often moves in and out of a whine.

References

Bakhtin, M.M. 1981. "Discourse in the Novel." In Michael Holquist, ed. *The Dialogic Imagination*. Austin: University of Texas Press, 259–331.

Booth, Stephen. 1998. *Precious Nonsense: The Gettysburg Address, Ben Jonson's Epitaphs on His Children, and Twelfth Night*. Berkeley: University of California Press.

Bressem, Jana, and Cornelia Müller. 2014. "The Family of Away Gestures: Negation, Refusal, and Negative Assessment." In Cornelia Müller, Alan Cienki, Ellen Fricke, Silva H Ladewig, David McNeill, and Jana Bressem, eds. *Body – Language – Communication: An International Handbook on Multimodality in Human Interaction*, vol. 2. Berlin: De Gruyter Mouton, 1592–1604.

Briggs, Charles, and Richard Bauman. 1992. "Genre, Intertextuality, and Social Power." *Journal of Linguistic Anthropology* 2 (2): 131–72.

CNN. 2021. "Transcript of New Day 14 January 2021." http://transcripts.cnn.com/TRANSCRIPTS/2101/14/nday.04.html, accessed January 14, 2021.

Hall, Kira, Donna Meryl Goldstein, and Matthew Bruce Ingram. 2016. "The Hands of Donald Trump: Entertainment, Gesture, Spectacle." *HAU: Journal of Ethnographic Theory* 6 (2): 71–100.

Hodges, Adam. 2020. "Plausible Deniability." In Janet McIntosh and Norma Mendoza-Denton, eds. *Language in the Trump Era: Scandals and Emergencies*. Cambridge: Cambridge University Press, 137–47.

Jakobson, Roman. 1960. "Closing Statement: Linguistics and Poetics." In Thomas A Sebeok, ed. *Style in Language*. Cambridge, MA: Technology Press of Massachusetts Institute of Technology, 350–77.

Kendon, Adam. 2004. *Gesture: Visible Action as Utterance*. Cambridge: Cambridge University Press.

Lakoff, Robin Tolmach. 2017. "The Hollow Man: Donald Trump, Populism, and Post-Truth Politics." *Journal of Language & Politics* 16 (4): 595–606.

Lempert, Michael. 2011. "Barack Obama Being Sharp: Indexical Order in the Pragmatics of Precision-Grip Gesture." *Gesture* 11 (3): 241–70.

McNeill, David. 2016. *Why We Gesture: The Surprising Role of Hand Movement in Communication*. Cambridge: Cambridge University Press.

Sclafani, Jennifer. 2018. *Talking Donald Trump: A Sociolinguistic Study of Style, Metadiscourse, and Political Identity*. London: Routledge.

Streeck, Juergen. 2008. "Gesture in Political Communication: A Case Study of the Democratic Presidential Candidates During the 2004 Primary Campaign." *Research on Language and Social Interaction* 41 (2): 154–86.

Streeck, Juergen, Charles Goodwin, and Curtis D. LeBaron, eds. 2011. *Embodied Interaction: Language and Body in the Material World*. New York: Cambridge University Press.

Woodbury, Anthony. 1985. "The Functions of Rhetorical Structure: A Study of Central Alaskan Yupik Eskimo Discourse." *Language in Society* 14: 153–90.

———. 1987. "Rhetorical Structure in a Central Alaskan Yupik Eskimo Traditional Narrative." In Joel Sherzer and Anthony Woodbury, eds. *Native American Discourse: Poetics and Rhetoric*. Cambridge: Cambridge University Press, 176–239.

Zito, Salena. 2016. "Taking Trump Seriously, But Not Literally." *The Atlantic*, accessed September 23, 2016.

7

TRUMP THE CAUDILLO

Tapping into already-existing populist unrest

Micah J. Fleck

In November of 2020, after four years of tumultuous domestic division and increasingly xenophobic foreign policy, Donald J. Trump was beaten by Joseph R. Biden in the US presidential race. Biden was elected the forty-sixth president of the United States, and there was much celebration. But this celebration, it became increasingly clear, was for the ousting of Trump and not for the election of Biden. In fact, despite his victory Biden significantly underperformed compared to the pre-election poll projections. In many key swing states, the margins were close enough that Trump was able to successfully demand legal recounts and audits, all the while using his typically incendiary rhetoric to rally his base and make claims of some kind of widespread conspiracy on behalf of government elites to fraudulently rig vote counts and construct an artificial Biden win. Yes, those claims were false and baseless, but the fact that the election was close at all considering Trump's tangible track record was something of an embarrassment in the eyes of many who looked to America for exemplary democratic process and celebration of individual liberty (something Trump's policies had stymied for many minority demographics during his term). Similar to how close things were in 2016 when Trump narrowly won the Electoral College in an upset victory over his opponent Hillary Clinton, the results of the 2020 election still showed quite prominently that America at large was not roused enough by the establishment Democratic Party's platform to crush Trump as expected. But why? What was it about the Democrats that seemed to consistently underwhelm American voters on the whole?

In short: the working class in the US has long been promised significant autonomy, reasonable wages, and social mobility by the establishment Democrats, but for decades those promises have gone largely unfulfilled. This is not a case where the majority of Americans actually want fascism; they are simply tired of neoliberalism. And the Democratic Party has the latter in droves. Ironically, of course, much of American neoliberal economic policy was born from the Republican

DOI: 10.4324/9781003152743-9

administration of Reagan, but as late capitalism has continued to collapse, the conservative working-class dissatisfaction with the state of things has caused the more populist elements of Republican talking points to accuse Democrats alone of such pro-establishment strokes. It is a revisionist view of economic policy, but it nevertheless was an angle the Trump campaign was able to exploit.

The victory of Joe Biden can and should be seen as a national rebuke of Donald Trump's fascistic policies and rhetoric, and that alone is worth celebrating. But in order for another Trump-like figure not to come along and woo his segment of the working class yet again, there needs to be more passion behind future Democratic votes. In summary, Democrats need to take the working-class plight much more seriously and consider genuinely radical changes to the economic status quo. Much of Trump's success in 2016 came from the fact that he was the only candidate in the national election talking like a populist at all. Bernie Sanders, the Democratic populist candidate, had been edged out of the running during the Democratic primary. Therefore, what voters were presented with come election day was a choice between a fake populist and a typical elitist Democrat. Many voters on the left saw right through Trump's faux-populist façade, but they were also unhappy with Clinton's business-as-usual platform. So, many stayed home. Many (but not all) Bernie Sanders supporters unfortunately felt personally betrayed by the Democrats and flipped to Trump as a protest vote of their own. And, of course, the conservatives and Republicans voted Republican as they always did. But this time, a special element of passion was there in many conservative Trump voters. They seemed genuinely rejuvenated by him, and they expressed that they saw Trump's campaign as a means of finally getting their voices heard by the elites in DC (the fact that Trump was an elite himself seemed to not register with them). Yes, there were plenty of racists, xenophobes, homophobes, transphobes, Islamophobes, etc. who wanted Trump to win simply so they could outwardly show their hate. But in my research regarding the specific working-class wing of conservatives who fancied themselves to be revolutionaries of sorts by voting for Trump, they seemed to genuinely want systemic change.

In my book that investigated the oft-misrepresented organic underbelly of right-wing populism, I went out of my way to give the benefit of the doubt to the most earnest among the Trump voters, as I saw time and again a kind of revolutionary urge present in the populist conservatives who voted for him. Through my own inquiry and conversations with this demographic, I found that the most fascistic elements of Trump's policies were not among the top appeal for many. Yes, it is true that undeniable ignorance on the part of these voters likely led to them being more or less indifferent to the more sinister aspects of Trump, but that is an argument best left for other chapters. The main interest for me regarding the working-class element to the Trump phenomenon has from the beginning been how so many of Trump's conservative working-class supporters often speak about authority and their present economic situation as if they were radical anarchists.

And it indeed became ever clearer to me over the course of my inquiry on this matter that much of the rationale behind the conservative working-class support for

Trump in the 2016 election was from a place of genuine grievance with the present socioeconomic system. Where the conservative brand of this radical populism ends up taking a misstep, however, is in regard to the general conservative attitude toward the history of radical labor movements. On the one hand, disgruntled working-class conservatives become just as radicalized by their financial situations as anyone else in the working class. On the other hand, however, all of the organic outcomes that result from that unrest have historically been leftist, or socialist, to one degree or another. Labor history is very clear on this (Weaver 2018). Therefore, the more truly organic response to their woes, even for conservatives, should lead them to a more leftward trajectory in their activism and voting direction. Why, then, does that not happen? Simple: conservatives in America are absolutely terrified of what they believe socialism is, namely, a gigantic superstate concerned with running everything about the economy from the top down, taking everyone's personal property away from them, and forcing behavior *en masse*. Despite this not being true, it has long been the main obstacle for otherwise well-meaning radical conservatives' pathways to affecting actual positive change for their own economic class.

But the unrest is still very real and present, even in the conservative wing of the working class. And without the willingness or the knowhow to move into actual pro-labor activist spaces for the reasons laid out above, substitutes must be offered in their place. The most popular among these substitutes currently is right-libertarianism, which hijacks rhetoric and terminology from *actual* libertarianism (once again, a leftist movement of old) and applies it to pro-capitalist initiatives that claim to be in favor of true free markets for working people. In effect, it gives the sensation of actually doing something radical while, in reality, it works to reinforce the economic status quo. The end result is that, despite populist conservatives' best efforts, nothing changes. And the aggravation with the state of things returns, only this time even more ferociously than before. The irony here is that Trumpism then manages to channel that aggravation toward a protectionist, nationalist direction instead of a truly pro-worker one. How that process occurs is outlined below.

Fellow researcher Noah Berlatsky and I, in an attempt to better illustrate this process, devised independently of one another alternative mechanisms to describe how populist rationale manifests in these propagandized spaces. Upon examining both models, I formulated them into one: The Populist Rationale Spectrum. Within that spectrum, shared populist unrest finds overlap within pockets of information gaps that more extreme forms of fake, distorted populism, ranging from center-right populism to outright fascism, take advantage of and propagandize. But once that initial propaganda takes hold, the process of initiating future generations in the misinformation about what it truly means to be radical or anti-elitist becomes organic and self-perpetuated. By the time of the 2016 election, that self-propagandizing process had been going strong for generations. Donald Trump's presidential campaign did not invent the platform it ran on. It merely tapped into the already-existing unrest within the conservative working class and chose to validate some of the most toxic fake populist narratives already floating around in the ether of the populist conservative world.

In fact, the seemingly everyman attraction to the Trump campaign's image as pro-working class mirrors that of the working-class populist attraction to the idea of the caudillo (political and military leaders who speak for the common people) in revolutionary Latin American countries. But to better understand how caudillos also take advantage of already-existing populist unrest in their respective regions, we should acknowledge Jacobinism and its effect on populism's trajectory throughout history.

Jacobinism, originating with the French revolutionary movement, was an origin point for modern populism's behavior and rhetoric. Many texts on the subject seem to credit modern populism's origins to more recent times and overlook the importance of Jacobinism for setting the true stage. Anthropologist Claudio Lomnitz described it once as a "fantasy of unmediated popular power; the will of 'the people' embedded in the law" (Lomnitz 2016).

Why and where this is relevant to the topic of populism and at large can be seen in *Dancing Jacobins: A Venezuelan Genealogy of Latin American Populism* by Rafael Sanchez, where he traces a genealogy of Jacobinist populist movements in Venezuela and Latin America on the whole (Sanchez 2016). One section of the book in particular that ties in with the sort of populism found on the American right is once again where a distinction is made between a group seen as the true "people" (which Sanchez calls "sovereign") and the more outlying "crowd" (which Sanchez calls "unfathomable")—reflecting in the process a similar distinction already put forth by Laclau in the form of the people versus plebs argument—in order to better delineate the idea of "excess" that went beyond and "continuously eluded its classificatory grid" (101).

As for the parallels between a populist figure like Trump and a caudillo, there lies an origin point for a culturally perpetuated concept of people's representation as an almost performative concept through physical representation—the body of the leader, as it is observed by Sanchez in the caudillos. Lomnitz again comments that the caudillo "has to embody something for there to be unity behind him—he is a physical placeholder for otherwise more abstract causes. The details cannot be reconstituted except by him" (101). In this way, a leader's presence can be somewhat immortalized and made identifiable and accessible more to the people themselves, which makes it much more likely for the population at large to stay subdued and pacified with the idea of a leader such as a caudillo, because said position is the very physical embodiment of a monument to the people's causes and wills.

This can be seen in a few specific examples in *Dancing Jacobins*, such as the caudillo, Simón Bolívar, who "turned himself into a living monument right before the masses" (294), thereby functioning as "a governmental tool" for bringing otherwise "formless, unruly crowds" to their knees in reverence to the caudillo, and uplifting a quasi-theological following, in this case "Bolivaranism," to the level of "obligatory horizon of rule in Venezuela" (293).

Another example of the body or form of the leader being utilized as a means of pacification and maintenance comes in the example of Bolívar not being able to be physically present everywhere he demanded praise. This necessitated that Bolívar make himself a living monument, in addition to erecting actual monuments of his likeness to serve as his surrogates in spaces where he was not available to be revered in person. For if Bolívar himself is now a monument, in some way, every monument of himself would therefore be Bolívar. And indeed, in the book's opening, Sanchez clarifies as much, stating that even "the statue of Bolivar… 'is the people'" and also that these statues are "orchestrated by the State" to serve as "the people's truest appearance when contemplated as a whole" (17).

In other words, the government seized upon the seeming need of the people to feel listened to and their wants embodied in something tactile and delivered on it by utilizing the concept of the leader's body being essentially the plebs incarnate. Through this lens, even the anti-political populists of the Jacobinistic sort are more likely to forgive the government mechanism because the politician himself so convincingly embodies their struggle. Once again, this suggests that the concept of the body of the leader is more about serving as a mechanism for governmental control rather than it is an actual desire to listen to the people.

This concept is not far removed from what we see in populist spaces in the United States and certainly within the conservative anti-political populist spaces I have been unpacking in my book and, to a more limited degree, in this chapter. That the majority of working-class Trump voters were simply decent, if misguided people who felt let down by the Democrats and desired a change is not a position unique to this essay. It was this very narrative that won the day when it came to how the Trump campaign *presented* itself as a symbolic embodiment of working-class unrest to the general public. Writing for *Foreign Affairs*, political theorist Omar G. Encarnacion muses on what he refers to as the "Latin-Americanization of US politics" and points out how Trump has much in common with "the typical caudillo," who "was a charismatic man on horseback with a penchant for authoritarianism" (Encarnacion 2016). And Trump was certainly behaving during his campaign like a traditional caudillo in the way in which he had appointed himself the guardian of this cause to bring America back to what is perceived as a "better" time in the eyes of the plebs who aimed to follow him and ultimately appoint him their representative leader.

To the earlier point of the leader's body actually being about control despite being pro-pleb in appearance, the most successful people to pull off such a feat would likely need to be incredible chameleons. And Trump is nothing short of an incredible chameleon.

However, Trump's working-class hero political persona started to take tangible shape when he abandoned his 2000 race, writing in an op-ed for *The New York Times* that while he felt the Reform Party was no longer a viable option for him, he still regretted not being able to continue running "a race against Mr. Bush and Mr. Gore, two establishment politicians" (Trump 2000). Playing up the role of an anti-elitist to the hilt, Trump went so far in his op-ed as to implicate both Bush and Gore as tone deaf elitists because they were both "Ivy League contenders." This narrative only worked, of course, if one chose to ignore the fact that Trump also went to an Ivy League college and likely had more money to his name than both of the gentlemen he was lambasting combined.

Still, elitist or no, Trump nevertheless played the part of the working-class spokesman well—just like the aforementioned caudillos. And while it is worth noting that even Encarnacion admits Trump would "blush" at just how much more of an extreme despot a caudillo such as the Dominican Republic's Rafael Leonidas Trujillo was, there are still some similarities between these two, as well (Encarnacion 2016). One standout that immediately comes to mind is how in the Trujillo regime, according to Trujillo scholar Robin Derby, women's identities were "based on shame, not honor," and Trump has infamously looked at women much in the same way—both privately as well as out in the open (Derby 2009: 167). Take, for instance, the leaked audio of Trump bragging about his ability to sexually assault women and get away with it due to his fame and cultural influence (Drum 2016).

Imagining oneself as holding the same kind of influence as a Donald Trump figure, how easy or difficult would it be to behave similarly? The answer might somewhat be colored by whether or not one always held this influence or if one started out lacking it and then acquired it later. But in either case, mass influence (i.e., power) itself seems to change the motivations and mindsets of people who hold it (Shea 2012).

But studies have suggested that this phenomenon, while real, is often misunderstood. In 2012, the *Journal of Applied Psychology* published a study (DeCelles et al. 2012) demonstrating that "people's 'moral identity'—the degree to which they thought it was important to their sense of self to be 'caring,' 'compassionate,' 'fair,' 'generous' and so on—shaped their responses to feelings of power" (Shea 2012). But the more nuanced outcome of this study was that power doesn't necessarily corrupt so much as it frees people to feel more comfortable in expressing their innermost proclivities without inhibitions. In other words, if one has displayed a tendency toward harshness for others and greed for oneself, giving that same person even more power and influence will likely simply push those already-present qualities to their extremes. The notion of Donald Trump, a lifelong millionaire born into his money and displaying no prior evidence of working-class empathy, being a working-class hero should have been quite transparently ridiculous from the start once one took this reality into account. Yet all of these red flags, all of these clear and present threats to traditionally conservative values and behavior, were not enough to stop the conservative working-class plebs from voting for Trump anyway.

After the failure of the Soviet Union and the subsequent growth of all the anti-socialist propaganda, arguably most everyday people in the West, even if they had issues with their present economic situations, abandoned any ideas of true socialist libertarian revolution against the capitalist system. The alternative, it was perceived, was too risky and could lead to another Soviet-style regime. And so, most people left behind their hopes for true revolution and began to accept more pacifying policy shifts (note the similarities to the subdued and pacified caudillo-run Venezuelans cited earlier) that would make daily existence within the machine more incrementally bearable. It was within these spaces of the moderates settling for less, and the conservatives self-deluding on the topic of what socialism and libertarianism even is in the first place, that the process outlined in the formulation the Populist Rationale Spectrum was able to unfold.

Succinctly, the process has been observed as happening in six key phases:

1. Organic populist unrest forms, which manifests historically as radical liberalism, socialism, and anarchism.
2. Elite forces formulate a distortion of these organic populist initiatives, forming information gaps along the shared populist narrative across all its political variants.
3. Hegemony is raised as a wall of informational obfuscation by neoliberal actors, pushing the centrists and conservatives within the populist experience away from even considering any anti-capitalist solutions.
4. Faux-populist strains, including everything from moderately right-leaning libertarianism and paleo-conservatism to nationalism and fascism, send out tendrils of narrative propaganda to fill the newly created information gaps.
5. Working-class leftists break through the hegemonic barrier and continue the trek toward organic populist activist initiatives; working-class conservatives are successfully propagandized and begin a new process of self-perpetuation of the propaganda which eventually becomes organic and truly believed.
6. The newly redirected working-class conservative populists now emerge from the various information gaps, form a new frontier of shared antagonism against manufactured enemies, and move more and more rightward each time their activism fails to change the economic system for the better.

This process of organic false consciousness was independently corroborated by anthropologist William Mazzarella, who described it as "an intensified insistence of collective forces that are no longer adequately organized by *formally* hegemonic social forms" but are instead an organic offshoot of past hegemony that acts as "a mattering-forth of the collective flesh" (Mazzarella 2019: 45). This process, specifically as parsed out above, is subsequently applicable to any economic system that has been propagandized long enough to start organically perpetuating its own false narratives about the true source of its economic unrest. This is not just applicable to the US. It also fits in very well with the circumstances that had befallen Venezuela shortly before Bolívar came along, dressed like one of the people, and presented himself as the one to voice the grievances of the true populists and take the mission to the governmental level (Sanchez 2016: 240). Trump, like a true caudillo, suddenly dressed himself as a common working-class man when he went to certain states during his 2016 campaign, such as in Mobile, Alabama when he donned a trucker hat and removed his necktie in an attempt to appear more relatable (Schleifer and Gray 2015). And further evidence of Trump's own participation in embodiment has also been found in the campaign rally setting. Take, for instance, Trump's pantomime style of imitation when quoting his political opponents, which anthropologists Kira Hall, Donna M. Goldstein, and Matthew Bruce Ingram (2016) describe as "bodily acts" that incorporate "dramaturgical replaying of an actual or imagined event, action or behavior" (in Trump's case, it is usually imagined being presented as actual).

It is within this exaggerated, extremist depiction of a high-stakes political drama, full of revolutionary-sounding rhetoric of "us versus them" sentiment, where Trump fully embodied not only his supporters' own ideological proclivities but the caudillo's tactics in full force. Late capitalism is said to favor style over substance, and Trump's vacuous claims of being part of some anti-political resistance certainly qualifies. In addition, Hall, Goldstein, and Ingram also point out that Trump's body language that accompanies his proof-starved tales accrues "visual capital," adding further seeming credence to his claims on an immediately digestible basis for those who do not bother (or have the time) to corroborate them independently.

Such play acting is further bolstered by another aspect of the caudillo's gallop: the persona of the strong man. When empty claims are made through means that embody the cause within its leader, the willingness to believe on behalf of the followers is heightened—when that embodiment is also accompanied by behaviors signaling especially confident, impenetrable strength, the sell becomes even more solidified in the minds of those looking to the leader for representation. This chapter earlier touched upon how in the face of dissatisfaction with neoliberal economic policy, Trump's campaign (and later, his administration) appealed to radical undemocratic means of forcing the hand of the system—supposedly in favor of the working people, but in reality favoring many of Trump's fellow economic elites.

Nevertheless, the question should still occur to anyone paying attention that it is innately contrary to claimed conservative and right-libertarian ideology to embrace statist moves away from actual democracy. Yet it remains the case that in high stakes, especially when it comes to one's fiscal existence, voters will at times throw their lot behind leaders who disregard democratic norms. So was the case with Trump and his conventionally conservative working-class voters. In a 2017 study by anthropologists Dinorah Azpuru, Mary Fran T. Malone, and Orlando J. Perez, circumstances were dissected under which pro-democratic citizens embrace undemocratic "strong man" leaders in times of economic crisis. They did this by comparing the post-election survey results for both caudillo-run Latin American countries and the US, with the former being the 2012 Latin American Public Opinion Project (LAPOP) "Americas Barometer" survey and the latter being the 2016 American National Election Studies (ANES) Post-Election Survey (Azpuru et al. 2017). The results were fascinating. In Latin America, the eight caudillos cited in the survey ended up appealing ideologically to many working-class voters on the left, despite the equivalent economic factors in the ANES survey ending up appealing to the Trump voters on the right. Yet the same rationale was given in both cases, proving true the two hypotheses that support for a strong leader who will bend the rules or limit the voice of the opposition to the perceived sociopolitical liberation of the voters was deemed worth it among the voters who felt the need to save their respective countries from disaster.

The fact that this pro-worker, anti-establishment sentiment was present on the left for the caudillo voters in Latin America and on the right for Trump voters in the US is further evidence that a type of populist distortion has been occurring in the latter's history, recasting historically leftist rhetoric as part of right-wing populist vernacular. But after that initial top-down insurgence, what followed was the self-driven, bottom-up form of organic false consciousness present in the working-class Trump votership today. No longer actively infiltrated, the conservative working class in America now honestly believes itself to be anti-establishment, when in reality it is simply anti-political. In the case of the 2016 election, many in this demographic managed, due to all the aforementioned factors, to be successfully taken in by Trump's rhetoric, borrowed heavily from caudillo tradition.

And so it was that, even in electoral defeat in 2020, Trump's caudillo act persisted. His cries of fraud and conspiracy on behalf of the government and fiscal elites were designed once again to appeal to those in his base who saw themselves as the plebs of America, who felt as if their voices had long been ignored, who had fallen unwittingly for the neoliberal propaganda that had blinded them to the real solutions. Blinded they were, but genuine they also felt. And in the face of losing their caudillo, their Jacobinistic representative, the embedder of their will into the law, the most earnest, passionate, and radical of Trump supporters chose to buy into the lie once more and believe the claim that some kind of nationwide conspiracy to take the election from Trump unfairly had somehow managed to be pulled off right from under everyone's nose. Even when faced with the overwhelming evidence to the contrary.

This is what radicalization can do to people, especially when the real solutions to the real problem are replaced by a fake savior. Moving forward, all working-class people can either strive to find new solidarity derived from the truth, or the division begun from the top down can continue to be perpetuated from the bottom up. How the country as a whole decides to learn from the Trump moment in its future treatment of workers will, in large part, serve as our indicator for which of these paths will ultimately be taken.

References

Azpuru, Dinorah, Mary Fran T. Malone, Orlando J. Perez. 2017. "American Caudillo: The Rise of Strongmen Politics in the United States and Latin America." *Conference of the Latin American Political Science Association*, ALACIP, Montevideo, Uruguay.

DeCelles, Katherine A. et al. 2012. "Does Power Corrupt or Enable? When and Why Power Facilitates Self-Interested Behavior." *Journal of Applied Psychology* 97 (3): 681–9.

Derby, Robin. 2009. *The Dictator's Seduction: Politics and the Popular Imagination in the Era of Trujillo*. Durham, NC: Duke University Press.

Drum, Kevin. 2016. "Trump on Tape." http://www.motherjones.com/kevin-drum/2016/10/trump-tape-grab-them-pussy-you-can-do-anything, accessed March 11, 2018.

Encarnacion, Omar G. 2016. "American Caudillo: Trump and the Latin-Americanization of U.S. Politics." http://www.foreignaffairs.com/articles/united-states/2016-05-12/american-caudillo, accessed December 9, 2020.

Hall, Kira, Donna M. Goldstein, and Matthew Bruce Ingram. 2016. "The Hands of Donald Trump: Entertainment, Gesture, Spectacle." *Journal of Ethnographic Theory* 6 (2): 71–100.

Lomnitz, Claudio. 2016. "Anthropology of Populism." *Seminar at Columbia University*, in which the author was a participant.

Mazzarella, William. 2019. "The Anthropology of Populism: Beyond the Liberal Sentiment." *Annual Review of Anthropology* 48: 45–60.

Sanchez, Rafael. 2016. *Dancing Jacobins: A Venezuelan Genealogy of Latin American Populism.* New York: Fordham University Press.

Schleifer, Theodore and Noah Gray. 2015. "30,000 Turn Out for Trump's Alabama Pep Rally." http://www.cnn.com/2015/08/21/politics/donald-trump-rally-mobile-alabama/index.html, accessed December 27, 2020.

Shea, Christopher. 2012. "Why Power Corrupts." http://www.smithsonianmag.com/science-nature/why-power-corrupts-37165345, accessed August 11, 2019.

Trump, Donald J. 2000. "What I Saw at the Revolution." http://www.nytimes.com/2000/02/19/opinion/what-i-saw-at-the-revolution.html, accessed December 8, 2020.

Weaver, Adam. 2018. "Outline of U.S. Labor History with a Focus on the Role of the Left." http://blackrosefed.org/outline-labor-history-left, accessed December 9, 2020.

8
LYING AS A CULTURAL SYSTEM

Jack David Eller

Throughout his career Clifford Geertz composed a series of essays treating various topics "as a cultural system," including art, ideology, common sense, and, most famously, religion. If he had lived long enough to witness Donald Trump in office (Geertz died in 2006), no doubt he would have added a piece on lying as a cultural system.

Trump is, by any estimation, a profligate and promiscuous liar. According to *The Washington Post*, by early April 2020, having served as president for 1,170 days, he had made eighteen thousand "false or misleading claims," averaging fifteen lies, exaggerations, or misstatements per day or approximately one every waking hour (Kessler, Rizzo, and Kelly 2020). In the seventy-five days immediately prior to that report, which corresponds to the outbreak of the coronavirus pandemic, his lying actually *increased* to twenty-three lies per day. And on November 6, 2020, when it appeared that he would lose his re-election bid, a CNN analyst accused him of giving "the most dishonest speech of his presidency" (Dale 2020). Many of these lies were repeated more than once, even when they had been thoroughly rebutted: at his return-to-campaign-mode rally in Tulsa, Oklahoma in June 2020, he once again claimed that he passed the Veterans Choice Bill, which was enacted during Barack Obama's administration. Almost two hundred times he took false credit for the largest tax cut in American history, and almost three hundred times he made the vague but inaccurate assertion that the American economy was better than it had ever been. Frequently, he denied saying something that he was clearly on the record saying. And when caught in a lie, he barged ahead, ignoring the charge, denying it, or attacking fact-checkers and the media as "fake news" and "Trump enemies."

Political scientist James Pfiffner categorized Trump's lies, concluding that Trump stands out from previous elected officials not only for the number but also for the nature of his untruths. Pfiffner assigns these fabulations to four sets—trivial lies, exaggerations and self-aggrandizing lies, lies to deceive the public, and egregious

DOI: 10.4324/9781003152743-10

lies. Trivial lies include his claim about the height of Trump Tower (58 stories, not 68 as he bragged); among his self-aggrandizing lies and exaggerations are the alleged size of his Electoral College majority and his inaugural crowd. His continued efforts to deceive the public include unsubstantiated accusations of voter fraud and illegal vote counting in the 2016 and 2020 elections, as well as that the United States has the highest tax rates in the world (while they are actually among the lowest in the developed world). But Trump really shines as an egregious liar, from his unrelenting "birther" attacks on Barack Obama (falsely maintaining that Obama was born outside the United States) to false statements to Canadian Prime Minister Justin Trudeau that the US has a trade deficit with Canada, not to mention his desperate pleading that he won the 2020 election that he lost. Pfiffner judges that his tireless perfidy illustrates "the cynicism with which Donald Trump approaches political leadership. It is one thing to spin news or to make exaggerated claims for credit for positive trends in the country, but it is quite another to make statements that are factually wrong and to persist in making the inaccurate claims" (Pfiffner 2019: 27).

Trump's prodigious prevarication has been attributed to sociopathy or brain damage, and there may well be some pathology at work, but insufficient attention has been paid to *lying as social action*. We should think of lying in the context of J. L. Austin's seminal *How to Do Things with Words*, since lying is doing something with words, as lies for aggrandizement and deception clearly indicate. We should also regard lying as a Goffmanian practice of self-presentation (and often enough self-obfuscation, which is a kind of presentation). Thus, an anthropology of Trump's equivocation cannot stop at pathology but must, as Carole McGranahan insists in her essay on the anthropology of lying, seek to "understand lies and liars in cultural, historical, and political context so that we can see clearly *the work of lies*" (2017: 243, emphasis added). And Trump surely does put his lies to work.

Anthropology meets lies

Treating lying as social action and cultural system requires recognizing its ubiquity and the prejudices against it. First, everyone lies, perhaps especially politicians but all people now and then in their professional and personal interactions. Second and closely related, the general assumption is that lying is always bad and anti-social and that truth is the point and essence of social (including political) discourse. This is simply not so, as Austin warned when he emphasized the *social efficacy* of language over its truth-value: sometimes an utterance has no truth-value (like "Close the window"), and sometimes not truth but rather social effect is the issue (like "I pronounce you man and wife"). It is exceedingly odd that Austin (1962) virtually ignores lying in his otherwise insightful study.

Further, we tend to assume that honesty is essential for trust and that trust is essential for social cohesion, but this is also not necessarily so. Georg Simmel over a century ago granted that a lie can be "an integrating element" in a social situation or relationship (1906: 448), insisting equally interestingly that a lie conceals more about the speaker than about the subject spoken of. Charles Barbour goes so far as to maintain that lying "is a paradigmatic example of interaction in Simmel's sense," which always entails "two or more individuals and a psychological inner world that remains private or is not exchanged" (2012: 226).

In societies where this inner mental world is more guarded, lying may be a pro-social tactic. For instance, in his study of mistrust among Berbers in Morocco, Matthew Carey explains how people employ dishonesty to facilitate social relations. Through various speech genres of joking, storytelling, and reportage, members envelop themselves in a cloud of ambiguous and dubious assertions and "apparently pointless lies" precisely in order *"to prevent one's interlocutor from being sure of the truth,* whatever that may be. In so doing, people preserve a space of psychic and moral autonomy by shrouding their actions in mystery" (2017: 35). In short, keeping others unsure about the veracity of one's talk makes one unpredictable, which maintains a zone of personal freedom in social action—that is, it is liberating to be not too trustworthy.

Likewise, on Nissan Atoll (Papua New Guinea) Steven Nachman encountered a lively culture of lying. Simultaneously condemning lying and accepting that there are "circumstances under which it is morally acceptable" (1984: 536), locals both lied and reproached others, including leaders, for lying. A rich vocabulary for misleading behaviors featured

> *bohopakapuk* ("feigning knowledge") and its opposite, *telteleboh* ("feigning ignorance"); *wolihkokop* ("pretending not to possess something one actually has"); *hingam Balil* (named after the village; "requesting something ostensibly for another, but actually for one's self"); *popolwonaboh* ("faking madness"); *bohototarbalakos* ("falsely claiming to be pregnant"); and *bangbangaboh* ("pretending to look," but more specifically described as "bending down supposedly to look for something, but with the actual intent of looking up a woman's loincloth."
>
> (541)

The motivation for dissimulation was often identical to Berber thinking, namely, "to create barriers between individuals and others' knowledge of them" (542). Finally, the norms of lying held that some individuals had no right to expect truthful statements, such as enemies, foreigners/Europeans, and at least sometimes women and children (543).

Anthropologists have become sensitive to lying as social practice, not least in our dealings with informants/collaborators in the field. Napoleon Chagnon (1992) famously and amusingly depicted the systematic deceptions he suffered at the hands of the Yanomamö (who also withhold certain knowledge, like personal names and kinship relations from each other). Peter Metcalf's fieldwork with the Berawan of Borneo was marked, he explained, by lies, "evasions, exaggerations, delusions, half-truths, and credible denials," including one elder's refusal to cooperate with him at all (2002: 1). But here too, withholding knowledge and providing false knowledge were strategic and cultural: reportedly, any local story would open with the formula

"*Malut dé, malut kita.* The verb *malut* means 'to lie,' *dé* is the third-person plural pronoun, and *kita* is the first-person plural pronoun: hence, 'they lie, we lie'" (7).

The list of culturally-defined deceits among the Nissan Atoll dwellers and the Berawan highlights the diversity of lying. All lies are mendacious, but they are not all malignant. Some lies, even in Western societies, grease the wheels of social interaction, such as the "white lies" we tell each other to spare feelings ("yes, I love the gift"; "no, you don't look fat in that outfit") as well as excuses, justification, lies in a crisis, lies to liars and enemies, lies protecting peers and clients, lies for the public good, lies in deceptive social science research, paternalistic lies, and lies to the sick and dying, collectively regarded as prosocial lies (Bok 1979). More, as a social skill lying is *acquired* or learned and consequently socially distributed, refined to a higher level for some social actors than others, for instance those in business and sales positions (Meibauer 2018: 371). In a study explicitly titled *An Anthropology of Lying*, Sylvie Fainzang (2015) explores the duplicitous communication that occurs between doctors and patients in the French healthcare context, but undoubtedly we could find it widely spread across careers and societies ostensibly dedicated to truth.

For these very reasons, Ina Rösing, in an essay on shamanic "amnesia," urged anthropologists not to disregard "lies, inventions, contradictory and fragmentary information." Rather, all of these untruths, partial truths, and missing truths should be treated not as "the 'waste' of research but [as] valuable information in its own right that can be recycled to constitute valid cultural information" (1999: 29). Particularly, they alert us to the social construction, the social appropriateness, and the social efficacy of the lie.

Anthropology, agnotology, agnomancy

For too long scholars, educators, and pundits alike have presumed that truth is the nature and goal of communication and that errors and false beliefs are simply a matter of insufficient knowledge; if only they knew the facts, people would jettison their misconceptions and gladly embrace the truth. Experience suggests otherwise—that false thinking is not just a matter of lack of knowledge and that such thinking is not individual in origin, perpetuation, or consequence.

As early as 1854, James Ferrier suggested that there ought to be a science of non-knowledge to accompany the science of knowledge or epistemology, for which he proposed the term "agnoiology." It would be more than a century before the cause was taken up again, in Michael Smithson's (1989) *Ignorance and Uncertainty*, which posited ignorance (in the sense of not-knowing) as a complicated social construct resulting from a plethora of innocent and not-so-innocent practices. He classified ignorance into two main types—error and irrelevance—the latter of which was subdivided into untopicality (data that are off-topic), undecidability, and taboo. Error was yet more complicated, consisting of distortion (including confusion and inaccuracy) and incompleteness (including absence of knowledge or uncertainty, uncertainly further containing vagueness, probability, or ambiguity). Interestingly, lies did not appear in his typology, although we can imagine a number of sites where they would contribute to ignorance, by making questions undecidable, by distorting or denying facts, and by sowing confusion, inaccuracy, and ambiguity.

The study of ignorance still lacked a name until Robert Proctor and Londa Schiebinger coined the term "agnotology" (*a-*, without; *gnosis*, knowledge) in their 2008 edited volume *Agnotology: The Making & Unmaking of Ignorance*. In the introduction to the volume, Proctor opined that ignorance is "more than a void" and often anything but natural or accidental. He proposed three ways to construe ignorance—as a state or a "resource," as a "lost realm" (i.e., that which was known and subsequently forgotten, sometimes by choice), and, most pointedly, as "a deliberately engineered and strategic ploy (or active construct)" (2008: 3). Additionally, ignorance overlaps with and emerges from a myriad of other terms and practices, such as "secrecy, stupidity, apathy, censorship, disinformation, faith, and forgetfulness" (2).

Most of the work in agnotology, including Proctor and Schiebinger's volume, focuses on industry and science, for justifiable reasons. Particular targets for agnotological examination have been tobacco companies and businesses that produce lead-based paint and gasoline, pesticides, and polyvinyl chloride for plastics. David Michaels, in his aptly titled *Doubt is Their Product*, perhaps most bluntly reveals how corporations engage in "manufacturing uncertainty," quoting a tobacco company executive who openly stated, "Doubt is our product since it is the best means of competing with the 'body of fact' that exists in the minds of the general public. It is also the means of establishing a controversy" (2008: x). Other similar investigations bear similar titles, such as *Merchants of Doubt* (Oreskes and Conway 2010) and *Deceit and Denial* (Markowitz and Rosner 2002). That is, it becomes clear that ignorance helps sell products and evade culpability for the negatives of production (e.g., worker health exposure, waste disposal) and use (e.g., consumer health exposure, product failure, accidents, addiction, etc.) of their goods.

Without possessing a word for it, what much of this literature is actually describing is *agnomancy*, the more-or-less (and often much more) intentional creation or "conjuring" of ignorance; agnomancy is one area or topic of agnotology, just as crime is one area or subtopic of criminology (along with policing, prisons, and so forth) but a very sizeable one, if not the preponderance of the subject. Following this analogy with crime and criminology, agnomancy is the commission of acts of ignorance-making (as crime is the commission of law violation), whereas agnotology is the general study of ignorance (as criminology is the general study of crime).

Research on corporations and other bad actors has unveiled an impressive and time-tested battery of tricks and tactics of the agnomancer, what we might rightly call agnomantic practices. The key to agnomancy is erecting obstacles against potentially disruptive information (illustrating that ignorance is not altogether a native or default state)—to flood believers with misinformation and disinformation and to sow confusion, doubt, and suspicion. Primary among these tactics is maligning any source of information that contradicts their claims and imperils their interests. Agnomancers may argue, for instance, that there is no scientific consensus or that the science is incomplete. They may stress that scientists were wrong in the past, so how can we trust them now? They may exaggerate disagreement or inconclusiveness on small or tangential matters while conveniently overlooking the consensus on the main or fundamental matters. At their most corrosive, they may question the quality or the very truth of facts while accusing the bearers of those facts of bias or self-interest. They may, for instance, vilify scientific findings as little more than opinion or majority rule, relegating scientific conclusions to the level of feeling or belief.

One crafty act of modern agnomancers is to sponsor "research" by their own "experts" and publish those results as what has come to be called "alternative facts." Tobacco companies notoriously pursued this line of attack by paying scientists to argue that cigarette smoking was not harmful, indeed may even be beneficial. On complex issues where ordinary citizens cannot distinguish between valid information and propaganda, or on any issue where reasoning is highly motivated and driven by ideological or pecuniary commitments (for example, Holocaust denial, evolution denial, or climate-change denial), these "alternative facts" give the partisans a license to reject information that they dislike and to disbelieve all further information that originates from the same sources. And agnomancers of all stripes comprehend that repeating a claim, including a false claim, over and over confers a kind of legitimacy, consciously or unconsciously exploiting cognitive biases like the confirmation bias (audiences selecting the data that support their pre-existing beliefs) and the basic tendency to remember and believe things that we have heard many times (variously known as the availability cascade, the mere exposure effect, or, most pointedly, the illusory truth effect).

When appropriate to the matter or industry at hand, agnomancers may shift responsibility from the product to the user. This is a common maneuver for "vice" industries, also known as "unhealthy commodity industries," such as alcohol, fast food, and gambling, as well as for the gun lobby. Agnomancers respond to data about the hazards of their fare by insisting that alcoholism or obesity or gambling addiction are complex issues and/or that the problem is not their product but how the consumers (mis/ab)use it. Corporations commonly offer to police themselves and to provide support services for users (alcohol and gambling counseling, for instance); what they resist is labeling (that is, information for the consumer), taxation, and regulation, which might hurt their sales.

Further agnomancy ploys include establishing false equivalencies, for instance insisting that schools or media present "both sides" of "controversies," like evolution, climate change, or the Holocaust. Accomplished agnomancers also understand that strong emotion affects (and impedes) thinking, primarily negative emotions such as anger and fear. Not entirely irrationally, anger toward individuals or groups and their ideas makes people antipathetic to those sources and facts, and fear spawns risk aversion and boundary formation and defense. Ample studies confirm that fear tends to inspire in-group solidarity, obedience to authority, and opposition to change or support for "the way things are." This response is so concrete that asking experimental subjects to imagine that they have superpowers (thereby enhancing their invulnerability to risk and danger) renders them more open to change. Conversely, it is no wonder that agnomancers frequently scream and threaten and scare, agitating their targets to close ranks and minds (Napier, Huang, Vonasch, and Bargh 2018).

There is tactical value in not only keeping others ignorant but in keeping oneself ignorant, or at least erecting a space of plausible ignorance. Linsey McGoey clarifies how pharmaceutical companies among many others practice "strategic ignorance" to shield themselves from liability. An "ignorance alibi" is "any mechanism that obscures one's involvement in causing harm to others, furnishing plausible deniability and making unawareness seem innocent rather than calculated" (2019: 56). Drug manufacturers, for instance, can allege that they did not know the risks or side effects of their products; they can also blame any bad outcomes on consumer abuse (say, in the case of opioids), underlying conditions, or drug interactions (trotting out again the "complexity" argument, that it is impossible to assign causal responsibility to just one variable). Of course, they may be lying about their ignorance, but this ignorance can be real if voluntary: they may rush a drug to market before it has been thoroughly tested, or they may keep themselves or regulators blissfully oblivious by not conducting certain tests or collecting relevant information in the first place or suppressing unfavorable information. Therefore, McGoey contends that, unlike secrecy which "hides," strategic ignorance "creates: constructing plausible rationale… for why problems should not exist, and therefore do not require closer investigation or penalization" (294).

Agnomancy is by no means restricted to industry, although it is especially common and urgent there as great wealth is at stake. Agnomancy is possible and likely wherever power is available and interest is in play, and one of the most likely domains for power-and-interest-driven agnomancy is politics. Indeed, in *The Open Society and Its Enemies* Karl Popper (1945: 150–1) recalls Plato's advice on political honesty:

> It is one of the royal privileges of the sovereign to make full use of lies and deceit: [Plato wrote that] "It is the business of the rulers of the city, if it is anybody's, to tell lies, deceiving both its enemies and its own citizens for the benefit of the city, and no one else must touch this privilege… If the ruler catches anyone else in a lie… then he will punish him for introducing a practice which injures and endangers the city."

And of course Machiavelli counseled the prince to break his word whenever expedient, instructing that "occasionally words must serve to veil the facts. But let this happen in such a way that no one become aware of it; or, if it should be noticed, excuses must be at hand to be produced immediately" (1882: 442).

Much more recently, the eminent political scientist Hannah Arendt (1967) noted that "truth and politics are on rather bad terms with each other, and no one, as far as I know, has ever counted truth among the political virtues. Lies have always been regarded as necessary and justifiable tools not only of the politician's or the demagogue's but also of the statesman's trade." Kings, prime ministers, and presidents have only too often proven this assessment valid. In the twentieth-century United States, Franklin Roosevelt misrepresented and obfuscated the Yalta agreement near the end of World War II, keeping his own vice-president uninformed. John F. Kennedy lied about the details of the Cuban missile crisis settlement (denying that the US also removed weapons pointed at the Soviet Union), and his successor, Lyndon Johnson, lied about the infamous "Gulf of Tonkin" incident to launch the Vietnam war, an act that was condemned as a "mixture of self-deception and deliberate dishonesty" (Alterman 2004: 213). Johnson so damaged his political credibility that he declined to seek re-election, but this did not prevent Richard Nixon from sanctioning illegal activities and then lying about it, leading to his resignation. Learning no lessons about truth in government, Ronald Reagan orchestrated an illegal program to sell weapons to Iran and funnel the proceeds to the "Contras" in Nicaragua, a plot that historian of presidential lies, Eric Alterman, judges "clothed in falsehoods from its inception"; worse, Reagan's CIA director, William Casey, "believed in lying to Congress as a matter of principle and genially referred to its denizens as 'those assholes on the Hill'" (262). Finally, the road to war with Iraq in 2003 was paved with lies; not only did the Bush administration knowingly mislead the public about Iraq's alleged "weapons of mass destruction" but his Department of Justice told the Supreme Court that the government demanded the right "to give out false information… incomplete information and even disinformation whenever it deemed necessary" (296).

Blatant lying is only one maneuver in the political agnomancy playbook; there are many subtler ways to refuse information to the citizenry. One classic method is "classifying" documents to make them secret; another is censorship. But a better technique for suppressing information is never to collect that information at all. Presidents Reagan, Bush II, and Trump crippled agencies like the Census Bureau, the Bureau of Justice Statistics, and the National Center for Health Statistics with budget cuts, understaffing, and unqualified and/or hostile directors. In 2020 Trump commanded that coronavirus data bypass the Centers for Disease Control, meanwhile removing information about climate change from federal websites, dismissing or never convening advisory panels, and muzzling scientists who receive federal grants; on more than a few occasions, industry representatives have been appointed to groups or agencies tasked to oversee those very industries and/or given veto power over reports about their businesses.

Finally, governments are perfecting their so-called "strategic communication," a tool or weapon normally unleashed against foreign adversaries but equally useful "to distort *domestic* or foreign sentiment, most frequently to achieve a strategic and/ or geopolitical outcome" by means of "false news, disinformation, or networks of fake accounts (false amplifiers aimed at manipulating public opinion)" (Weedon, Nuland, and Stamos 2017: 5). That Russia is more advanced in "reflexive control"— deploying knowledge about enemies against them—gives no comfort whatsoever.

Trump's lies and the specious construction of reality

This brief sojourn through the realm of political agnomancy proves that Trump's lies, while extraordinary, were not unprecedented. Trump lied like leaders before (and surely after) him, although not to sneak the country into war or for any single purpose; rather than a surgical strike, his perfidy was a carpet-bombing of the society and the consensus of thought on which it stands.

It is settled that lying—by anyone, not just politicians—is a social practice, but the lying of leaders (governmental, corporate, or other) is a specifically political act, if not what Marlies Glasius terms an *authoritarian practice*. Authoritarian practices are "patterns of action that sabotage accountability to people over whom a political actor exerts control, or their representatives, by means of secrecy, disinformation, and disabling voice" (Glasius 2018: 517). By such means, including but not limited to shameless lying, a leader can interfere with normal democratic processes in two ways: (a) by *disabling questioning*, e.g., avoiding press conferences, refusing interviews, and attacking verbally or otherwise as with police searches, lawsuits, and tax investigations or, in the worst cases, arrest and torture, anyone who does or might dare to raise a question or objection; and (b) by *disabling passing of judgment*, which tends to require more muscular maneuvers like disbanding legislatures, ignoring or co-opting courts, or corrupting or canceling elections.

If we consider the social motivations and effects of Trump's extravagant and reckless lying, we can identify five areas of political and anthropological importance. First, *his guile was and is actually a sign of authenticity to his followers*. As perverse as it may sound to Trump non-supporters, when his lying was acknowledged (and it was not always acknowledged), it was often perceived as a good thing. For followers of a certain ilk, Trump's lies verified his contempt for "political correctness" and proved that he was not an ordinary politician who minces words to avoid controversy. He "says what he means," they cheered. And he would not be gagged by the "reality-based community," who, after all, only conspired with alleged "facts" to obstruct him and his populist agenda.

Oliver Hahl, Minjae Kim, and Ezra Zuckerman Sivan try to make sense of "the authentic appeal of the lying demagogue." They reason that when a constituency has lost faith in the political system as hopelessly corrupt and/or deaf to their interests, "a lying demagogue can appear as a distinctively *authentic champion* of its interests"; he may be appreciated for "bravely speaking a deep and otherwise suppressed truth," one that is more true or at least more relevant than ordinary mainstream truth (2018: 3). Of course, the liar must withstand the fury of the establishment that denounces his lies, but "his willingness to antagonize the establishment by making himself *persona non grata*" is part of the appeal; it "lends credibility to his claim to be an authentic champion for those who feel disenfranchised by that establishment" by proving that he is not one of *them* but one of *us* (8). Worse for his detractors, every attack on his pretenses reinforces the confidence among his base that the system is out to get him and cannot be trusted, making it appear that his critics are the liars and not him.

Just as Trump's lying was a performance of faithfulness to his people (who are allegedly *the* people), couched in the vernacular and vulgarity of the common folk, so his people's assent to those lies was a performance of faithfulness to him. In a study whose title sums up the situation—"They Might Be a Liar But They're My Liar"—Briony Swire-Thompson et al. describe how Trump supporters presented with facts that debunk Trump's misinformation tended to continue to trust his lies, but even if they surrendered their belief in the misinformation, they did "not change their voting preferences nor feelings towards him" (2020: 72). It is as if they said to themselves, "Yes, he was wrong/lying, but he is still my guy." Equally distressing, in another study (Swire et al. 2017) the same team finds that a week after the test-subjects were shown facts that disconfirmed Trump's lies, they had begun to "re-believe" him and to forget the true facts of the matter. Jennifer Hochschild and Katherine Levine Einstein pass along a comment by a Tea Party member who said it succinctly when asked about Trump's fallacious insistence that Barack Obama was born outside the United States:

> The birther issue definitely isn't part of our core values, but what Donald Trump is doing is questioning things and saying, "Why do we have to just accept everything?"… To hold the birther view is to affiliate oneself with an attitude, not a truth claim… Your average Trump supporter may think that the proper attitude to have toward America's politicians is contempt.
> (2015–16: 608–9)

Second and obviously related to the first, *Trump's lies were a demonstration of power*. The fabrications of a leader like Trump make him appear not only authentic to certain audiences but also dominant. As Pfiffner posits, "Telling lies and expecting others to believe or at least to accept false claims can also be an assertion of power" (2019: 11) They make him look like a tough guy, someone who will not concede to anyone, who will not be deterred by experts, elites, or any denizens of the reality-based community. And every time he survived an onslaught from the fact-checkers, he illustrated once again his strength and the strength of his convictions. He showed, in a word, that he could lie and get away with it, which licensed him to lie again. He was, as they said of Reagan, Teflon.

Various observers have noted that today's populist figures, almost all of them male (with the exception of France's Marine Le Pen), typically exude machismo, which is part of what Miguel Diaz-Barriga and Margaret Dorsey dub the "dictator aesthetic" (2017: e84). Lying is just one element of this role, which also features "loud, gaudy, imposing, and golden" speech and actions like Trump's "beautiful" border wall. Along with sexism, the dictator aesthetic is marked by "cruelty, menace, violence and arbitrariness," including arbitrariness with the facts, all of which "is meant to impress and express absolute power."

Tellingly, Masha Gessen, the author of several books on Vladimir Putin and Russia, christens this constellation of behaviors the "Putin paradigm." "Both Trump and Putin," Gessen (2016) finds, "use language primarily to communicate not facts or opinions but power: it's not what the words mean that matters but who says them and when. This makes it impossible to negotiate with them and very difficult for journalists to cover them." In a prophetic essay written before Trump's inauguration, Gessen notes Trump's "admiration" for strong men like Putin, which has only been repeated in his bromance with Kim Jong Un and his praise for Jair Bolsonaro and Rodrigo Duterte. As for truth, in a paraphrase of Marshall McLuhan, Gessen concludes, "Lying is the message. It's not just that both Putin and Trump lie, it is that they lie in the same way and for the same purpose: blatantly, to assert power over truth itself." In addition to a direct display of power, inveterate lying has an indirect power-effect: it keeps opponents off-balance and distracted by the project of countering lies, always in reactive mode while Trump moves on to the next fiction.

More than demonstrating power, such lying also facilitates power. Like the tobacco executives who manufacture doubt, Trump's lies generated a dense fog of ignorance and unreality, a region of freedom of action and thought for him and his followers—free from facts that contradict their beliefs and impede their action, filled with falsities that sustain their beliefs and enable their action. Such conjured ignorance is highly liberating and empowering, rendering its followers nearly immune to counterargument. For instance, no matter how many court challenges and vote recounts failed, they remained determined to "stop the steal."

Third, the pervasiveness—but, more importantly, *the success*—of Trump's cozenage *increased the likelihood of embedding the habit of lying and distortion in social and political discourse.* Trump may have thought he was clever, wielding strategic communication so effectively against his own populace, but he showed utter disregard for the lasting damage that such cavalier disregard for truth did and will have on America. Adam Hodges argues that Trump's lies "serve to prop up the problematic worldview he peddles to his base," a worldview where "factual fidelity is superseded by ideological fidelity to one or more axioms that undergird the system of beliefs of Trumpism" (2018: e189–90). At a bare minimum, shielding their worldview from disconfirmation freed Trump's minions to slumber in their (anti-)epistemological daydream. Worse yet, it invited them to join him in ignoring and disparaging reality—and in ignoring and disparaging the "reality-based community" of journalists, scientists, and anyone else who disagreed—which short-circuited any possibility of a civil and reasoned debate and of potentially changing supporters' attitudes (so much for Habermas' model of the public square as a site of rational discourse).

And, of course, Trump was far from alone in perpetrating this attack on and delegitimation of opponents and of civil discourse itself. The right-wing media mendacity machine has pumped falsehoods and delusions into the body social for years, softening it for a character like Trump; according to a 2015 analysis, fully 60 percent of the "information" featured on Fox News was false, from mostly false (21 percent) to totally false (31 percent) to blatantly false (9 percent) (Sharockman 2015). By comparison, CNN reporting was 80 percent half-, mostly- or completely-true, a finding that Fox and Trump fans no doubt decried as another sign of elite/liberal bias and fakery. But thanks to Fox News and the likes of Rush Limbaugh and Alex Jones—all sources and echo chambers for Trump's baloney—the national information "ecosystem is so polluted" (Wardle 2017) that we do not know how, or if, we can clean it again. Such a polluted information ecosystem has the deleterious effect for society but advantageous effect for Trump of scrambling public judgment and discernment. After saturation with lies, denials, hoaxes, and other agnomancy practices, people are unable to distinguish what is true or false and whom to trust. On such unstable ground, trust itself may seem impossible or unwise.

But the Trump effect extends beyond Trump himself. He also attracted and promoted extremists and absurdists. Steve Bannon was one of the early fringe figures on the Trump team. Then there was Dr. Stella Immanuel, praised by Trump for advancing his discredited promotion of hydroxychloroquine as a "cure" for COVID-19 while dismissing the use of masks (since there is a cure!). This same physician attributed gynecological conditions to sex with demons ("demon semen"), alleged that extraterrestrial DNA is used in mainstream medical treatments and that scientists are devising a vaccine to prevent religion, and repeated the bizarre conspiracy that the government is run by reptilians.

Worst of all, Trump's example inspires political imitators. The complicity of formerly relatively sensible figures like Lindsey Graham is incomprehensible enough, but others have more dishonorably hopped the unreality train. One truly reprehensible example was Cynthia Brehm, a Texas county Republican party chairperson, who actually posted on Facebook that the death of George Floyd at the hands of the police, which launched weeks of street protests, was a "staged event." Previously, Republicans and conservatives questioned the reality of school shootings, as in Newtown, Connecticut (Alex Jones called the Sandy Hook shooting "synthetic, completely fake with actors") and then dismissed the coronavirus as a hoax and a political stunt to subvert Trump, despite the rising numbers of infections, hospitalizations, and deaths. Elsewhere, Republican governor of West Virginia Jim Justice, another billionaire businessman with no political experience, forced the resignation of long-time state health officer, Dr. Cathy Slemp, on the grounds that she was over-reporting COVID-19 cases and impeding his efforts to accelerate the reopening of the state. Meanwhile, in late 2019, a Texas Republican party plot was uncovered to purchase domain names similar to those of their Democratic rivals and hijack traffic to decoy websites stocked with false and inflammatory (dis)information.

Given this pattern, and his unwavering support among the lunatic fringe of the alt-right and QAnon, we can expect to see more Trump-like politicians and tactics in his wake. In fact, the "QAnon candidates" are already here, marching in the footsteps of Trump: Angela Stanton-King (congressional candidate, Georgia) tweeted about "global elite pedophiles" and a supposed child-trafficking ring operated by an online furniture store (shades of Pizzagate); Lauren Boebert (congressional candidate, Colorado) praised QAnon, saying, "Everything I've heard of Q—I hope this is real"; Jo Rae Perkins (senatorial candidate, Oregon) trumpeted, "I stand with Q and the team" and swore the QAnon "digital soldier oath"; and Marjorie Taylor Greene (congressional candidate, Georgia) lauded the "once-in-a-lifetime opportunity to take this global cabal of Satan-worshipping pedophiles out" (Rosenberg and Steinhauer 2020). And lest we laugh these irrational pretenders away, two of them—Boebert and Taylor Greene—won their races and serve in the post-Trump Congress.

Fourth and more pernicious than the mere muddying of political discourse, *Trump's lies contributed to, and ostensibly aimed at, the erosion of democratic norms and institutions.* Every executive chafes against the limitations of institutions and constitutions, none more so than the populist, demagogue, or authoritarian. Many circumvent the strictures of checks-and-balances, legislative oversight, judicial review, and popular approval through various acts of agnomancy, including, as we have seen, secrecy, information suppression, and outright deceit. A democracy can perhaps operate with small doses of dishonesty, but a steady diet of ignorance and denial is toxic; citizens and government agencies alike cannot make informed choices if they are uninformed, misinformed, disinformed. But the leader who aspires, consciously or instinctively, to Carl Schmitt's image of the sovereign seeks to monopolize the act of decision through manipulation of the exception. Here Schmitt's political theology becomes immediately relevant, since laws, traditions, institutions, and constitutions are explicitly designed to apply to "normal" circumstances and to attempt to normalize, if not depoliticize those circumstances (i.e., there is no "decision" to make; "procedure" will suffice). Chipping away at normality, including and especially factuality, is a way of achieving an ironic permanent state of exception, in which the leader may and must act, unfettered by the truth.

No assault on institutions was more egregious and potentially more dangerous than Trump's denigration of the 2020 election. It illustrated how a big lie—that the Democrats are trying to steal the election, that there is a conspiracy against him—depends on many small lies, of voter fraud and illegal ballots and counting irregularities, ad infinitum. The effect, if not the purpose—other than retaining power at all costs—of such behavior was to so discredit the election that its outcome, or at least *the legitimacy of the outcome*, would forever be in doubt; simultaneously, the opposition was so maligned (*they* are the enemies of democracy, not *us*) that *an armed assault on the Capitol during vote-counting seemed justified to them*. Trump supporter Brenden Dilley was unusually forthcoming about the goal of his lies: he proudly admitted that "he doesn't care about the truth of the things he says and that he has no problem 'making shit up'"; "I don't give a fuck about being factual… I make shit up all the time." And why would anyone be so indifferent to the truth of his statements? Because he is not in the business of informing but of warring: "My objective is to destroy Democrats, OK? To destroy liberals, liberalism as an idea, Democrats, and anything that opposes President Trump" (Mantyla 2020). Such are the wages of agnomancy.

Fifth and finally, and most germane to anthropology and other social sciences, *Trump's lies were an exercise in the control and construction of reality*. For the leader of a certain breed, it simply does not matter what is true. Indeed, we would do well to dispel the notion that politics is about truth in any substantial way. The truth, besides being restrictive (facts are tyrannical, after all), is largely about the past, or rather, about what already is. Politics, only most overtly in Schmitt's moment of exception and decision, is about the future, about acting to change and construct society, including laws, institutions, and constitutions. For this purpose, a good myth, a good ritual, or frankly a good lie is just as productive as the truth, if not more so. As Roland Boer puts it in his study of political myth and biblical themes, following the philosopher Alain Badiou, the grammar of politics is "the future perfect": by "forcing a truth" through political discourse and decision-making, what we say today—even if it is a lie—"will have been true" (2009: 17).

Another Republican operative, sometimes purported to be Karl Rove, revealed as much when he told Ron Suskind (2004) of *The New York Times Magazine*—as if speaking directly to anthropologists—that the United States is "an empire now, and when we act, we create our own reality. And while you're studying that reality… we'll act again, creating other new realities, which you can study too." This should come as no surprise to us, familiar since the days of Berger and Luckmann with the social construction of reality. Who would naively assume that truth is the only, or best, tool in the constructor's kit? Subsequently deconstructionists, postmodernists, postcolonialists, and critical theorists all taught that reality is not stable but highly fluid and malleable. We can be reasonably sure that Trump never read Derrida (or, by some accounts, hardly anything else), but the plasticity of reality, of what counts as a "fact" and as "reality" at all is apparent now, especially to those with authoritarian or megalomaniac intuitions. Accordingly, speaking again of the Putin paradigm but completely applicable in Trump's America, the lying leader is "able to say what he wants, when he wants, regardless of the facts. He is the president of his country and *king of reality*" (Gessen 2016, emphasis added).

Reality is constructed by all members of society but most thoroughly by those with the power *and the will* to impose their impression on the world. Here we pass from Berger and Luckmann and even from Schmitt to Schopenhauer, who taught that the world ultimately is a representation or idea of will, and the more that will is willing to foster and foist a (non)reality on it, and on us, the more it takes the shape that the person, the executive, the sovereign would give it. Like a mythical trickster, Trump joyously broke one truth or reality to make another. This is why Ruth Marcus (2017) opines that Trump was not a post-truth president but a *pre-truth* one, in the sense that truth did not exist until he spoke it into existence; it was not that Trump denied reality, "it is that he bends it to his will. In this Trump tower of dreams, if he tweets it, the truth—or some asserted version thereof—will come." That leaves us anthropologists to study his lie-truths before the next liar/truth-teller emerges.

References

Alterman, Eric. 2004. *When Presidents Lie: A History of Official Deception and its Consequences*. New York and London: Viking.

Arendt, Hannah. 1967. "Politics and Truth." https://idanlandau.files.wordpress.com/2014/12/arendt-truth-and-politics.pdf. Originally published in *The New Yorker*, 25 February, accessed June 23, 2020.

Austin, J. L. 1962. *How to Do Things with Words*. London and New York: Oxford University Press.

Barbour, Charles. 2012. "The Maker of Lies: Simmel, Mendacity and the Economy of Faith." *Theory, Culture & Society* 29 (7/8): 218–36.

Boer, Roland. 2009. *Political Myth: On the Use and Abuse of Biblical Themes*. Durham, NC: Duke University Press.

Bok, Sissela. 1979. *Lying: Moral Choices in Public and Private Life*. New York: Vintage.

Carey, Matthew. 2017. *Mistrust: An Ethnographic Theory*. Chicago, IL: HAU Books.

Chagnon, Napoleon. 1992. *The Yanomamö*, 4th ed. Fort Worth, TX: Harcourt Brace College Publishers.

Dale, Daniel. 2020. "Fact Check: Trump Delivers the Most Dishonest Speech of his Presidency as Biden Closes in on Victory." https://www.cnn.com/2020/11/05/politics/fact-check-trump-speech-thursday-election-rigged-stolen/index.html, accessed November 9, 2020.

Diaz-Barriga, Miguel, and Margaret Dorsey. 2017. "Trump's Wall and the Dictator Aesthetic." *Anthropology News* 58 (4): e83–6.

Fainzang, Sylvie. 2015. *An Anthropology of Lying: Information in the Doctor–Patient Relationship*. Surrey, UK: Ashgate.

Gessen, Masha. 2016. "The Putin Paradigm." https://www.nybooks.com/daily/2016/12/13/putin-paradigm-how-trump-will-rule, accessed November 11, 2020.

Glasius, Marlies. 2018. "What Authoritarianism Is… and Is Not: A Practice Perspective." *International Affairs* 94 (3): 515–33.

Hahl, Oliver, Minjae Kim, and Ezra W. Zuckerman Sivan. 2018. "The Authentic Appeal of the Lying Demagogue: Proclaiming the Deeper Truth about Political Illegitimacy." *American Sociological Review* 83 (1): 1–33.

Hochschild, Jennifer, and Katherine Levine Einstein. 2015–16. "Do Facts Matter? Information and Misinformation in American Politics." *Political Science Quarterly* 130 (4): 585–624.

Hodges, Adam. 2018. "How Trump's Lying Affirms a Worldview." *Anthropology News* 59 (1): e189–92.

Kessler, Glenn, Salvador Rizzo, and Meg Kelly. 2020. "President Trump Made 18,000 False or Misleading Claims in 1,170 Days." https://www.washingtonpost.com/politics/2020/04/14/president-trump-made-18000-false-or-misleading-claims-1170-days, accessed November 9, 2020.

Machiavelli, Niccolo. 1882. *The Historical, Political, and Diplomatic Writings of Niccolo Machiavelli*, vol. 4. Boston, MA: J. R. Osgood and Company.

Mantyla, Kyle. 2020. "Brenden Dilley Doesn't 'Give a F★ck About Being Factual'." https://www.rightwingwatch.org/post/brenden-dilley-doesnt-give-a-fck-about-being-factual, accessed November 11, 2020.

Marcus, Ruth. 2017. "Forget the Post-Truth presidency. Welcome to the Pre-Truth Presidency." https://www.washingtonpost.com/opinions/welcome-to-the-pre-truth-presidency/2017/03/23/b35856ca-1007-11e7-9b0d-d27c98455440_story.html, accessed November 11, 2020.

Markowitz, Gerald and David Rosner. 2002. *Deceit and Denial: The Deadly Politics of Industrial Pollution*. Berkeley, CA: University of California Press.

McGoey, Linsey. 2019. *The Unknowers: How Strategic Ignorance Rules the World*. London: Zed Books.

McGranahan, Carole. 2017. "An Anthropology of Lying: Trump and the Political Sociality of Moral Outrage." *American Ethnologist* 44 (2): 243–8.

Meibauer, Jörg. 2018. "The Linguistic of Lying." *Annual Review of Linguistics* 4: 357–75.

Metcalf, Peter. 2002. *They Lie, We Lie: Getting on with Anthropology*. London and New York: Routledge.

Michaels, David. 2008. *Doubt is Their Product: How Industry's Assault on Science Threatens Your Health*. New York: Oxford University Press.

Nachman, Steven R. 1984. "Lies My Informants Told Me." *Journal of Anthropological Research* 40 (4): 536–55.

Napier, Jaime L., Julie Huang, Andrew J. Vonasch, and John A. Bargh. 2018. "Superheroes for Change: Physical Safety Promotes Socially (but not Economically) Progressive Attitudes among Conservatives." *European Journal of Social Psychology* 48 (2): 187–95.

Oreskes, Naomi, and Erik M. Conway. 2010. *Merchants of Doubt: How a Handful of Scientists Obscured the Truth on Issues from Tobacco Smoke to Global Warming*. New York: Bloomsbury.

Pfiffner, James P. 2019. "The Lies of Donald Trump: A Taxonomy." In Charles M. Lamb and Jacob R. Neiheisel, eds. *Presidential Leadership and the Trump Presidency: Executive Power and Democratic Governance*. Cham, Switzerland: Palgrave Macmillan, 17–40.

Popper, Karl R. 1945. *The Open Society and Its Enemies, Volume 1 The Age of Plato*. New York and Evanston, IL: Harper Torchbooks.

Proctor, Robert N. 2008. "Agnotology: A Missing Term to Describe the Cultural Production of Ignorance (and Its Study)." In Robert N. Proctor and Londa Schiebinger, eds. *Agnotology: The Making & Unmaking of Ignorance*. Stanford, CA: Stanford University Press, 1–33.

Rosenberg, Matthew, and Jennifer Steinhauer. 2020. "The QAnon Candidates Are Here. Trump Has Paved Their Way." https://www.nytimes.com/2020/07/14/us/politics/qanon-politicians-candidates.html, accessed November 11, 2020.

Rösing, Ina. 1999. "Lies and Amnesia in Anthropological Research: Recycling the Waste." *Anthropology of Consciousness* 10 (2): 13–34.

Sharockman, Aaron. 2015. "MSNBC, Fox, CNN Move the Needle On Our Truth-o-meter Scorecards." https://www.politifact.com/article/2015/jan/27/msnbc-fox-cnn-move-needle-our-truth-o-meter-scorec, accessed November 11, 2020.

Simmel, Georg. 1906. "The Sociology of Secrecy and of Secret Societies." *The American Journal of Sociology* 11 (4): 441–98.

Smithson, Michael. *Ignorance and Uncertainty: Emerging Paradigms*. New York: Springer-Verlag, 1989.

Suskind, Ron. 2004. "Faith, Certainty and the Presidency of George W. Bush." *The New York Times Magazine*, 17 October.

Swire, Briony, Adam J. Berinsky, Stephan Lewandowsky, and Ullrich K. H. Ecker. 2017. "Processing Political Misinformation: Comprehending the Trump Phenomenon." *Royal Society Open Science* 4: 1–21.

Swire-Thompson, Briony, Ullrich K. H. Ecker, Stephan Lewandowsky, and Adam J. Berkinsky. 2020. "They Might Be a Liar But They're My Liar: Source Evaluation and the Prevalence of Misinformation." *Political Psychology* 41 (1): 21–34.

Wardle, Claire. 2017. "Fake News: It's Complicated." https://medium.com/1st-draft/fake-news-its-complicated-d0f773766c79, accessed November 11, 2020.

Weedon, Jen, William Nuland, and Alex Stamos. 2017. "Information Operations and Facebook." https://fbnewsroomus.files.wordpress.com/2017/04/facebook-and-information-operations-v1.pdf, accessed November 10, 2020.

9
ORANGE CANDLES AND SHRIVELED CHEETOS

Symbolic representations of Trump in the anti-Trump witchcraft movement

Julia Coombs Fine

Introduction: Symbolic representations of Trump within and outside the #MagicResistance movement

Roughly a year after the election of Donald Trump, the forty-fifth president of the United States, I attended an exhibit at an art gallery in downtown Santa Barbara. I remember only one of the pieces: a large, gold spray-painted swastika surrounded by a border of bright orange Cheetos. Even without reading the accompanying explanation, I immediately recognized it as a critique of the president.

The golden swastika and Cheetos, as I interpreted them, symbolically alluded to Trump's connections to the alt-right (see, for instance, Love 2017: 263–264) and his extravagant (if at times fraudulent) displays of wealth (Regilme 2019: 13, 29; Johnston 2017: 115) in a time of rising income inequality in the United States (Hoffman, Lee, & Lemieux 2020). As one of the most white supremacist (McHendry 2018: 5), misogynistic (Harp 2018: 189–207), and corrupt (Buchanan & Yourish 2019) presidents in recent memory—yet as the object of cult-like devotion among his supporters (Hassan 2020: xvii–xviii)—Trump has inspired an outpouring of derisive nicknames and symbolic representations. Political cartoons, protest art, and online discourses often represent him as, among other things, a toddler or a deranged king. For instance, in an article in Salon.com, Blotcky, Norrholm and Scaramucci (2020) write, "Just like a *screaming and defiant young child*, Trump needs to be put in timeout—indefinitely. [...] Frankly, the media must stop normalizing his behavior, must stop trying to fit an ordered framework around his mentally disordered mind, and must stop using charming, storytelling descriptions such as '*Mad King*'" [emphasis added]. Satirical portrayals often imitate Trump's idiosyncratic speech style, including his gestures (Hall, Goldstein, & Ingram 2016) and trademark phrases such as "Believe me" (Fea 2018: 12–13), *yuge* ([juʤ]; a variant of *huge* [hjuʤ]—e.g., Trudeau 2016), and "Stand back and stand by" (an

DOI: 10.4324/9781003152743-11

instruction to the white nationalist group the Proud Boys in response to a debate question asking him to disavow white supremacy; see Holden 2020: 148). In everyday conversation and online discourse, too, I have witnessed many people avoiding Trump's name in favor of other terms, such as *forty-five, Drumpf* (the Trump family's ancestral last name, popularized by comedian John Oliver via the hashtag #makedonalddrumpfagain; see Ulrich 2019: 314), *tRump*, and *SCROTUS* (see Graefer, Kilby, & Bore 2019: 183).

While symbolic representations of Trump abound in many progressive contexts, they are especially apparent in the #MagicResistance movement. Stemming from author Michael Hughes' viral 2016 ritual "A Spell to Bind Donald Trump and All Those Who Abet Him," the #MagicResistance movement (also including the #BindTrump hashtag) consists of self-identified witches and secular witchcraft practitioners (henceforth referred to as "practitioners") who perform monthly rituals to symbolically bind Trump in order to prevent him from doing harm (Asprem 2020; Magliocco 2020). The movement takes place across a variety of social media platforms, including Twitter, Facebook, and TikTok, and has received substantial media attention (see, for instance, Burton's 2017 article in *Vox*, Ellis' 2019 article in *Wired*, and Jackson's 2020 article in *VICE*). Both humorous and serious (Hughes, quoted in Fine 2019: 80), "carnivalesque" (Bakhtin 1984) and ritualesque (Santino 2011), the #MagicResistance movement also promotes secular forms of political action, such as signing petitions, calling officials, and voting.

Symbolic representations of Trump permeate both online discourse and ritual practice in the #MagicResistance movement. In online discourse, practitioners refer to Trump using nicknames, and they share visual representations of Trump such as cartoons, art, and memes. In ritual practice, practitioners represent Trump using objects suggested in Hughes' binding spell (including photos of Trump, orange candle stubs, baby carrots, fool's gold, and Tower Tarot cards), but also using a range of other symbols that vary according to individual preference (including, among other things, Cheetos). Some practitioners share photographs and descriptions of their ritual altars online, furthering the dialogic relationship between ritual practice and online discourse, and thus between material and linguistic symbolic representations of Trump.

In this chapter, I examine the sociocultural significance of symbolic representations of Trump in the #MagicResistance movement. Combining social media analysis with an online survey of 11 practitioners, I consider practitioners' motivations for using visual, material, and linguistic symbols to represent Trump and their reasons for choosing specific symbolic representations over others—that is, what do they seek to critique, change, or avoid through the use of these symbols? I further consider relationships between linguistic and visual/material representations of Trump, showing how these representations influence and elaborate each other within and across media texts. Finally, I analyze how symbolic representations of Trump in anti-Trump witchcraft partially overlap with, yet are in some ways distinct from, representations of Trump in other progressive movements.

"Voldemort politics": Political symbols in spiritual practice

In an article in *Dissent*, historian Timothy Shenk refers to the avoidance of Trump's name as "Voldemort politics" (Shenk 2019: 4). He recounts how a "finance bro" told him, "I don't even say his name," adding, "Not that we would need to. He's Donald J. Drumpf, Adolf Twitler, Covfefe in Chief, and whatever else the #Resistance has come up with to avoid directly referring to its own personal Voldemort." (The epithet "Adolf Twitler" refers to Trump's alt-right and dictatorial bent and his extensive use of Twitter; "Covfefe in Chief" refers to the notorious typographical error in Trump's 2017 tweet, *Despite the constant negative press covfefe*—see Rippeon 2020: 57–59). Voldemort is a fantasy villain in J. K. Rowling's *Harry Potter* series, whose name other characters avoid saying out of fear. Shenk (2019: 4) attributes the avoidance of Trump's name to disgust rather than fear, however, linking this practice to people who (like his "finance bro") financially benefit under the Trump administration: "It's an odd thing, how the people who most aggressively perform their personal disgust with Trump—'*I don't even say his name*'—also seem to be the ones most likely to have received a hefty tax cut. But if the system was already working for you, returning to normalcy must be an appealing prospect. Just remove the Trump-sized tumor from the body politic, and the patient will be healthy again." Shenk concludes, "The real debate should be over whether there's a cure for a disease that's infected the entire political establishment. I think the answer is yes, but only if we acknowledge the scope of the challenge. If that reckoning does not take place, then President Cheeto—sorry, I mean Donald Trump—will be the least of our problems."

The nicknames Shenk includes (*Donald J. Drumpf*, *Adolf Twitler*, *Covfefe in Chief*, and *President Cheeto*) are only a small subset of the many that have been coined to refer to Trump. Many, like *President Cheeto*, focus on Trump's orange skin tone: examples include *Agent Orange* (a play on the name for an herbicide that critiques Trump's orange skin tone; used by rapper Busta Rhymes—see Chen 2017), *Cheeto Jesus* and *Cheeto Christ* (see Harvey 2019), and *Orange Julius* (a play on a drink of the same name and "Julius Caesar"; see Lopez 2020). Other nicknames and symbolic representations discussed by Graefer, Kilby and Bore (2019) portray Trump as impotent (for instance, by representing him as having "tiny hands"; 176–177) or associate him with excrement to symbolize his untruthfulness (for instance, by representing his mouth as an anus with feces spewing out of it—also a reference to his comments about "shithole countries"; 176–177). Trump is, of course, not the only US president to be the subject of unflattering nicknames: according to Gladkova (2002), others include "Teddy the Meddler" for Roosevelt (5), "Tricky Dicky" for Nixon (5), and "His Fraudulency" for Hayes (8). However, nicknames for Trump seem to be especially numerous and vitriolic.

Nicknames and other symbolic representations of Trump within the #MagicResistance movement may be considered as a subtype of these broader practices of political satire—and indeed, as I will show, there is significant overlap between symbolic representations of Trump within #MagicResistance and elsewhere. Yet symbolic representations of Trump within the #MagicResistance movement are multivalent: in addition to their parodic function, they can also be considered as forms of spiritual practice. This spiritual significance is perhaps most obvious in the case of the material symbols used to represent Trump in witchcraft rituals, such as orange candle stubs and photographs of Trump. By altering these objects during rituals (e.g., by burning them, sticking pins in them, or binding them with string), practitioners aim to diminish or bind Trump's power. These alterations are forms of sympathetic magic (Frazer 1983: 215–220), a type of spiritual practice in which a practitioner seeks to influence a person or entity by manipulating a representation of it.

In view of the interrelatedness of material, visual, and linguistic symbols for Trump in the #MagicResistance movement (which I will demonstrate), linguistic representations of Trump might also be expected to have spiritual as well as political significance. The survey data analyzed in this chapter demonstrate that, at least for some practitioners, their use of nicknames and their avoidance of Trump's real name are indeed motivated by beliefs about the spiritual power of names. From this perspective, #MagicResistance practitioners' nicknaming and name avoidance practices can be understood as similar to other spiritually-motivated practices of name avoidance, a kind of linguistic taboo found in many cultural contexts. For instance, Stasch (2011: 104) describes how Korowai speakers avoid saying the names of priests and priestesses before feasts in order to avoid problems that would disrupt food production; Wojtylak (2015) describes how Witoto hunters avoid saying animals' names when hunting in order to avoid alerting the animals' spirits; and Fomin (2020: 56–58) describes how Irish fishermen avoid saying the names of red-colored animals while fishing due to beliefs about red being unlucky. More so than these linguistic avoidance practices, #MagicResistance practitioners' avoidance of Trump's name is entwined with an affective stance of disgust and a refusal to affirm him as a political leader. Nevertheless, these practices of political nicknaming and name avoidance share a perception of names as powerful and potentially influential. Like magical activism more generally, #MagicResistance practitioners' symbolic representations of Trump carry both political, spiritual, and affective significance, highlighting the simultaneously communicative and experiential nature of symbolic expression.

Methods

To examine symbolic representations of Trump in the #MagicResistance movement, I conducted a media analysis of posts on the #BindTrump and #MagicResistance Instagram and Twitter hashtags. Although this analysis is grounded in my previous participant observation of the Facebook groups *Bind Trump, Witches Against White Supremacy*, and *The Witches Against Trump (TWAT)* (Fine 2019: 72), I chose to focus primarily on Instagram and Twitter for several reasons. First, some of these Facebook groups adopted a policy banning surveys, suggesting that my presence as a researcher might be intrusive. The Instagram and Twitter hashtags, in contrast, are visible to the public, partially allaying these concerns of intrusiveness. Secondly, the image-focused format of Instagram lends itself to identification and analysis of visual and material symbols more readily than the format of Facebook and other platforms.

Thirdly, I concentrated on Instagram in particular because it was possible to direct message (DM) posters in order to request image use permission and ask questions about the significance of symbols. Twitter formerly also offered this option but now only allows comments on Tweets unless the poster allows otherwise (or unless the poster follows the person who sends the direct message).

To inform my analysis of the Instagram and Twitter media examined here, I also conducted an online open-response survey, which I publicized through my existing contacts in the #MagicResistance movement and by posting on groups that allowed surveys. In the survey, I asked about respondents' engagement in the #MagicResistance movement, their use of material symbols and nicknames for Trump, and their reasons for using these symbols and nicknames. I also asked optional questions to determine demographic information about the survey respondents, including gender, ethnoracial identity, and affiliation with spiritual traditions. Of the eleven respondents, ten chose to disclose their gender. Seven of these ten respondents identified as female, two identified as non-binary, and one identified as male. Eight respondents chose to disclose their race; seven of these respondents described themselves as "White" or "Caucasian" (with one respondent also noting "1/4 Semitic heritage"), and one self-described as an "Eastern European mutt."

Of the ten practitioners who chose to disclose an affiliation with a particular spiritual tradition, four used the term "Wiccan," replying "solitary wiccan," "Im a practicer of Wicca, though I unlike some others see that binding does not harm but instead helps and therefore use it in my craft," "For the bind I work in a very Wiccan fashion, In my own practice I am a ceremonial magician with a pantheist belief system," and "A blend of pagan wiccan, not dark magick." In addition to this last respondent, who used both "pagan" and "wiccan" to describe their spiritual tradition, two other respondents also used the term "Pagan," replying, "Earth Based, Pagan" and "Grey Neo-Pagan for 13 years. Specialize in astral projection, energy work, and parapsychology." Two respondents described themselves as atheistic or non-religious, replying, "Atheist who finds the ritual, symbolism, and framework of traditional religions occasionally meditative" and "I'm not religious. I've always been weird. Manifesting intent is beyond religious beliefs." Of the remaining two respondents, one replied "traditional and family gift," and the other replied, "Desperate when so shocked Trump got COVID. Otherwise nonexistent." The sample as a whole is therefore predominantly white, female, and Wiccan or Pagan. While not necessarily representative of the #MagicResistance movement as a whole, this sample is demographically fairly similar to the interviewees who participated in my 2019 study (Fine 2019: 72–73).

Material symbols used to represent Trump in #MagicResistance rituals

Michael Hughes' (2017) ritual, "A Spell to Bind Donald Trump and All Those Who Abet Him," is the inspiration for many symbolic representations of Trump in the #MagicResistance movement and is itself rich in material and linguistic symbolism. The spell calls for three representations of Trump: an "unflattering photo of Trump (small)," a "Tower tarot card (from any deck)," and a "tiny stub of an orange candle," which the practitioner is instructed to inscribe with Trump's full name using a pin or nail. The spell further lists two more representations of Trump as optional ingredients: a piece of fool's gold and a baby carrot (Gault 2017, writing for *Defiant*, alternatively proposes "a shriveled Cheeto, preferably the smallest one in the bag"). Also included are a white candle (to represent the element of fire), a bowl of water (to represent the element of water), a bowl of salt (to represent the element of earth), and a feather (to represent the element of air).

Over the course of the spell, the practitioner is instructed to perform actions to change the position or material state of each symbol representing Trump. The practitioner is instructed to prepare the Tower card by standing it up vertically, then turn it upside down; then light the orange candle stub, use it to burn the photo of Trump, and snuff it out. Each of these symbolic actions is synchronized with the spoken ritual, the material symbolism reinforcing the meaning of the words. As the practitioner lights the orange candle stub inscribed with Trump's name, they are told to say, "I call upon you/To bind/Donald J. Trump/So that his malignant works may fail utterly." As they ask elemental, heavenly, and demonic spirits to "Strike down their towers of vanity," they are instructed to turn the Tower Tarot card upside down. At the culmination of the spell, when the practitioners ask the spirits to "Bind them in chains/Bind their tongues/Bind their works/Bind their wickedness," they are instructed to light the photo of Trump on fire, burn it, then blow out the orange candle, "visualizing Trump blowing apart into dust or ash." Originally, the spell instructed practitioners to end with three repetitions of the phrase "So mote it be," but this has been eclipsed in favor of what Hughes terms "The Use-His-Pet-Phrase-Against-Him Variant"—"You're fired!" Hughes notes, "This should be particularly beautiful as the flames consume his image," emphasizing the play on words between the verb *fire* (to dismiss from one's employ) and the material fire consuming the photograph. After the ritual, practitioners are further instructed to bury the orange candle stub at a crossroads, or to discard it in running water. In a variation proposed by a rootworker (see Mathews 1987), which Hughes terms the "Traditional Binding Variant," the practitioner ties Trump's photo to the orange candle stub using black thread. Another variation suggests substituting a baby carrot in place of the orange candle stub.

#MagicResistance practitioners generally include at least some elements suggested in Hughes' spell but recombine them in novel and varied ways. The following images of ritual altars uploaded to Instagram and Twitter under the hashtags #MagicResistance and #BindTrump illustrate this variation (Figures 9.1, 9.2, and 9.3). In Figure 9.1, the altar contains the suggested orange candle stub, the small, unflattering photo of Trump, the feather, and the bowl of salt, but there are other objects present as well that are not called for in Hughes' ritual: small stones and crystals, a seashell, a pendant of a sigil (magical symbol) created by Hughes, and a photograph of Democratic House speaker Nancy Pelosi pointing a finger at Trump. Additionally, the practitioner has drawn X's over Trump's eyes and straight

Orange candles and shriveled Cheetos 147

FIGURE 9.1 Orange candle stub and unflattering photograph. Image credit: Kaleigh Donnelly @901Tarot

FIGURE 9.2 Tarot cards. Image credit: Amber Love, @amberunmasked; Cards copyright MJ Cullinane (@crowtarotmjcullinane)

FIGURE 9.3 Baby carrot. Image credit: @boredofwords

lines over his mouth. Figure 9.2 includes a candle and the Tower Tarot card, which Hughes suggests as a representation of Trump Tower (Hughes 2018: 58), but also the Emperor, Hierophant, and Justice cards. Figure 9.3 includes the Tower Tarot card as well, along with the suggested bowl of salt, bowl of water, white candle, and baby carrot variation; however, there are also two other white candles, and the photograph of Trump is on the practitioner's mobile phone rather than printed out.

The use of material symbols for Trump, whether those suggested by Hughes or others chosen by practitioners, is widespread within the #MagicResistance movement. When asked if they used a specific object or objects to represent Trump in their rituals, all survey responses said that they did. Five respondents said that they used an orange candle, citing a range of reasons for this choice (1–5).

(1) *ritual magic kinda just uses candles, y'know?*—Respondent 1
(2) *He's kind of orange and it's my least favorite color, so it invokes the same feeling*—Respondent 2
(3) *It was a suggestion in the script.*—Respondent 3
(4) *It was easy to carve his name into.*—Respondent 6
(5) *I like to imagine his influence waning as the candle reduces.*—Respondent 7

While Respondent 1 attributes the choice to use an orange candle to a more general use of candles in ritual magic ("ritual magic just kind of uses candles"), Respondent 2 orients to the orange color of the candle specifically, citing its resemblance to Trump ("He's kind of orange") and noting a dislike of both the color and, by implication, the president ("it's my least favorite color, so it invokes the same feeling"). Respondent 3 links their choice to Hughes' ritual ("It was a suggestion in the script"), adding that they also use a baby carrot because of the color and because it, too, was suggested in the script. Respondent 6 comments on the practicality of a candle as an item that can be inscribed with Trump's name, as Hughes' ritual suggests ("It was easy to carve his name into"). Respondent 7 comments that they enjoy the parallel between the candle's reduction in size as it burns and their imagination of Trump's diminishing influence, highlighting the spiritual link between the alteration of a symbol for Trump and a desired alteration in Trump himself.

The Tower Tarot card, also suggested in Hughes' ritual, was another popular choice among survey respondents. As with the use of the orange candle, practitioners' reasons for using the Tower card were varied, though there are some shared themes (6–10).

(6) *Scripted. It represents the collapse of trump agenda*—Respondent 1
(7) *The symbolism of "power" works there*—Respondent 2
(8) *it represents the fall of his Trump tower and his climb to fame/power that should be torn down*—Respondent 4
(9) *It represents the chaos he has nurtured*—Respondent 6
(10) *Real estate mogul, trump tower—physical representation of things representing him that can be manipulated in a way that manifests intent.*—Respondent 7

Like Respondent 3 in (3), Respondent 1 notes that the Tower Tarot card was suggested (or "scripted") in Hughes' ritual. Respondents 2 and 4 both touch on the theme of power ("The symbolism of 'power' works there"; "his climb to fame/power that should be torn down"), while Respondent 9 instead sees the Tower Tarot card as a symbol of "the chaos he has nurtured." Both Respondent 8 and Respondent 10 mention Trump Tower ("it represents the fall of his Trump tower"; "Real estate mogul, trump tower"), framing the card as a representation of Trump specifically in addition to the more general meanings they discuss. Respondent 10 further adds that the card is a "physical representation of things representing him that can be manipulated in a way that manifests intent." This emphasis on manipulability is similar to Respondent 6's comments about candles being easy to inscribe. Respondent 3 similarly notes, "Paper pictures can be burned."

Perhaps because Hughes included it as an optional rather than required component, fewer respondents reported using fool's gold, or pyrite, in their rituals. However, those who did linked it to meanings of foolishness, greed, and falseness: Respondent 1 said that they "use [it] occasionally to symbolize foolish greed," and Respondent 7 said, "He falsely represents himself, as does the pyrite."

When asked if they had any additional comments about their use of ritual objects to represent Trump, two respondents reported that they viewed the objects as unnecessary or secondary to their intention. Respondent 7 said, "I have done the ritual so many times that I don't always use physical items. It's easy to visualize an altar and set intention with even just the 'schema primed' in the brain. Though props are fun, when practical." Respondent 6 commented, "In my practice, it is my will and words that direct the ritual. The tools are objects that focus my intent and have no intrinsic power in themselves. The objects I used to represent him were a only conduit to direct my focus." These comments demonstrate that, although material symbols for Trump are highly visible and prevalent in the #MagicResistance movement, we cannot assume that practitioners conceptualize the symbolic objects themselves as spiritually powerful. Instead, these practitioners locate the source of spiritual power in themselves ("set *intention*"; *"my will and words"*; "focus *my intent*" [emphasis added]).

Furthermore, for many practitioners, the ritual objects serve a dual purpose: they are used both to attempt to influence some aspect of Trump and to critique him. In response to the multiple-choice question *Which of the following best fits your use of this object/these objects to represent Trump?*, two respondents selected, *I use the object/these objects to CRITIQUE something about him*, three respondents selected *I use the object/these objects to CHANGE something about him (for instance, using a small or shriveled object to lessen his power)*, and six respondents selected, *I use these objects to both CHANGE and CRITIQUE him*. Previous analyses of political nicknames focus mainly on their use as means of critiquing or parodying their referents, and theories of magical practice focus mainly on practitioners' manipulation of representations to alter referents. These respondents' comments suggest that some #MagicResistance practitioners conceptualize ritual symbols for Trump as primarily a means of critiquing him; others, as primarily a means of altering him; and others, as a means of achieving both change and critique. These results align with the alternately, and sometimes simultaneously, spiritual and political significance of the #MagicResistance movement.

Nicknaming and name avoidance in the #MagicResistance movement

Motivations for nicknaming and name avoidance

In addition to using material symbols for Trump during rituals, many survey respondents reported that they used nicknames for Trump, avoided saying or writing his name, or both. In response to the multiple choice question *Which of the following is true of how you refer to Trump? Please check all that apply*, three respondents (Respondent 3, Respondent 5, and Respondent 9) said that they both avoided saying Trump's name and used nicknames for Trump. Respondent 7 and Respondent 8 said that they used nicknames for Trump, though they did not say that they avoided saying his name, and Respondent 6 said that they avoided saying Trump's name, although they did not say that they used nicknames for him. Two respondents, Respondent 1 and Respondent 10, shared alternative naming practices that they did not consider nicknames: "lowercase lettering. intentional mangling of name" (Respondent 1) and "I call him Drumpf, his original family name" (Respondent 10). Three respondents, Respondent 2, Respondent 8, and Respondent 11, mentioned that they used Trump's real name and did not add that they used any nicknames. Respondent 11 commented, "I use his name. May it be mud in the book of life." Respondent 2 and Respondent 8 both commented that they used Trump's name but avoided saying "President" or "his job title" (11, 12).

(11) *I say his name. I do avoid putting "President" in front of it because I really don't want people to pick up on that symbolic reverence toward him. God knows he's trying to cultivate it.*—Respondent 2
(12) *I avoid his job title.*—Respondent 8

Though Respondent 8 does not specify why they avoid Trump's job title, Respondent 2 specifies that they choose to avoid because they do not want others to afford Trump the "symbolic reverence" that the title "President" conveys, especially because they perceive this reverence as important to Trump ("God knows he's trying to cultivate it").

When asked an open-response question about their reasons for avoiding Trump's name (*If you avoid saying Trump's name, why do you avoid it?*), three of the respondents said that they did so in order to avoid giving Trump power (13–15).

(13) *to not give him power*—Respondent 9
(14) *Names have power. And trump is highly sensitive to insult.*—Respondent 1
(15) *He values himself and his name over all others. It gives him pleasure to see and hear his name. I will not give him more power by saying it. I will not direct more attention to him than I need to in order to work the binding*—Respondent 6

Respondent 1 explicitly states that "Names have power"; this assertion is implicit also in the other responses (e.g., "I will not give him more power by saying it"). Respondent 1 and Respondent 6 also mention their perceptions of Trump's reactions to their naming and avoidance practices ("trump is highly sensitive to insult"; "It gives him pleasure to see and hear his name"), framing their choices as contrary to Trump's interests.

Respondent 5 attributes their avoidance of Trump's name not to perceived spiritual power but to the intense emotional response Trump's name evokes in them, saying, "I despise him so much his name is a curse word to me." Respondent 3 says that they avoid his name "To avoid affirming him," and Respondent 8 says they do so "Because i [sic] see he is not fit for the job, and i did not vote for him." Respondent 7 identifies their desire to avoid targeted advertising as their reason for avoiding Trump's name, saying, "I only avoid it on social media so I don't get targeted advertising associated with his campaign, etc." These responses exemplify the many different reasons for avoidance of Trump's name within the #MagicResistance movement, including affective and practical considerations as well as beliefs about the spiritual power of names.

When asked separately about their motivations for using nicknames for Trump (*If you use nicknames for Trump, why do you use them?*), respondents likewise reported various motivations. Respondent 1 and Respondent 4 said that they used nicknames in order to insult or belittle Trump: "Used for insulting effect" (Respondent 1) and "to belittle him and to show others how I feel about him" (Respondent 4). Respondent 4's answer suggests that part of this belittlement is for the benefit of audiences other than Trump ("to **show others** how I feel about him"). Respondent 7 says that they use nicknames for Trump as part of their avoidance of targeted ads ("Avoid social media targeted ads, as stated above"). Respondent 3 links their motivation to a strong stance of disgust, using the simile, "His name is like offal in my mouth." In summary, respondents report that they use nicknames for Trump and avoid his real name for spiritual reasons (not wanting to give Trump power by saying or writing his name), communicative reasons (i.e., wanting to insult and belittle Trump in order to influence other people's perceptions of him), emotional reasons (i.e., experiencing intense hatred or disgust when saying or writing his name), and practical reasons (i.e., wanting to avoid targeted ads).

The significance of particular nicknames

In addition to asking about practitioners' motivations for using nicknames or other strategies of name avoidance, I also asked which nicknames they used and why they chose those specific ones (*If you use nicknames for Trump, which nicknames do you use?* and *Why do you use these particular nicknames for Trump instead of others?*). Respondents reported using the following nicknames (16–20).

(16) *"tmurp" "turnip" "trunt"*—Respondent 1
(17) *DT, Toddler in Chief, Don the Con*—Respondent 3
(18) *Cheeto*—Respondent 4
(19) 🍊🤡💩 *(orange clown shit emoji's)*—Respondent 7
(20) *scrotus the impeached*—Respondent 9

Several of these nicknames, including *Cheeto*, *Toddler in Chief*, *Don the Con*, 🍊🤡💩, and *Scrotus*, are also used outside of the #MagicResistance movement. Some of these names critique Trump's physical characteristic of orange skin (e.g., *Cheeto*); others, his infantile, criminal, and clownlike behavior (*Toddler in Chief*, *Don the Con*); and others, both appearance and behavior (🍊🤡💩). As Respondent 1 notes, they use lowercase letters and deliberate misspellings as part of their "intentional mangling" of Trump's name (*tmurp, trunt*) as well as the somewhat orthographically and phonetically similar word *turnip*. *Scrotus the impeached* is based on the term *Scrotus* (a portmanteau of *scrotum* and *POTUS*, the acronym for *President of the United States*; see Bivens and Cole 2018: 20–21). The addition of *the impeached* satirizes a naming convention typically used for monarchs, e.g., *Alexander the Great*. Respondent 1 added, "In addition to the nicknames, I sometimes refer to him formally as 'The Pig God.' That term is about the only one which I will capitalize the first letters." This name may be an allusion to Trump's perceived greed, since pigs are often used as a metaphor for greed, or could also evoke the sense of "pig" as "police."

Orange candles and shriveled Cheetos   153

In response to the question about their motivations for using these specific nicknames, two respondents again linked them to their avoidance of Trump's name: "I do not want to affirm his name" (Respondent 3), "so I don't give the name Trump power" (Respondent 9). Two others responded with an analysis of the meanings behind the nicknames: "Because he's a orange, and a clown, and a turd" (Respondent 7) and "Not sure, but I think the cheeto powder is a good metaphor for Trump being dirty on the outside like he is on the inside" (Respondent 4). Respondent 6, who did not use nicknames for Trump, explained, "He likes to give hateful nicknames to those who oppose him. I will not stoop to his level."

These nicknames are entwined with the ritual symbols for Trump in multiple ways. Similar critiques underlie many of them: the color orange, smallness, and ugliness emerge as common themes. During Hughes' ritual, practitioners link material and linguistic symbols of Trump, synchronizing ritual actions with ritual speech (for instance, by igniting a photo of Trump while chanting "You're fired"). Coordination of multimodal symbols occurs via social media, as well. For instance, in the Instagram post in Figure 9.4, @cameragirlsf shares an image of a ritual featuring the Tower Tarot card, an orange candle, a feather, and a burning photo of Trump, captioning it #latergram #trumpresistance #bindtrump #trump #resistance #ritual #spell #bind #yourefired #fired #notmypresident #angrycheeto #trumpvoodoo #resisttrump #magicresistance.

A commenter replies, *Amen! And So IT is! Blessed Be THAT Fire!* Both @cameragirlsf and this commenter explicitly comment on the fire in the photograph, and @cameragirlsf uses hashtags (#yourefired, #fired) to circulate the transmodal pun between the ritual chant of "You're fired!" and the physical fire igniting Trump's photo.

Similarly, in the Tweet in Figure 9.5, @SeebeeNarra posts a sigil (a symbol created by combining and stylizing orthographic letters representing a phrase that encapsulates the practitioner's intention—see Hughes 2018: 72) drawn on a bag of Cheetos, with the caption, **Digest** *the Cheeto-in-Chief then* #DumpTrump

FIGURE 9.4   "#yourefired". Image credit: @cameragirlsf

154 Julia Coombs Fine

FIGURE 9.5 "#CheetoInChief". Image credit: @SeebeeNarra

on 11/03/2020 #sigil #SympatheticMagick #chaosmagick #DumpTrump2020 #VoteHimOut2020 #DumpTrumpDayNov3 #MagicResistance #CheetoInChief #BindTrump [emphasis added].

Here, @SeebeeNarra combines a nickname for Trump (#*CheetoInChief*) with an image of a bag of Cheetos, also used to symbolize Trump. Through the phrase **Digest** the *Cheeto-In-Chief*, @SeebeeNarra extends the metaphor of TRUMP = CHEETO, urging audiences to vote Trump out of office. These multimodal practices show the extent to which nicknaming and material symbolism are intertwined in the #MagicResistance movement, with each reinforcing the other. Practitioners' survey responses, furthermore, suggest that there are parallels between their uses of material symbols and nicknames. Material symbols are used not only to change aspects of Trump, but to critique him; linguistic symbols such as nicknames are used not only to critique Trump, but to lessen his power.

Discussion

Examining symbolic representations of Trump in the #MagicResistance movement, this analysis finds that many practitioners use material, visual, and linguistic symbols for Trump, and avoid saying Trump's name, for a range of spiritual, affective, communicative, and practical reasons. When asked about their reasons for using ritual symbols such as orange candles and the Tower Tarot card, practitioners cited Hughes' 2016 ritual as influential, also describing the use of symbols as enjoyable and a way to focus their spiritual intentions. Their choice of specific material symbols is reportedly also due to Hughes' ritual, to the manipulability (e.g., flammability or ease of carving) of certain objects over others, to perceived resemblances between the objects and Trump, and to similarities in practitioners' emotional orientations to both. When asked why they avoided saying Trump's name, practitioners who did so cited a desire to avoid increasing Trump's power or affirming him as president, intense disgust or hatred for him, and an avoidance of targeted social media ads. When asked why they used nicknames for Trump, practitioners mentioned similar reasons of wanting to lessen Trump's power, lessen others' esteem of him, and avoid saying his name. Though political nicknames and linguistic avoidance are largely treated as separate phenomena in previous literatures, these results suggest that they may be practiced by the same, or overlapping, groups of actors and may be motivated by similar concerns and desires. Additionally, semantic overlaps between linguistic, visual, and material symbols (e.g., the overarching theme of orangeness), their co-use in Hughes' ritual text and social media discourses, and the similar motivations practitioners mention for using them suggest that these different modalities of symbols are closely intertwined within the #MagicResistance movement.

In view of the overlap between nicknames for Trump in the #MagicResistance movement and other anti-Trump resistance movements, we might further ask whether practitioners' spiritual and emotional reasons for nicknaming and name avoidance apply to some non-practitioners as well. With respect to emotional motivations, this seems likely. Many non-practitioners have mentioned that they experience intense feelings of disgust and loathing with regards to Trump. It is therefore plausible that this emotional aversion drives name avoidance among some non-practitioners, as well as practitioners; similarly, the "cheerful vulgarity" (Wertmüller, quoted in Biskind 1974: 11) of "carnivalesque" nicknames for Trump might provide non-practitioners, as well as practitioners, with joy and amusement. And perhaps some non-practitioners also perceive, at some level, that "names have power"—be it spiritual power, power to influence public opinion, power to trigger targeted ads, or all of the above.

In anthropological and linguistic analysis, language and culture are often examined primarily as outward-facing semiotic displays rather than affective, and indeed at times spiritual, experiences. In linguistic anthropology, for instance, we often ask how actors use language to produce sociocultural worlds, or how their language use is affected by sociocultural factors. We rarely ask how specific instances of language impact those who produce them. Yet this analysis demonstrates that, in at least some contexts, language use (as well as ritual practice) may be motivated not only by actors' communicative goals, or their sociopolitical goals as mediated through communication, but also by their desire to directly cause change through the perceived spiritual power of symbolic practice and to experience emotional states brought about through it. Potentially intersecting with language ideologies, psychology, and cognitive linguistics, this area of inquiry might provide a fuller picture of the role of linguistic and material symbols in political protest and spiritual practice.

References

Asprem, Egil. 2020. "The Magical Theory of Politics: Memes, Magic, and the Enchantment of Social Forces in the American Magic War." *Nova Religio: The Journal of Alternative and Emergent Religions* 23 (4): 15–42.

Bakhtin, Mikhail M. 1984 [1965]. *Rabelais and His World*. Helene Iswolsky, trans. Bloomington: Indiana University Press.

Biskind, Peter. 1974. "Lina Wertmuller: The Politics of Private Life." *Film Quarterly* 28 (2): 10–16.

Bivens, Kristin Marie, and Kirsti Cole. 2018. "The Grotesque Protest in Social Media as Embodied, Political Rhetoric." *Journal of Communication Inquiry* 42 (1): 5–25.

Buchanan, Larry, and Karen Yourish. 2019. "Tracking 30 Investigations Related to Trump." https://www.nytimes.com/interactive/2019/05/13/us/politics/trump-investigations.html, accessed December 16, 2020.

Burton, Tara I. 2017. "Each Month, Thousands of Witches Cast a Spell Against Donald Trump." https://www.vox.com/2017/6/20/15830312/magicresistance-restance-witches-magic-spell-to-bind-donald-trump-mememagic, accessed December 16, 2020.

Cheng, Susan. 2017. "Donald Trump Dubbed 'President Agent Orange' By Busta Rhymes." https://www.buzzfeednews.com/article/susancheng/busta-rhymes-called-out-donald-trump, accessed December 16, 2020.

Ellis, Emma G. 2019. "Trump's Presidency Has Spawned a New Generation of Witches." https://www.wired.com/story/trump-witches, accessed December 16, 2020.

Fea, John. 2018. *Believe Me: The Evangelical Road to Donald Trump*. Grand Rapids, MI: William B. Eerdmans Publishing.

Fine, Julia Coombs. 2020. "#MagicResistance: Anti-Trump Witchcraft as Register Circulation." *Journal of Linguistic Anthropology* 30 (1): 68–85.

Fomin, Maxim. 2020. "Name-Avoidance and Circumlocutory Terms in Modern Irish and Scottish Maritime Memorates." *Studia Celto-Slavica* 11 : 51–67.

Frazer, James George. 1890. *The Golden Bough*. London: Macmillan.

Gault, Matthew. 2017. "Use This Spell to Bind Trump and His Cronies." https://medium.com/defiant/use-this-spell-to-bind-trump-and-his-cronies-a5b6298f5c69, accessed December 16, 2020.

Gladkova, Anna. 2002. "The Semantics of Nicknames of the American Presidents." *Proceedings of the 2002 Conference of the Australian Linguistic Society* 2: 1–11.

Graefer, Anne, Allaina Kilby, and Inger-Lise Kalviknes Bore. 2019. "Unruly Women and Carnivalesque Countercontrol: Offensive Humor in Mediated Social Protest." *Journal of Communication Inquiry* 43 (2): 171–93.

Hall, Kira, Donna M. Goldstein, and Matthew Bruce Ingram. 2016. "The Hands of Donald Trump: Entertainment, Gesture, Spectacle." *HAU: Journal of Ethnographic Theory* 6 (2): 71–100.

Harp, Dustin. 2018. "Misogyny in the 2016 US Presidential Election." In Jacqueline R. Vickery and Tracy Everbach, eds. *Mediating Misogyny*. London: Palgrave Macmillan.

Harvey, Josephine. 2019. "'Cheeto Christ' Trends After Randy Rainbow Releases Video Mocking Trump's God Complex." https://www.huffpost.com/entry/cheeto-christ-randy-rainbow-trump-satire-music-video_n_5d6858ece4b06beb649b96a7, accessed December 16, 2020.

Hassan, Steven. 2020. *The Cult of Trump: A Leading Cult Expert Explains How the President Uses Mind Control*. New York: Free Press.

Hoffmann, Florian, David S. Lee, and Thomas Lemieux. 2020. "Growing Income Inequality in the United States and Other Advanced Economies." *Journal of Economic Perspectives* 34 (4): 52–78.

Hughes, Michael M. 2017. "A Spell to Bind Donald Trump and All Those Who Abet Him: December 12th Mass Ritual." https://extranewsfeed.com/a-spell-to-bind-donald-trump-and-all-those-who-abet-him-february-24th-mass-ritual-51f3d94f62f4, accessed December 16, 2020.

——— 2018. *Magic for the Resistance: Rituals and Spells for Change*. Portland, OR: Llewellyn Publications.

Jackson, Gita. 2020. "Witches Are Trying to Figure Out Whose Spell Gave Trump COVID-19." https://www.vice.com/en/article/bv8wvv/witches-are-trying-to-figure-out-whose-spell-gave-trump-covid-19, accessed December 16, 2020.

Johnston, David Cay. 2017. *The Making of Donald Trump*. Brooklyn: Melville House.

Lopez, Steve. 2020. "Column: Why can't President Orange Julius be more like Queen Elizabeth?" https://www.latimes.com/california/story/2020-04-05/column-joe-exotic-and-donald-trump-both-center-stage-is-this-what-acid-trips-were-like, accessed December 16, 2020.

Love, Nancy S. 2017. "Back to the Future: Trendy Fascism, the Trump Effect, and the Alt-Right." *New Political Science* 39 (2): 263–68.

Magliocco, Sabina. 2020. "Magical Responses to the 2016 Presidential Election in the United States." *Nova Religio: The Journal of Alternative and Emergent Religions* 23 (4): 43–68.

Mathews, Holly F. 1987. "Rootwork: Description of an Ethnomedical System in the American South." *Southern Medical Journal* 80 (7): 885–91.

McHendry Jr. George F. 2018. "White Supremacy in the Age of Trump: An Introduction to a Special Issue of the Journal of Contemporary Rhetoric." *Journal of Contemporary Rhetoric* 8 (1/2): 1–5: 5.

Regilme Jr. Salvador Santino F. 2019. "The Decline of American Power and Donald Trump: Reflections on Human Rights, Neoliberalism, and the World Order." *Geoforum* 102: 157–66.

Rippeon, Andrew. 2020. "'Lighght' and 'Covfefe': Reading Media and Misspellings from Mimeo to Twitterverse." https://read.dukeupress.edu/the-minnesota-review/article/2020/95/57/167265, accessed December 16, 2020.

Santino, Jack. 2011. "The Carnivalesque and the Ritualesque." *The Journal of American Folklore* 124 (491): 61–73.

Scaramucci, Anthony. 2020. "Donald Trump is Acting Like a Spoiled Toddler—America Must Give Him a Permanent Timeout." https://www.salon.com/2020/12/03/donald-trump-is-acting-like-a-spoiled-toddler--america-must-give-him-a-permanent-timeout, accessed December 16, 2020.

Shenk, Timothy. 2019. "Voldemort Politics." *Dissent* 66 (1): 4.

Stasch, Rupert. 2011. "Word Avoidance as a Relation-Making Act: A Paradigm for Analysis of Name Utterance Taboos." *Anthropological Quarterly* 84 (1): 101–20.

Thorp, H. Holden. 2020. "Words Matter." *Science* 370 (6513).

Trudeau, Garretson B. 2016. *Yuge!: 30 Years of Doonesbury on Trump*. Kansas City, MO: Andrews McMeel Publishing.

Ulrich, Anne. 2019. "Attention through Distraction: Basic Modalities and Rhetorical Medialities of Last Week Tonight." *Poetics Today* 40 (2): 299–318.

Wojtylak, Katarzyna Izabela. 2015. "Fruits for Animals: Hunting Avoidance Speech Style in Murui (Witoto, Northwest Amazonia)." *Proceedings of the Annual Meeting of the Berkeley Linguistics Society* 41: 545–63.

PART III
Donald Trump versus social institutions

10
"I DON'T THINK THE SCIENCE KNOWS, ACTUALLY"

The biocultural impacts of Trump's anti-science and misinformation rhetoric, the mishandling of the COVID-19 pandemic, and institutionalized racism

Benjamin J. Schaefer

Introduction

On April 23, 2020, President Donald Trump suggested during a coronavirus White House press briefing that people should "inject themselves" with bleach and other household disinfectants to cleanse their body of the SARS-CoV-2 (henceforth as COVID-19) virus (Funke 2020). This suggestion came after William Bryan, the Undersecretary for Science and Technology at the Department of Homeland Security, presented a study that found sun exposure and typical household cleaning agents have adverse effects on the coronavirus (Funke 2020). Bryan was referring to the disinfectants being used on surfaces, such as door knobs and other commonly touched areas, and in aerosols; however, Trump *legitimately* asked whether the chemicals in these disinfectants could be used as a potential treatment against COVID-19. Even though Trump has since rescinded his comments about injecting household disinfectants, doctors, state agencies, and companies that produce these products had to issue statements that "under no circumstance" should these products be ingested, injected, or inhaled (Nierenberg 2020). Though President Trump said that he was "asking a very sarcastic question," a survey conducted by the Centers for Disease Control and Prevention (CDC) found that about 4 percent of respondents consumed or gargled with diluted bleach solutions, soapy water, and other disinfectants in an effort to protect themselves from the coronavirus (Gharpure et al. 2020) at Trump's suggestion. To this point, it is not clear what part of Trump's comments were sarcastic.

In this chapter, I illustrate the various ways in which Trump disseminated "anti-scientific" and misinformation rhetoric in the final years of his presidency, their detrimental effects on society, and their legacies post-presidency. I draw from peer-reviewed, evidence-based, hypothesis-tested published data and from news outlets that meticulously archived Trump's political interference in the spread of misinformation about the COVID-19 pandemic. Specifically, I focus on the mishandling of

DOI: 10.4324/9781003152743-13

the COVID-19 pandemic in the United States. I also discuss how Trump's spread of anti-science misinformation exacerbated a parallel pandemic: institutionalized racism. I weave together the direct and indirect ways Trump's racist rhetoric has been used as ammunition by supporters in the increased volume of hate crimes during his presidency. I conclude by theorizing the role of biological anthropology and the legacy of Trump's political interference with science post-presidency.

Fake news, misinformation, and political interference with science

At the midpoint of Trump's presidential term in 2018, I was teaching Introduction to Biological Anthropology to university students in Atlanta, Georgia. While this course served to introduce bioanthropology theory and method, many students enrolled in the course to get their first exposure to the theory of evolution.[2] Other students wanted to use this class as a countermeasure to pro-Trump ideology regurgitated by family members; few had even privately requested that I petition the course title to not include "biological" on their transcripts so that their parents would not know they enrolled in a science course. While these were shocking requests, it is very reminiscent of the type of underground learning that Queer, Black, Indigenous, and People of Color must do in order to survive. Around the same time, teenagers in the United States were posting on Reddit forums asking how to safely get vaccinated due to their parent's anti-vaccine stance (Doubek 2019). During class, I allowed time for students to submit questions about science topics that they were too afraid to search on their computer or ask family. In doing so, a range of topics from vaccines to ancient aliens naturally came up (Schaefer 2018). To answer the questioned posed by students, we walked through the various ways to fact-check and critically interrogate the information presented in controversial popular science news articles or family conversations. At the time, I felt that these measures were simple and easy to reproduce outside of the course once the Spring semester had ended.

The final two years of Trump's presidency proved that the spread of "fake news," misinformation, and their legacies were more far-reaching than I expected. In May 2018, the Trump administration disbanded the White House pandemic response team (Chang 2020). Admitted to fabricating data on the aetiology of AIDS in the 1980s (Sifferlin 2018), in the same month Trump would appoint Dr. Robert Redfield as the director of the Centers for Disease Control and Prevention.

The term "fake news" was first used to describe fabricated news stories from websites that would publish hoaxes as satire or yellow journalism (Quandt et al. 2019; Tandoc et al. 2018). These fabricated stories would be picked up by hyper-partisan websites and marketed as if they were verified stories and news coverage. These stories ranged from Pope Francis endorsing both former President Donald Trump and former United States Secretary of State Hillary Clinton during their 2016 presidential campaigns to Clinton selling weapons to ISIS. These fabricated articles would then go viral on social media platforms such as Facebook and Twitter in the final months leading up to the 2016 presidential election.

Once elected, the term "fake news" became weaponized by Trump and his supporters. Previously used to describe corrupt phenomena, first in politics and then subsequently in other areas such as science, it swiftly became a form of ammunition that discredited news outlets critical of his policies and for Trump to maintain his power. This shift in the phrase's meaning was aided by his 48 million Twitter followers[3] who would liken his words to holy gospel, transforming the phrase "fake news" into a general put-down used by many—in seriousness or in jest. Since gaining worldwide popularity, the term "fake news" has exploded in its usage. It can refer to biased media, scientific findings that are antagonistic to Trump's benefactors, or any kind of news that Trump simply does not like. A Gallup Survey found that while the majority of Americans believe that "fake news" poses a threat to democracy, about 42 percent of Republicans consider any news critical of a politician to be "fake news" (Jones and Ritter 2018). After losing the election to Joe Biden, Trump continued to tweet and share conspiracy theories about the election being stolen from him and his supporters. The reality and legacy of Trump's rhetoric would become fully realized on January 6, 2021 at the #StopTheSteal rally for instigating violence and rioting at the United States Capitol after Vice President Mike Pence refused to overturn the Electoral College votes and name Trump as the re-elected president for another term. At the time of writing this chapter (February 2021), Trump has been impeached twice and acquitted for instigating violence at the Capitol.

The Trump administration was known to repeatedly politicize science by pressuring health and science agencies to change their reporting and recommendations in order to conform to Trump's policies and tweeted public comments (Diamond 2020). Trump and his administration also pressured federal health and science agencies to take actions that would favor Trump in the media (Colvin 2020); though it is unethical of scientists to fold to these requests, federal agencies must abide by the instructions from Trump (Reardon 2016). While this is true throughout his presidency, it became more apparent in regard to his handling of the COVID-19 pandemic in the United States. Additionally, Trump shared the infamous and debunked "Plandemic" and COVID-19 treatment conspiracy videos that were published on YouTube in summer 2020. In an attempt to conspire and fabricate data in order to receive "good ratings" among his supporters, Trump also purported his own conspiracy theory that there is a "Deep State" among federal scientists to hurt him politically and prevent his re-election (Gross 2020). Regardless, by sewing together a mistrust in science and xenophobic fears of the BIPoC "other" purported by saying "the China Virus" and that BLM is a hate group (Cohen 2020), Trump's role in the spread of anti-science misinformation during his presidency is quite evident.

Political interference with health agencies

"You just inject the bleach?": COVID-19 testing and treatments

The COVID-19 virus was originally thought to be similar to Severe Acute Respiratory Syndrome (SARS), with many governments labelling it as a mild illness which resulted in few national-level initiatives to stop the spread (Piguillem and Shi

2020). Soon after outbreaks in China, Italy, and Iran, it become clear that COVID-19 was substantially more contagious than SARS and similar viruses. In order to combat the spread of COVID-19, many health agencies and government administrations began to take aggressive measures to reduce the spread and slow the disease diffusion. However, the required reagents for COVID-19 testing were already in short supply, and testing centers reported additional barriers in acquiring the necessary materials (Esbin et al. 2020). Due to the novel status of the COVID-19 virus, established testing measures were not readily available. Researchers attempted to refine testing measures in order to obtain the most accurate results; however, a number of cultural barriers affected the ability of some to get tested, such as unclear information of those that are not heritage English speakers.[4] While burnt-out scientists and healthcare workers were refining testing and validating measures, the world watched science happen in real time at a greater speed than is commonly shown in television, movies, and media.

In early March, Trump directed the Food and Drug Administration (FDA) to test a variety of medications in order to elucidate whether they could be used as a potential COVID-19 treatment (FDA 2020a). The two promising drugs were chloroquine and hydroxychloroquine, which have been used to treat malaria for decades. By April, the FDA issued an Emergency Use Authorization (EUA) that allowed doctors in hospitals to begin clinical drug trials and research their efficacy in reducing the COVID-19 viral load. In the same month, Trump suggested that people should "inject themselves" with bleach and other household disinfectants to slow the virus. By mid-June, the FDA revoked the EUA, and the clinical trials and distribution for chloroquine and hydroxychloroquine ceased. The FDA (2020b) published results suggesting that there are "no benefits for decreasing the likelihood of death or speeding recovery" and safety issues associated with taking these drugs outside their intended use. While Trump promoted baseless ideas about potential treatment options, many Americans listened and either injected themselves with bleach or hoarded chloroquine and hydroxychloroquine, while some simply gargled with soap and water.

On June 20, 2020 at a campaign rally in Tulsa, OK, Trump claimed he had instructed his administration to reduce the volume of COVID-19 testing in order to keep the number of confirmed cases low. Prior to this rally, Trump repeatedly reported that COVID-19 cases were low during the first part of the national quarantine; however, this false claim was due to his administration undermining the number of COVID-19 tests that were administered and resulted in skewed data (Stolberg 2020). In doing so, many Americans and his supporters disregarded or practiced a very relaxed version of health mandates instructed by numerous state and federal health agencies. In late August, the CDC testing guidelines were quietly changed from their earlier testing recommendations to only test people who have been exposed to COVID-19. The new guidelines stated that people did not need to be tested if they did not have symptoms; the site has since been updated (CDC 2020a). Multiple public health experts expressed concerns about this change, as early testing is considered an essential method to track and mitigate the spread of viruses and other diseases (Ng et al. 2020). Additionally, infected people can still be contagious even if they are not experiencing symptoms, as in the famous case of Typhoid Mary who was asymptomatic and spread the disease through her cooking (Soper 1939).

Rat-lickers and anti-maskers

Masks are a popular public health measure in Asia and are intended to reduce the spread of germs and disease while going about typical daily life. During the COVID-19 pandemic, health professionals and political authorities recommended the use of surgical and cloth face masks to reduce the risk of COVID-19 spread and disease transmission (CDC 2020b). Face coverings reduce the transmission of viruses and other pathogens from the wearer to others and also provide some degree of personal protection to the wearer against infection. Kai-Wang et al. (2020) identified COVID-19 in salivary and respiratory droplets and concluded that the virus may be transmitted directly or indirectly without symptoms. The rationale for wearing masks is to reduce asymptomatic transmission (Prather et al. 2020), an additional buffer if there is difficulty in appropriately social distancing (Eikenberry et al. 2020), and the cost-benefit of reducing the spread of the virus in order to overcome high transmission rates. While the growing evidence-based data suggest that masks do work in slowing the spread and flattening the curve, the mask has become a site of political contention.

Riding on the back of the anti-vaxxer movement, people who chose not to wear a mask in public spaces were quickly labeled "Anti-Maskers" and "Rat-Lickers," a name that metaphorically links the COVID-19 pandemic to the Black Death (1346–1353 CE). In various countries such as Canada and the United Kingdom, large, congregated rallies took place in protest against public health mask mandates and compulsory mask wearing in shops and businesses. Some protests also co-opted the feminist slogan "my body, my choice" and the Black Lives Matter slogan that Eric Garner and George Floyd gasped as they were choked to death by police: "I can't breathe." Others have taken a more inappropriate perspective by comparing "wearing a mask" to being "enslaved" and their "freedom" taken away (Morales 2020). A rudimentary search about the trans-Atlantic slave trade and the lasting legacies of colonialism prove that these anti-masking sentiments are completely unhinged, incomparable, and unfounded by any credible source. Though opposition to wearing masks is not new in the United States,[5] the politicization of science and mask wearing during the pandemic became a focal point of Trump and his anti-science agenda.

As the pandemic continues, mask-wearing holds a form of cultural capital that communicates a certain type of ideology. Ideology cannot be separated from language and socially constructed sign-systems such as symbols (Voloshinov 1973). Thus, to some, wearing a mask symbolizes the commitment to practice COVID-19 safety guidelines and ensure the wellbeing of themselves and others, while Trump supporters who do not wear a mask use the absence as a social litmus test to communicate that they are invulnerable and that they are not anxious about COVID-19 despite the exponential rise in cases. To this point, many believe that not wearing a mask communicates their proximity to Trump and are thus "more American" (Vargas and Sanchez 2020). The growing sentiment of anti-science measures also influenced people's behaviors toward wearing a mask as Trump fomented mistrust in scientists. The denial in wearing a mask also communicates that those not wearing one have little remorse for their role in the spread of COVID-19, to communities that have a higher susceptibility to disease and those that are immunocompromised. The sentiment behind the public health slogan "We are all in this together" provided a positive outlook on the pandemic. Trump supporters and those who chose not to wear masks made it clear that we are not in this together to reduce the spread and prolonging any safe way to open the United States (and the world) back up.

Reopening the United States and the vaccine

A 17-page report from the CDC (2020c) titled "Guidance for Implementing the Opening up America Again Framework" *surprisingly* provided clear, detailed guidelines for the reopening of businesses, public transit, restaurants, schools, and public areas. However, the Trump administration barred the distribution of the report and told the CDC scientists affiliated with the statement that their report would "never see the light of day" (Dearen and Stobbe 2020). Between April and May 2020, the Associated Press published an unauthorized version of the 60 page guidelines which included 6 additional guideline flowcharts that were not previously distributed. This release occurred weeks after many states began to reduce their lockdown procedures and reopen. As Trump publicly urged for schools to fully reopen for the 2021–2022 academic school year, the White House Coronavirus Task Force continued to downplay any risk associated with in-person instruction, stressing the need for children to be in school to prevent the development of mental health issues. Before being distributed to parents to make an informed opinion about sending their children back to in-person instruction, White House officials were allowed to make edits to the report and include unfounded scientific claims that the virus was less deadly to children (Chuck 2020). By suggesting this, it is clear that the children are a demographic that can be tested on as tribute so long as it furthers Trump's political platform. Ultimately, what seems like a chapter out of Goebbels' playbook (Culbert 1995), the final title of the official document was "The Importance of Reopening America's Schools this Fall" (CDC 2020d).

Radiologist Scott Atlas was appointed as a White House advisor on the coronavirus task force by Trump in August (Morrison 2020). Atlas quickly became influential in Trump's administration and garnered popularity as Trump's and Atlas' ideologies aligned. Atlas opposed the closure of schools and businesses, stating that the best approach was to let younger people get the virus and live with the unknown lasting detrimental effects in order to protect those most vulnerable (Abutaleb and Dawsey 2020). While Atlas suggested state-sanctioned violence as an appropriate

COVID-19 response, his proposal was never enacted (Weiland et al. 2020). In October, Atlas pushed to focus less on the expansion of national COVID-19 testing, supported the belief that social distancing is worthless, masks do not work, and the end of the pandemic and development of a vaccine was eminent (Abutaleb et al. 2020). Ultimately, Twitter removed Atlas' posts for violating their policy against the spread of misinformation.

Trump publicly stressed the need for a COVID-19 vaccine and that pharmaceutical companies were attempting to develop one at "warp speed" under Operation Warp Speed (HHS 2020). Trump repeatedly suggested that the vaccine would be ready before the end of 2020 or before the presidential election, in an attempt to showcase his vaccine development response and persuade voters. At a congressional committee meeting, CDC director Redfield is reported to have said that wearing a mask can be more effective than a vaccine because it was unlikely to distribute vaccines before middle to late 2021. Despite Redfield's efforts, Trump dismissed his vaccine timetable as "incorrect information" (Forgey 2020a). Though Trump continued to say that a vaccine was coming in the next few weeks (Forgey 2020b), lead member of the White House Coronavirus Task Force, Dr. Anthony Fauci, stated that the efficacy of the vaccine would be unknown until December 2020 or January 2021 due to the necessary blind-clinical trials (Hodgson et al. 2021).

In early October 2020, after spending months downplaying the severity of the pandemic that had killed more than 500,000 in the United States and more than 2.36 million people worldwide (CDC 2020f), Trump and First Lady Melania Trump tested positive for COVID-19. In the middle of the night, Trump disclosed their positive test results on Twitter (Trump 2020). There was no immediate word at the time on how far the infection spread among senior White House officials, many of whom did not wear masks in solidarity with Trump's disdain for them. Even though Trump publicly addressed the nation while showing signs of tremendous bodily fatigue from COVID-19 (Weiland et al. 2021), the positive test results *and* acknowledging the severity would have hurt him politically. Downplaying his own symptoms, the symbol of an infected American president could have undermined his political agenda and disrupted his political and economic supporters' plans for reopening. Weiland et al. (2021) reported that Trump was in fact sicker than he allowed the public to know, with medical doctors suggesting that he be put on a ventilator—the same technology he suggested hospitals obtain on their own rather than using federal funds. According to CDC data (2020e), 8 out of 10 COVID-19 deaths in the United States have been in adults 65 years old and older, the age category including Trump. When discussing whether he or others would get sick, he described it as essentially a roll of the dice (Weiland et al. 2021), which is an illogical probability example when compared to reported official data.

In the weeks leading up the 2020 presidential election, public mistrust in the COVID-19 vaccine began to grow. Dr. Ashish Jha, Dean of Brown University School of Public Health, said that the Trump campaign created a "veneer of political meddling" which reduced public confidence in the vaccine.[6] In late October, Health and Human Services chief Alex Azar attempted to obtain permission to remove FDA administrator Dr. Stephen Hahn due to his insistence that the COVID-19 vaccine meet safety standards prior to being approved and distributed. A month after losing the election in mid-December, a peer-reviewed standing committee of outside scientists reviewed the Pfizer-BioNTech vaccine application and recommended the FDA authorize it for emergency use. In order to augment public confidence in the vaccine, politicians including both Vice President Mike Pence and House Speaker Nancy Pelosi received the vaccine during a nationally-televised broadcast, while healthcare professionals, essential workers, and those who were sheltering-in-place wondered when they would be eligible.

Exposing the original pandemic: institutional racism

The World Health Organization (WHO) developed guidelines for best practices for naming new human infectious disease in collaboration with the World Organization for Animal Health (OIE), the Food and Agriculture Organization of the United Nations (FAO), and with leading experts of the International Classification of Diseases (ICD) (WHO 2015). Using names such as "swine flu" for the H1N1 influenza variant and "Middle East Respiratory Syndrome" (MERS) has had unintended negative impacts by stigmatizing certain communities and economic sectors. The best practices for applying the WHO guidelines consist of generic descriptive terms based on the symptoms (e.g., respiratory) and more specific terminology (e.g., juvenile or severe) once more robust information is available. Despite these established guidelines recommended by multiple international health organizations prior to Trump's presidency, Trump continued to label COVID-19 as the "China virus" or "Chinese virus" as an attempt to assign the disease's origin. This resulted in an increase of hate crimes against Asian communities across America (Tessler et al. 2020) and internationally (Plaga and Büchenbacher 2020), regardless if they are ethnically Chinese.

Between January and February 2020, over a few thousand incidents of xenophobia and racism against Asian peoples were reported in the United States. These incidents of anti-Asian racism exponentially increased, as Trump refused to use the proper nomenclature and perpetuated anti-Asian rhetoric about COVID-19. Trump was quoted saying that his reference to COVID-19 as the "China virus" is "not racist at all" (Forgey 2020b). Trump's xenophobic and racist actions would detrimentally affect Asian-owned restaurants and businesses by about 80 percent across the United States (Alcorn 2020). In some cities, Han (2020) reported that Koreans were hesitant to wear masks in public due to the rise in hate crimes and racism toward Asians who wore masks. It is clear that the anti-scientific rhetoric and xenophobic remarks made by Trump are co-constituted, resulting in the rise in hate crimes brought about by Trump's misinformation. On April 10, 2020, Surgeon General Jerome Adams suggested that people of color were "socially predisposed" to coronavirus. Adams asked Black, Indigenous, and People of Color (BIPoC) communities to abstain from drugs and alcohol with condescending language saying, "Do it for your *abuela*. Do it for your granddaddy, do it for your Big Mama, do it for your pop-pop." Adams' public statements would be broadcast in television advertisements across the nation as his message failed to directly name racism as a main cause for health disparities and these violent attacks. Institutional racism is a form of racism that is embedded into normal practices and behaviors, and the major contributing factor that disproportionately affects Black, Indigenous, and communities of color in the United States. According to Pew Research Center, Ruiz et al. (2020) found that 58 percent of Asian-Americans and 45 percent of Black Americans believe that racist views toward them had increased since the onset of the pandemic.

In May 2020, people around the world watched the body camera footage showing former Minneapolis police officer Derek Chauvin[7] kneeling on George Floyd's neck for nearly 9 minutes while Floyd pleaded for his life, repeating "I can't breathe." As a result, Black Lives Matter (BLM) protests sparked up in major cities like Chicago and rural areas like Great Barrington, Massachusetts in the United States, to worldwide protests in solidarity against police brutality, during the global COVID-19 pandemic. BLM is a decentralized political and social movement that protests against incidents of police brutality and racially motivated violence against Black people (Rickford 2016). While activists protested in the streets across the United States demanding an end to police brutality, many non-Black Americans took this statement as their lives somehow did *not* matter.

The BLM movement began in July 2013 with the use of the #BlackLivesMatter hashtag on social media following the acquittal of George Zimmerman in the shooting of Black teen Trayvon Martin in February 2012 (Thomas and Blackmon 2015). This movement became nationally recognized in 2014 after street demonstrations and protests following the deaths of Michael Brown in Ferguson, Missouri (Ray et al. 2017), and Eric Garner in New York City. Since the inception of this movement, numerous demonstrations against the unjust killing of Black Americans by police while in custody or their proximity to police have continued to this day. While BLM comprises many different views and a breadth of demands, BLM primarily centers around criminal justice reform and transformative justice. Black people are disproportionately policed at higher rates than those in other demographic groups. The legacy of white supremacy has resulted in centuries of unjust policing (Chaney and Robertson 2013; Cooper and Fullilove 2016), as well as nutritional (Allen et al. 2018), psychosocial (Krieger et al. 2011), and environmental stressors (Murry et al. 2018) that continue to affect BIPoC communities.

While the pandemic continued to ravage the world, the news coverage of the racial violence exacerbated burnout and stress. Stress is a precarious concept. Stress is defined as a physiological change caused by strain on an organism from environmental, nutritional, psychological, and other pressures (Reitsema and McIlvaine 2014). Here, the body responds to the threatening external stressors, via cortisol secretion, which, while beneficial in the short term, can have adverse health outcomes if experienced over a long period of time (Schaefer 2017). Thus, in the absence of stress, the optimal health profile is one in which basal cortisol levels are low (Sapolsky 2012). For example, cortisol levels appear to be lower in dominant rather than subordinate animals in species in which high rank is maintained by intimidation and high-ranking individuals can aggressively displace frustrations onto subordinates with impunity. In contrast, it is the subordinate individuals who have the lowest levels of cortisol in species in which maintaining high rank requires frequent fighting (McEwan 2007). However, humans belong to multiple hierarchies and have a multitude of psychological means to rationalize the meanings of their rank (Sapolsky 2012). Sherman et al. (2012) suggest that military leaders had substantially lower resting cortisol levels and lower levels of self-reported anxiety. Despite both low cortisol and anxiety correlated with leadership, neither was correlated with each other; rather leadership was associated with an elevated personal sense of power insofar that it was associated with an enhanced sense of control (Sapolsky 2012). Building on these foundational concepts, the study of stress and health outcomes in relation to the oppressive structures provides a broader understanding of the imperial enterprise among peoples under subjugation and their lack of control. By creating climates of fear through the public display of choreographed killings, these climates of fear reinforce elite power in politics and become embodied, further legitimizing state control over the middle and lower classes, and social inequity (Foucault 1995).

Anthropology of embodiment evaluates how social interactions and the social become incorporated biologically and molecularized. Scholars have studied this phenomenon in contemporary populations by examining body proportions between Black and white people (Cobb 1947) and the incidence of diseases in relation to systemic racism (Gravlee 2009); others have examined the role of stress and psychological trauma in alterations of the human genome (Non and Thayer 2015; Zhang et al., 2021), epigenetic modifications to external stressors (Zhang et al., 2021), and human and nonhuman primate social hierarchies (Sapolsky 2012).

Anthropological inquiry of embodiment formulated the body as not solely biological but inherently social as well (Scheper-Hughes 1990). Aiding in this approach, Sofaer (2006) incorporated these ideas of embodiment into bioarchaeological studies to interpret human remains (and the body) as historically and contextually produced entities. The unique experiences mark the body not only as a biological object but a cultural object that can tease out the effects of individuals' social and historical contexts. The molecularized social life provides unique insights into individual lives which can empirically elucidate the embodiment of psychosocial stressors. Integrating these theoretical frameworks allows for a nuanced perspective of Black social life as biological and cultural subjects that are inherently affected by structures of imperial inequity and subjugation. Uniquely poised to address the intersections between human biology and culture, we can weave together ethnohistorical (see Crenshaw 1991; Hartman 1997; Mbembe 2006; Spillers 1987), archaeological (see Battle-Baptiste 2011; Blakey 2020), and biological datasets (Fernando 2017) to elucidate the biocultural effects and health outcomes from the embodiment of racism and white supremacy endured over generations.

Between July 2013 and 2021, more than 2000 Black Americans and Americans of color were killed by police using excessive force.[8] Following the death of Michael Brown Jr., the US Congress passed the Death in Custody Reporting Act (H.R.

1447 Public Law No: 113–242), which mandates police departments to report deaths while in custody (US Congress 2013). While the intent was to acquire more data to elucidate why Black people were dying in police custody in order to prevent future deaths, currently there is neither a functional reporting system in place for this data to be collected or stored nor repercussions for failing to report. The official state data of police killings, both on and off duty, still do not exist. Fortunately, grassroots efforts such as Mapping Police Violence (Sinyangwe et al. 2015) constructed this database of police brutality from 2015 to the present. Some of their key findings highlight that

- There have only been eighteen days in 2020 where police did not kill someone.
- Black people are most likely to be killed by police.
- Police killed Black people at higher rates than white people in 47 of the 50 largest US cities; Chicago police killed Black people at 22 times the rate of white people per population from 2013 to 2020.
- Black people are five times more likely to be killed by police in Oklahoma than in Georgia, suggesting that where Black people live does matter.
- Police violence is changing over time, demonstrating that police killings have decreased in cities (generally), but increased in suburban and rural areas.
- Zero people were killed in Buffalo, NY[9] compared to 13 in Orlando, FL[10] despite Buffalo having a higher violent crime rate (12 per 1000 compared to 9 per 1000, respectively).

This is not an exhaustive list but depicts the police brutality in the United States and disproportionate policing of Black Americans simply living their lives.

In the months prior to George Floyd's unjust death, racial profiling and hate crimes continued and led to three specific events. On February 23, 2020, 25-year-old Ahmaud Arbery was fatally shot while jogging in Glynn County, Georgia. Arbery was pursued and confronted by three white residents driving two vehicles. Notably, the murderers included Gregory McMichael (father) and Travis McMichael (son) who were armed, and William "Roddie" Bryan. They would ultimately be indicted months later after Arbery's murder on nine counts. On March 13, plain-clothes Louisville police officers Jonathan Mattingly, Brett Hankison, and Myles Cosgrove knocked down the apartment door of 26-year-old Breonna Taylor, fatally unloading six rounds while she was in the hallway. During this situation, Taylor's boyfriend Kenneth Walker shot back and called the police, saying, "someone kicked in the door and shot my girlfriend" (Albert 2020). While the police did have a no-knock search warrant for drug suspicions, it became clear that the Louisville police kicked down the door at the wrong house. More than a month after Breonna Taylor's death, prosecutors offered a plea deal if Walker would commit perjury, saying that Taylor was part of his drug-dealing operations; Walker rejected this deal. The officers were charged with three counts of wanton endangerment.[11]

Lastly, hours before the death of George Floyd, Christian Cooper was birdwatching at New York's Central Park when he was confronted by Amy Cooper (no relation). Christian Cooper asked Amy Cooper to leash her dog while in The Ramble, a no-dogs-off-leash area, who ultimately called the police stating that C. Cooper was threatening her, despite clear video evidence contesting A. Cooper's claim. By the time police arrived, both people had left. While this situation ended very differently compared to others who encounter police while Black, the climate of fear generated by white fright conjures exponential possibilities that could have happened.

The events that were triggered from the tragic death of George Floyd, Breonna Taylor, and Ahmaud Arbery were a much-needed awakening across institutions and communities to disrupt institutionalized racism. At the same time, these events collided with the disproportionate number of Black, Indigenous, and People of Color dying from COVID-19 (Titanji and Swartz 2020). Understanding the unique relationship of Black and Indigenous peoples to "whiteness" highlights how communities of color experience racism and the social determinants of health. Recognizing the shared experiences between communities of color provides a nuanced understanding that BIPoC communities are not homogenous and have unique histories that shape their lived experiences in response to racism. The histories of medical experimentation on BIPoC communities further exacerbated the already lingering mistrust in the American medical system. Early data from the vaccine rollout starkly show that those who have been vaccinated are predominantly white (64.1 percent) while Black (6.4 percent) and Indigenous (2 percent) peoples are severely underrepresented (CDC 2020g) despite having a higher number of deaths. Additionally, when mapping testing and vaccination centers, they are concentrated in white neighbourhoods and make it more difficult for Black communities to access the same treatments (Tye and Hacker 2020). Specifically in Illinois, in a state that is about 14 percent Black overall, 30 percent of all COVID-19 cases and 41 percent of deaths are attributed to Black residents. These disparities are not limited to Chicago or Illinois and likely mirror similar metrics for other major cities throughout the United States. Regardless, where an individual lives should not determine how long they live.

Concluding remarks

After President Biden's inauguration, Wade Davis opined in *Scientific American* "Why Anthropology Matters" (Davis 2021). In this essay, Davis explored the role of early American anthropology from its inception to the current era, while completely erasing the contributions of Black and Indigenous peoples' knowledge production, how they also shape contemporary American anthropology, and that all anthropologies have histories.[12] Notably, Davis states that,

> Anthropology is the antidote to nativism, the enemy of hate, a vaccine of understanding, tolerance and compassion that silences the rhetoric of demagogues, inoculating the world from the likes of the Proud Boys and Donald Trump. As the events of the last months have shown, the struggle long ago

championed by Franz Boas is ongoing. Never has the voice of anthropology been more important.

Anthropology allows scholars and non-scholars to weave together theory and method to scientifically study and think about culture in various ways. However, Davis' perspective lacks a nuanced understanding of colonialism and its ties to anthropology. Rather Davis writes that anthropology is history's antidote *to* colonialism and not the arbiter of colonialism and its contemporary legacies to racism and white supremacy. For anthropology to be anything close to a vaccine to its own virus, anthropology would have to recanonize anthropological theory and method outside the contributions of early anthropologists, move Black, Indigenous, and scholars of color's scholarship up on the syllabus, and engage with their scholarship critically instead of performatively.

If (biological) anthropology were the antidote to nativism and the vaccine of understanding, the efficacy has been well below typical vaccine standards during former President Trump's administration. This is not to say that there is no credence to anthropology breaking Trump's legacy, but anthropologists must first contend with the issue that early anthropology is part of the modern problem. Leading up to his final days in office, Trump tweeted "The BIG Protest Rally in Washington D.C. will take place at 11 A.M. on January 6 Location details to follow. StopTheSteal!" This became a call to action for Trump supporters, QAnon conspiracy theorists, the Proud Boys, and other white supremacists' groups to descend on Washington, DC for the "Save America" and #StopTheSteal rally on the National Mall. Many supporters did not wear masks and held signs suggesting that the pandemic was manufactured in a lab, reinforcing Trump's anti-science rhetoric.

The #StopTheSteal rally highlighted that this insurrection was about upholding white supremacy and Trump's influence in politics and not solely about electoral votes. As a political symbol, Trump gave power to those who followed him, instilling a form of control over non-white people, a belief in "fake news," and mistrust in science. Protestors around the world typically erect a guillotine as a political symbol against the government and ties to the historic memory of the French Revolution; the insurrectionists erected gallows with a noose, a stereotypical method used to lynch enslaved Africans and Black people up to the end of the Jim Crow Era (1965),[13] demanding former Vice President Mike Pence's head. While many admonished the attack on the Capitol and Trump's racist rhetoric as anti-American, Trump's legacy proves that racism and white supremacy are as American as apple pie. The growing concern that racism is a public health issue continues to be a divisive political issue, despite the growing scholarship that has shown how racism and racist systems are embedded in the American medical system (Feagin and Bennefield 2014; Yele 2008), housing (Sadler and Lafreniere 2017), food deserts (Howerton and Trauger 2017) and swamps (Hager et al. 2017), to breathing (Fikes 2012; Górska 2016; Graham et al. 2015).

After his inauguration, President Biden signed 17 executive orders on his first day in office, and the legacies of Trump's political interference post-presidency are slowly coming to light. As new COVID-19 variants have mutated in countries around the world due to mosaic lockdown orders, the Pfizer-BioNTech, Moderna, among other vaccine rollouts continue. Guidelines for COVID-19 vaccine eligibility have been determined by individual state health officials. Despite the public mistrust in the vaccine, Americans have found loopholes to obtain a vaccine ahead of their eligibility date. For example, non-eligible people in Massachusetts posted Craigslist ads requesting to bring and pay the elderly to get vaccinated and themselves. While attempting to cheat the system and receive vaccines ahead of their eligibility, some healthcare professionals suggest that it *does* show that there is a growing public trust in the vaccine (pers. comm. Pansecchi and D. Schaefer 2021). However, there is a growing shadow market for fabricated COVID-19 vaccination cards to bypass vaccination all together. Some parents have even lied about their children's ages in order to obtain a vaccine despite unapproved uses for children under 12 years of age. While the vaccine distribution continues, most of the world will not be eligible for the vaccine until middle to late 2021. In a recent interview about safely reopening schools in autumn and new CDC guidelines, vaccinated President Biden distantly sat about 10 feet away from the reporter.

In this chapter, I discussed the shortcomings of former President Trump and his administration's political interference to science and the pandemics in the United States: the global COVID-19 pandemic and institutionalized racism. While my aim was to highlight the issues between Trump and his rudimentary understanding of science, Trump, the power of his rhetoric, and his supporters illuminate the nefarious legacies of an exasperated anti-science period in American history. While it is easy to draw similar conclusions, the legacies of colonialism, white supremacy, and racism are more far-reaching than Trump's infamous presidency, stretching to the European colonialization of Turtle Island. Ultimately, I hope that this chapter serves as a launching point for others to think about how science, politics, economy, among other institutions are co-constituted and affect people instead of bounded stand-alone categories. The full spectrum of Trump and his administration's political interference with science agencies is unquantifiable in the limits of this chapter. Though this chapter has come to a close, the final chapters on Trump and his anti-science legacy are far from complete.

Acknowledgements

I would like to thank Olivia Perry, Achsah Dorsey, Jenail Marshall, Lindsay Clayson, Elsie How, Caitlin Mayer, Lakshita Malik, Donielle Perry, and Patrick Carberry for providing feedback on earlier drafts of this chapter. You all helped me make this chapter stronger and I cannot thank you enough. I would also like to acknowledge all of those that have been disproportionately affected by Trump's political interference with science agencies and his mishandling of the COVID-19 Pandemic in the United States. We have lost an incalculable amount of people under his "guidance." All errors in this chapter are mine alone.

Notes

1. I was asked to write about "Trump and Science." I decided to focus on the pandemic as I am not a specialist in environmental policy and would much rather see scholars who specialize in these areas focus on the long lasting effects on those agencies.
2. In Georgia, it is quite common for school districts to tape, use a sticker, or completely tear out the evolution chapter in biology textbooks.
3. At the time in 2016, since following the events of the insurrection on 6 January 2021 at the US Capitol, Twitter has since permanently banned Donald J. Trump (@realDonaldTrump).
4. On my first day at the Illinois Department of Public Health in Chicago, I was asked to speak to a woman who only spoke Spanish. In my conversation, she told me that she was told to call the office to obtain COVID-19 results and asked if being in close contact meant that she should not report to work. In this conversation, it was fairly clear that she was not provided with adequate care when getting tested for COVID-19 and that the information was not presented clearly for her to fully understand the next steps. I neither had her results nor would I be able to give them over the phone due to it being a HIPPA violation.
5. During the Spanish Influenza pandemic in the United States (1917–1920), masks were politicized and opposed by the Anti-Mask League that was established in San Francisco, California.
6. Though there was a reduced public confidence in the vaccine, history tells us that American medical scientists readily experimented prior to IRB approval on Black communities, Indigenous communities, and forced sterilization of Puerto Rican Women, among other BIPoC communities.
7. Former police officer Derek Chauvin was eventually charged on second degree murder following his body camera footage going viral on social media and backlash against the Minneapolis police for not reprimanding Chauvin. Additionally, J. Alexander Kueng, Thomas K. Lane, and Tou Thao were charged with aiding and abetting second degree murder Chauvin following Black Lives Matter protests sparked around the United States and other countries in solidarity against police brutality against Black people.
8. This is a conservative estimate as many Black deaths in the United States are either underreported or happen in police custody and are not part of the official count. The total number of Black people murdered in the United States is unquantifiable.
9. The population of Buffalo, New York is about 258,959, with about fifty percent of the population being Black, Indigenous, People of Color.
10. The population of Orlando, Florida is about 255,483 with about forty-two percent of the population being Black, Indigenous, People of Color.
11. In Kentucky, wanton endangerment is defined as a person acting wantonly with respect to a result or to a circumstance described by a statute defining an offense when he is aware of and consciously disregards a substantial and unjustifiable risk that the result will occur or that the circumstance exists. The risk must be of such nature and degree that disregard thereof constitutes a gross deviation from the standard of conduct that a reasonable person would observe in the situation.
12. For more complete commentary, see @Rickwasmith's twitter thread.
13. In 2016, a Black man was discovered hanged in Piedmont Park, Atlanta, Georgia. Public consensus agreed that this was done by the Ku Klux Klan which still holds meetings in Stone Mountain, Georgia; former Atlanta mayor Kasim Reed said that there was no evidence of "foul play" ruling the man's death as dying by suicide.

Peer-Reviewed References

Allen, Nickolas L., Benjamin J. Becerra, and Monideepa B. Becerra. 2018. "Associations Between Food Insecurity and the Severity of Psychological Distress among African-Americans." *Ethnicity & Health* 23 (5): 511–20.

Battle-Baptiste, Whitney. 2011. *Black Feminist Archaeology*. London: Routledge.

Blakey, Michael L. 2020. "Archaeology Blinding Light of Race." *Current Anthropology* 61 (S22): S183–97.

Centers for Disease Control and Prevention. 2020a. "Your Guides to Mask." https://www.cdc.gov/coronavirus/2019-ncov/prevent-getting-sick/about-face-coverings.html, accessed February 15, 2021.

———. 2020b. "Testing for COVID-19." https://www.cdc.gov/coronavirus/2019-ncov/symptoms-testing/testing.html, accessed February 15, 2021.

———. 2020c. "Guidance for Opening Up American Again Framework." https://archive.org/details/guidance-for-opening-up-america-again-framework, accessed February 16, 2021.

———. 2020d. "Importance of Reopening Schools." https://web.archive.org/web/20200929191545/https://www.cdc.gov/coronavirus/2019-ncov/community/schools-childcare/reopening-schools.html, accessed February 16, 2021.

———. 2020e. "Older Adults." https://www.cdc.gov/coronavirus/2019-ncov/need-extra-precautions/older-adults.html, accessed February 16, 2021.

———. 2020f. "COVID View Summary Ending on October 3, 2020." https://www.cdc.gov/coronavirus/2019-ncov/covid-data/covidview/past-reports/10092020.html, accessed February 22, 2021.

———. 2020g. "Demographic Characteristics of People Receiving COVID-19 Vaccinations in the United States." https://covid.cdc.gov/covid-data-tracker/#vaccination-demographic, accessed February 22, 2021.

Chaney, Cassandra and Ray V. Robertson. 2013. "Racism and Police Brutality In America." *Journal of African American Studies* 17 (4): 480–505.

Cobb, William Montague. 1947. *Medical Care and the Plight of the Negro*. New York: National Association for the Advancement of Colored People.

Cooper, Hannah and Mindy Fullilove. 2016. "Excessive Police Violence as a Public Health Issue." *Journal of Urban Health* 93 (1): 1–7.

Crenshaw, Kimberle. 1991. "Mapping the Margins: Intersectionality, Identity Politics, and Violence Against Women of Color." *Stanford Law Review* 43 (6): 1241–99.

Culbert, David. 1995. "Joseph Goebbels and His Diaries." *Historical Journal of Film, Radio and Television* 15 (1): 143–9.

Eikenberry, Steffen E., Marina Mancuso, Enahoro Iboi, Tin Phan, Keenan Eikenberry, Yang Kuang, Eric Kostelich, and Abba B. Gumel. 2020. "To Mask or Not To Mask: Modeling the Potential for Face Mask Use by the General Public to Curtail the COVID-19 Pandemic." *Infectious Disease Modelling* 5: 293–308.

Esbin, Meagan N., Oscar N. Whitney, Shasha Chong, Anna Maurer, Xavier Darzacq, and Robert Tjian. 2020. "Overcoming the Bottleneck to Widespread Testing: A Rapid Review of Nucleic Acid Testing Approaches for COVID-19 Detection." *RNA* 26 (7): 771–83.

Feagin, Joe, and Zinobia Bennefield. 2014. "Systemic Racism and US Health Care." *Social Science & Medicine* 103: 7–14.

Fernando, Suman. 2017. *Institutional Racism in Psychiatry and Clinical Psychology: Race Matters in Mental Health*. Cham, Switzerland: Palgrave Macmillan.

Fikes Jr., Robert. 2012. "Breathing While Black: Rude And Frightful Encounters with the Police Recalled by Distinguished African Americans, 1860–2012." *Journal of Pan African Studies* 5 (5): 41–66.
Food and Drug Administration. 2020a. "Coronavirus (COVID-19) Update: FDA Revokes Emergency Use Authorization for Chloroquine and Hydroxychloroquine." https://www.fda.gov/news-events/press-announcements/coronavirus-covid-19-update-fda-revokes-emergency-use-authorization-chloroquine-and, accessed February 15, 2021.
———. 2020b. "FDA Cautions Against Use of Hydroxychloroquine or Chloroquine for COVID-19 Outside of the Hospital Setting or a Clinical Trial Due to Risk of Heart Rhythm Problems." https://www.fda.gov/drugs/drug-safety-and-availability/fda-cautions-against-use-hydroxychloroquine-or-chloroquine-covid-19-outside-hospital-setting-or, accessed February 15, 2021.
Foucault, Michel. 1995 [1977]. *Discipline and Punish: The Birth of the Prison*. Alan Sheridan, trans. New York: Vintage.
Gharpure, Radihika, Candis M. Hunter, Amy H. Schnall, Catherine E. Barrett, Amy E. Kirby, Jasen Kunz., Kristen Berling , Jeffrey W. Mercante, Jennifer L. Murphy, Amanda G. Garcia-Williams. 2020. "Knowledge and Practices Regarding Safe Household Cleaning And Disinfection for COVID-19 Prevention—United States, May." *Morbidity Mortality Weekly Report* 69: 705–709. http://dx.doi.org/10.15585/mmwr.mm6923e2.
Górska, Magdalena. 2016. *Breathing Matters: Feminist Intersectional Politics of Vulnerability*. Linköping, Sweden: Linköping University Press.
Graham, Jessica R., Amber Calloway, and Lizabeth Roemer. 2015. "The Buffering Effects of Emotion Regulation in the Relationship between Experiences of Racism and Anxiety in a Black American Sample." *Cognitive Therapy and Research* 39 (5): 553–63.
Gravlee, Clarence C. 2009. "How Race Becomes Biology: Embodiment Of Social Inequality." *American Journal of Physical Anthropology* 139 (1): 47–57.
Hager, Erin R., Alexandra Cockerham, Nicole O'Reilly, Donna Harrington, James Harding, Kristen M. Hurley, and Maureen M. Black. 2017. "Food Swamps and Food Deserts in Baltimore City, MD, USA: Associations with Dietary Behaviors among Urban Adolescent Girls." *Public Health Nutrition* 20 (14): 2598–2607.
Hartman, Saidiya V. 1997. *Scenes of Subjection: Terror, Slavery, and Self-Making in Nineteenth-Century America*. Oxford: Oxford University Press.
Hodgson, Susanne H., Kushal Mansatta, Garry Mallett, Victoria Harris, Katherine RW Emary, and Andrew J. Pollard. 2021. "What Defines an Efficacious COVID-19 Vaccine? A Review of the Challenges Assessing the Clinical Efficacy of Vaccines against SARS-CoV-2." *The Lancet Infectious Diseases* 21 (February): e26–35.
Howerton, Gloria and Amy Trauger. 2017. "'Oh Honey, Don't You Know?' The Social Construction of Food Access in a Food Desert." *ACME: An International Journal for Critical Geographies* 16 (4): 740–60.
Kai-Wang, Kelvin To, Owen Tak-Yin Tsang, Cyril Chik-Yan Yip, Kwok-Hung Chan, Tak-Chiu Wu, Jacky Man-Chun Chan, Wai-Shing Leung, Thomas Shiu-Hong Chik, Chris Yau-Chung Choi, Darshana H. Kandamby, David Christopher Lung, Anthony Raymond Tam, Rosana Wing-Shan Poon, Agnes Yim-Fong Fung, Ivan Fan-Ngai Hung, Vincent Chi-Chung Cheng, Jasper Fuk-Woo Chan, and Kwok-Yung Yuen. 2020. "Consistent Detection of 2019 Novel Coronavirus in Saliva." *Clinical Infectious Diseases* 71 (15): 841–3, https://doi.org/10.1093/cid/ciaa149.
Krieger, Nancy, Anna Kosheleva, Pamela D. Waterman, Jarvis T. Chen, and Karestan Koenen. 2011. "Racial Discrimination, Psychological Distress, and Self-Rated Health among

US-Born and Foreign-Born Black Americans." *American Journal of Public Health* 101 (9): 1704–13.

Mbembe, Achille. 2006. "Necropolitics." *Raisons Politiques* 21 (1): 29–60.

McEwen, Bruce S. 2007. "Physiology and Neurobiology of Stress and Adaptation: Central Role of the Brain." *Physiological Reviews* 87 (3): 873–904.

Murry, Velma McBride, Sheretta T. Butler-Barnes, Tilicia L. Mayo-Gamble, and Misha N. Inniss-Thompson. 2018. "Excavating New Constructs for Family Stress Theories in the Context of Everyday Life Experiences of Black American Families." *Journal of Family Theory & Review* 10 (2): 384–405.

Non, Amy, and Zaneta. Thayer. 2015. "Epigenetics for Anthropologists: An Introduction to Methods." *American Journal of Human Biology* 27 (3): 295–303.

Ng, Boon Hau, Nik Nuratiqah Nik Abeed, Mohamed Faisal Abdul Hamid, Chun Ian Soo, Hsueh Jing Low, and Yu-Lin Andrea Ban. 2020. "What Happens When We Treat the 'Typhoid Mary' Of COVID-19." *Respirology Case Reports* 8 (6): e00604.

Piguillem, Facundo, and Liyan Shi. 2020. "Optimal COVID-19 Quarantine and Testing Policies." Centre for Economic Policy Research Discussion Papers, no. 14613.

Prather, Kimberly A., Chia C. Wang, and Robert T. Schooley. 2020. "Reducing Transmission of SARS-CoV-2." *Science* 368 (6498): 1422–4.

Quandt, Thorsten, Lena Frischlich, Svenja Boberg, and Tim Schatto-Eckrodt. 2019. "Fake News." In Tim P. Vos and Folker Hanusch, eds. *The International Encyclopedia of Journalism Studies*. Hoboken, NJ: Wiley-Blackwell, 1–6.

Ray, Rashawn, Melissa Brown, Neil Fraistat, and Edward Summers. 2017. "Ferguson and the Death of Michael Brown on Twitter: #BlackLivesMatter, #TCOT, and the Evolution of Collective Identities." *Ethnic and Racial Studies* 40 (11): 1797–1813.

Reitsema, Laurie J., and Britney Kyle McIlvaine. 2014. "Reconciling 'Stress' And 'Health' in Physical Anthropology: What Can Bioarchaeologists Learn from the Other Subdisciplines?" *American Journal of Physical Anthropology* 155 (2): 181–5.

Rickford, Russell. 2016. "Black Lives Matter: Toward a Modern Practice of Mass Struggle." *New Labor Forum* 25 (1): 34–42.

Sadler, Richard Casey and Don J. Lafreniere. 2017. "Racist Housing Practices as a Precursor to Uneven Neighborhood Change in a Post-Industrial City." *Housing Studies* 32 (2): 186–208.

Sapolsky, Robert M. 2012. "Importance of a Sense of Control and the Physiological Benefits of Leadership." *Proceedings of the National Academy of Sciences* 109 (44): 17730–1.

Schaefer, Benjamin J. 2017. "Sacrifice Reconsidered: Interpreting Stress from Archaeological Hair at Huaca De Los Sacrificios." Atlanta: Georgia State University, Master's thesis. https://scholarworks.gsu.edu/anthro_theses/124.

——— 2018. "Fake News, Fake Science?: Reflections of Teaching Introduction to Biological Anthropology in the Era of Trump." *Teaching and Learning Anthropology Journal* 1 (1): 1–9.

Scheper-Hughes, Nancy. 1990. "Three Propositions for a Critically Applied Medical Anthropology." *Social Science & Medicine* 30 (2): 189–197.

Sherman, Gary D, Jooa J. Lee, Amy J.C. Jonathan Renshon, Christopher Oveis Christopher Oveis, James J. Gross, and Jennifer S Lerner. 2012. "Leadership is Associated with Lower Levels of Stress." *Proceedings of the National Academy of Sciences* 109 (44): 17903–17907.

Sofaer, Joanna R. 2006. *The Body as Material Culture: A Theoretical Osteoarchaeology*. Cambridge: Cambridge University Press.

Soper, George A. 1939. "The Curious Career of Typhoid Mary." *Bulletin of the New York Academy of Medicine* 15 (10): 698.

Spillers, Hortense J. 1987. "Mama's Baby, Papa's Maybe: An American Grammar Book." *Diacritics* 17 (2): 65–81.

Tandoc Jr, Edson C., Zheng Wei Lim, and Richard Ling. 2018. "Defining 'Fake News': A Typology of Scholarly Definitions." *Digital journalism* 6 (2): 137–153.

Thomas, Anita Jones and Sha'Kema M. Blackmon. 2015. "The Influence of the Trayvon Martin Shooting on Racial Socialization Practices of African American Parents." *Journal of Black Psychology* 41 (1): 75–89.

Titanji, Boghuma K., and Talia H. Swartz. 2020. "A Diverse Physician-Scientist Pipeline to Fight Structural Racism." *Clinical Infectious Diseases* ciaa1387, https://doi.org/10.1093/cid/ciaa1387.

US Congress. 2013. "H.R. 1447 Public Law No: 113–242." https://www.congress.gov/bill/113th-congress/house-bill/1447, accessed February 16, 2021.

Voloshinov, Valentin. 1973 [1929]. *Marxism and the Philosophy of Language*. Ladislav Matejka and I.R. Titunik, trans. Cambridge, MA: Harvard University Press.

World Health Organization. 2015. "WHO Issues Best Practices for Naming New Human Infectious Disease." https://www.who.int/news/item/08-05-2015-who-issues-best-practices-for-naming-new-human-infectious-diseases, accessed February 16, 2021.

Yele, Aluko. 2008. "American Medical Association Apologizes for Racism in Medicine." *Journal of the National Medical Association* 100 (10): 1246.

Zhang, Haocheng, Jing-Wen Ai, Wenjiao Yang, Xian Zhou, Fusheng He, Shumei Xie, Weiqi Zeng, Yang Li, Yiqi Yu, Xuejing Gou, Yongjun Li, Xiaorui Wang, Hang Su, Zhaoqin Zhu, Teng Xu and Wenhong Zhang. 2021 "Metatranscriptomic Characterization of Coronavirus Disease 2019 Identified a Host Transcriptional Classifier Associated With Immune Signaling." *Clinical Infectious Diseases* 73 (3): 376–385.

News and Media References

Abutaleb, Yasmeen and Josh Dawsey. 2020. "New Trump Pandemic Advisor Pushes Controversial 'Herd Immunity' Strategy, Worrying Public Health Officials." https://www.washingtonpost.com/politics/trump-coronavirus-scott-atlas-herd-immunity/2020/08/30/925e68fe-e93b-11ea-970a-64c73a1c2392_story.html, accessed 16 February 2021.

Abutaleb, Yasmeen, Philip Rucker, Josh Dawsey, and Robert Costa. 2020. "Trump's Den of Dissent: Inside the White House Task Force as Coronavirus Surges." https://web.archive.org/web/20201025205233if_/https://www.washingtonpost.com/politics/trumps-den-of-dissent-inside-the-white-house-task-force-as-coronavirus-surges/2020/10/19/7ff8ee6a-0a6e-11eb-859b-f9c27abe638d_story.html, accessed 16 February 2021.

Albert, Victoria. 2020. "911 Call from Breonna Taylor's Shooting Death Released: 'Somebody Kicked in the Door and Shot My Girlfriend'." https://www.cbsnews.com/news/breonna-taylor-kenneth-walker-911-call-police-shooting, accessed 16 February 2021.

Alcorn, Chauncey. 2020. "Coronavirus Anxiety is Devastating Chinese Businesses in New York City." https://www.cnn.com/2020/03/02/business/chinese-business-new-york-city-coronavirus/index.html, accessed 16 February 2021.

Chang, Ailsa. 2020. "Member of Now-Disbanded National Security Council Pandemic Response Team Speaks." https://www.npr.org/2020/03/27/822728420/member-of-now-disbanded-national-security-council-pandemic-response-team-speaks, accessed 14 February 2021.

Chuck, Elizabeth. 2020. "CDC Quietly Releases Detailed Plan for Reopening America." https://www.nbcnews.com/news/us-news/cdc-quietly-releases-detailed-plan-reopening-america-n1211316, accessed 16 February 2021.

Cohen, Max. 2020. "Trump: Black Lives Matter is a 'Symbol if Hate'." https://www.politico.com/news/2020/07/01/trump-black-lives-matter-347051, accessed 22 February 2021.

Colvin, Jill. 2020. "Trump Lashes Out at Scientists Whose Findings Contradict Him." https://apnews.com/article/30b35bfadcc9e827c81986e86ced4b15, accessed 14 February 2021.

Davis, Wade. 2021. "Why Anthropology Matters." https://www.scientificamerican.com/article/why-anthropology-matters, accessed 16 February 2021.

Dearen, Jason and Mike Stobbe. 2020. "Trump Administration Buries Detailed CDC Advice on Reopening." https://apnews.com/article/7a00d5fba3249e573d2ead4bd323a4d4, accessed 16 February 2021.

Diamond, Dan. 2020. "Trump Officials Interfered with CDC Reports on COVID-19." https://www.politico.com/news/2020/09/11/exclusive-trump-officials-interfered-with-cdc-reports-on-covid-19-412809, accessed 14 February 2021.

Doubek, Jamies. 2019. "18-Year-Old Testified About Getting Vaccinated Despite Mother's Anti-Vaccine Beliefs." https://www.npr.org/2019/03/06/700617424/18-year-old-testifies-about-getting-vaccinated-despite-mothers-anti-vaccine-beli, accessed 14 February 2021.

Forgey, Quint. 2020a. "Trump's Allies Back Up His Attacks On CDC Chief." https://www.politico.com/news/2020/09/17/trump-allies-cdc-chief-attacks-417046, accessed 16 February 2021.

———. 2020b. "Trump Claims Vaccine Coming 'Within a Matter of Weeks,' Contradicting Health Officials." https://www.politico.com/news/2020/09/21/trump-contradicts-health-officials-vaccine-419330, accessed 16 February 2021.

Funke, Daniel. 2020. "In Context: What Donald Trump Said about Disinfectants, Sun and Coronavirus." https://www.politifact.com/article/2020/apr/24/context-what-donald-trump-said-about-disinfectant, accessed 14 February 2021.

Gross, Terry. 2020. "'In Deep' Challenges President Trump's Notion of a Deep-State Conspiracy." https://www.npr.org/2020/04/15/834874400/in-deep-challenges-president-trump-s-notion-of-a-deep-state-conspiracy, accessed 14 February 2021.

Han, Jane. 2020. "Mask Dilemma Troubles Koreans in US." https://www.koreatimes.co.kr/www/world/2020/03/683_286453.html, accessed 16 February 2021.

Health and Human Services, US Department. 2020. "Trump Administration Announces Framework and Leadership for 'Operation Warp Speed'." https://www.hhs.gov/about/news/2020/05/15/trump-administration-announces-framework-and-leadership-for-operation-warp-speed.html#, accessed 16 February 2021.

Jones, Jeffrey M. and Zacc Ritter. 2018. "Americans See More News Bias; Most Can't Name Neutral Source." https://news.gallup.com/poll/225755/americans-news-bias-name-neutral-source.aspx, accessed 14 February 2021.

Morales, Christina. 2020. "Mask Exemption Cards from The 'Freedom To Breathe Agency'? They're Fake." https://www.nytimes.com/2020/06/28/us/fake-face-mask-exemption-card-coronavirus.html, accessed 15 February 2021.

Morrison, Cassidy. 2020. "Critic of Coronavirus Lockdowns and School Closures Made Adviser to President Trump." https://www.washingtonexaminer.com/news/critic-of-coronavirus-lockdowns-and-school-closures-made-adviser-to-president-trump, accessed 16 February 2021.

Nierenberg, Amelia. 2020. "Please Do Not Eat Disinfectant." https://www.nytimes.com/article/coronavirus-disinfectant-inject-ingest.html, accessed 14 February 2021.

Plaga, Corrine, and Katrin Büchenbacher. 2020. "Es Bricht Mir Das Herz, Dass Ich als Schweizerin Aufgrund Meines Asiatishcen Aussehens Beliedigit Werde – Wie Menschen in Zeiten des Coronavirus Diskriminierung Erfahen." https://www.nzz.ch/panorama/coronavirus-rassismus-gegen-asiaten-nzz-ld.1543322?reduced=true, accessed 16 February 2021.

Reardon, Sara. 2016. "The Scientists Who Support Trump." https://www.nature.com/news/the-scientists-who-support-donald-trump-1.20827, accessed 14 February 2021.

Ruiz, Neil G., Juliana Menasce Horowitz, and Christine Tamir. 2020. "Many Black and Asian Americans Say They Have Experienced Discrimination Amidst The COVID-19 Outbreak." https://www.pewresearch.org/social-trends/2020/07/01/many-black-and-asian-americans-say-they-have-experienced-discrimination-amid-the-covid-19-outbreak/, accessed 16 February 2021.

Sifferlin, Alexandra. 2018. "AIDS Researcher Robert Redfield is the New CDC Director. Here's Why the Pick is Controversial." https://time.com/5211143/robert-redfield-cdc-director, accessed 14 February 2021.

Sinyangwe, Samuel, DeRay McKesson, and Johnetta Elzie. 2015. "Mapping Police Violence." https://mappingpoliceviolence.org, accessed 16 February 2021.

Stolberg, Sheryl G. 2020. "Trump Administration Strips C.D.C. of Control of Coronavirus Data." https://www.nytimes.com/2020/07/14/us/politics/trump-cdc-coronavirus.html, accessed 14 February 2021.

Trump, Donald. 2020. "Tonight, @FLOTUS And I Tested Positive for COVID-19. We Will Begin Our Quarantine and Recovery Process Immediately. We Will Get Through This TOGETHER!" https://twitter.com/realDonaldTrump/status/1311892190680014849, accessed 16 February 2021.

Tye, Chris and Chris Hacker. 2020. "African Americans Make Up More than 70 Percent of Chicago's COVID-19 Deaths." https://chicago.cbslocal.com/black-chicagoans-make-up-70-of-coronavirus-deaths-in-chicago, accessed 22 February 2021.

Vargas, Edward D. and Gabriel R. Sanchez. 2020. "American Individualism is an Obstacle to Wider Mask Wearing in the US." https://www.brookings.edu/blog/upfront/2020/08/31/american-individualism-is-an-obstacle-to-wider-mask-wearing-in-the-us, accessed 15 February 2021.

Weiland, Noah, Maggie Haberman, Mark Mazzetti, and Annie Karni. 2021. "Trump was Sicker than Acknowledged with COVID-19." https://www.nytimes.com/2021/02/11/us/politics/trump-coronavirus.html, accessed 16 February 2021.

Weiland, Noah, Sheryl Gay Stolberg, Michael D. Shear, and Jim Tankersley. 2020. "A New Coronavirus Adviser Roils the White House with Unorthodox Ideas." https://www.nytimes.com/2020/09/02/us/politics/trump-scott-atlas-coronavirus.html, accessed 16 February 2021.

11
TRUMPING THE PAST, TRUMPING THE FUTURE

How political messianism and violent conspiracy cultism come front and center in American politics

Bruce Knauft

FIGURE 11.1 Life-sized gilded statue of Donald Trump holding the US Constitution and a star scepter, at the Conservative Political Action Conference (CPAC), Orlando, FL, February 26, 2021.

Widely reproduced Reuters photo by Octavio Jones, including in the U.S. News & World Report, February 26, 2021 accompanying the article by Steve Holland and David Morgan "With Gold-Colored Trump Statue, Conservatives Show Fealty to Former President."
https://www.usnews.com/news/top-news/articles/2021-02-26/trumps-hold-on-republican-party-on-display-as-conservatives-gather. Accessed September 29, 2021.
Also published online in the New York Post, February 27, 2021 in a news article by Jon Levine "Gold Trump Statue on Sale at CPAC for $100,000." https://nypost.com/2021/02/27/gold-trump-statue-on-sale-at-cpac-for-100000/. Accessed September 29,. 2021.

DOI: 10.4324/9781003152743-14

How is it that Trump supporters can live in such a parallel world, a world incomprehensible to most of those who would be reading this book? It seems bizarre that a political system, and a Republican Party, that just a few years ago seemed obstreperous and recalcitrant but still largely "mainstream" could have morphed so quickly into a party, and a movement surrounding Trump, that so completely upends core standards of American politics as known in our lifetimes. On the one hand, seeds of the present have been long brewing and fermenting, in many ways quite explicitly, in American society and especially in the Republican Party. Trump himself has of course been key, especially since the run-up to the 2016 election and his term as president. But so also is the increased susceptibility of many Americans to alt-right outlandishness. At present, this susceptibility informs the vulnerability of the Republican Party as a whole to institutional takeover from within, with Trump's instigation and repeated incitement.

Now that Trump has been removed from power by election, if with great difficulty, what does the future bring? In addressing this we draw upon anthropological understanding of reactionary extremism, of millenarian and chiliastic movements, and radical Christian and political cults of violent resistance. But in the present case, Trumpism and conspiracy theories, including those related to QAnon, are not outside or refractory to but at the heart of institutional Republican Party politics. Virulent reactionary politics are not unprecedented in American politics. One may be reminded of Red Scare McCarthyism of the 1950s (Fried 1997) or, on the other hand, the violent Leftist Weather Underground movement of the late 1960s and early 1970s (Eckstein 2016). But the present appears to bring oppositional and conspiracy theory dynamics together by means of the very presidency of the US itself. This provides a continuing, if not central legacy for many millions of staunch Trump supporters who form a principal base of one of America's two main political parties.

These dynamics are largely outside or beyond the narrower purview of received academic scholarship in political science, sociology, anthropology, or cultural studies—or critical race or gender theory. Here we enter largely uncharted waters: the prognosis of extremist politics vis-à-vis Republicanism amid generally chaotic social conditions in the contemporary US. Based on what we can glean concerning millenarism and extremist populist politics historically and comparatively, including from within the US, and especially in relation to racism and xenophobia (e.g., Wilkerson 2020a), these paths are uncertain and yet in larger ways knowable. It now seems important to develop critical conceptual understanding that can provide initial frames of reference for these emerging developments—to help us begin understanding them, however unstable and shifting their future may be (see Knauft 1996, 2014). These issues connect the subjective core and zeitgeist of Trumpism among angry, economically marginalized, and yet previously privileged white voters with the institutional and demographic trajectories of Republican Party politics in the US today.

The challenge of the history of the future in the present

Scholarship is always challenged to engage the present, its social and political immediacies, in a timely manner. Time works against us: The pace of events is quick, the need for social and political understanding high, but the pace of scholarly reflection, not to mention publication, is slow, typically years (Knauft 2004). In practical terms, knowledge delayed is often knowledge denied; it becomes a never-ending race to keep present developments in scholarly focus. The time-space compression of twenty-first-century hypermodernity greatly accentuates this risk (cf., Harvey 1990). Yet the pressure and import of contemporary issues—their historical context, emerging developments, and potential futures—beg understanding beyond the quick and thinner analyses of most journalists, on the one hand, and off-the-cuff assessments by media pundits, on the other. The slow pace of considered scholarship easily disconnects us from current relevance and, in the process, from public intellectualism.

Added to this is the challenge of projecting complicated present trends into the trajectories of an unknown future. Easily a fool's errand, this remains important lest we give up critical purchase on the relevance of the past and the present for what is presently in the making. We can't know or predict the specifics of the future. But we can try to be critical seismologists assessing tectonic stresses across political, economic, and cultural fault lines. We cannot predict exactly when and how ruptures and explosions will occur, their specific magnitude or location. But we can size up their tendencies, relative likelihoods, and emergent patterns of overdetermined causation.

In early August 2020, I posted a blog entry, "Marching Towards an Uncivil War in America" (Knauft 2020). It foresaw Trump's attempt to abrogate the 2020 election and the likelihood of armed alt-right resistance and violence in its wake. I couldn't then see the specifics of this expression, including the Trumpist storming of the US Capitol on January 6, 2021—or the preceding attempt of the Michigan Wolverine militia to kidnap and torture Michigan Governor Gretchen Whitmer. Three months before the election, in a context of ongoing urban racial strife, it looked possible that violence would be fomented by Trump to disrupt voting itself in key swing states, upon which Trump could then call in federal troops and declare the election compromised. He was also then on the cusp of succeeding in his attempts to prevent the US Postal Service from effectively handling mail-in ballots (Cole 2020). Instead, the election went ahead relatively peacefully—only to be nearly abrogated by Trump in its aftermath. This obviously included his #StoptheSteal campaign, his relentless voter fraud lawsuits, his blatant pressure on officials in states such as Georgia to have election results summarily overturned, and his inciting a mob of armed protesters to storm the Capitol in an attempt to prevent the Congressional approval of the Electoral College count.

The timing, location, and magnitude of these events could not have been forecast. But the virulent build-up of their deeply incited expression was palpably evident, a violent tornado approaching clearly if through an idiosyncratic path on the national horizon. So, too, there ended up being a systematic and uncanny parallel between Trump's ploys and those I had comparatively described concerning how tin-pot dictators in developing countries steal or attempt to steal elections: fomenting social tension and violence based on identity politics; projecting state-incited violence as if it originated from the opposition; accusations of fraud and denial of electoral results; pressuring electoral officials to overturn and reverse electoral vote tallies; and spectacularist domination of public attention through claims and threats that disaster will ensue if the incumbent is not maintained in power.

It can be useful to assess trajectories in a general way even though specific forecasts or predictions cannot be accurately made. This is what the present essay attempts in the wake of Trump's contested defeat and the continuing poignant implications of Trumpism and its spin-offs during the succeeding Biden Presidency.

Trumpist diversity

Though one finds substantial sub-cultural commonality across many Trump supporters, their differences are vitally important—especially if one wants to begin distinguishing their more extreme and potentially or actually violent members. Setbacks or failure of a conservative agenda—such as the re-election of Trump—can cause at least some adherents to become more than less committed to their cause in a hardline manner. And yet, this is not invariable or inevitable.

What drives some people to become more extreme or violent in social resistance movements, and others not, is a question that has long bedeviled social scientists; it is hard to find causal factors that discriminate such alternative outcomes. Among QAnon supporters waiting for the apocalyptic crushing of the Deep State by Trump and his allies, some have felt betrayed and abandoned by Trump following his electoral defeat and the declining prospect of his #StoptheSteal campaign (e.g., O'Sullivan 2021). But others double down in their conspiracy theory commitments, claiming to have found special coded clues that explain just why the predicted success of Trump and the defeat of the Deep State cabal have not yet taken place (Naik 2021). In some cases, families have been torn apart by competing acceptance or rejection of QAnon and associated conspiracy theory beliefs (Batchelor 2021).

In the study of terrorism, recent work distinguishes importantly between "supporters," "facilitators," and "principal actors" (e.g., Horgan, Shortland, and Abbasciano 2018). On the one hand, the sliding scale of tolerance of and commitment to extremist belief results in distinct differences in which participants are not all equally willing or complicit. On the other hand, a key issue remains how larger networks of extremist supporters, some of whom do not explicitly avow or pursue violence, nonetheless support larger movements that alternatively allow, accept, or tacitly accept it. In the January 6, 2021 attack on the US Capitol, for instance, it has become evident that the general mob insurrection effectively enabled small groups of highly dedicated militants, especially those associated with Oath Keepers and Proud Boys, to play an outsize role in the attack (Valentino-DeVries et al. 2021). The broader implication is that a better understanding is needed of the relationship between more generally oppositional political culture and the more ardent extremist elements within it. As suicide bombing expert Robert Pape and colleague Kevin Ruby (2021: 11) suggest,

> What's clear is that the Capitol riot revealed a new force in American politics—not merely a mix of right-wing organizations, but a broader mass political movement that has violence at its core and draws strength even from places where Trump supporters are in the minority. Preventing further violence from this movement will require a deeper understanding of its activities and participants, and the two of us do not claim to know which political tactics might ultimately prove helpful…

Mainstream Republican Party, millenarian cult heroism, or violent extremism?

Social movements have often informed US party politics, including the influence of the Civil Rights movement and movements of opposition to the Vietnam war on the Democratic Party in the 1960s and early 1970s (e.g., Thompson 2009). As has often been noted, the Republican Party has for several decades courted social conservatism and combined it with fiscal conservatism to mobilize its political base—and align it with the economic interests of wealthy white Americans and Republican donors (see Hacker and Pierson 2020). In some cases, populist movements spawned or amplified by politicians have developed a committed social base, as in McCarthyism—the anti-Communist Red Scare inquisitions led by Senator Joseph McCarthy during the 1950s—and the Tea Party movement within the Republican Party beginning in 2009, drawing on the strident fiscal and social conservatism of Newt Gingrich, Republican Speaker of the House between 1995 and 1999. By 2013, more than 10 percent of Americans supported the Tea Party movement, which in its heyday staged large-scale protests (Bowman and Marsico, 2014). So, too, various conspiracy theories have filtered through and informed American politics to a greater or lesser degree for decades (Merlan 2019).

Trumpism has drawn upon this strain of Republican politics but personalized and polarized it against Democrats and mainstream Republicans to an unprecedented degree (Abramowitz 2018). During the run-up to the 2020 presidential election and even more in its aftermath, Trump made personal loyalty and unwavering support for him not just the litmus test for presidential favors and preferences but the *sine qua non* for acceptance and support in the Republican Party as a whole. Even in the wake of electoral defeat, full-throated Trump supporters hold control of the national Republican Party and many of its most important state party organizations (e.g., Isenstadt 2021). Many Republicans in Congress are privately said to be horrified at Trump but unwilling to admit the slightest break in their fealty to him—for fear of incurring his revenge and the vitriol of his supporters, including in upcoming primaries and elections (e.g., Pengelly 2020). He reinforced this fear by calling out a "hit list" of mainstream Republicans in his first major speech as ex-president—those who voted for his impeachment or otherwise did not unflinchingly support him (Martin and Haberman, 2021; see Holland and Morgan 2021). Never in our lifetimes, perhaps in all of American political history, has a defeated ex-president held such sway in a major party whose members are personally so politically uncomfortable with him.

Here we must complement the calculus of party politics by considering Trump's political base as an increasingly independent social movement of ardent supporters. To many of his most fervent followers, Trump is not an ex-president but a cult hero, the leader of a deeply informed movement to forestall the takeover of government by forces of Evil associated with so-called Liberals and Democrats. This is explicitly evident in conspiracy theory movements such as QAnon. QAnon holds that a Deep State cabal of nefarious leaders has conspired to secretly overtake the US government from within, corrupt society through exploitative politics, and sow Evil through pedophilia and the killing of children, drinking their blood to increase their own life force (see Roose 2021; Beverly 2020; Quinn 2020; Smith 2020; cf., Knight 2017). QAnon's undying and heroic paragon, the savior who will expose and destroy this Cabal of Evil, is Donald Trump. QAnon supporters were highly visible and among the most extreme in the insurrection and pillaging of the US Capitol on January 6, 2021 (Rubin et al. 2021).

Though Donald Trump was defeated in the 2020 election, the reluctance of Republicans to dissociate themselves from him—even after his bald attempts to subvert the election, and even after his inciting a violent mob to storm the Capitol—reveals the continuing deep purchase among his supporters of his flagrant disregard not just of liberal values but of democracy itself. Trump retains his alt-right status as a cult hero of seething white anger, now intertwining increasingly with preposterous conspiracy theories that foment violence and anti-government terrorism (see Homans 2021; Thompson 2021). These notions are not just tolerated but virulently propagated by highly visible Republican members of Congress. Influential Congresswoman, vehement Trump supporter and QAnon adherent Marjorie Taylor Greene has endorsed the assassination of Democrats (Edmonson 2021a; Steck and Kaczynski 2021), has asserted that mass school shootings in the US were merely staged (Edmonson 2021b), and has suggested that California wildfires were caused by a Jewish space laser (Chait 2021). In significant ways, Trumpism is now morphing into an anti-liberal millenarian cult, seemingly resistant to any semblance of fact or reason. As studies of millenarian cults have consistently shown since at least the 1950s (see Festinger et al. 1956), proponents of outlandish conspiracy theories may not be dissuaded by factual disconfirmation. Instead, they may be driven to validate their claims as a socially constructed reality, oftentimes affirmed by the intensified recruitment of yet more people to their cause.

Given the stoking of rank conspiracy theories by the alt-right media and Trump himself as an acceptable means of violent resistance, it is not surprising that alt-right men under siege are also not uncommonly warriors armed with assault weapons. Alt-right talk show paragons such as Sean Hannity openly encourage the prospect of armed resistance against a Democratic regime (see Hannity 2020). Even prior to Trump's defeat, in fall 2020, 13 men of the Wolverine Watchmen white supremacist group followed up on Trump's incitement to "liberate" Michigan from its Democratic governor, Gretchen Whitmer, by attempting to kidnap, torture, and potentially execute her (Gray and Tompkins 2020). In the aftermath of this plot, Trump encouraged a campaign crowd not to disavow the attempted kidnappers but rather to incarcerate Whitmer herself. He even incited them to chant, "Lock her up! Lock her up!" (Martin 2020). The Michigan Republican Party has actively cultivated ties with or otherwise tolerated initiatives by its state's paramilitary groups (Kirkpatrick and McIntire 2021). Members of Oath Keepers, a right-wing militia group, started setting up training sessions for urban warfare within a week of Election Day, and they discussed a plot to ferry heavy weapons into Washington across the Potomac River while "awaiting direction" from Trump about how to respond to the election results (Feuer 2021). Since shortly after Trump's election in 2016, and fueled by him, anti-government militia groups such as Electric Boogaloo began planning armed insurrection, which they described as "Civil War 2" (Mogelson 2020; cf., Blight 2017).

Since 2017, the percentage of Americans who think it is justified for their political party to use violence to advance their goals has increased from 8 percent to more than 30 percent (Prideaux 2020). The sale of guns as "protection"—against the feared results of a fraught election—fueled their purchase to record-breaking levels, including a 91 percent increase of guns sold in the pre-election period of 2020 vis-à-vis the same period in 2019 (Searcey and Oppel Jr., 2020). As noted by Harkin (this volume), active participation in gun culture is a highly important aspect of male identity in "Trumplandia." Sixty percent of Americans now believe that domestic terrorism poses either an immediate or a somewhat serious threat (Economist Weekly Chart, February 5, 2021). Recently, the US Department of Homeland Security has issued a National Terrorism Advisory System Bulletin which warns that "ideologically-motivated violent extremists with objections to the exercise of governmental authority and the presidential transition, as well as other perceived grievance fueled by false narratives, could continue to mobilize to incite or commit violence" (DHS 2021).

In hindsight, QAnon may be, at least in larger historical terms, something of a current flash in the pan; it could conceivably decline and wither as its core beliefs and prophecies are increasingly disconfirmed. However, it is also possible or likely that some segments of QAnon supporters will intensify their beliefs, disguise their efforts, become more removed from public scrutiny, and become more extremist and violent. In any case, it is evident that religiously inflected cult political conspiracy theories such as QAnon and related alt-right militia movements connect with deeper strains of evangelical radicalism, often associated with the biblical book of Revelation and the so-called Great Awakening (Quinn 2020). This strain of millenarian political thought in ongoing political context is apt to morph and continue, potentially in increasingly extreme ways over time. A key issue is how likely it is for these developments to strongly influence or even define the core dimensions and base of support of the Republican Party in future years.

Before considering these issues specifically, we should step back and consider the larger contours of Trumpism and Trump supporters, not limiting consideration to their most radical and extreme adherents.

Stigma and its displacement: the spirit of Trumpism

Several papers in the present volume plumb the subjective sense of disenfranchisement among Trump supporters, including Harkin's chapter on Trump supporters in Wyoming, Westermeyer's contribution concerning Tea Party members transition to Trumpism in North Carolina, and Pied's consideration of Trump-related political tensions in rural Maine. A common theme across these cases, and in the consideration of Trumpism more generally, concerns working-class and rural white Americans, especially men, who feel left out and deeply stigmatized in relation to mainstream "Blue" values of humanitarian progressivism and liberality (see Vance 2016; Wuthnow 2018). As suggested elsewhere (Knauft in press), these opposed values associate with what I call the "Blue Bourgeoisie." The Blue Bourgeoisie can be defined as the American cultural class largely composed of highly educated professionals who are not as rich as the upper 2 percent in America, but richer than the lowest 85 percent of the nation's socio-economic pyramid. As described by Matthew Stewart (2018) using a slightly more restrictive economic benchmark (the uppermost 9.9 percent), this class tends to be politically liberal, progressive, and at least moderately, if not entirely successful in the digital economy. Families in this demographic typically have enough wealth to support their children through college and professional training degrees and to help them through the challenges of buying and owning a home, paying medical bills, child-care expenses, and meeting other financial needs.

All this contrasts starkly, if not diametrically, with the values and circumstances of many Trump supporters. Westermeyer (this volume, p. 1), suggests that, "These… 'deplorables' view their communities as suffering from deindustrialization that has favored the coastal, urban areas containing liberal elites advocating multiculturalism. However, instead of being silenced through symbolic violence, the deplorable label becomes the foundation for the fashioning of activist political identities." Among these supporters, "Paul," says, "You watch MSNBC or read some of the newspapers on the left… we're just buffoons, we're morons, we're idiots. We're deniers, whatever. We are intellectually racist. Whatever. And it's just not true. We may disagree on some things but were not stupid people. There are intelligent people on both sides" (Westermeyer, p. 9). As "Linda" puts it (Westermeyer, p 14), "It's one thing to have money. But it's different for you to feel you're smarter and know best. And there is an elite element in our world. People that know best and they run everything. They're the public masters." Against this, Westermeyer (p. 15) describes T-shirts proclaiming one to be a "PROUD MEMBER OF THE BASKET OF DEPLORABLES" and a Facebook group titled "UNITED DEPLORABLES FOR TRUMP" with over a quarter of a million likes.

Concerning Trump supporters in rural Maine, Pied (this volume, p. 3) finds that, "Trump voters described feeling controlled, belittled, or patronized by liberal politicians and their liberal neighbors." In Wyoming, Harkin (p. 15) suggests that Trump, "has instilled a sense of victimhood in Whites who culturally identify with a rural, Christian identity. His rallies provided a cathartic expression of this White identity in a way that had not been socially acceptable before." Further, "This culture—the 'liberal' side of neoliberalism—is at odds with the traditional culture of rural White America." (Harkin, this volume, p. 25).

It is not hard to see how the generally declining economic conditions and cultural privilege of rural and working-class Trump supporters grate against the values and lifestyle of the Blue Bourgeoisie and align with racist and xenophobic resentment against the growing demographic ranks of American persons of color. Indeed, one of Trump's great political results has been to firmly ally the interests of lower-class and hyper-conservative upper-class whites in racist opposition to People of Color, on the one hand, and bourgeois liberals, on the other (see Knauft in press). One need but tune in to Fox News or alt-right talk radio to feel the deep vitriol and ridicule of Trumpist diatribes against those associated with liberal and humanitarian progressivism.

The deeper cause of Trumpist discontent is not hard to find. As discussed elsewhere (Knauft in press), Trump's racist alliance of white privilege between rich and poor whites is fueled by their shared anxiety about current demographic and economic trends. Within a few years, whites will become a minority of the American population, surpassed by the demographic growth of non-whites (US Census Bureau 2015; see Wilson 2016). The possibility that this will result in persons of color holding increased political and economic power is an outcome that Republicans appear to be deeply afraid of—and dedicated to politically forestalling, if not reversing. In this context, the racial resentment and polarization stoked by Trump have distracted lower-class whites from opposing the economic inequality that has skyrocketed extremely between them and wealthy Americans under twenty-first-century capitalism (Abramowitz 2018).

In the mix, the social structure of the US economy has become deeply skewed, with so much wealth concentrated in so few hands while the rest of the population is left so far behind, with little effective chance of economic advancement. The Great Recession of 2007–09 nearly halved the wealth of lower-income whites, and this decline has not reversed, though upper-class recovery has mushroomed (Kochhar and Cilluffo 2017). The richest fifty Americans are now worth as much as the poorest 165 million (Steverman and Tanzi 2020), and the pay of American CEOs is now 278 times greater than that of the average worker (Cox 2019). More than 160,000 small businesses closed in the US between March and November 2020, including 100,000 that have closed permanently (see Nichols 2021).

Given changes in the new gig economy and advances in machine learning, combined with the increasing cost and challenges of higher education, it has become more difficult for a person with a low-level job or contract work that does not include benefits to work her or his way to higher-class status (see Shapiro 2017; Kessler 2018). All of these challenges are greatly intensified by COVID-19 isolation conditions, which disproportionately impact the middle and lower classes. Even before the pandemic, as Williams (2017) suggests, many white Americans now considered "poor" or "working class" were downwardly sinking members of the middle class who resented both the professional elite and the historically poor. "[M]any people have conflated 'working class' with 'poor'—but the working class is, in fact, the elusive, purportedly disappearing middle class. They often resent the poor and the professionals alike. But they don't resent the truly rich" (Williams 2017: frontispiece). This is because, "Their dream is not to join the upper middle class, with its different culture, but to stay true to their own values in their own communities—just with more money" (see details in Williams 2017: Ch. 3). What results, as titled in Robert Wuthnow's (2018) penetrating book, is *The Left Behind: Decline and Rage in Rural America*. This deeply shared, but inchoate failed middle-class aspiration, this combined sense of desire, entitlement, and resentful neglect, has been effectively used by Trump to fuel virulent racism, sexism, and xenophobia.

White working-class men, in particular, are angry; their received double privilege of being male and white in an America that used to afford them the status of upward mobility has been effectively shattered (see Kimmel 2017). But when they blame others, they don't blame the wealthiest, who often use their wealth to promote a politics of resentment against Blacks, women, immigrants, and other Persons of Color (see Wilkerson 2020b; Knauft in press). Instead, it is the urbane sensibilities, multiculturalism, and elite intellectualism of liberal professionals that are anathema to Trump's base, who feel degraded, condescended to, and denigrated by patronizing liberal values. These sentiments inform the deep antipathy and resentment—if not loathing—that Trump supporters typically feel toward the Blue Bourgeoisie.

Self-described hillbilly J. D. Vance (2016: 191) described the reaction of lower-class whites he knows to Barack Obama as president:

> [T]he president feels like an alien to many Middletonians for reasons… Nothing about him bears any resemblance to the people I admired growing up: His accent—clean, perfect, natural—foreign; his credentials are so impressive that they're frightening; he made his life in Chicago, a dense metropolis; and he conducts himself with a confidence that comes from knowing that the modern American meritocracy was built for him.

Compare this with life in white rural working-class America. As highlighted by Wuthnow (2018), lives in this context are shot through with population decline and brain drain; teen pregnancy; drugs; lack of jobs; and cultural threats, including by the demographic and occupational rise of immigrants and Persons of Color. In terms of upbringing and socialization, as Vance (2016: 226) describes it, experience is pervaded by euphemistically termed "adverse child experiences," including: being sworn at, insulted, or humiliated by parents; being pushed, grabbed, or having something thrown at you; feeling that your family didn't support each other; having parents who were separated or divorced; living with an alcoholic or drug user; living with someone who was depressed or attempted suicide; watching a loved one be physically abused.

Westermeyer (this volume, p. 11) describes the common features of the right-leaning men he interviewed:

> One factor is common: almost all have experienced failed marriages and relationships, and all who have children are estranged from them, often by court order. That is, they feel a strong sense of both being victims of forces beyond their control (notably lawyers and the courts), as well as being unable to fulfill the paternal responsibilities that they believe to be a central part of masculine identity. There exists a wound at the center of their being, which they attempt to compensate for in various ways, in particular through the possession of guns and other markers of a blue-collar masculine ideal, such as large pickup trucks.

Into this context strode the persona of Trump. His racism and sexism, his double standard of macho pride and insecurity, resonated with what the white working-class and rural men so often themselves experience. This involves life*style*, fundamentalist values, and conservative ethics and morality. If you experience life as a hardscrabble struggle, a mean existence of defending yourself and fighting back, then Trump is easily your man. (In this case, you probably haven't read the *New York Times*' scathing exposé of Trump's financial and family background; see Barstow et al. 2018.) That Trump managed to get where he is *despite* who he is can make him all the more of a hero. He speaks his mind and does "what needs to be done." Batting away liberal niceties with presidential disdain, he roundly mocks PC punditry in ways that delight and energize his political base. If he's a scoundrel, at least he's one his followers can identify with. Even his racism and sexism, his double standard of macho pride and insecurity, resonate with what the white rural and working-class men so often experience themselves. Life as such is not always pretty. But it has a value that is more than economic. And the deeper fears and resentments of less well-off and less educated whites were shared by Trump as president of the United States as a whole.

As against this, as Vance (2016: 191) describes it,

> President Obama came on the scene right as so many people in my community began to believe that the modern American meritocracy was not built for *them*. We know we're not doing well. We see it every day. In the obituaries for teenage kids that conspicuously omit the cause of death (reading between the lines: overdose), in the deadbeats we watch our daughters waste their time with. Barack Obama strikes at the heart of our deepest insecurities. He is a good father while many of us aren't. He wears suits to his job while we wear overalls, if we're lucky enough to have a job at all.

Illegibility: a key issue—and methodological problem

An important factor in analyzing the potentials for more violent extremism in the US is that its capacities develop largely beneath the radar of standard public opinion, awareness, or investigation; they are covered over by metaphoric and tacit expressions of alt-right oppositionalism. At one level, this is true of practically all violent state-opposition resistance movements: they strive to be illegible and outside the scope of official awareness. Though the US has often tried to pride itself on a tradition of peaceful public protest movements (e.g., Risen 2015), the planning and strategy of anti-governmental violence is underground practically by definition. However, the covering of this potential with a fervent and potential volatile public movement that, on the surface, "denies violence," makes complicity hard to definitively assess. Such assessments are themselves contended, including at the highest levels of government. Hence, for instance, the stark divide between most Republicans and Democrats as to whether Trump was or was not responsible for inciting the January 6, 2021 storming of the Capitol.

Anthropologist James Scott (e.g., 1999, 2010) has emphasized the significance of remaining illegible to state awareness and intervention. In the present case, the illegibility of conspiracy theories that champion the destruction of so-called Deep State is magnified by the manifest outlandishness of their beliefs from a mainstream perspective. These appear to emerge from a mystical and frankly crazy worldview that is ridiculous to most Americans, and especially to most Democrats. And yet anthropologists, as well as critical theorists of subjectivity such as Foucault (1984, 1995, see Knauft 1996, 2017, 2018), have long shown the penchant of people to willfully not understand or identify with those designated as Other within their own societies. As such, illegibility can in the present case be reinforced, as it were, from both sides.

The problem of "illegibility" is compounded by the sliding scale of opposition to mainstream US government—from peaceful conservatism to tolerance of aggressive oppositionalism to facilitating or participating in activities that incite or expressly perpetrate violence. This sliding scale is itself integral to the larger effectiveness of alt-right Trumpism and its relation to conspiracy theories. Adherents can present their dispositions "both ways": non-violent and "peaceful" and yet emphasizing the importance of being able to take action, including armed action.

At a higher and more official organizational level, in the national Republican Party, the ability of Trumpist adherents or "tolerators" to slide between condoning versus merely tolerating or being a by-stander to violence was palpably illustrated during Trump's second impeachment proceedings. In these, the vast majority of Republican legislators, including 197 of 211 Republican House members and 43 of 50 Republican Senators, refused to find Trump responsible for significantly inciting the insurrection against the US Capitol.

This process is extended further by turning around legitimate accusations against Trump or Trump supporters and simply redirecting them onto liberals. This was graphically reflected in the alt-right claim after and even during the insurrection itself that the insurgents against the Capitol were leftist "antifa" vigilantes rather than Trump supporters. This false re-direction (there is no evidence at all that any antifa members or other leftist group members took part in the insurrection) was quickly fomented by alt-right media.

> By day's end, Laura Ingraham and Sarah Palin had shared it with millions of Fox News viewers, and Representative Matt Gaetz of Florida had stood on the ransacked House floor and claimed that many rioters "were members of the violent terrorist group antifa." Nearly two months after the attack, the claim that antifa was involved has been repeatedly debunked by federal authorities, but it has hardened into gospel among hard-line Trump supporters, by voters and sanctified by elected officials in the party. More than half of Trump voters in a Suffolk University/USA Today poll said that the riot was "mostly an antifa-inspired attack." At Senate hearings last week focused on the security breakdown at the Capitol, Senator Ron Johnson, a Wisconsin Republican, repeated the falsehood that "fake Trump protesters" fomented the violence.
>
> (Grynbaum et al. 2021)

As the flipside of conspiracy theory beliefs, many well-documented findings and that are critical of Trump are dismissed by alt-rightists as completely fake "hoaxes," including the impeachment accusations against Trump, the investigation into Russian election-meddling, and the 2020 presidential election itself.

The "cultification" of Trump, the Republican Party, and the violent fringe: how bad will it get?

On Christmas morning 2020, Anthony Q. Warner drove his explosive-rigged RV to a posh downtown street in the center of Nashville, Tennessee, and detonated the vehicle—and killed himself. The blast damaged some fifty buildings, many historic. A few collapsed, and the antique brick faces were sheared off others, destruction that will take years and tens of millions of dollars to restore (Cavendish et al. 2021). What was his motive?

> Though Mr. Warner's motive remains shrouded in mystery, false information and outlandish tales had poisoned his mind, apparently driving him to spectacular violence. This mind-set has become alarmingly familiar to law enforcement officials now reckoning with the destructive force of conspiracy theories that mutate endlessly online and played a role in the January 6 attack on the US Capitol. Mr. Warner, who was 63 when he died, was not among the angry QAnon followers who came to believe the unlikely theory that Donald J. Trump would hold on to power by defeating a satanic cabal. He was a computer specialist with a deep distrust of government, according to his own writings and to those who knew him. A loner… he had cultivated a

bizarre obsession with shape-shifting alien lizards and a dense thicket of other peculiar ideas.

(Cavendish et al. 2021)

Warner's case illustrates how difficult it is to pinpoint the factors that could distinguish in advance those who might commit acts of extreme violence, those loosely (or more tightly) associated with armed resistance groups, and those who are devoted to Trump as a QAnon cult hero. How are we to discriminate between those who only dabble or flirt with outlandish conspiracy theories and those who get sucked into them more violently, such as Mr. Warner?

In larger terms, we confront overlapping chain-links of identification, and potential action, across a whole spectrum. On the one hand this spectrum includes dedicated alt-right militia groups devoted to exercises and rehearsals of potential violent extremism, or actually carrying them out. It also includes enablers and toleraters of hard-core alt-rightism, those who believe in an eminent Christian apocalypse of violent Armageddon, and those who only dabble or toy with conspiracy theories as a kind of fantasy or side-line hobby. These, in turn, articulate with mainstream Make America Great Again (MAGA) supporters not associated with QAnon but who, for example, may be sympathizers or active supporters of Trump's "#StoptheSteal campaign. Then there are an increasing number of radical conspiracy theory foundational texts, some which have been known for a number of years, that are now being rediscovered and reinterpreted in newly virulent ways (Economist 2021).

Whatever their initial orientation, the spectrum of those attracted to Trumpism is easily channeled by alt-right influence to become more extreme over time. In addition to Trump-friendly cable networks and talk radio, this is reinforced by Republican politicians at the local, state, and federal levels, including prominent alt-right members of Congress. Sympathy with deeper conspiracy theory leanings can easily be flagged, as it was by Trump, by particular phrasings, metaphors, or allusions which have strong meaning and intent for those "in the know," but which seem innocuous or just strange to the uninitiated. As such, alt-right politicians can "pass" as mainstream while still reflecting and re-stoking hard alt-right conspiracy-based oppositionalism. At the least, virulent opposition against views associated with the Blue Bourgeoisie is a powerful organizing principal and strategic tactic. Following the vote of Republican representative Liz Cheney to impeach Donald Trump, 66 of the 74 members of the Wyoming Republican Central Committee voted to censure her (Gruver 2021).

Direct Republican ties to extremist groups are increasingly evident, and "a number of members of Congress have links to organizations that played a role in the January 6 assault on the Capitol" (Broadwater and Rosenberg 2021). Publicizing the Oath Keepers' video "The Coming Civil War," Arizona chapter leader Jim Arroyo recounted a visit to the group by one of the far-right members of Congress, Representative Paul Gosar of Arizona. When asked about the coming Civil War, Arroyo said that the congressman's "response to the group was just flat out: 'We're in it! We just haven't started shooting at each other yet.'" Far from being shunned by his Party, Gosar's actions have been applauded, if not lionized by many Republicans, and he was chosen to give the keynote address at the much-heralded CPAC convention at which Trump gave his first major speech as ex-president (Steakin 2021).

Yet, it is hard to know how deeply or materially these connections will be extended to violent action in coming months and years. In this sense, the illegibility of core violent extremists is also a challenge to the Republican Party. Disavowing die-hard alt-right conspiracy activists risks compromising Trump's base and alienating his continuing power, especially his power of revenge, within the Republican Party. But actively tolerating or pandering to them risks backlash from more centrist party members and from the American electorate more generally. At larger issue is the present likelihood that the Republican Party will be more fully co-opted by its far-right conspiracy theory elements.

One can presently see these dynamics playing out in alt-right media. Following Fox News' surprise calling of the presidential election for Joe Biden in Arizona, Trump harshly criticized Fox and urged his supporters toward alternative alt-right media outlets. Following this, Fox viewership plummeted, and the network suffered its worst ratings in twenty years (Sommerlad 2021a). Conversely, the ratings of new alt-right competitor NewsMax soared, along with those of One America News (OAN) (Sommerlad 2021b). Whether analogous splintering will occur within the Republican Party itself over lock-step fealty to Trump is an important question. For now, however, the yet-further rightward march of the Republican Party seems painfully evident, as reflected in their Conservative Political Action Conference (CPAC) in February 2021. Once a melting pot of conservative ideas, proposal, and ideologies, CPAC in 2021 was reduced to a festive celebration and lionization of Trump's white nationalism (Lerer 2021; Plott 2021).

In the present case, much will likely depend on whether Trump himself emerges as the master, or becomes the slave, of a new generation of alt-right stridency. Current evidence is that Trump will fight strongly to keep his influence and leadership in the Republican Party. At the above-mentioned CPAC gathering, Trump continued to debunk the 2020 election results and claim leadership of a unified Republican Party. He declared, "I may even decide to beat them [Democrats] for a third time"—signaling the active possibility that he will run for the presidency again in 2024 as well as the Trumpist belief that the 2020 election was stolen from him. One can hardly imagine the deep threat and discreditation of American democracy that a further Trumpist presidential campaign would entail. This would put the terms and veracity of the election itself under deep suspicion and doubt by Republicans and Trump supporters from the very start. If Trump was not elected—and given the resistance against him by Democrats and others, it is quite likely he would be defeated—it could easily, if not likely sow the seeds of widespread discontent and violence, a new kind of twenty-first-century civil war. At present, it appears that half or more Americans still take Trump to be the leader of the Republican Party (Rynor and Lowenstein 2021). Perhaps as significantly, he appears to have no viable contenders poised to supplant him in this capacity. If American politics has been Trumped in the past, it may well be Trumped more stridently in the future—regardless of whether Trump runs again for the presidency and is re-elected, or not.

Conclusions

Virulent right-wing extremism and its relationship with QAnon and other conspiracy theories are likely to continue as a prominent part of both mainstream Republican politics and less legible "fringe" groups that disguise their intent and activities. Much remains at stake in whether these oppositional elements come to dominate the Republican Party more fully, or whether non-conspiracy theory Republicans grow in strength and influence. At present, the former outcome seems far more likely than the latter.

Much depends on the role of Trump himself in future months and years—if he gains more support by remaining the effective leader of the Republican Party, with few viable contenders to supplant him, or if he attacks Republicanism more fully and compromises the Party by championing more radical organizations and initiatives outside of and opposed to it. The deeper structural causes of seething discontent that have fueled Trumpism, and that Trump continues to stoke as ex-president, articulate effectively with extremist conspiracy theories and with virulent racism and xenophobia. These remain deeply ensconced and intensifying in major portions of the white American electorate.

Yet, it is difficult to assess the likely future trajectory of specific American groups or types of individuals in relation to morphing alt-right extremism. Of particular and often-overlooked significance is the chain-link network of overlapping connection between hard-core extremists, those who sympathize with or tolerate violent extremism without themselves participating in or explicitly condoning it, and those, including politicians, who borrow from and reflect the beliefs and coded language of extreme alt-right adherents while not explicitly endorsing their violent intent or activities.

Anthropologists seem especially well-positioned to understand and assess the deeper dynamics of Trumpist sensibilities through ethnographic research of the kind reflected in several chapters of the present volume. This understanding of subjectivity in relation to particular alt-right constituencies and their relation to centrist Republicanism and other vantage points across the political spectrum seems particularly important at the present time.

We cannot yet see the future of specific developments in relation to Trumpist extremism, conspiracy theory adherence, and violent opposition to mainstream US government and politics. But it is strongly evident that changes in the American electorate, especially the rising demographic tide of Persons of Color, is deeply threatening and mobilized by Trump and Trumpism to stoke racism and xenophobia among whites who fear loss of their privilege. These structural forces are apt to become stronger in future years, and they are exacerbated by the increasing loss of large numbers of the middle- and lower-class jobs amid the twenty-first-century march of high tech, AI (artificial intelligence), the "gig" work of temporary self-employment, and the increasing dominance of the digital attention economy. This larger context provides fertile ground for intensifying present trajectories of racist white reactionism, anti-democracy, and radical conspiracy opposition, not to mention the potential, if not likely continuing role of Trump himself as a galvanizing and intensely polarizing figure. These trends are highly troubling and of grave concern for the future of American politics and American democracy.

References

Abramowitz, Alan I. 2018. *The Great Alignment: Race, Party Transformation, and the Rise of Donald Trump*. New Haven, CT: Yale University Press.

Barstow, David, Susanne Craig, and Russ Buettner. 2018. "Trump Engaged in Suspect Tax Schemes as He Reaped Riches from His Father." *The New York Times*, Special Investigation, October 2. https://www.nytimes.com/interactive/2018/10/02/us/politics/donald-trump-tax-schemes-fred-trump.html, accessed February 28, 2021.

Batchelor, Tom. 2021. How QAnon Conspiracy Theorists are Tearing American Families Apart. *Newsweek*, February 11. https://www.newsweek.com/qanon-conspiracy-theorists-capitol-riot-american-families-1568664, accessed February 28, 2021.

Beverly, James A. 2020. *The QAnon Deception: Everything You Need to Know About the World's Most Dangerous Conspiracy Theory*. Seattle, WA: Amazon Books.

Blight, David. 2017. "'The Civil War Lies on Us Like a Sleeping Dragon': America's Deadly Divide – and Why it Has Returned." *The Guardian*, August 20. https://www.theguardian.com/us-news/2017/aug/20/civil-war-american-history-trump, accessed February 28, 2021.

Bowman, Karlyn and Jennifer Marsico. 2014. "As the Tea Party Turns Five, It Look a Lot Like the Conservative Base." *Forbes Magazine*, February 24. https://www.forbes.com/sites/realspin/2014/02/24/as-the-tea-party-turns-five-it-looks-a-lot-like-the-conservative-base/?sh=218e1a91f0cc, accessed February 28, 2021.

Broadwater, Luke and Matthew Rosenberg. 2021. "Republican Ties to Extremist Groups Are Under Scrutiny." *The New York Times*, January 29. https://www.nytimes.com/2021/01/29/us/republicans-trump-capitol-riot.html, accessed February 28, 2021.

Cavendish, Steve, Neil MacFarquhar, Jamie McGee, and Adam Goldman. 2021. "Behind the Nashville Bombing: A Conspiracy Theorist Stewing About the Government." *The New York Times*, February 24. https://www.nytimes.com/2021/02/24/us/anthony-warner-nashville-bombing.html, accessed February 28, 2021.

Chait, Jonathan. 2021. "GOP Congresswoman Blamed Wildfires on Secret Jewish Space Laser." *New York Magazine, Intelligencer*, January 28. https://nymag.com/intelligencer/article/marjorie-taylor-greene-qanon-wildfires-space-laser-rothschild-execute.html, accessed February 28, 2021.

Cole, Steve. 2020. "Is the Postal Service Being Manipulated to Help Trump Get Re-elected?" *The New Yorker*, July 29. https://www.newyorker.com/news/daily-comment/is-the-postal-service-being-manipulated-to-help-trump-get-reelected, accessed February 28, 2021.

Cox, Jeff. 2019. "CEOs See Pay Grow 1000% in the Last 40 years, Now Make 278 Times the Average Worker." *CNBC News Online*, August 16. https://www.cnbc.com/2019/08/16/ceos-see-pay-grow-1000percent-and-now-make-278-times-the-average-worker.html, accessed February 28, 2021.

DHS (US Department of Homeland Security). 2021. "National Terrorism Advisory System Bulletin—January 27." https://www.dhs.gov/ntas/advisory/national-terrorism-advisory-system-bulletin-january-27-2021, accessed February 28, 2021.

Eckstein, Arthur M. 2016. *Bad Moon Rising: How the Weather Underground Beat the FBI and Lost the Revolution*. New Haven, CT: Yale University Press.

The Economist. 2021. "Deadly Inspirations: What Their Chosen Reading Says About America's Far-Right." *The Economist*, February 20. https://www.economist.com/

united-states/2021/02/20/what-their-chosen-reading-says-about-americas-far-right, accessed February 28, 2021.

Edmonson, Catie. 2021a. "Marjorie Taylor Greene Reportedly Endorsed Executing Democrats on Facebook Before She was Elected to Congress." *The New York Times*, January 27. https://www.nytimes.com/2021/01/27/us/marjorie-taylor-greene-executing-democrats.html?searchResultPosition=4, accessed February 28, 2021.

———. 2021b. "Pelosi Savages GOP Leaders for Giving Education Committee Seat to Congresswoman Who Called School Shootings Staged." *The New York Times*, January 28. https://www.nytimes.com/2021/01/28/us/pelosi-marjorie-taylor-greene.html?searchResultPosition=5, accessed February 28, 2021.

Festinger, Leon, Henry W. Riecken, and Stanley Schachter. 1956. *When Prophecy Fails: A Social and Psychological Study of a Modern Group that Predicted the Destruction of the World*. New York: Harper.

Feuer, Alan. 2021. "Oath Keepers Plotting Before Capitol Riot Awaited 'Direction' from Trump, Prosecutors Say." *The New York Times*. February 11. https://www.nytimes.com/2021/02/11/us/politics/oath-keepers-trump-investigation.html?searchResultPosition=1, accessed September 29, 2021.

Foucault, Michel. 1984. *The Foucault Reader*. Edited by Paul Rabinow. New York: Pantheon.

———. 1995. *Discipline and Punish: The Birth of the Prison*. New York: Vintage.

Fried, Albert. 1997. *McCarthyism: The Great American Red Scare – A Documentary History*. New York: Oxford University Press.

Gray, Kathleen and Lucy Tompkins. 2020. "Kidnapping Plot Against Whitmer Becomes Part of Michigan Politics." *The New York Times*, October 18. https://www.nytimes.com/2020/10/11/us/whitmer-kidnapping-plot-michigan.html, accessed February 28, 2021.

Gruver, Mead. "Wyoming GOP Censures Liz Cheney Over Impeachment Vote." *Associated Press*, February 6. https://apnews.com/article/donald-trump-capitol-siege-censures-rawlins-wyoming-3d2a5ad3377bb748c22f632642ba23f1, accessed February 28, 2021.

Grynbaum, Michael M., Davey Alba, and Reid J. Epstein. 2021. "How Pro-Trump Forces Pushed a Lie About Antifa at the Capitol Riot." *The New York Times*, March 1. https://www.nytimes.com/2021/03/01/us/politics/antifa-conspiracy-capitol-riot.html?referringSource=articleShare, accessed March 1, 2021.

Hacker, Jacob S. and Paul Pierson 2020. *Let Them Eat Tweets: How the Right Rules in an Age of Extreme Inequality*. New York: Norton/Liveright.

Hannity, Sean. 2020. *Live Free Or Die: America (and the World) on the Brink*. New York: Threshold Editions.

Harvey, David. 1990. *The Condition of Postmodernity*. London: Blackwell.

Holland, Steve and David Morgan. 2021. "With Gold-colored Trump Statue, Conservatives Show Fealty to Former President." *KLS.com*, February 27. https://www.ksl.com/article/50115169/with-gold-colored-trump-statue-conservatives-show-fealty-to-former-president, accessed February 28, 2021.

Homans, Charles. 2021. "How Armed Protests are Creating a New Kind of Politics." *The New York Times Magazine*, January 26. https://www.nytimes.com/interactive/2021/01/26/magazine/armed-militia-movement-gun-laws.html?searchResultPosition=1, accessed February 28, 2021.

Horgan, John, Shortland, Neil, and Abbasciano, Suzzette. 2018. "Towards a Typology of Terrorism Involvement: A Behavioral Differentiation of Violent Extremist Offenders." *Journal of Threat Assessment and Management* 5(2): 84–102.

Isenstadt, Alex. 2021. "Trump Allies Reelected to Lead RNC as Party Faces Reckoning." *Politico*, January 8. https://www.politico.com/news/2021/01/08/ronna-mcdaniel-tommy-hicks-reelected-rnc-456625, accessed February 28, 2021.

Kessler, Sarah. 2018. *Gigged: The End of the Job and the Future of Work*. New York: St. Martin's Press.

Kimmel, Michael. 2017. *Angry White Men: American Masculinity at the End of an Era*. New York: Nation Books.

Kirkpatrick, David D. and Mike McIntire. 2021. "'Its Own Domestic Army': How the G.O.P. Allied itself with Militants." *The New York Times*, February 8. https://www.nytimes.com/2021/02/08/us/militias-republicans-michigan.html?action=click&module=Spotlight&pgtype=Homepage, accessed February 28, 2021.

Kochhar, Rakesh and Anthony Cilluffo. 2017. "How Wealth Inequality Has Changed in the US Since the Great Recession, By Race, Ethnicity, and Income." *Pew Research Center Fact Tank*, November 1. https://www.pewresearch.org/fact-tank/2017/11/01/how-wealth-inequality-has-changed-in-the-u-s-since-the-great-recession-by-race-ethnicity-and-income, accessed February 28, 2021.

Knight, Michael. 2017. *President Trump and the New World Order*. Mendota Heights, MN: North Star Publishing.

Knauft, Bruce. 1996. *Genealogies for the Present in Cultural Anthropology*. New York: Routledge.

———. 2004. "Scholarship in Time." *Academic Exchange (Emory University)* 7 (2): 1–4.

———. 2014. "Critical Theory." In R. Jon McGhee and Richard Warms, eds. *Theory in Social and Cultural Anthropology*. Thousand Oaks, CA: Sage.

———. 2017. "What is Genealogy? An Anthropology/Philosophical Investigation." *Genealogy* 1 (5): 1–16.

———. 2018. "On the Political Genealogy of Trump After Foucault." *Genealogy* 2 (4): 1–18.

———. 2020. "Marching Towards an Uncivil War in America." https://scholarblogs.emory.edu/bknauft/files/2020/08/Marching-Towards-Uncivil-War-in-America.pdf.

———. In Press. "Trump's Corruption and the Virus of Polarization: Race, Class, and the Reign of the Wealthy." In Donna M. Goldstein and Kristin K. Drybread, eds. *Corruption and Illiberal Politics in the Trump Era*. London: Routledge.

Lerer, Lisa. 2021. "CPAC and the New Republicanism." *The New York Times*, February 27. https://www.nytimes.com/2021/02/27/us/politics/cpac-trump-republicans.html?referringSource=articleShare, accessed February 28, 2021.

Martin, Jonathan. 2020. "'Lock Them All Up': Trump's Whitmer Attack Fit a Damaging Pattern." *The New York Times*, October 18. https://www.nytimes.com/2020/10/18/us/politics/trump-whitmer-michigan.html, accessed February 28, 2021.

Martin, Jonathan and Maggie Haberman. 2021. "Trump's Republican Hit List at CPAC Is a Warning Shot to His Party." *The New York Times*, February 28. https://www.nytimes.com/2021/02/28/us/politics/trump-cpac-republicans.html?action=click&module=Top%20Stories&pgtype=Homepage, accessed February 28, 2021.

Merlan, Anna. 2019. *Republic of Lies: American Conspiracy Theories and Their Surprising Rise to Power*. New York: Metropolitan Books.

Mogelson, Luke. 2020. "Nothing to Lose But Your Masks: Groups Protesting Lockdown See the Pandemic as a Pretext for Tyranny—And as an Opportunity for Spreading Rage." *The New Yorker*, August 24, pp. 32–45. https://www.newyorker.com/magazine/2020/08/24/the-militias-against-masks, accessed February 28, 2021.

Naik, Richa. 2021. "'They're Unrecognizable': One Woman Reflect on Losing Her Parents to QAnon." *CNN Business*, February 12. https://www.cnn.com/2021/02/12/tech/qanon-followers-family-lost-loved-ones, accessed February 28, 2021.

Nichols, Chris. 2021. "Fact-Check: Have One-Third of US Small Businesses Closed During Pandemic?" *Austin American-Statesman*. June 8. https://www.statesman.com/story/news/politics/politifact/2021/06/08/kamala-harris-small-business-closures-covid-fact-check/7602531002, accessed September 29, 2021.

O'Sullivan, Donie. 2021. "She was Stunned by Biden's Inauguration: How this South Carolina Mom Escaped QAnon." *CNN Business*, February 3. https://www.cnn.com/2021/02/03/tech/qanon-mom-former-believer/index.html, accessed February 28, 2021.

Pape, Robert and Keven Ruby. 2021. "The Capitol Rioters Aren't Like Other Extremists." *The Atlantic*, February 2. https://www.theatlantic.com/ideas/archive/2021/02/the-capitol-rioters-arent-like-other-extremists/617895, accessed February 28, 2021.

Pengelly, Martin. 2020. "Bernstein Names 21 Republican Senators Who Privately Expressed Contempt for Trump." *The Guardian*, November 23. https://www.theguardian.com/us-news/2020/nov/23/carl-bernstein-21-republican-senators-expressed-contempt-for-trump, accessed February 28, 2021.

Plott, Elaina. 2021. "At CPAC, A Golden Image, a Magic Wand, and Reverence for Trump." *The New York Times*, February 28. https://www.nytimes.com/2021/02/28/us/politics/cpac-trump-statue.html?referringSource=articleShare, accessed February 28, 2021.

Prideaux, John. 2020. "Checks and Balance." *The Economist*, October 2. https://www.economist.com/podcasts/2020/10/02/reality-wreck-misinformation-and-how-the-truth-became-a-partisan-issue, accessed February 28, 2021.

Quinn, Michael D. 2020. *QAnon – The Great Awakening Explained: An Objective Guide to Understanding QAnon, the Deep State, and Related Conspiracy Theories*. Seattle: Amazon Books.

Risen, Clay. 2015. *The Bill of the Century: The Epic Battle for the Civil Rights Act*. New York: Bloomsbury.

Roose, Kevin. 2021. "What is QAnon, the Viral Pro-Trump Conspiracy Theory?" *The New York Times*, February 4. https://www.nytimes.com/article/what-is-qanon.html, accessed February 28, 2021.

Rubin, Olivia, Lucien Bruggeman, and Will Steakin. 2021. "QAnon Emerges as Recurring Theme of Criminal Cases Tied to US Capitol Siege." *ABC News*, January 19. https://www.nytimes.com/article/what-is-qanon.html, accessed February 28, 2021.

Rynor, Morgan and Jack Lowenstein. 2021. "Polls Show Many Believe Trump Remains Leader of Republican Party." *WINK News*, February 10. https://www.winknews.com/2021/02/09/polls-show-many-believe-trump-remains-leader-of-republican-party, accessed February 28, 2021.

Scott, James C. 1999. *Seeing Like a State: How Certain Schemes to Improve the Human Condition Have Failed*. New Haven, CT: Yale University Press.

——— 2010. *The Art of Not Being Governed: An Anarchist History of Upland Southeast Asia*. New Haven, CT: Yale University Press.

Searcey, Dionne and Richard A. Oppel, Jr. 2020. "A Divided Nation Agrees on One Thing: Many People Want a Gun." *The New York Times*, October 27. https://www.nytimes.com/2020/10/27/us/guns-2020-election.html, accessed February 28, 2021.

Shapiro, Thomas M. 2017. *Toxic Inequality: How America's Wealth Gap Destroys Mobility, Deepens the Racial Divide, and Threatens Our Future*. New York: Basic Books.

Smith, Simon. 2020. *QAnon and the Dark Agenda. The Illuminati Protocols Explained and the Arrival of a New World*. Seattle: Amazon books.

Sommerlad, Joe. 2021a. "'We are Lost': FOX News Suffers Worst Ratings in 20 Years." *Independent*, February 11. https://www.independent.co.uk/news/world/americas/us-politics/fox-news-ratings-trump-newsmax-b1798081.html, accessed February 28, 2021.

———. 2021b. "NewsMax and OAN: How Are the Ultra-Conservative Cable Channels Coping without Trump in the White House?" *Independent*, February 2. https://www.independent.co.uk/news/world/americas/us-politics/newsmax-oan-trump-fox-biden-b1796458.html, accessed February 28, 2021.

Steakin, Will. 2021. "GOP Congressman Headlines Conference Where Organizers Push White Nationalist Rhetoric." *The New York Times*, February 27. https://abcnews.go.com/US/gop-congressman-headlines-conference-organizers-push-white-nationalist/story?id=76152780, accessed February 28, 2021.

Steck, Em and Andrew Kaczynski. 2021. "Marjorie Taylor Greene Indicated Support for Executing Prominent Democrats in 2018 and 2019 Before Running for Congress." *CNN KFile*, January 26. https://www.cnn.com/2021/01/26/politics/marjorie-taylor-greene-democrats-violence/index.html, accessed February 28, 2021.

Steverman, Ben and Alexandre Tanzi. 2020. "The Fifty Richest Americans Are Worth as Much as the Poorest 165 Million." *Bloomberg*, October 8. https://www.bloomberg.com/news/articles/2020-10-08/top-50-richest-people-in-the-us-are-worth-as-much-as-poorest-165-million, accessed February 28, 2021.

Stewart, Matthew. 2018. "The 9.9 Percent Is the New American Aristocracy." *The Atlantic*. June. https://www.theatlantic.com/magazine/archive/2018/06/the-birth-of-a-new-american-aristocracy/559130, accessed March 5, 2021.

Thompson, Heather Ann. 2009. *Speaking Out: Activism and Protest in the 1960s and 1970s*. New York: Pearson.

Thompson, Stuart A. 2021. "Three Weeks Inside a Pro-Trump QAnon Chat Room." *The New York Times*, January 26. https://www.nytimes.com/interactive/2021/01/26/opinion/trump-qanon-washington-capitol-hill.html, accessed February 28, 2021.

US Census Bureau. 2015. "Projections of the Size and Composition of the US Population: 2014 to 2060." Washington, DC: United States Census Bureau, Report #P25-1143.

Valentino-DeVries, Jennifer, Lu, Denise, Lutz, Eleanor, and Matthews, Alex Leeds. 2021. "A Small Group of Militants' Outsize Role in the Capitol Attack." *The New York Times*, February 21. https://www.nytimes.com/interactive/2021/02/21/us/capitol-riot-attack-militants.html?searchResultPosition=1, accessed September 29, 2021.

Vance, J. D. 2016. *Hillbilly Elegy: A Memoir of a Family and Culture in Crisis*. New York. Harper Collins.

Wilkerson, Isabel. 2020a. *Caste: The Origins of our Discontent*. New York: Random House.

———. 2020b. "America's Enduring Caste System: Our Founding Ideals Promise Liberty and Equality for All Our Reality is an Enduring Racial Hierarchy that has Persisted for Centuries." *The New York Times*, July 1. https://www.nytimes.com/2020/07/01/magazine/isabel-wilkerson-caste.html, accessed February 28, 2021.

Williams, Joan C. 2017. *White Working Class: Overcoming Class Cluelessness in America*. Cambridge, MA: Harvard Business Review Press.

Wilson, Valerie. 2016. "People of Color Will Be a Majority of the American Working Class in 2032." *Economic Policy Institute*, June 9. https://www.epi.org/publication/the-changing-demographics-of-americas-working-class, accessed February 28, 2021.

Wuthnow, Robert. 2018. *The Left Behind: Decline and Rage in Rural America*. Princeton, NJ: Princeton University Press.

12
HINDUTVA AND DONALD TRUMP
An unholy relation

Raj Kumar Singh

Introduction

In 2016, the citizens of the United States elected Donald J. Trump, the Republican Party nominee, as president of the world's oldest democracy. Trump's victory was not expected by the political pundits of the whole world. Trump was an outsider to the American political arena. His election campaign was based on the slogan of "America First," which expanded on the thesis of American identity and on identifying the enemies of American civilization and portraying himself as the savior of American identity and civilization. The context of the election campaign was almost similar to the election campaign of Narendra Modi in India.

Hindu nationalists in India had a very strong centralized organization, but they were lacking a good political leader who can unite the whole of Hindu community to vote for him. The task was given to Narendra Modi, who was a long-time Swayam Sewak of RSS. He had established himself as a leader among the masses and was elected as chief minister of Gujarat for three consecutive terms. The election of Modi as prime minister of India in 2014 was a big event and was seen as the acceptance of Hindu nationalism by a majority of Indians.

The electoral successes of Modi and Trump in India and America, respectively, are two of the major events of the past decade. The election of these two right-wing leaders as the heads of their respective countries created a rift between the secular and liberal nature of democracies in both countries. The idea of one nation under one God and one flag became the foundation of Trump's politics in America. His vision of creating a global civilizational alliance against terrorism synchronizes with Modi's vision of forming an alliance to destroy terrorists and terrorism in the world. In this chapter I discuss how the rise of Trump to the American presidency has given a rise to the right-wing politics in India and how it symbolically helped

DOI: 10.4324/9781003152743-15

the cause of Hindu nationalism in India to achieve the aim of building a Hindu nation in India.

Methodology

The methodology through which I build my arguments includes a range of methods, such as discourse analysis of speeches of the leaders of Hindu organizations in India and policies of the Trump administration in the US. I have also analysed the speeches of leaders of organizations which act as a connecting link between the Trump supporters in America and Modi supporters in India, various blogs such as Hindus for Trump, and media articles related to the news regarding the support of Hindu organizations in India for Trump. The time frame for analysing the news, blogs, and articles spans the period from Trump's nomination as a presidential candidate for the Republican Party in 2015 up to the 2020 election. I will be analysing the statements and policies of Trump, who has helped the Hindu nationalists in India to achieve their goal and as a counter against their secular and liberal opponents.

The emergence of Hindu nationalism in India

Hindu nationalism in India took its inspiration from white nationalism which, as an ideology, was adopted by Adolf Hitler. Hitler believed in creating a nation for the pure white race of Aryans. He further believed that the Jewish community was an inferior race and was one of the obstacles to achieving his racial goal. The propaganda deployed against the Jewish community by Nazi Germany came into action in the form of Nuremberg laws, which stripped the Jews of their citizenship rights. The law forbade marriages between Jews and Christians with the view of protecting the pure German race. This was further extended by the Jewish genocide in which millions of Jews were killed in the concentration camps of Poland and Nazi Germany (Badri 2020).

The ethnic cleansing of the Jews by Nazi Germany was very much applauded by the Hindutva forces in India. However, fundamentalist ideologues of Hindu nationalism adopted the ideology, transformed it accordingly and replaced white nationalism with Hindu nationalism and Jews with the Muslim community. The belief of creating a separate and pure land for the Hindus was the final motive of Hindu nationalism in India.

The term "Hindutva" was coined by Vinayak Damodar Savarkar in 1923. Coincidentally, this was the same year that Hitler attempted to seize power in Munich, Germany by marching Nazi followers into the city center. The resultant confrontation led to the deaths of sixteen Nazis and four police officers, and Hitler was later arrested by German police on sedition charges (Evans 2003). Savarkar, in his major work, "Essentials of Hindutva," gave three distinct criteria for identifying Hinduness— "common-race," "common-nation," and "common-civilization"— which became the basis for exclusion of both Indian Muslims and Indian Christians (Savarkar 1923: 41–3). Savarkar insisted on creating British India as a Hindu state for

Hindus. Savarkar believed that all non-Hindus were foreigners who were a threat to the society, and if Hindus grew stronger in number, then Muslims should be treated in a similar way to that in which the Jews were being treated by the Nazis (124–5).

RSS was formed by Keshav Balram Hedgewar in 1925 through the inspiration of B. S. Moonje in order to establish a Hindu Rashtra. The direct connection between Italian fascism and the Hindu nationalist organization took place through the meeting of B.S. Moonje with Mussolini in Italy in 1931. Hindu nationalist fascism was a perfect example of a revolution which is conservative in nature, and its application on India would result in making India a superpower in the near future (Casolari 2000: 218–28). Savitri Devi (or Maximiani Portas), a supporter of Hitler, moved to India in 1932 and remained an influential figure among the Hindutva groups like Rashtriya Swayamsevak Sangh, Bajrang Dal, Vishwa Hindu Parishad etc. until her death in 1982. She advocated for a synthesis of Neo-Nazis, white supremacists, and Hindutva and proclaimed Hitler as an Avatar of Lord Vishnu, a Hindu deity. She also regarded Jews as evil. She worked at the Hindu Mission in Calcutta for 18 months and shared Savarkar's concept of Hindutva. In her book *A Warning to Hindus*, she cautioned Hindus about the threat of Islam and Christianity and advised Hindus to assert themselves in order to save their religion and civilization. She saw upper-caste Hindus as symbols of Aryan purity and superiority and envisioned that India should revive Aryan supremacy in the world. She advocated for the militarization of the Hindu community and systematic and organized violence against the Muslim community (Clarke 1998).

The Hindutva movement continues to regard fascism and Nazism with a lot of goodwill in spite of knowing about the atrocities committed by dictators like Hitler and Mussolini. Their believe in totalitarian regimes and their policy with regard to the so-called internal enemies of the state has always inspired the Hindu nationalist organization in India.

The Rise of the Bharatiya Janata Party and Hindutva in India

The agenda of building a Hindu nation in India seems to be impossible in the absence of a political party with a Hindutva ideology. The Bharatiya Janata Party (or BJP) came into existence as a successor to Jan Sangh. Atal Bihari Vajpayee was the first president of BJP and in their first election, in 1984, only two candidates were able to win parliamentary elections. The demolition of the Babri mosque in 1992 by Hindu nationalists in Ayodhya, Uttar Pradesh was a crucial milestone in Indian politics. The destruction was followed by Hindu-Muslim riots in Mumbai, which resulted in approximately 2000 deaths. The terrorist attack in 1993 was believed to be coordinated by Indian Muslims, who were also part of the Indian criminal underworld (Heath 1999).

The terrorist attacks created an environment of fear among Hindus who started re-evaluating the constitutional enshrinement of secularism. The Vishwa Hindu Parishad (VHP) and Shiv Sena rose in popularity as quasi-military to fight against what they believed was an attack on the Hindu community by Muslim extremists. In the 1996 election the BJP became the party with the highest number of parliamentarians in the Lok Sabha (Lower House) due to the rise of Hindutva ideology in the country. However, they were unable to form a government as the BJP didn't have the adequate majority required. The coalition of local parties, with the support of Indian National Congress (INC), was able to form a government, but the coalition didn't last long and another election took place in 1998, as a result of which BJP was able to form a coalition government with around 15 other parties and rule India for five years. However, with the coalition government their major agenda was put aside and the party was not able to execute any of their Hindutva agenda (Kantha 1997).

The hardcore BJP voters felt cheated as the BJP was not able to fulfil any promise during its regime. In the next general election in 2004, the Indian National Congress (INC) emerged as the single largest party. The coalition led by Indian National Congress governed India for a decade (2004–14). However, the involvement of their leaders in corruption charges and terror attacks in India fuelled the rise of the BJP which discovered, in Narendra Modi, a leader who came from a Rashtriya Swayamsewak Sangh (RSS) background and was from the Other Backward Caste (OBC) community. From now on, the agenda of development was mixed with the agenda of Hindutva, and this formula was able to win BJP a clear majority in the 2014 parliamentary election.

Hindu nationalism in the US: Nationalism beyond borders

The growth of Hindu nationalism among the Hindu-American community was led by Hindu organizations such as Vishwa Hindu Parishad (VHP), which has developed an organizational structure in the US. The effort of the VHP's wing in America has been to build support for Hindu supremacy in India since its formation in 1970 (Rajagopal 2000). The VHP also helped in reorienting Modi in the American political establishment after the ban for his role in the 2002 Gujarat riots (Sud 2008).

The Republican Hindu Coalition (RHC) has been the common link between Hindu nationalist organizations in India and the Republican Party in America. The RHC was founded by Indian-American businessman Shalabh Kumar, who claimed his political inspirations from Ronald Reagan, John F. Kennedy, and Narendra Modi. Shalabh Kumar arranged a meeting in 2013 between American congressmen and Modi who was at that time the Chief Minister of Gujarat and was banned from traveling to the US after allegations of his role in the Gujarat anti-Muslim riots. The RHC supported the immigration policies of Trump and organized a gathering to show their support for Trump. The members of the RHC believe in strengthening the political and trade ties between America and India through promoting "Made in America" and encouraging Modi's "Make in India" as an alternative for China (Mandavailli and Swamy 2019).

Trump, Muslims, and right-wing aspirations

As the world's largest economic and military power, the United States is the country against which all of the world's nations, including India, measure themselves. America has always stood as an advocate for democracy, human rights, and economic liberalization. Trump's campaign appeal to tradition and his vow to destroy the Islamic State resonate with the policies of Hindu nationalists in India. Hindu nationalism is built on hate against Pakistan and the minorities in the country, especially the Muslim community. After the partition of India and the creation of Islamic Republic of Pakistan, the patriotism of Indian Muslims has been always questioned by both secular and Hindu nationalists. The ill-treatment of minorities in Pakistan also acts as fuel for Hindu nationalists in India who believe that Muslims should be treated as second-class citizens in India or should move to Pakistan as they demanded a separate nation for themselves (Danziger 2020).

Any policy which works for the betterment of the Muslim community in India is always suspected as minority appeasement by Hindu nationalists. The celebration of the Iftar dinner party during Ramadan was started by the Indian National Congress during the era of Indira Gandhi in the early 1970s at Rashtrapati Bhavan (President House) and became a tradition thereafter. However, the hosting of the Iftar dinner party at Rashtrapati Bhavan was halted during the regime of APJ Abdul Kalam and the funds of the Iftar dinner party were transferred to an orphanage, but the tradition was again re-started by Pratibha Patil and later continued by Pranab Mukherjee. Prime Minister Modi remained absent from the Iftar dinner party, which was hosted by President Pranab Mukherjee from 2014 to 2017. However, the new incumbent Indian president Ram Nath Kovind ended this tradition. The celebration of the Iftar dinner party in Rashtrapati Bhavan was never appreciated by the Hindu nationalists in India as the celebration of Iftar was always understood as the policy of appeasing the Muslim community to cement the minority voting bloc at public expense (Subramaniam 2017).

Donald Trump broke the twenty-year-old tradition of hosting an Iftar during Ramadan in the White House, which had been started by Hillary Clinton in 1996. Iftar was hosted even after the terrorist attack of September 11, 2001 by George W. Bush in order to show the whole world the inclusiveness of America and sent a message that the US is at war with terrorism, but that it respects Islam and Islamic traditions (Hunt and Smith 2017). The decision to discontinue the celebration of Iftar by President Trump was very much appreciated by the right-wing community in India and also gave backing for BJP to revoke this tradition, and later the same policy was adopted by the Indian president.

The anti-Islamic campaign of Trump in 2016 promised to ban Islam; after winning the presidential election, he attempted to ban Muslim entry into the United States (Husain 2018). The decision to ban travel by individuals from six Muslim-majority countries on the grounds of national security was very much a celebrated affair by his Hindu nationalist supporters in India as they believed that Trump has realized the radical nature of Islam and Muslims, who they regarded as a threat to the whole world. They believe that Trump as a world leader has acted firmly against radical Muslims and that it showed the whole world how to deal with Islamic radicalism (Choi 2018). The Hindu Sena, a right-wing organization in India, celebrated Trump's birthday and prayed for his victory in the 2016 election. A *yagna* was performed and a *Tilak* was placed on the forehead of Trump's portrait, which was adorned with flowers and garlands. For Hindu Sena and other right-wing Hindu nationalists in India, Trump is the personification of a strongman brand of politics that believes in taking hard stances against the Muslim community (Parikh 2017).

The Kashmir question and Hindu nationalism

Kashmir has been a bone of contention between India and Pakistan since 1947. The accession of Jammu and Kashmir in India happened between Maharaja Hari Singh, the last ruler of Jammu and Kashmir, and the Indian government. A special provision was granted to the newly acceded state by the government of India through Article 370 (which provided a special autonomous status to Jammu and Kashmir), and as a result the state of Jammu and Kashmir has its own constitution and make its own rules relating to permanent residency, ownership of property, and fundamental rights. The constitution also bars Indians from outside Jammu and Kashmir from purchasing land in the state (Kronstadt 2019). Hindu nationalist leaders have always opposed this kind of accession of the state which allows the state to have its own flag and constitution as it prevents the complete integration of the state with the country, Jammu and Kashmir being the only Indian state where the majority of the population is Muslim. This has always offended the right-wing Hindu nationalists in the country.

The insurgency in Kashmir started in 1989 and had directed a lot of terrorist activities in Kashmir valley. The genocide of the Kashmiri pandits in 1990 by terrorists made them refugees in their own country. The demand for a separate country by the Kashmiri separatist leaders and the rise in terrorist activities resulted in the deployment of the Indian army in the region of Kashmir. The Armed Forces Special Powers Act (AFSPA) enables Indian troops to hold a prisoner without trial, and on many occasions international NGOs such as Amnesty International have accused the Indian security forces of violating human rights in Kashmir (Huey 2011).

This special status of Kashmir was always seen as a part of the terrorist problem in Kashmir by right-wing organizations in India. Abrogation of special status of Jammu and Kashmir by the government of India on August 5, 2019 was one of the major resolutions of BJP leaders since the party's formation in the country. The revocation of special status changed Jammu and Kashmir from one autonomous state to a three-union territory—Jammu, Kashmir, and Ladakh. The revocation of special status for Kashmir led to extensive protest by various NGOs and advocacy groups around the world. The Islamic Society of America also protested, and in its fifty-sixth convention Senator Bernie Sanders, one of the Democratic frontrunners in the 2020 US presidential election, also criticized the Indian government for its communication blockade and demanded that the US government speak out in support of international humanitarian law in Kashmir (Strickland 2019). The stance of Democrats on the issue of Kashmir backfired, while the hands-off attitude of Trump led to a shift in the position of Indian American voters in favor of Republicans. The soft attitude of Trump toward India and Prime Minister Narendra Modi on the issue of abrogation of special status of Kashmir elevated the status of India on the world stage. The deep silence of the Trump administration was also a signal of the impact of long-distance nationalism of the right-wing Hindu community in America (Myers 2019).

Donald Trump, American Hindus, and Hindu nationalism in the United States

The identity of India as a nation of Hindus and the identification of Indians as Hindus was the common narrative in the US. The rise of Modi in India, and his engagement with the Indian diaspora around the globe, has helped in cementing their identity as Indians which is difficult to distinguish from Hindu identity. The presence of a large Hindu Indian diaspora in America and their support for Modi and Hindu nationalism in India was first realized by Donald Trump during his election campaign in 2016. Trump addressed his love for India and Hindus in an event called "Humanity against Terrorism," in which he sought votes from the American Hindu community. This was the first time in history when an American presidential candidate attended a rally of the Indian community (Kumar 2017; Thobani 2018).

The tradition of celebrating Diwali in the White House was started by Barack Obama in 2009 to show inclusiveness and respect for all religions and to celebrate the diversity of America. The tradition was continued by Trump to display his admiration for the American Hindu community. However, the decision behind abandoning the celebration of the Iftar dinner on Ramadan while celebrating Diwali was more an appeasement of the Hindu community than an act of inclusiveness (Melton 2017).

Trump also organized a sacred Vedic *shanti* path or prayer in the White House on the National Day of Prayer for the wellbeing of everyone (Jha 2020). The hosting of sacred *shanti* path in the White House was applauded by Hindu nationalists in India who found a new topic for debating and demonstrating the influence of the Hindu religion in the world. Whenever these kinds of events are hosted outside India, they are used to taunt the Muslim community in India and are seen as empowerment of the Hindu religion and Hindu nationalism in the country. Moreover, it also comes as an approval and acceptance of their hate against the Muslim community in the country and acts as a question mark for the patriotism for the Muslim community in India who follow Islamic tradition. The common notion that has developed among Hindu nationalists in India about Muslims is that they always oppose Hindu traditions. Muslims in India opposed the celebration of International Yoga Day on the basis that Yoga was un-Islamic and was an imposition of Hindutva ideology in the country (Khan 2015).

Islamic organizations in India were criticized by Hindu nationalists who believed that Islamic theology is just an excuse, as most of the Muslim countries in the world supported Yoga and the problem of an Islamic body in India is because of their hatred toward Hindu community and Hindu religion. The international acceptance of Indian traditions like Yoga gives a push to Hindu nationalists for their aim of forming a Hindu nation by removing the secular nature of the Indian constitution (Gupta and Jacob 2019).

US entangled between Chinese aggression and Indian resistance

The American economy is intensely tangled with Asian countries, especially China and Japan. The trade deficit between America and China has always been a concern for the US government, and Trump advocated for a balancing of this trade deficit by imposing tariffs on Chinese products and also in order to provide protection for American industries (Tankersley 2019). The economic and military power of China exceeds any other nation in Asia, and because of its economic and military superiority in Asia, China has developed territorial disputes with almost all its neighbors. The influence of the People's Republic of China in Asia has been a vital subject in shaping the US-India relationship. Today, the relationships between China, America, and India vary from cooperation to competition to conflict. Chinese aggression in the South China Sea and in Ladakh has always escalated the tension between America and China and between China and India.

As president, Trump imposed tariffs on Chinese products, thereby increasing the friction between China and America. During Trump's reign, there has been a tilt toward the Indian position regarding border disputes with China. There has been significant progress in building alliances for balancing China. The formation of QUAD, the signing of COMCASA, and the joint naval exercise in the South China Sea have all heightened tensions in the region (Lee 2020).

The Indian government has always looked to the United States as a partner for balancing Chinese aggression in Asia, as America is a superpower with one of the largest militaries in the world. The defeat of the Indian armed forces in the Sino-India war in 1962 continues to trouble the Indian community. Chinese aggression on India's border and the financial support for Pakistan have always bothered India (Madan 2020:). The Chinese policy of One Belt One Road (OBOR), which passes through Pakistan Occupied Kashmir (POK), was opposed by India on the grounds of territorial sovereignty, and the concerns of India over OBOR were supported by America on economic grounds (Jain 2018).

President Trump, in his speech at the United Nations General Assembly, accused China of transmitting the coronavirus to the whole world, as Beijing had allowed people to leave China in the early stages of the outbreak to infect the world while simultaneously shutting down its own domestic travel. Trump's speech played a major role in damaging the global credibility of China and demanded action against China via the United Nations forum. He also criticized the World Health Organization (WHO) for being virtually controlled by China, and his disregard for WHO resulted in America leaving WHO (Trump 2020). The US Justice Department suspected Chinese hackers and researchers of stealing intellectual property and trade secrets of the companies working to develop a vaccine for coronavirus (Barnes 2020).

The faceoff between Chinese and Indian troops in Galwan valley in Ladakh led to the death of twenty Indian soldiers while the scale of Chinese causalities remains unknown (Chaturvedi 2020). This incident increased tension between China and India, to which the Indian government responded by banning many Chinese mobile applications in India. The government of India terminated many contracts previously provided to Chinese companies for building infrastructure in India. Although the policy of banning Chinese apps was criticized by some of the left-wing intellectuals in the country, the ban was appreciated by the right-wing Hindu nationalists. This confrontation also led to the movement to boycott Chinese goods by Indian citizens in the Indian markets (Shenoy and Mahendher 2020).

The American Secretary of State, Mike Pompeo, extended condolences to the Indian soldiers who lost their lives due to Chinese aggression (India Today Web desk 2020). In the US, President Trump signed an order to end Hong Kong's special status after China enacted a new security law in Hong Kong. The diplomatic ties between America and China then sank to a new low decades after America gave China three days' notice to close the Chinese consulate in Houston (Press Trust of India 2020c). The sanctions on Chinese diplomats were widely reported in the Indian media, which elevated the status of Trump among the Hindu nationalists, as for the first time in decades China was on its back foot against any country. The aggression of the Trump administration against China created a positive atmosphere among the Hindu community in India and America. The American Hindu community drew closer to Trump because of his support for India against Chinese aggression. The US action against China provided a psychological relief for Hindu nationalists. Their belief in Trump as an ally against Chinese aggression consolidated the Hindu community to support him.

From India to America: Political responses vis-à-vis undocumented immigrants

There is a similarity in the opinions of the Trump and Modi administrations with regard to dealing with the crisis of undocumented immigrants. The hard rhetoric of Trump called these undocumented immigrants criminals and rapists, despite the fact that studies related to immigrants reveal that they are less involved in criminal activities (Light, He, and Robey 2020). Similar language was used by the Indian home minister who promised to expel illegal immigrants whom he branded termites and infiltrators from India and especially from West Bengal, which shares a border with Bangladesh. The Ministry of Home Affairs had issued a camp manual for implementation and compliance for prescribing the amenities to be provided in the model detention center (Thomas 2019). The government of India denied all these allegations about the construction of detention camps, but construction is still ongoing in Assam (Loiwal 2019), while the Trump administration defended the construction of detention camps in America for undocumented migrants (Kassie 2019).

The new amendments to the citizenship laws for undocumented migrants echo the German Nuremberg laws. The new law provides a fast-track citizenship for non-Muslim migrants from neighboring countries, especially from Bangladesh and Pakistan, and thus discriminates against the Muslim community on the grounds of religion. The next move of the government, after the discriminatory Citizenship Amendment Act (CAA), was the proposed National Register of Citizenship (NRC). This requires every Indian citizen to prove their citizenship with legal documents, which many citizens lack. Most non-Muslim Indian citizens are safe from the CAA since even if they don't have any documents their citizenship won't be questioned, while the NRC and CAA jeopardized the position of many Muslim citizens without any legal documents. These laws are a privilege to the non-Muslims while they are problematic for the Muslim community in India, subjecting them to suspicion of being illegal citizens. Although the Indian government has denied reports of building detention centers for ineligible Muslim residents, the notion has psychologically impacted Indian Muslims and created an atmosphere of fear among them (Mahmudabad 2020).

The protest by the Muslim community in India against the discriminatory CAA and the formation of a movement like Shaheen Bagh in Delhi were almost ignored by the central government, and the movement was also framed as anti-India and anti-Hindu by the leaders of the ruling party in India. The organizers of the Shaheen Bagh movement were framed as conspirators, who were funded by the anti-nationalistic forces which wanted to destroy the peace in India. The hate speeches of leaders of the ruling party ignited hatred against Muslims and led to Hindu–Muslim riots in February 2020. The riots were totally overlooked by the Indian media, which were busier covering the visit of Trump in the country, as it was a bigger event and fetched them better television ratings. The Indian media houses didn't ask any questions during Trump's press conference regarding the ongoing protests of the Muslim community over the discriminatory CAA and over the ongoing riots. However, the question about the ongoing protest was raised by an international reporter, to which Trump responded with reluctance and stated that he had firm belief in the policy of the Indian government and Prime Minister Modi over the issue of rights of minorities in India. His statement was represented as support for Hindu nationalism in the country. The media coverage of the riots after Trump's visit in Delhi portrayed them as anti-Hindu riots, and the blame of the riots was put on the Muslim community (Rao 2020).

America, Pakistan, and Hindu nationalism

The relationship between Pakistan and America is primarily a military and governmental relation as compared to India and America, which is also a civilian relationship, and there is more person-to-person contact among the citizens of the latter countries. As an Islamic republic, Pakistan has an aggressive state policy based on the Islamic agenda of jihad against Western nations which are hostile to Islamism. In the last few years, the major focus of Trump's administration was withdrawing US troops from Afghanistan. In the first two years, the major focus of Trump's administration action in this area was against the Haqqani network. Trump accused Pakistan of lying and deception by taking American aid for counter terrorism but eventually doing nothing. The administration took actions against Pakistan by cutting American security assistance and placing Pakistan on the grey list through the Financial Action Task Force (FATF), causing financial harm and obstructing economic investment in Pakistan (Hathaway 2019).

The policy of Trump's administration on the Kashmir crisis between India and Pakistan has been non-alignment, while the Obama administration believed that both nations should engage with each other through bilateral talks. Trump's approach of dealing with terrorism with more force and seeing no distinction between separatism and terrorism made his administration more tolerant toward India's action of surgical strikes against terrorist camps in Pakistan in retaliation to terrorist activities in India (Bouton, 2017). The Hindutva forces in India were extremely comfortable with the policy of the Trump administration. The shift in Kashmir policy during the Trump era can be marked through the decision to declare Hizbul Mujahideen a global terrorist organization, which favored the Hindutva doctrine of Modi. The engagement between Trump and Modi finds no distinction between indigenous militants and transnational terrorist groups, and Trump's policy and statement against Islamic terrorism has allowed Modi's government pursue a clean sweep in Kashmir rather than in engaging with the separatist leader of Kashmir.

India as a bigger military power needs better weaponry systems for security purposes. This makes India a lucrative market for US companies to sell their arms and ammunition. The shift in the last few years in foreign policy tilted more toward buying weapons from America. India has acquired more weapons from the US during the Trump regime; weapons procurement rose from US$6.2 million to US$3.4 billion (Press Trust of India 2019). India utilizes this market potential to induce the US administration to apply pressure to Pakistan on the issue of terrorism. The partnership between America and India was one of the major reasons for the US to pressure Pakistan to arrest Hafiz Saeed (Press Trust of India 2020b).

Conclusion

The rise of Narendra Modi and Donald Trump has been due to nationalist and protectionist politics. The sloganeering of "Make in India" and "*Sabka Sath Sabka Vikas*" attracted Indian middle-class voters to the BJP. Similarly, the slogans of "America First" and "Make America Great Again" motivated many American voters to vote for the Republican Party. Hindu nationalists and white nationalists have found a common opponent in Islamic extremism which they believe is represented by the Muslim community and illegal immigrants who are a threat to their culture and society.

Donald Trump was a perfect American president for right-wing nationalists in India, as he ignored the Hindu nationalist agenda of the Indian government. Trump had been a strong supporter of Hindu nationalist policies in India, as the policies of the Trump administration complement those of the Indian government. The travel ban on six Muslim countries, restrictions on undocumented migrants, the statement on Pakistan, and increased tariffs against China are among the major decisions which came as a referendum for Modi's policy on illegal migrants and on the

Muslim community in India. Most of the populist decisions by Trump's administration resonate with the sentiments of Hindu nationalists in India.

Trump's muteness on the Hindu–Muslim riots in Delhi during his visit to India made him the most admired US president among Hindu nationalists. Trump's policies against Muslims are used as a justification for the radical acts of Hindu nationalists in India against Muslims. Hindu nationalists have a firm belief in Trump as the world leader of the right-wing community, which shares a common belief in Islamophobia.

The support of Hindu nationalists in India for Donald Trump was evident in the voting strategy of the American Hindu diaspora and their support for Trump in the 2016 presidential election (Varghese, 2018). The partnership between Modi and Trump appealed to many Hindu Americans who wholeheartedly supported Trump in the 2020 election. Trump's disregard for the world order in the form of leaving the WHO had opened opportunity for India to become a leading power. The transition in US politics from Barack Obama, who was very vocal about human rights in India and reminded Modi about the Indian constitution on his visit to India, to Trump, who is hardly bothered by the US Constitution and even human rights violations in America, could not be starker.

The alliance between Hindu nationalist supporters of Modi and right-wing activists in American is bridged through the diasporic Hindu community in the US. Hindu nationalists in India had supported the right-wing nationalists in America during the "Black Lives Matter" protest, which they believed was motivated by nothing more than robbery and the destruction of state and personal property. The assertive attitude of Trump during the movement was appreciated by Hindu nationalists in India who in the past have detected a similar protest by the Muslim community in India over new citizenship laws. For example, the state government in Uttar Pradesh, which is headed by Chief Minister Yogi Adityanath of the BJP, seized and auctioned the property of the rioters who were mostly from the Muslim community to compensate destruction of public and private assets. The actions were ordered to curb the voice of the activists protesting against the new citizenship laws (Kumar 2019). The support among India's right wing for Trump's actions against the Black Lives Matter movement comes from the writings of Savarkar, the founder of Hindutva ideology in India. In an interview with war correspondent Tom Treanor, Savarkar equated Muslims with African-Americans and believed that Muslims in India should be treated in a similar manner as blacks are being treated in the West (Treanor 1944).

The supremacist agenda of the right-wing community in both countries complements each other, with a common goal of establishing a totalitarian nation where minorities are treated as second-class citizens. The BJP was formed with the agenda of achieving the three major purposes, one of which—the revocation of Article 370 from Kashmir and the formation of Ram Mandir—has been achieved while the third, of achieving a Uniform Civil Code (UCC) in the country, is still pending. With the BJP in the clear majority in both houses of the parliament, UCC as a constitutional bill might be the next target to achieve in order to reach their ultimate goal of the Hindu Rashtra. The National Register of Citizens (NRC) was unable to gain any momentum due to the COVID-19 pandemic. However, as the NRC was part of the BJP's manifesto in the 2019 parliamentary election it might well be introduced in the near future. The application of NRC in the country might generate the same amount of protest against the government as occurred with the passage of the Citizenship Amendment Act (CAA).

The 2020 US presidential election was the most discussed overseas election in Indian media, including social media. The news channels continuously provided news and electoral results from America. However, with the new Democratic administration of Joe Biden as president and Kamala Harris as vice-president, who in their election campaign advocated for restoring the rights of Kashmiris and had voiced their dissatisfaction over implementation of CAA and NRC in Assam, it might be tough for the Indian government to carry out their hyper-nationalistic agenda (Press Trust of India 2020a). The common concerns of both countries, including their fight against terrorism and counterbalancing Chinese aggression in Asia, require co-operation. It will be interesting to see how the US–India partnership develops in the future, and how the two governments find ways to work together.

References

Badri, Adarsh. 2020. "The Rise and Rise of Hindutva: Narratives, Visualised Communities, and the Hindu Nation". https://ssrn.com/abstract=3608686, accessed December 4, 2020.

Barnes, Julian. 2020. "US Accuses Hackers of Trying to Steal Coronavirus Vaccine Data for China." https://www.nytimes.com/2020/07/21/us/politics/china-hacking-coronavirus-vaccine.html, accessed October 23, 2020.

Bouton, M. Marshall. 2017. "The Trump Administration's India Opportunity". *Asia Society Policy Institute*, https://asiasociety.org/files/ASPIIssueBriefTrumpIndia_FINAL_0.pdf accessed November 20, 2020.

Casolari, Marzia. 2000. "Hindutva's Foreign Tie-Up in the 1930s: Archival Evidence." *Economic and Political Weekly* 35(4): 218–28.

Chaturvedi, Amit. 2020. "Face-off between India and China in Galwan valley: Here's what we know" https://www.hindustantimes.com/india-news/face-off-between-india-and-china-in-galwan-valley-what-we-know-so-far/story-NNjwanbGiNiyAhQhnmj25I.html, accessed November 18, 2020.

Choi, Seung-Whan. 2018. "Does Restrictive Immigration Policy Reduce Terrorism in Western Democracies?" *Perspectives on Terrorism* 12 (4): 14–25.

Clarke, Nicholas G. 1998. *Hitler's Priestess: Savitri Devi, the Hindu-Aryan Myth, and Neo-Nazism*. New York: New York University Press.

Danziger, Sunaina. 2020. "Dividing Lines: What India's Hindu Nationalist Turn Portends for Relations with Pakistan." https://www.stimson.org/2020/dividing-lines-what-indias-hindu-nationalist-turn-portends-for-relations-with-pakistan, accessed November 25, 2020.

Evans, Richard J. 2003. *The Coming of the Third Reich*. New York: Penguin Books.

Gupta, Bhuvi and Jacob Copeman. 2019. "Awakening Hindu Nationalism through Yoga: Swami Ramdev and the Bharat Swabhiman Movement." *Contemporary South Asia* 27 (3): 313–29.

Hathaway, Robert M. 2019. "Power without Leverage, Leverage without Power: Pakistan and the United States in the Era of Trump." *Journal of South Asian and Middle Eastern Studies* 42 (2): 1–19.

Heath, Oliver. 1999. "Anatomy of BJP's Rise to Power: Social, Regional and Political Expansion in 1990s." *Economic and Political Weekly* 34 (35): 2511–17.

Huey, Caitlin. 2011. "Amnesty International Cites Human Rights Abuse in Kashmir." *Report. Usnews.com*, accessed September 5, 2020.

Hunt, Elle and David Smith. 2017. "Donald Trump Abandons Traditional White House Ramadan Celebration." https://www.theguardian.com/us-news/2017/jun/26/donald-trump-abandons-traditional-white-house-ramadan-celebration, accessed November 20, 2020.

Husain, Nausheen. 2018. "Timeline: Legal Fight over Trump's 'Muslim Ban' and the Supreme Court Ruling".https://www.chicagotribune.com/news/data/ct-travel-ban-ruling-time-linehtmlstory.html, accessed October 6, 2020.

India Today Web desk. 2020. "On Galwan Clash with China, Mike Pompeo Says US Stands with India." https://www.indiatoday.in/india/story/galwan-valley-clash-with-china-mike-pompeo-usa-stands-with-india-1735554-2020-10-27, accessed November 16, 2020.

Jain, Romi. 2018. "China's Economic Expansion in South Asia: Strengths, Challenges and Opportunities." *Indian Journal of Asian Affairs* 31(1/2): 21–36.

Jha, Lalit. 2020. "Vedic Shanti Path recited at White House on National Day of Prayer Service." https://in.news.yahoo.com/vedic-shanti-path-recited-white-235311725.html, accessed December 10, 2020.

Kantha, Pramod K. 1997. "General Elections. 1996: BJP Politics: Looking beyond the Impasse." *Economic and Political Weekly* 32 (48): 3090–100.

Kassie, Emily. 2019. "How the US Built the World's Largest Immigrant Detention System." https://www.theguardian.com/us-news/2019/sep/24/detained-us-largest-immigrant-detention-trump, accessed September 21, 2020.

Khan, Atiq. 2015. "Muslim Body says Yoga is Unacceptable." https://www.thehindu.com/news/national/yoga-is-unacceptable-muslim-body/article7351189.ece, accessed September 22, 2020.

Kumar, Abhishek. 2019. "CAA Protests: UP Government Starts Process to Seize Property of Protesters Involved in Violence." https://www.indiatoday.in/india/story/yogi-govt-rioters-shocked-up-cm-police-crackdown-violent-properties-seized-1632116-2019-12-28, accessed October 25, 2020.

Kumar, Rashmee. 2017. "Hindus for Trump: Behind the Uneasy Alliance with Right-wing US Politics." https://www.theguardian.com/us-news/2016/oct/17/donald-trump-hindu-nationalism-india, accessed September 20, 2020.

Kronstadt, K. Alan. 2019. "Kashmir: Background, Recent Developments, and US Policy" https://sgp.fas.org/crs/row/R45877.pdf, accessed November, 15, 2020.

Lee, Lavina. 2020. *Assessing the Quad: Prospects and Limitations of Quadrilateral Cooperation for Advancing Australia's Interests Assessing the Quad*. Sydney: Lowry Institute for International Policy.

Light, Michael T., Jingying He, and Jason P. Robey. 2020. "Comparing Crime Rates Between Undocumented Immigrants, Legal Immigrants, and Native-Born US Citizens in Texas." *Proceedings of the National Academy of Sciences* 117 (51): 32340–7.

Loiwal, Manogya. 2019. "Detention Centre Near Guwahati Nears Completion as PM Modi Denies Construction of Any." https://www.indiatoday.in/india/story/assam-detention-centres-goalpora-illegal-immigrants-nrc-caa-1631003-2019-12-23, accessed September 21, 2020.

Madan, Tanvi. 2020. *Fateful Triangle: How China Shaped US–India Relations During the Cold War.* Washington, DC: Brookings Institution Press.

Mahmudabad, Ali. 2020. "Indian Muslims and the Anti-CAA Protests: From Marginalization Towards Exclusion." *South Asia Multidisciplinary Academic Journal* 24/25: 1–19.

Mandavailli, Anu, and Raja Swamy. 2019. "Trump, 'Howdy, Modi!' and the Diaspora: Do Indian Americans Support a Hindutva Agenda?" *Economic & Political Weekly* 54 (47): 1–11.

Melton, Marissa. 2017. "Trump Celebrates Diwali, Hindu Festival of Lights." https://www.voanews.com/usa/us-politics/trump-celebrates-diwali-hindu-festival-lights, accessed October 14, 2020.

Myers, David N. 2019. "Trump's Silence on Kashmir Sends a Dangerous Signal to the World's Autocratic Leaders." https://www.latimes.com/opinion/story/2019-08-29/india-kashmir-modi-trump-russia-putin-israel-netanyahu, accessed October 2, 2020.

Parikh, Tej. 2017. "Why India's Hindu Nationalists Love Donald Trump." https://thediplomat.com/2017/02/Why-India's-Hindu-Nationalists-Love-Donald-Trump, accessed November 5, 2020.

Press Trust of India. 2019. "India's Weapons Procurement from the US Jumps to USD 3–4 billion in 2020." https://economictimes.indiatimes.com/news/defence/indias-weapons-procurement-from-the-us-jumps-to-usd-3-4-billion-in-2020/articleshow/79637410.cms, accessed October 14, 2020.

———. 2020a. "Biden Seeks Restoration of Peoples' Right in Kashmir, Disappointed with CAA-NRC." https://www.thehindu.com/news/international/biden-seeks-restoration-of-peoples-rights-in-kashmir-disappointed-with-caa-nrc/article31921284.ece, accessed October 26, 2020.

———. 2020b. "Pak Court Sentences JuD Chief Hafiz Saeed to Over 15 Years in Jail in One More Terror Financing Case." https://timesofindia.indiatimes.com/world/pakistan/pak-court-sentences-jud-chief-hafiz-saeed-to-over-15-years-in-jail-in-one-more-terror-financing-case/articleshow/79943439.cms, accessed October 19, 2020.

———. 2020c. "Chinese Consulate in Houston Shuts After Four Decades." https://www.thehindu.com/news/international/chinese-consulate-in-houston-shuts-after-four-decades/article32188467.ece#, accessed November 23, 2020.

Rajagopal, Arvind. 2000. "Hindu Nationalism in the US: Changing Configurations of Political Practice." *Ethnic and Racial Studies* 23(3): 467–96.

Rao, Rahul. 2020. "Nationalisms by, against and beyond the Indian state." *Radical Philosophy* 2 (7): 17–26.

Savarkar, Vinayak Damodar. 1923. *Essentials of Hindutva.* New Delhi: Global Publishing House.

Shenoy, Veena and Sheetal Mahendher. 2020. "Virtual Strike: Ban of 59 Chinese Apps in India and Users and Non-Users Perceptions." *High Technology Letters* 26: 841–8.

Strickland, Patrick. 2019. "Islamic Group Hosts Sanders and Castro as Right Wingers Protest." https://www.theguardian.com/us-news/2019/aug/31/houston-islamic-society-sanders-castro-far-right, accessed September 15, 2020.

Subramaniam, Samanth. 2017. "India Tradition of Multipartisan Iftars in Danger of Vanishing." https://www.thenationalnews.com/world/india-tradition-of-multipartisan-iftars-in-danger-of-vanishing-1.47021, accessed November 15, 2020.

Sud, Nikita. 2008. "Tracing the Links between Hindu Nationalism and the Indian Diaspora." *St Antony's International Review* 3(2): 50–65.

Tankersley, Jim. 2019. "Trump's Love for Tariffs Began in Japan's 80's Boom." https://www.nytimes.com/2019/05/15/us/politics/china-trade-donald-trump.html, accessed October 15, 2020.

Thobani, Sitara. 2018. "Alt-Right with the Hindu-Right: Long-Distance Nationalism and the Perfection of Hindutva." *Ethnic and Racial Studies* 42 (5): 1–18.

Thomas, K.V. 2019. "The Politics of NRC and its Pan-Indian Dimensions." https://www.cppr.in/wp-content/uploads/2019/12/The-Politics-of-NRC-and-its-Pan-Indian-Dimensions.pdf, accessed November 28, 2020.

Treanor, Tom. 1944. *One Damn Thing After Another: The Adventures of An Innocent Man Trapped Between Public Relations and the Axis*. Garden City, NY: Doubleday, Doran & Company.

Trump, Donald. 2020. "Donald Trump's Letter to the World Health Organization." https://zhongguoinstitute.org/donald-trumps-letter-to-the-world-health-organization-who-full-text-pdf, accessed September 10, 2020.

Varghese, George. 2018. "Jostling and Arrests at World Hindu Congress,". https://www.thehindu.com/todays-paper/tp-national/jostling-and-arrests-at-world-hindu-congress/article24905904, accessed October 16, 2020.

13
THE EVENTS AT THE CAPITOL AND THE TRUMP MEDIATION

America's uncivil war and new authoritarian totalitarian possibilities[1]

Bruce Kapferer and Roland Kapferer

The Trump phenomenon as a whole, his election, his presidency, the events at the Capitol, Biden's accession, and Trump's impeachment are moments of radical process. They form a dynamic in and of themselves. They express the chaos and transition of the moment, but they are also, and at the same time, forces in the transformation and transmutations of capitalism and world history—perhaps, with the complications of the COVID-19 pandemic, virtually an axial moment, a switch or turning point of crisis. This involves a reconsideration of what is fast becoming the master narrative concerning Trump, with its own ideological implications. Trump is presented as a specter of a fascist past rather than a foretaste, a mediation into, the potential of an authoritarian totalitarian future involving major transmutations in capitalism. What follows concerning the Trump phenomenon is written with all this very much in mind.

Our guess (a risky gamble in these times when almost anything seems possible) is that Trump will fade. There are doubtless many other political figures similar or worse who could take his place. With the exit of Trump his "movement" may follow. What crystallized around him was more an assemblage, a loose-knit heterogeneous, motley collection of diverse persons and groups, ranging from the extreme far right to the more moderate, whose organizational cohesion may be more illusory than real. Not yet a "Party Trump," it is as likely to melt into air and go the way of most populist movements as congeal into a longer-lasting force of opposition headed by Trump.

This is not to gainsay the shock of the storming of the Capitol on the otherwise ritualistic day of the confirmation of Biden's victory that concludes the liminal transitional period conventional in the American democratic cycle. Such a liminal space (Turner 1969) is a relative retreat and suspension of the state political order as the presidency is renewed or changed. This is often a festive time given to all kinds of political excess when the people vent their potency in the selection of those who

DOI: 10.4324/9781003152743-16

are to rule them. Trump encouraged and intensified the potential chaos of liminality at its peak when, ideally, it should subside and political order should be fully restored. He aimed to disrupt this critical moment and to maintain his uncertain presence as the Lord of Misrule, if not necessarily to effect a coup. Named as "God's chaos candidate" by some of the evangelicals who supported him, Trump promoted, even if unwittingly, a moment of extreme chaos that was all the more intense for the liminal moment of its occurrence when the participants themselves blew out of control.

Night of the world, pandemonium at the Capitol

In the nightmare of the event, newscasts presented visions of a fascist future filled with Fascist and Nazi images and other commonly associated symbols. There was a strong sense of dialectical collapse along the lines of Hegel's "Night of the World," disconnected flashes of the demonic when forces in opposition dissipate against each other and lose their meaning. The representatives of the nation cowered under their desks fitting gas masks, while those who would challenge them in festive mood and drunk with brief power put their feet up on desks aping their masters and carried off the mementos and spoils of their invasion. Exuberant chants of "This is our house" echoed down the corridors of power.

Shades of the past paraded in the present, foremost among them that of the enduring trauma of the rise of Nazi Germany. What Sinclair Lewis had warned in *It Can't Happen Here*—a Hitler-esque rise to power at the center of the democratic world—anticipated by all sides from the early days of Trump's apotheosis, seemed to be actually materializing. This accounts for the excitement on the steps of the Capitol—"This is America 2021, y'all!!" Arlie Hochschild captured the millenarian Nuremberg feel of his campaign rallies when researching *Strangers in Their Own Land: Anger and Mourning on the American Right* (Hochschild 2016), her excellent ethnography of the white far right and their sympathizers in Louisiana, America's poorest state and a Donald Trump heartland. Hochschild recounts at a lecture to the Rosa Luxemburg Foundation in Berlin a scene, reminiscent of the opening frames of Leni Riefenstahl's *The Triumph of the Will*, when Trump's plane, "Trump Force One," appears through the clouds and, as if from heaven, descends "down, down, down" to the waiting crowd electrified in expectation of the savior's endlessly repeated sermon of redemption of the deep resentment that they felt for having been pushed aside from the promise of the American Dream.

But here is the point: The immediate reaction to the storming of the Capitol gave further confirmation to the real and present danger of Trump's fascist threat, fuelled in the rumblings of class war which Trump has inflamed and exploited. It is a liberal fear, mainly of the Democrats but including some Republicans, who are the chief targets of Trump's attacks. His demonization of elite liberal values (marked by accusations of moral perversities aimed at unmasking the claims to virtue) is at one with his condemnation of the liberalism of federal political and social economic policies which he presents as contributing to the abjection of mainly white American working class and poor and to be seen in the rapidly increasing power of global corporations, policies of economic globalization, the privileging of minorities, refugees, recent immigrants, etc. It might be remembered at this point that the violence of the Capitol invasion, the marked involvement of military veterans, the carrying of weapons, baseball bats, the reports of pipe bombs, that shocked so many, reflect the fact that all modern states are *founded on violence*. This is particularly the case in the US where the US Constitution's Second Amendment protects the right to bear arms in defense of democratic rights. In an important sense the violence of those invading the Capitol refracts back at the middle class, and especially the ruling elite, the very violence that underpins the structure of their rule. If liberal virtue was shocked by the events on January 6 it was also confronted with the violent paradox deep in its democratic heart (see Palmer 2021). Thus, this paradox slips into paroxysm at this critical moment in American political history.

The transitional figure of Trump feeds on the prejudices of his intended constituencies and exploits an already ill-formed class awareness building on ready commitments and vulnerabilities—the well-rehearsed fascist and populist technique—creating indeed a false consciousness (there is no other way to say it) that is not only destructive but, in the hands of the likes of Trump, integral to intensifying the feelings of impotence and the miseries that give Trump his relative popularity. Slavoj Žižek (2021) says as much in what he describes as "Trump's GREATEST TREASON."

Arnold Schwarzenegger, "The Governator," was quick to counter the white supremacist, macho, Proud Boy, Oath Keeper and Three Percenter elements highly visible in media newscasts with a Conan the Barbarian performance. This was his take on the dominant brand of Make America Great Again. (Really, all those along the political spectrum participate in MAGA—*Democrat Party* badges and hats from the recent election read "Dump Trump Make America Great Again.") He focussed on his own immigration away from his native Austria and its Nazi associations to the liberated American world of his success. For Schwarzenegger, the Capitol invasion and its vandalism equated to Kristallnacht. Noam Chomsky likens the storming to Hitler's Beer Hall Putsch of 1923, observing that it effected a greater penetration to the heart of power than did Hitler's failed attempt. But Chomsky, with characteristic acuity, adds that the fascist danger lies in the anti-democratic class forces (including electoral and political manipulations on all sides) that provide the fertile ground for fascism.

At this point we take brief stock.

The Capitol invaders or rioters or protestors were a cross-class assemblage but overwhelmingly white. Their whiteness gave them a coherence, especially in an America where the politics of class refracts major divisions of race and color affecting most specifically African-Americans whose enslavement acts as a continual reminder of the basis of American democracy and capital in the subversion of the highest democratic and egalitarian ideals. Such a scandal is behind much of the outrage at the Capitol events and particularly in the context of ongoing Black Lives Matter activism. The participants in the Capitol were from diverse socio-economic backgrounds, from the wealthy to the poor, with multiple affiliations and other than those of the right-wing militias that provided the dominant images for the news media. Nonetheless, their whiteness indicated the cross-class force of color in America as a major ongoing contradiction of the democratic ideal, a fascist potential. Trump exploited such racism, even as he denied it, and provided a point for its crystallization. But we suggest that the assemblage character of his following is also his weakness. While his fan appeal extended beyond marginalized extremist groups, the ties linking them were not strong and easily dissipate as a function of the conflicts and contradictions of class alone.

Jacob Chansley, the QAnon Shaman, whose image went viral, embodies the character of the assemblage (and certainly the fascist potential) and an internal tension to dissolution. Indeed confronted by the reactive power of the state, a scapegoat, perhaps, for the evasive criminality of Trump at the edge of impeachment, the Shaman began to dissolve and fragment, pixilate, as Trump's so-called movement may also fade. Nonetheless, the Shaman's body deserves further consideration not only as an assemblage but also as what Gilles Deleuze would recognize as a plane of immanence for the expression of all manner of extremism in the historical formation of contemporary American cultural realities. This is so from the left-ist hippie folk rock pacifist but rebellious sixties, through the primitivist mysticism and religious cultism often fundamentalist in orientation of working-class and middle-class America to the radical overtly macho and violent rightist groups. The Shaman manifests the cultural field in which Trump (still) worked and which was subject to his hegemonic magic in the context of the challenges and changes confronting capital in the context of American democratic ideology.

Thus, Chansley's body and costume are a postmodern hybrid of multiple directions, a constellation that articulates heterogeneous elements: he wore American flag face-paint, a fur hat made of coyote skins and bison horns, and displayed a bare torso covered in various Norse tattoos and runic letters—a large Mjolnir or Thor's Hammer and an image of the Norse tree Yggdrasil. Above these was a Valknot, a symbol possibly related to Odin and fallen warriors at the extreme point crossing into Valhalla, but now deterritorialized by white supremacists and referred to by the Anti-Defamation League as a "hate symbol." Chansley proudly offered up his body to the assembled media, screaming and bellowing his celebration of America "land of the free home of the brave!" This is a body as a dynamic system or, as Deleuze and Guattari (1987) might say, a body that goes to the limit, that is deterritorializing and reterritorializing, in flow and whose component parts are not fixed but selected according to exterior relations. This is an extreme body—the new American individual multiplied and *in extremis*. In the aftermath of the Capitol events Chansley increased his infamy when he refused to eat prison food because of his delicate physical constitution: he refused to eat for seven days until he was provided with proper organic food. This was the subject of many memes, and many commented on the irony of his claiming constitutional rights after attempting to impede the constitutional recognition of the president.

But returning to Chomsky's observation which we want to take further. New class formations are in the making right now and they are being driven in the explosive nature of technological revolution. This is something Marx himself was very much aware of and why he wrote more than one hundred pages on the machine and the human in *Capital*. This is also the concern of Marcuse in *One Dimensional Man* (2002) and the continued focus of today's accelerationists such as the Deleuzian Nick Land (1993) and Nick Srnicek (2017) with his idea of platform capitalism.

Creative destruction, the transmutation in capital, and corporate state formation

The Rise and Fall of Trump (not discounting the possibility that Humpty Dumpty might come together again, which is the fear of the master narrative[2]) may be understood as expressing a transition between two moments of capital during which one formation morphs into another. Trump is the embodiment, instrument, and anguish of this transition, a tragic figure in a theater of the absurd. Grand Guignol almost but in Gothic *American Horror Story* style. The accession of Biden is the apotheosis of the new: in the hopes of most, he is a vehicle for healing the divisions in America that Trump brought to a head and are still very much present. But Biden's rise has ominous oppressive indications of its own.

The events Trump have all the hallmarks of the crisis and rupture of transformation or, better, *transmutation*. The millenarian spirit that Hochschild captures in her account is one born in the capitalist ideology of the American Dream, fortified in the religious fundamentalism of Trump's many followers that revitalizes their hopes in the Dream in the face of abject failure. The rallies and the impassioned actions of those invading the Capitol are filled with revitalizing energy. Such millenarian explosions, distinct in their own historical contexts, occur at many other points in global history. It was apparent at the dawn of capitalism in Europe, at later moments of crisis and redirection in capital up to the present—indeed at the inception of the Nazi horror—and at points of the disruptive expansion of capital in the western imperial/colonial thrust as in the cargo movements of the Pacific (Cohn 1970; Lanternari 1963; Worsley 1968).

The rupture of transmutation in capital, the crisis that the Trumpian progress manifests, is an instance of what Marx and others have understood to be the creative/destruction dynamic of capital whereby it reproduces, renews, revitalizes its potency against contradictions and limitations to its profit motive that capital generates within itself as well as those thrown up against it in the very process of its own expansion and transformation.

The circumstances underpinning the current transmutation in capital relate to the revolutions in science and technology (those associated particularly with the digital age and advances in biotechnology) to a large extent driven by capital and motivated in profit. The rapid development of capital (and especially that of the still-dominant, if declining, American form) was driven by the innovations in knowledge and technology (something that Marx and many others admired in America). What became known as the nation-state (the dominant political form that nurtured capital) and the class orders that were generated in capital and necessary to it (not to mention the overpopulation and ecological disasters that grew in capital's wake) *also* constituted barriers and limitations to capital's growth.

The new technological revolutions are a response to the limitations on capital emergent within its own processes. Technological innovations enabled revolutions in production and consumption (creating new markets and increasing consumption, reducing the need for human labor *and the resistances it brings with it*, overcoming problems, and opening up novel lines, of distribution), forcing the distress of unemployment (especially among the erstwhile working class), creating impoverishment and uncertainties reaching into once-affluent middle classes (as captured in the neologism, the precariat), shifting class alignments, redefining the nature and value of work, of the working day (the expansion of zero hours and its returning sense of a bygone era).

The current technological revolution is a key factor in the extraordinary growth of the monopolizing strength of corporations such as Google, Amazon, or even Tencent. The dot.com organizations (the flagships and spearheads of capitalist transformation with huge social transmutational effect) have wealth that dwarfs many states, and they are functioning in areas once controlled by the state (e.g. in the current race to colonize space). Indeed the corporate world has effectively invaded and taken over the operation of nation-states (Kapferer 2010; B. Kapferer 2016; Kapferer and Gold 2018). This is most noteworthy in those state orders influenced by histories of liberal social democracy in Europe and Australia, for example, which tended to draw a sharp demarcation between public interest and private enterprise. The nation-state and its apparatuses of government and institutions for public benefit have been corporatized (so much so that in many cases government bureaucracies have not only had their activities outsourced to private companies but also have adopted managerial styles and a ruthlessness along the lines of some business models). The corporatization of the state has aligned it much more closely with dominant economic interests in the private (now also public) sectors than before and enables a bypassing of state regulation, even that which once sustained capitalist interest, but which became an impediment to capitalist expansion.

These changes have wrought socio-economic and political disruption and distress globally, and most especially in the Western hemisphere. This is not merely collateral damage. The revolution in science and technology has been a key instrument in effecting social and political changes via destruction, for the regenerative expansion of capital. It is central to the re-imagination of capital in the opening of the twenty-first century.

This is particularly so in the United States whose sociopolitical order is historically one of corporate state formation which accounts for its long-term global political economic domination. Some renewal in leftist thought (e.g. with Bernie Sanders) is an index of the depth of distress that is being experienced although the ideological and counteractive potency of the American Dream fuelled, especially in fundamentalist Christianity, suppresses such potential, contributing to the intensity and passion of the Trump phenomenon. The ideological distinction of the Trump event aside, its dynamic of populism is reflected throughout the globe.

One common feature of this is the rejection of the political systems associated with nation-state orders and, to a marked extent, the largely bipartite party systems vital in the discourses of control and policy in nation-states. Trumpism and other populist movements (in Europe notably) complain of the alienation of the state and its proponents from interests of the mass. The expansion of corporatization and the further hollowing out of the state, the corruption of its public responsibilities by corporate interests, is effectively what Trump was furthering in his presidency. It is a potent dimension of the Trump paradox and a major irony of the Capitol invasion that, for all the apparent fascist tendencies, it was the spirit of reclaiming democracy (admittedly of the freebooting kind) in an already highly corporatized establishment (subject to great corporate capitalist interest) that Trump's actions were directed to expanding. An important figure in this respect is the Silicon Valley venture capitalist Peter Thiel. The tech billionaire, early investor in Facebook and founder of PayPal, was an early Trump supporter and named a part of Trump's transition team in 2016. His book, *Zero to One*, based on his lecture courses at Stanford University, argues for a corporate-technocratic governance beyond older systems of government (Theil 2014).

From panopticon to coronopticon

COVID-19 has highlighted the social devastation of the destructive/creative dynamic of capitalism's transmutation. The class and associated ethnic inequities have everywhere been revealed and probably intensified by a pandemic that is starting to equal, if not surpass, the depressing and devastating effect of two world wars. Like them it is clearing ground for capitalist exploitative expansion—something like Naomi Klein's disaster capitalism (Klein 2007). Under the shadow of the virus, labor demands are being rationalized, the cutting back of employment and its benefits legitimated, governments are pumping capital into the economies in a way that protects consumption in an environment where there is declining occupational opportunity and income. The idea of the Universal Basic Income is being seriously discussed which would offset some of the contradictions in a transformation of capitalism that is reducing our dependence on labor and endangering consumption through automation and digitalization. While the poor are getting poorer the rich are getting richer, most notably those heading the revolutionary technologies of the digital age and biotechnology, the competitive race to secure viable vaccines against the virus being one example.

There is a strange synchronicity linking the pandemic with the dynamic of capitalism's transmutational corporatization of the state. The virus reproduces and spreads in a not dissimilar dynamic. Indeed, COVID-19 in some ecological understandings is the product of the acceleration of globalization effected in those processes of capitalism's transmutation associated with corporate expansion and the corporatization of the nation-state. As a crossover from animal to human bodies, the virus is one manifestation of increased human population pressure on wild animal territory, the closer intermeshing of animal and human terrain. The scale of the pandemic is, of course, a direct consequence of the time-space contraction and intensity of the networked interconnections of globalization.

State surveillance has intensified as a by-product of combatting COVID, which is also its legitimation, with digitalization as the major surveillance instrument. The digital penetration into every nook and cranny of social life (see Shoshana Zuboff *The Age of Surveillance Capitalism* [2019] or Netflix's *The Social Dilemma*) is interwoven with the commodification of the social and personal for profit—economizing individuals calculating the costs and benefits of their social "interactions" (the YouTube or Kuaishou "influencer," the hype TED talker as Foucault's entrepreneurial self, cut, pasted, uploaded and remixed). The management of COVID, demanding social isolation and the disruption of ordinary social life, has exponentially increased the role of the digital as the primary mediator of the social and a commanding force in its very constitution. COVID has been revealed as a kind of social particle accelerator. As such, and ever more exclusively so, the real of the social is being re-imagined, re-engineered and re-mastered as a digital-social, a "Digisoc" or "Minisoc," constrained and produced within algorithmically preset parameters. Here is Peter Weir's film, *The Truman Show*, radically updated. And, as with Truman, the space of freedom is also *and at the same time* experienced as a space of unfreedom. This manifests in the deep ambivalence many feel about the new technologies they daily live with and through. The digitized social is often presented as a new agora, a liberating "space" in which new, progressive ideas and directions are enabled, operationalized, and, indeed, *optimized*. The internet has become a site of multiple struggles in which class forces and new potentials for social difference and proliferating identity-claims are continually emerging. The freedom of the internet has provided exciting opportunities for many. Such freedom also and at the same time contributes to conspiracy on all sides. As has been made clear in the two elections featuring Trump, the superpower of corporations like Google and Facebook threatens to install a domain of hyper-control. Digital walls and electronic fences are appearing everywhere in the age of the global "splinternet."

A digital fascism: towards the machinic materialization of being

An essay by Thomas Klikauer and Norman Simms on the new "digital fascism" argues along similar lines to us: they claim that the internet makes a new form of fascism possible in an emerging and original socio-historical dispensation (Klikauer and Simms 2021). They make the simple and important point that social media and online sociality is not itself socially created. We develop and extend: online sociality is truly a corporate zone.

Digi-sociality is a strange, uncanny new form of "sociality" that is engineered through a still barely understood and technically complex process whereby huge masses of individuals are collected as "big data," digitized and algorithmically ordered—dividualized—by software engineers building and designing mega-corporate platforms and new multi-media "environments" or "spaces" (for want of much better words).[3]

Unlike older forms of fascism and totalitarianism, the re-formatting of human existence creates an open horizontal and de-hierachialized plane that is de-centralized and leaderless; it is a totally equalized and individuated plane or any-space-whatever in which truth is radically relativized—your truth, my truth, any-truth-whatever—and facts become fictions or fictions become facts and reality becomes indiscernible from fantasy. This is what Gilles Deleuze (2013) has called the crystalline "power of the false." As we move into the new space-times of what may be called a crystalline capitalism, we learn to live with and adjust our senses to the emerging digital domain. And the digital domain is the domain of fake news. The plat-forming of human lives flattens sociality, fragmenting individuals into dividuals or "bits" of individuals—byte-sized chunks—organizes them into sets and groups them according to tastes and likes and clicks and then folds and refolds according to the needs of various corporate interests—human being as commercial dataset.

It is this radical datafication of the world that humans are currently learning to live with and adjust to. And it is this "world" or nonworld or night of the world which provides the fertile ground for new mythologies that attempt to grasp it, control it, and bring it to order. Truth collapses into lies and lies into truth. This is a context that is ripe for Klikauer and Simms' (2021) digital fascism and ripe for the era of conspiracy. On this flattened and individualized or personalized plane new theories and myths, each as good as any other, multiply and proliferate wildly. Trump operates on this plane. And he is as much a product or symptom of this as he is an expert player within it: he "games" this system certainly but, equally, anybody can.

The hegemonic and totalizing potential for the ruling bodies of the corporatizing state who control the digital is as never before. This is so not just in the global scale of the network reach but in the heightened degree to which controlling bodies can form the ground of the social, radically remodel, engineer and design reality in accordance with dominant interests, and where motivated shut out that which threatens their order. The awareness of this has driven the fury of censorship and self-censorship on all sides—Trump's threatened TikTok ban becomes Twitter's actual Trump ban.

A fascism of the future: from 1984 into brave new world

Trump and Trumpism are moments in the transitional, transmutational process of capitalism outlined above and of the formation of new social and political orders. Echoing the past they express its transmutation (and its agonies) rather than repeat it. Trump and Trumpism manifest the contradictions of such processes, agents, and agencies for the transmutations in the social and political circumstances of life that are in train, themselves forces in the bringing forth of a future that, in some aspects, is already being lived.

Trump himself can be described as an In-Betweener, a bridge into the new realities, both a force in their realization *and* a victim.

His manner and style, the brutal no-holds-barred amorality is that familiar from the captains of industry and robber barons of an earlier age, who built capitalist

America and crushed working-class resistance by all means, more foul than fair. Trump maintains the style but in reverse redemptive mode. In his shape-shift he presents as supporter of the working classes, not their nemesis as did his forerunners. However, his authoritarian business manner, of *The Apprentice's* "You're fired" fame, matches well the managerialism of the present. He is an exemplar of contemporary venture capitalism and, most especially, of profit from non-industrial production (often anti-production) gained from real estate, property transfer, asset stripping, and the expanding gaming and gambling industries (symptoms of the crises of transformation in capital) from which some of Trump's key supporters come.

Trump's reactive anti-immigrant nationalism and Make America Great Again rhetoric not only appeal to the white right of his constituency but are an engagement of past rhetoric to support new political and economic realities. Trump's economic war with China stressed re-industrialization, but it was also concerned with counteracting China's technological ascendancy, especially in the realm of the digital, a major contradiction born of the current globalizing transmutation in capitalism involving transfers of innovatory knowledge.

Trump anticipated the risk to his presidential re-election, and it manifested the dilemmas of his in-betweenness. His inaction with regard to the pandemic was consistent with the anti-Big Government policies of many Republicans and the American Right who are so much a part of QAnon conspiracies, but also concerned to reduce government interference and modify regulation in capitalist process, a strong emphasis in current transitions and transformations of the state and of capital. Trump's cry that the election was being stolen was excited in the circumstances of the pandemic. His attack on postal votes related to the fact that the pandemic gave the postal vote a hitherto unprecedented role in the election's outcome by by-passing and neutralizing the millenarian populist potency of his mass rallies already reduced in numbers by fear.[4] Trump sensed that the COVID-inspired move to "working from home" and "voting from home" would challenge fence in and fence out his base of support.

Trump has always taken advantage of the digital age, his use of Twitter and Facebook the marked feature of his style of rule. His practices looked forward to the politics of the future ever increasingly bounded and conditioned in societies of the image. Following the events at the Capitol, Trump's own Custer's last stand to allay his fate, his cyberspace and internet accounts were switched off. He has been cancelled by the new digitally authoritarian corporate powers (who arguably benefitted the most from the Trump era and profited[5] greatly under pandemic conditions) who are behind the growing new society of the image, in which he was a past master and within which he had in the main established his identity (R. Kapferer 2016; Kapferer in press).

The overriding image of the Capitol invasion, carried across most networks, is that of the occupation of the heart of American democracy by those who would threaten its ideals. The media have concentrated on what was the dominating presence of the extremist macho white American far right violently parading symbols of a racist past combined with clear references to the not-so-distant memories of fascism and Nazism. There were others there more moderate in opinion and representative of other class fractions, if still mostly white, whose presence does not reduce the fear of fascism, possibly as in Nazi Germany when what seemed to be small groups of extremists hijacked power (and the events of the Capitol evoke such memory) to unleash the horrors to follow. Something similar could be said for what happened in Russia leading to Stalinism. These were the worlds of George Orwell's *1984*, in which some of the major ideals of the time flipped in their tragic negation. Such events were very much emergent in realities of the nation-state, its imperialist wars, and the class forces of that particular historical moment in the history of capitalism and the formations of its social and political orders. There is no statement here that this could not happen again.

What we are saying is this: a different authoritarian and oppressive possibility may be taking shape—not of the fascist past but of the future. This is a future that Trump was mediating but which may be coming into realization, despite the great hope to the contrary in the accession of President Biden. Perhaps this prospect can be seen as more akin to Aldous Huxley's *Brave New World* born in the current transmutations of capital (and its agonies of class) and in the circumstances of the radical technological revolutions of the digital era, involving the apotheosis of the corporatisation of the state, the corporate state emerging out of the ruins of the nation-state.[6]

Aldous Huxley depicted a world centered on production and efficiency, a biotechnologically conditioned global system of perfect rational, optimized order. The class conflicts of the past are overcome here; everyone accepts their predetermined place. It is a post-human reality in which the foundation of human beings in their biology and passions is transcended. It is a somatized, artificially intelligent world of the image and promiscuity. Indeed, the American Dream. Those who do not fit or who resist are fenced out. Time and space are being reconfigured, incurring around the individual and "personalized."

Biden's inauguration for all its upbeat ceremonial spirit had some intimation of such a future, taking into full account the security constraints of its moment: to protect against the murderous unchecked rampage of the virus and the threat of the attack of right-wing militias. The stress on this, it may be noted, had an ideological function to distance what was about to come into being from, for example, the definitely more visceral world of Trump and thoroughly evident in the invasion of the Capitol—what Biden in his inauguration speech called an "uncivil war."

The scene of the perfectly scripted inauguration was virtually devoid of people, apart from the dignitaries and all-important celebrities, the highly selected order of the society of the corporate state. Where the general populace would normally crowd was an emptiness filled with flags and protected by troops, more than were stationed in Afghanistan at the time. Those who might disrupt, Hillary Clinton's "deplorables" and Aldous Huxley's "resistant savages," were fenced out. It was a totalizing and constructed digital media image presenting a reality of control, harmony, and absolute surveillance.

We claim that something like Trump and the events surrounding him would have happened regardless of the specific phenomena we have focused on here. The events Trump are a moment, perhaps among the most intense, in the transitional transmutation of the history of capitalism and the socio-economic and political orders which build and change around it. The apparent chaos indicates a major axial moment in world history—a chaos driven in the emergence of a cybernetic techno-capitalist apparatus on a global scale. What might be augured in the Biden accession is already taking vastly different shape in China and elsewhere around the globe. New and diverse formations of totalitarian authoritarianism are emerging. The Trump phenomenon is crucial for an understanding of some of the potentials of a future that we are all very much within and that an overconcentration on the parallels with the past may too easily obscure.

Notes

1 We are grateful to David Eller who invited our contribution to this volume. He asked us to expand an argument we initially published in Focaalblog.com/2021/03/02 "The Trump Saga and America's Uncivil War: New Totalitarian Authoritarian Possibilities." This we have done here with a particular focus on Trump's role in in political economic changes related to digitalization. We are very grateful to David Eller for his critical considerations.
2 Trump made an official state visit to the United Kingdom on July 13, 2018. He was greeted in central London by tens of thousands of protestors and a now-famous six-meter wide caricature blimp depicting Trump as a baby wearing a nappy. Along with the "Trump baby," protestors installed a sixteen-foot high Trump robot sitting on a golden toilet sending tweets. Protestors wore hats and t-shirts emblazoned by Trump as Humpty Dumpty. The American actor John Lithgow has released a poem entitled "Trumpty Dumpty Wanted a Crown" that perfectly captured the liberal fear of what they felt would be Trump's post-constitutional and aristocratic power grab.
3 It is possible that there has been too much focus on the notion of "spaces" and "worlds" as metaphors for understanding what is happening in the current convergence of human and machine. When the internet was first developing the dominant metaphors were spatial—web-*sites*, cyber-*space*, the information super-*highway* we meet in internet-*rooms* or *town-halls*. This radically new situation could only be made sense of using previous experiences. This was how the internet was made "user-friendly." The same can be said about the idea of digital "worlds." But just as the cinema was first limited by the theater as a means of understanding it—strange new things called movies were shown as if they were theatrical performances or movie-*theaters*—more recent developments in technology seem to be leaning on previous systems to help people make sense of them. Perhaps the internet is not a space at all or at least may not be fully attended to if understood as a place or a space? Software developers and computer engineers who design platforms and apps are designing augmented sense organs and perception is being augmented or transmuted by new technologies. And when perception is augmented and stimulated in these strange new ways certain shifts in human relations must occur. The internet is merged and entangled with hyper-stimulated nervous systems and bloodshot retinas and may well be re-structuring basic human orientations.
4 There were 65.6 million postal votes cast in the 2020 election, many more than ever before. Overall, 159,690,457 people voted. So only 94,083,951 voted non-virtually, only thirty million more than voted by post. The overall number of people eligible to vote is 257,605,088. Of course, a substantial number of eligible voters didn't vote at all:

94,083,951 people who could have voted didn't. Many states are starting to limit voting to only postal votes: Colorado, Hawaii, Oregon, Utah, and Washington no longer have any other means of voting except by post. Clearly, there will be a move over the next few years to entirely virtual systems. There is an effort to move states toward postal voting despite the fact that the National Vote at Home Institute recently found that 32 states are missing major policies, infrastructure and best practice that will ensure secure mail-in ballots. Fifteen states cannot even verify voter addresses before they are sent out. Seventeen states do not have a voter verification system. And 30 states do not have options to fix problems in voter signatures and often voters have no way to fix signature mismatch.

5 A pandemic of profit: In the 2021 financial reports on tech company profits Apple went beyond all analysts' expectations, reporting a record revenue and a net profit of $28.8bn. Sales rose in all regions, most of all in China. Apple's quarterly sales exceeded $100bn for the first time. Microsoft reported record sales. Facebook also reported record quarterly revenues and Tesla recorded its first-ever profit of $721m on news of Biden's election. Amazon, of course, still maintains the biggest annual revenues. See *The Economist*, January 30, 2021.

6 John Lanchester (2019) writes, in an insightful essay we discovered after completing our own, of the "overlapping warnings" in the dystopic visions of both Orwell and Huxley in relation to the Trump presidency. He concludes that we exist today in a strange mix of Huxley's soma-like anti-depressants and sexual promiscuity combined with Orwell's post-sexual celibacy, never-ending war, and increasingly authoritarian political leaders. In a sense the different presidencies push out to greater extremes. If the Obama legacy was Donald Trump's anti-presidency then Trump's legacy is the Biden–Harris "Community. Identity. Stability" which appears to be a return to the normalcy that many crave but promises, more, a hyper-normalization (see Curtis 2021).

References

Cohn, Norman. 1970. *The Pursuit of the Millennium: Revolutionary Millenarians and Mystical Anarchists of the Middle Ages*. Oxford: Oxford University Press.
Curtis, Adam. 2021. "Can't Get you Out of my Head." *BBC Documentary Series*. February 11.
Deleuze, Gilles. 2013. *Cinema II: The Time Image*. London: Bloomsbury.
Deleuze, Gilles and Felix Guattari. 1987. *A Thousand Plateaus: Capitalism and Schizophrenia* Minneapolis, MN: University of Minnesota Press.
Hochschild, Arlie. 2016. *Strangers in their Own Land: Anger and Mourning on the American Far Right*. New York: New Press.
Kapferer, Bruce. 2010. "The Aporia of Power: Crisis and the Emergence of the Corporate State." *Social Analysis* 54 (1): 125–51.
———. 2016. "Brexit and Remain: A Pox on All their Houses." *Focaal Blog*, https://www.focaalblog.com/2016/08, accessed March 5, 2021.
Kapferer, Bruce and Marina Gold. 2018. "A Nail in the Coffin." *Arena*, https://arena.org.au/informit/a-nail-in-the-coffin, accessed March 5, 2021.
Kapferer, Roland. 2016. "Trump as Singularity." *Arena*, https://arena.org.au/trump-as-singularity-by-roland-kapferer, accessed March 5, 2021.
———. In press. *Shock Ontology: From Being-In-The-World to (Non) Being in the West World*. New York and Oxford: Berghahn Books.
Klein, Naomi. 2007. "Disaster Capitalism: The New Economy of Catastrophe." *Harper's Magazine* (October): 47–58.
Klikauer, Thomas and Norman Simms. 2021. "What is Digital Fascism?" *Counterpunch* (February 18).

Lanchester, John. 2019. "Orwell vs. Huxley: Whose Dystopia Are We Living in Today?" *The Financial Times*, https://www.ft.com/content/aa8ac620-1818-11e9-b93e-f4351a53f1c3, accessed March 5, 2021.

Land, Nick. 1993. "Machinic Desire." *Textual Practice* 7 (3): 471–82.

Lanternari, Vittorio. 1963. *Religions of the Oppressed: A Study of Modern Messianic Cults*. New York: Alfred A. Knopf.

Marcuse, Herbert. 2002 [1964]. *One Dimensional Man: Studies in the Ideology of Advanced Industrial Society*. London: Routledge.

Palmer, Bryan. 2021. "01/06.21: The Insurrection That Wasn't." *Socialist Project*, https://socialistproject.ca/2021/02/01-06-21-the-insurrection-that-wasnt, accessed March 5, 2021.

Srnicek, Nick. 2017. *Platform Capitalism*. Cambridge, UK and Malden, MA: Polity.

Theil, Peter. 2014. *Zero to One: Notes on Startups or How to Build the Future*. New York: Random House.

Turner, Victor. 1969. *The Ritual Process*. New York: Aldine Publishing.

Worsley, Peter. 1968. *The Trumpet Shall Sound*. New York: Schocken Books.

Žižek, Slavoj. 2021. "'Trump's GREATEST TREASON' is the Betrayal of Populism." https://www.rt.com/op-ed/512165-slavoj-zizek-trump-treason-populism, accessed March 7, 2021.

Zuboff, Shoshana. 2019. *Surveillance Capitalism: The Fight for a Human Future and the New Frontier of Power*. New York: Hachette.

AFTERWORD

Authoritarianism after Trump

Jeff Maskovsky

Anthropologists are not exceptional in our concerns about the presidency of Donald Trump. As with other liberal-left-leaning academics, we have felt compelled to raise the alarm about his hateful and violent political rhetoric; we have condemned his corruption, xenophobia, sexism, and racism; and we have detailed his policy failures and the effects of his at-first gleeful and then toward-the-end panicked abrogation of liberal-democratic norms. From the very early days of his political rise, anthropologists have taken Trump seriously. We have drawn on our ethnographic expertise on political cultures around the world to explain the basis and durability of his popularity, the power and effectiveness of his political style, and the institutional and social damage that his self-dealing, authoritarian posturing, corruption, and illiberal and kleptocratic governing practices have caused inside and outside of the United States. Now that Trump has been politically defeated (at least for the moment) and the immediate threat of his reign has receded, it becomes crucial to explain in more depth what the Trump phenomenon is all about. We need to get Trump right—to illuminate what Trumpism signals about current-day US and global political culture and also to understand the limits and limitations of both his political program and those to which he is opposed—if we are to play our part, as academics ought, in imagining, and helping to bring about, a more positive, just and equal future.

This theme of getting Trumpism right is borne out in the chapters published in Jack David Eller's important anthology, *The Anthropology of Donald Trump: Culture and the Exceptional Moment*, in which twelve scholars, including Eller himself, locate Trumpism within contemporary political-economic and cultural life in the United States and worldwide. In this volume, the authors eschew easy, popular, and commonsensical understandings of Trumpism and instead highlight the "exceptional" aspects of Trump's reign, treating him as a significant transitional political figure whose style of rule is both a reflection of a deepening crisis in the current-day social

DOI: 10.4324/9781003152743-17

order and a catalyst for a more authoritarian future. In this Afterword, I reflect on the multiplicity of forces, antagonisms, conflicts, and emergent political forms that mark the present as a moment of crisis, building on the essays anthologized in this volume to paint a picture of the present as a transitional moment that is rife with new (but by no means wholly unprecedented) dangers, uncertainties, and possibilities.

In the introduction to this anthology, Jack David Eller makes a compelling case for treating Trumpism as a cultural system comprised of deeply held beliefs, values, and sentiments. Trump is good to think with, Eller tells us, because he exposes the fragility and vulnerabilities of US political institutions and because his words and gestures inspire unexpected enthusiasm for a right-wing political program built on conspiracies, grievances, and lies. He is important as well because his political project poses challenges to the actually-existing liberal order of which Trump himself is very much a part. This order was built on systems of colonialism, slavery, exploitation, oppression, war, and violence at a scale that had never been seen before in human history. But Trump's intervention into liberalism is authoritarian to its core and offers no hope for repair to the damage done by liberal regimes, past or present. Furthermore, anthropologists are, as with other scholars and intellectuals, broadly implicated in the regimes of power and truth against which Trump and his supporters define themselves. Thinking about Trump thus requires us to confront the history, flaws, failures, weaknesses, limitations, and contradictions of the liberal order, the political and cultural positionings of Trump's followers within it, and the extent of our investments in liberal academic knowledge formations, among other important political issues in which we cannot pretend to be disinterested (Maskovsky in press). The anthropology of Trump is thus a very tricky undertaking.

The essays gathered in this volume rise to the challenge of getting Trumpism right by illuminating the ways that class, race, and gender politics, shifts in global and regional capitalist political economy, and disenchantment with, and disaffection from, mainstream liberalism came together to enable Trump's political rise. The ethnographic accounts of "Trump country" offer important perspectives on these matters. In contrast to popular and academic explanations that characterize Trump enthusiasts as either "deplorables" or dupes, William Westermeyer, Michael Harkin, Ariana Hernandez-Reguant, and Claudine Pied offer nuanced accounts of highly constrained and precarious people who are nonetheless engaged, as are their liberal counterparts, in pleasurable acts of political self-creation. Westermeyer describes Tea Partiers' reluctant journey into the Trump political base. Although they were suspicious of Trump's bombastic political style and worried about his immorality and his lack of concern for, or even knowledge of, founding constitutionalism, they nonetheless shared with Trump a deep disdain for the liberal establishment. It turns out that Tea Partiers were just as politically passionate about the evils of immigration as they were about controlling the federal deficit (Williamson et al. 2011). So Trump's xenophobia also played an important role in recruiting them to his cause. Harkin finds a similar situation in rural Wyoming, where white working-class men beset by physical injury, economic precarity, and social isolation embrace Trump also as a way of lashing out at the liberal elite. Engulfed by a crisis in masculinity rooted in their inability to fulfill their roles as family breadwinners, rural white men support Trump, Harkin explains, to express their superiority to those whom they see as less socially isolated and less precarious than themselves. In a brilliant piece on Cuban Americans in Miami, Florida, Hernandez-Reguant accounts for Cuban exile community support of Trump in connection to a different kind of loss and alienation: that experienced by exiles and their descendants who are searching for a way to free themselves from the weight of the Cuban expatriate experience and of the burdens of multicultural belonging offered by the liberal establishment. As with other white ethnics, Trumpism offers Cuban exile community members the possibility of transcending their off-white, in-between immigrant racial status and of embracing whiteness through the phantasmagoria of the good life associated with the American dream (Berlant 2011). Finally, Claudine Pied gives us an up-close view of what political polarization actually looks like in rural Maine. Unsettling accounts presuming that Trump supporters and their liberal opponents live in entirely separate Red State/Blue State political, social, and cultural universes, Pied finds instead dense networks of people connected to each other across the political divide. Rural residents, she shows us, are careful not to allow pro- and anti-Trump sentiments to fully saturate the political or social scene. Taken together, these four pieces help us to understand the ways that geography, race, class, and gender shape the form that pro-Trump politics takes. To be clear, the political scenes that these authors describe are certainly animated by what Rancière (2021) calls a "passion for inequality, the passion that allows both rich and poor to find a multitude of inferiors over whom they must at all costs maintain their superiority." They make clear also the extent to which patriarchal white nationalist political sensibilities shape white working- and middle-class politics in many regions of the United States. But these scenes are also shaped by other concerns and suggest that Trumpism may be less monolithic than outside observers tend to imagine.

Trump's ability to perform racialized resentments and grievances is crucial to his political success, as is his capacity to invoke a public image of himself as a glitzy showman, a successful corporate boss, and a strongman who is uniquely capable of rescuing a weak and feminized nation from its enemies within and without. In this collection of essays, Daniel Lefkowitz, Micah J. Fleck, and Jack David Eller are brilliant in tracing the unique and disturbing ways that Trump brings together entertainment, entrepreneurial triumphalism, white community resentment, sexist claptrap, and mockery of the political establishment into a unique communicative style. In an analysis of a 2019 Trump v. Biden debate performance, Lefkowitz identifies an important semantic disconnect between the words Trump speaks and the gestures he makes. Unlike Biden, who coordinates his words and gestures in an effort to assert his political authority, Trump is literally all over the place. But his confusing political performance works in his favor, Lefkowitz explains, because Trump's gestures introduce mockery and confusion into a formal political ritual the very authority of which he seeks to undermine. Along similar lines, Micah J. Fleck traces the roots of Trump's populist political style to the caudillo figure from the revolutionary populist tradition in Latin America. Knowingly or not, Trump appears to be appropriating this style in order to create a working-class hero political persona. Fleck sees at work here a *faux* populism that dupes working-class voters who feel let down by the Democratic Party. I see in this persona an attempt to appeal to white working- and middle-class Americans in explicitly racial—and racist—terms, and in terms also of retrograde gender and sex politics. Indeed, perhaps what looks like *faux* populism with respect to class politics is more organically an expression of patriarchal white supremacy. Jack David Eller tackles one of the most vexing aspects of Trump's political performance: his incessant lying. In a very astute study on this theme, Eller shows the work that lying does for Trump. Among its many uses, it serves up a defiant comeuppance against the liberal establishment, who insist on the truthiness of *their* truths over those of Trump's supporters. It works also to shore up Trump's anti-intellectual bona fides and confuses his political opponents, who expect a certain kind of accountability from elected officials. Ultimately, as Eller argues, lying is a performance of seemingly unbridled political power, forcing political deliberation into a fantastical dreamland space that Trump can dominate with his false assertions, disinformation, and self-serving tall tales. And Trump's lying is contagious as politicians from across the political spectrum incorporate lying into their political repertoires without accountability or consequences. Julie Fine gives us an example of the creative political style of some of Trump's opponents—in this case #MagicResistance practitioners—who manipulate material, visual, and linguistic symbols to perform political opposition to the Trump presidency. For example, they use linguistic avoidance—in this case, refusing to say Trump's name—to deny him power and legitimacy. The close analysis of performances such as these helps us to understand better why Donald Trump's embrace of many patriarchal white nationalist and corporate boss ideological precepts makes good political sense in the twenty-first-century United States and, perhaps most importantly, what political strategies and tactics can be used to undermine his political authority and short-circuit his populist appeal.

    The final section of this anthology devotes itself to studies of the Trump regime's impact on public institutions. Benjamin Schaefer uses an abolitionist lens to explain the biocultural impact of Trump's mishandling of the COVID crisis. He documents the ways that Trump's anti-science political stance worked to weaken the public health response to the COVID epidemic, emphasizing how the Trump administration's refusal to promote social distancing, mask wearing, or widespread testing serves as a racist form of political interference that puts Black and Brown people at disproportionate risk from COVID. This, in turn, increased their stress and their exposure to illness. This kind of public health failure is a form of institutional racism that has unhealthy consequences for Black and Brown people living under the yoke of multiplicative oppressions, including mass incarceration, political disenfranchisement, and housing and labor market discrimination. In his piece, Bruce Knauft explains Trump's disastrous influence on the Republican Party. Trump worked hard at both symbolic and institutional levels to legitimate right-wing extremism in US party politics and political culture. Knauft argues that racism and xenophobia are *structural forces* that are likely to propel American politics and democracy in authoritarian directions even if Trump himself is displaced from his current position of power within the Republican Party. This argument should give pause to anyone who is tempted to treat Trump's reign as an aberration and who sees his electoral defeat as a definitive solution to the authoritarian turn taken during his reign. Raj Singh sees similar trends happening at the geopolitical level. He shows how Trumpism in the United States and the Hindutva forces in India are mutually constitutive and provides a detailed discussion of the authoritarian political sensibilities that Indian prime minister Narendra Modi shares with Donald Trump. Again, the issue of Trump's personal political future is less important than are geopolitical realignments. The effort to thwart China's global economic influence, for example, aligns India and the United States in a way that encourages the spread of authoritarianism populism in Modi's India. Post-cold war geopolitical realignments, and the decline of the US empire, combine with local and regional dynamics to spur on similar developments in the Philippines, Turkey, Russia, the UK, Hungary, Colombia, and elsewhere (Maskovsky and Bjork-James 2020). In the final chapter of this anthology, Bruce Kapferer and Roland Kapferer make a compelling case for seeing Trump as a transitional figure in a period of dramatic capitalist transmutation. The global economic system, they argue, is shifting away from the US-led neoliberal capitalism of the past four decades and toward a new order dominated, in deeply anti-democratic ways, by cybernetic technology firms such as Google and Facebook (see also Maskovsky and Bjork-James 2020). Accompanying this shift is a great deal of political disorder, as the political elites of the past have lost legitimacy. In this situation, Trump sensed and exploited frustrations that some fractions of the US white middle and working classes felt at the upheavals they are witnessing. But Trump is a paradoxical figure, according to Kapferer and Kapferer. He tapped into right-wing resentments and anger, but he has thus far not been able to elaborate a compelling economic program for his constituents. He may represent the managerial spirit of the emerging anti-democratic digital age (he's more proficient than most politicians at using social media and is a paragon of mass-mediated popularity), but his political base is comprised mostly of the white people who feel acutely disoriented by the deeper shifts in capitalist political economy and culture of which Trump's own enterprises and his transactional style of governing are a part. Trump is thus best understood not a specter of a fascist past but as a mediating figure pointing toward a new authoritarian totalitarian future.

 The chapters collected in this anthology paint a bleak picture of US politics in the present. This volume is important not just for revealing the damage Trump's political reign has caused but also for unhiding the subterranean flows of nationalism and class-, race-, and gender-inflected authoritarianism that Trump dragged to the surface as part of a long-term political crisis and the right-wing ascent of the post-cold war period. The volume makes clear the need to address concerns about growing economic inequality and the persistence of inequalities around race, sex, and gender in ways that also discourage the resurfacing of dangerous and exclusionary form of authoritarian rule. While keeping the dangers of a brave new authoritarian future in mind, it is also important to consider the broader set of political possibilities, including those that are elaborated as anti-racist, queer, social democratic, socialist, or feminist or that strive to bring about a more positive, just and equal future. It is essential to consider what it might take to advance durable forms of emancipatory politics and to help create and sustain spaces of egalitarian political experimentation (Swyngedouw 2018) and anti-racist repair (Thomas 2019). Keeping in mind the lessons learned from the essays collected here, I have a keen sense of the formidable challenge we face in displacing the increasingly hard-edged authoritarian populism that is taking hold in a variety of places. As Antonio Gramsci told us long ago, there is something very hopeful in taking full stock of exactly what we are up against.

References

Berlant, Lauren. 2011. *Cruel Optimism*. Durham, NC and London: Duke University Press.
Maskovsky, Jeff. In Press. "Engendering White Nationalism." In Christine A. Kray and Uli Linke, eds. *Formations of Political Culture in the Trump Era*. London and New York: Routledge.
Maskovsky, Jeff and Sophie Bjork-James. 2020. *Beyond Populism: Angry Politics and the Twilight of Neoliberalism*. Morgantown: West Virginia University Press.
Rancière, Jacque 2021. "The Fools and the Wise." *Verso Blog Post*. https://aoc.media/opinion/2021/01/13/les-fous-et-les-sages-reflexions-sur-la-fin-de-la-presidence-trump/?fbclid=IwAR3WAntDPOwHkhjR8dAW6DKVTceGBUh8UFD4j8yS4sO6ciD2EKNoPjN8iro, accessed March 13, 2021.
Swyngedouw, Erik. 2018. *Promises of the Political: Insurgent Cities in a Post-Political Environment*. Cambridge, MA: MIT Press.
Thomas, Deborah A. 2019. *Political Life in the Wake of the Plantation: Sovereignty, Witnessing, Repair*. Durham, NC and London: Duke University Press.
Williamson, Vanessa, Theda Skocpol, and John Coggin. 2011. "The Tea Party and the Remaking of Republican Conservatism." *Perspectives on Politics* 9 (1): 25–43.

INDEX

agnomancy 128–32, 135, 137
agnotology 128–29
alt-right 12, 59, 68, 71, 136, 141, 143, 183–84, 187–88, 190, 192–93, 195–97
American agitator 8–9
América TeVé 59–60, 68, 71
antifa 75, 80–2, 193–94
Arbery, Ahmaud 171–72
Arendt, Hannah 57, 131
Atlas, Scott 166–67
Austin, J.L. 126
authoritarian(ism) 3, 8, 12, 37, 43–4, 66, 119, 136, 138, 219, 228–30, 233–34, 237–38; aggressiveness 6; family 48; personality 14; practice 133

Babri mosque 205
Badiou, Alain 64, 72, 137
Bakhtin, Mikhail 10, 96, 108, 142
Bannon, Steve 55, 136
"basket of deplorables" 6, 33, 189
Berawan 127–28
Berger and Luckmann 138
Bharatiya Janata Party (BJP) 205–08, 213–15
Biden, Joe 1, 55, 65, 96, 106, 115–16, 163, 172–74, 185, 195, 215, 219, 223, 229–30, 235; gestures of 100–05; hand; "Sleepy Joe" 9
Black Lives Matter (BLM) 15, 28, 49, 71, 75, 79–80, 82, 87, 163, 165, 169, 214, 221
Blue Bourgeoisie 189–91, 195
Boas, Franz 5, 14, 50–2, 173
Boebert, Lauren 136
Bolívar, Simón 118–19, 121

Booth, Stephen 97, 106–08
Bourdieu, Pierre 28, 32, 45–6
Brown, Michael 169–70
Bush, George W. 6, 11, 24, 119, 132, 207
Bush, Jeb 63

capitalism/ist 12, 22, 41, 60, 66, 117, 120, 190, 219, 223–25, 227–30, 234, 237; *The Age of Surveillance Capitalism* 226; anti-capitalist 121; crystalline 227; disaster 225; late 116, 122; platform 223
capitol 12, 71, 75, 95, 137, 163, 173, 184–85, 187, 193–95, 219–23, 225, 228–29
Carson, Ben 26
Centaur state 44, 47, 52–3
Centers for Disease Control (CDC) 161–62, 165–67, 172, 174
Chansley, Jacob 222
Charlottesville 43, 108
Cheney, Liz 195
China 66, 104–05, 109, 164, 228, 230, 237; relations with India 206, 210–11, 213; virus 163, 168
Chinese 70, 168; relations with India and America 210–11, 215
Chomsky, Noam 221
Christian/ity 4, 12, 24, 28, 32, 41–2, 48, 183, 189, 204–05; apocalypse 195; evangelical 6; fundamentalists 7, 224; Judeo-Christian values 35; rural 50; *see also* evangelical
Clinton, Bill 31, 43
Clinton, Hillary Rodham 6, 26–7, 33, 46, 60, 66, 79, 115–16, 162, 207, 229; "Crooked Hillary" 9

CNN 11, 95, 125, 135
Conservative Political Action Conference (CPAC) 2, 182, 195–96
Constitution 21–2, 25–30, 214, 221; of Jammu and Kashmir 208
"continuity thinking" 4
coronavirus 61, 79, 125, 132, 136, 161, 168, 210; White House Task Force 166–67; *see also* COVID-19
COVID-19 12, 34–6, 57, 82–3, 85, 136, 145, 161–69, 172, 174, 190, 215, 219, 225–26, 228, 236; *see also* coronavirus
Cruz, Ted 9, 26, 63

Davis, Wade 172–73
Dean, Howard 101–02
Deep State 163, 185, 187, 193
Deleuze, Gilles 227; and Guattari 222
Democratic Party 56, 61, 79, 115, 236
Derrida, Jacques 44, 138
Durkheim, Émile 41, 50

electoral college 43, 115, 126, 163, 184
Encarnacion, Omar G. 119–20
evangelical 1, 6, 14, 188, 220
Evans-Pritchard, E.E. 3–4

facebook 4, 36, 48, 56, 75, 83, 86, 136, 162, 225–26, 237; anti-Trump magic on 142, 144; United Deplorables for Trump on 33, 189
fascism/ist 10, 12, 53, 56–7, 115–17, 121, 219–22, 225, 227–29, 237; anti-fascist 80; digital 226–27; Hannah Arendt on 57; Hindu nationalist 205; Italian 205; neofascism 55
Fauci, Dr. Anthony 167
Floyd, George 79, 87, 136, 165, 169, 171–72
Foucault 170, 193, 226
Fox News 24, 36, 67, 135, 190, 193, 195–96
Freud, Sigmund 41, 53
fundamentalism/ist 7, 22, 25–6, 36, 192, 222–24; cultural 24; Hindu 204; market 35; Tea Party 27, 31

Gadsden flag 21, 35, 50
Garner, Eric 165, 169
Geertz, Clifford 2, 4, 125
German(y) 204, 211, 220, 229; Romanticism 51
Gessen, Masha 134, 138
Gingrich, Newt 31, 186
globalization 3, 12–3, 23, 221, 225–26
Gosar, Paul 195

Hall, Kira, Donna Goldstein, and Matthew Ingram 9–10, 33–4, 96–7, 101, 108, 121–22, 141
Hall, Stuart 23
Hannity, Sean 187
Hindutva 204–06, 209, 213–14, 237
Hitler, Adolf 42, 204–05, 220–21
Hochschild, Arlie 29, 45, 61, 68–9, 220, 223
Hodges, Adam 9, 96, 108, 135
Hughes, Michael 142, 145–46, 148–49, 153, 155
Hungary 13, 40, 44, 237

Iftar 207, 209
illiberal 14, 44, 77, 233
Indian National Congress 206–07
Instagram 144–46, 153
Islam(ic) 205, 207–09, 212; Islamic Republic of Pakistan 207; Islamic Society of America 208; terrorism 43, 213; *see also* Muslim
Islamophobia 6, 116, 214

Jacobin(ism) 118–19, 123
January 6, 2021 12, 54, 75, 95, 163, 173, 184–85, 187, 193–95, 221
Jew(ish) 12, 68, 204–05; space laser 187
Jha, Ashish 167
Jones, Alex 135–36

Kant, Immanuel 51
Kashmir 208–10, 213–15
Kendon, Adam 96–8, 102, 104–06, 108
Kennedy, John F. 43, 131, 206

Laclau, Ernest 12, 23, 118
Lakoff, George 48, 54
Lakoff, Robin 108
Latin America(n) 10, 60, 62, 118–19, 122, 235; Latin American Public Opinion Project 122
Lennon, Myles 7, 77
Le Pen, Marine 14, 134
Levitsky, Steven and Daniel Ziblatt 41–3, 45
Lewis, Sinclair 220
libertarian 68, 72, 117, 120–22
Limbaugh, Rush 56, 135
Los 3 de La Habana 61, 65, 67, 72

MAGA, *see* Make America Great Again
Make America Great Again (MAGA) 15, 35, 50, 61, 75, 83, 195, 213, 221, 228

Malinowski, Bronislaw 2, 4–5
Martin, Trayvon 169
Marx, Karl 32, 41, 223
McCain, John 6, 30
McCarthy(ism) 183, 186
McGoey, Linsey 131
Modi, Narendra 12–3, 203–04, 206–07, 209, 211–14, 237
Morgan, Lewis Henry 41
Morton, Gregory 13
Mudde, Cas 11, 25
Muslim 12, 36, 87, 204–09, 211–14; ban 207; *see also* Islami(ic)
Mussolini 42, 205

Nazi 204–05, 220–21, 223, 228–29; neo-Nazi 43
neoliberal(ism) 3, 12–3, 40, 44–6, 50, 56–7, 59, 77–8, 88, 115, 121–23, 189, 237
Newsmax 36, 196
Nissan Atoll 127–28
Nixon, Richard 132, 143

Oath Keepers 14, 185, 187, 195, 221
Obama, Barack 22, 26, 34, 60, 64, 66, 71, 78, 125–26, 191–92, 209, 213–14; birther accusations against 126, 134; hand gestures of 99–100
One American News (OAN) 36, 196
Orbán, Viktor 13–4, 44

Pakistan 207–08, 210–13; Pakistan Occupied Kashmir 210
Parler 14, 36, 56
Pelosi, Nancy 146, 168
Pence, Vice President Mike 1, 35, 163, 168, 173
Pfiffner, James 125–26, 134
Pfizer-BioNTech 168, 174
Plato 40–1, 131
populism/ist 3, 10–2, 22–5, 35–6, 42, 52, 55, 66, 68, 71–2, 115–19, 121, 123, 133–34, 136, 183, 186, 214, 219, 221, 224–25, 235–38; alt-right 59; backlash 14; Cas Mudde and Cristóbal Kaltwasser's definition of 11; conservative 77; Ernest Gellner on 11; Ernest Laclau on 12; as illiberal democracy 14; Latin American 118; millenarian 228; *Populism: Its Meaning and National Characteristics* 11; Populist Rationale Spectrum 117, 121; right-wing 13, 25, 77–8; Tea Party movement as 24–5; William Mazzarella on 11

Proctor, Robert 129
Proud Boys 14, 71, 142, 172–73, 185
Putin, Vladimir 13, 134, 138

QAnon 56, 64, 95–6, 136, 173, 183, 185, 187–88, 194–96, 228; shaman 222

Radcliffe-Brown, A.R. 3–4
Ramsey-Elliot, Morgan 7
Rancière, Jacques 71, 235
Rashtriya Swayamsevak Sangh (RSS) 203, 205–06
Reagan, Ronald 13, 22, 31, 44, 59, 116, 132, 134, 206
Redfield, Dr. Robert 162, 167
Republic 40–1
Republican Party 1–2, 12, 14, 29, 62, 64, 66, 136, 182–83, 186–88, 193–96, 203–04, 206, 213, 236–37
Riefenstahl, Leni 220
Romney, Mitt 6, 30
Rorty, Richard 43, 51, 53
Rubio, Marco 63

Sanders, Bernie 46, 116, 208, 224
Savage, Michael 55–6
Savarkar, Vinayak Damodar 204–05, 214
Scheper-Hughes, Nancy 5, 15, 170
Schmitt, Carl 10, 13, 137–38
Schwarzenegger, Arnold 221
Sclafani, Jennifer 10, 96, 100
Scott, James 193
Second Amendment 61, 80, 221
Shenk, Timothy 143
Smithson, Michael 128
Soviet Union 59, 62–3, 120, 132; post-Soviet 59, 70
StopTheSteal 135, 163, 173, 184–85, 195
Streeck, Juergen 97, 101

Tarot 142, 146–49, 153, 155
Taylor, Breonna 171–72
Taylor Greene, Marjorie 136, 187
Tea Party 7–8, 21–37, 68, 71, 77–8, 83, 134, 186, 188, 234
Thatcher, Margaret 13, 44
TikTok 142, 227
Trumpism 2, 22, 24, 50, 52, 59–61, 64, 66, 71, 73, 117, 135, 183, 185–89, 195, 197, 225, 227, 233–35, 237; alt-right 193
Turkey 13, 44, 237
Twitter 9, 11, 14, 33–4, 36, 142–46, 162–63, 167, 227–28

Vance, J.D. 189, 191–92
Venezuela 118, 121

Wacquant, Loïc 44–7
Walley, Christine 7
Warner, Anthony Q. 194
Whitmer, Gretchen 184, 187
Woodbury, Anthony 97, 106–07

World Health Organization (WHO) 13, 168, 210, 214
Wuthnow, Robert 189, 191

YouTube 60, 71, 163, 226

Zimmerman, George 169

Ingram Content Group UK Ltd.
Milton Keynes UK
UKHW022113040523
421267UK00007B/82